PITCHSIDE

Amrit Mathur was Manager of the Indian team that toured South Africa in 1992. Four years later, he was part of PILCOM, the organising committee for the 1996 Cricket World Cup, which was conducted across India, Pakistan and Sri Lanka. He became Chief Operating Officer of the Delhi Daredevils and General Manager, BCCI, and also held administrative positions in the state associations of Railways, UP, MP, Delhi and Uttarakhand.

Amrit was Secretary, Sports Authority of India, and Advisor, Ministry of Sports and was instrumental in conceptualising and executing TOPS (Target Olympic Podium Scheme), India's flagship programme for supporting elite athletes. Currently, he is Advisor, Federation of Indian Fantasy Sports. His column, Straight Drive, appears in the *Hindustan Times*.

PITCHSIDE

My Life in Indian Cricket

AMRIT MATHUR

SPORT

First Published by Westland Sport, an imprint of Westland Books, a division of Nasadiya Technologies Private Limited, in 2023

No. 269/2B, First Floor, 'Irai Arul', Vimalraj Street, Nethaji Nagar, Allappakkam Main Road, Maduravoyal, Chennai 600095

Westland Sport, the Westland Sport logo, Westland Books and the Westland Books logo are the trademarks of Nasadiya Technologies Private Limited, or its affiliates.

Copyright © Amrit Mathur, 2023
Photographs by Pradeep Mandhani and Ashutosh Sharma

Amrit Mathur asserts the moral right to be identified as the author of this work.

ISBN: 9789357765572

10 9 8 7 6 5 4 3 2 1

Typeset by Jojy Philip, New Delhi 110 015
Printed at Parksons Graphics Pvt. Ltd

For all the players, fans, officials,
ground staff, umpires, scorers, media and
sponsors who together make cricket a great sport

CONTENTS

1

OPENING THE ACCOUNT

Cricket is bat versus ball, eleven versus two. For players, it is about the decisions they must make all the time.

Captains agonise over the pitch and often get it wrong. They stress about the toss. Bat first, always—that's what experience suggests. But bat first even when it's a bit damp? That's a tough call. They fret about the final eleven—and make mistakes about the team combination. Sourav Ganguly lost sleep—and possibly hair and weight—choosing between Anil Kumble and Harbhajan Singh. Virat Kohli, otherwise so decisive, couldn't make up his mind about Ravichandran Ashwin. Rohit Sharma thought hard before picking Yuzvendra Chahal ahead of Kuldeep Yadav.

Batsmen worry about the caught-behind appeal when they haven't nicked the ball. Or the leg-before when there was bat on it. Or the unplayable one which bends in before moving out a shade to hit off. Bowlers have nightmares thinking of what to do on a flat wicket against two set batsmen. It's hard to decide what to bowl in the crucial eighteenth over—yorker, wide yorker, back-of-the-hand pace off, slow bouncer? Or just anything after a quick prayer.

For cricketers, the most difficult time is just before the start of a match. The wait and the uncertainty ahead of a game are killing. It's the same when it comes to writing a book. Doubts arise: is anyone interested? Will people read?

My friends urged me to write. It's a good idea to record facts and preserve memories, I was told. But after careful consideration and listening to a sane voice (my own), I decided to do what is called a 'well left'.

I did so with good reason. I am no celebrity. I have no great controversy or scam to reveal. I don't have any deep wisdom to share. Basically, no 'breaking news' that the nation might want to know. Why would anyone, I asked myself, connect with someone on the fringes of the cricket world?

There was also fear. Compared to the short newspaper columns that I was used to writing, a book seemed daunting. It was like asking someone who takes ten steps to his flat every day to climb a mountain. Newspaper columns are transient; your message, good or bad, is read and quickly forgotten. Books stay on the shelf and are more permanent; someone years later can spot errors and fault its content. I dreaded a situation where a clever dude would confront me to say I had written rubbish. There was also the minor matter of hard work. Books take effort and on the *mehnat* versus reward *tarazoo*, it was too much pain for too little gain. Writing a book is similar to a Cheteshwar Pujara Test innings, the runs made with sacrifice and sweat. Certainly, it's far from a breezy Surya Kumar Yadav or Hardik Pandya T20 slog.

Yet, here I am. After carefully analysing the (few) pros and (several) cons, and many rounds of group discussions between me and myself, I decided to pad up and put my fingers to the keyboard.

This book is about my innings of thirty-five years in and around cricket. I take the reader beyond the boundary, into the boardroom of the Board of Control for Cricket in India (BCCI), the Indian Premier League (IPL) dugout, the Indian team's dressing room and the offices of various cricket associations. It is an account of Indian cricket based on what I have seen, heard and observed over the years. A direct, first-hand, eyewitness experience, not a someone-heard-something-and-told-me account.

I was a part of many 'firsts' and landmark moments in Indian cricket, including the BCCI's first-ever media rights sale to the South African Broadcasting Corporation (SABC); Team India's historic tour to South Africa in 1992, when television technology was introduced to aid line decisions; the first commercial sponsorship of a Ranji team in 1988; the creation of the IPL blueprint a decade and a half before its 2008 launch; and the first-ever domestic day–night game, the Delhi–Mumbai Ranji final in Gwalior in 1997.

As a BCCI official, member and employee, I had a season ticket to events that shaped Indian cricket. I attended BCCI meetings where officials were elected and cricket matters were discussed, debated and decided. I toured with the Indian team and saw the players up close. I sat in IPL auctions and the team dugout. I was in the Lord's balcony in 2002 when Sourav Ganguly took off his shirt, at the SuperSport Park Stadium in Centurion when Sachin Tendulkar took down Waqar Younis and Wasim Akram in the 2003 World Cup, and in the Indian dressing room in 2004 when Virender Sehwag scored 309 at Multan.

I have watched cricket matches in different countries and in various settings. A Test match seated in Kotla's concrete stands with *aam janta*, World Cup finals from plush hospitality suites in Lahore and at the Wanderers and Wankhede, several games from the Indian dressing room and—believe it or not—India–Pakistan matches sitting in the Pakistan team's dressing room.

During my journey I met legends of the game, superstars I admired from afar and dreamt about. I shook hands with prime ministers and presidents, and met politicians and public figures, corporate czars and media moghuls, celebrities and social influencers, democrats and dictators, as well as cricketers-turned-politicians, politicians who wanted to be cricketers, cricketers who became top administrators—and a cricketer who went on to become the prime minister of his country.

This is Indian cricket's story seen through my eyes.

As a BCCI member, I found myself in the company of stalwarts such as Fatesinghrao Gaekwad, M.A. Chidambaram, Raj Singh Dungarpur, P.M. Rungta and N. Srinivasan. Working closely with BCCI presidents Madhavrao Scindia and Jagmohan Dalmiya was a private tuition in cricket administration. And PILCOM (the Pak–Indo–Lanka Joint Management Committee for the 1996 World Cup) gave me the opportunity to learn the subtle play of global cricket.

It became clear to me quite early on that the BCCI leans towards control rather than cricket. At one level, the game is not only about bat and ball but also power and patronage. Contrary to common understanding, cricketers were always part of governance, but the BCCI assigned them peripheral roles. The players were junior artistes in a show dominated by non-cricket actors, while the BCCI was led by political bigshots, business leaders and career administrators—some smart ones who were on the ball, others who played and missed, and still others who didn't know short leg from slip.

Later, the wheel turned full circle for me when I worked for the BCCI as general manager (communication and coordination), based out of Mumbai. My role changed from member to employee in this second innings. The BCCI, too, had changed but its core remained unaltered. It was still about control, cash—and cricket.

I worked with many state associations, the Railways being the first, where I made policy and executed it without any interference. In Rajasthan, as the high court appointed administrator following Lalit Modi's suspension, I had complete freedom and was answerable to the court, not to state association officials. As CEO at Uttarakhand, I dealt with greedy members who knew little about cricket and had no interest in finding out more.

This is a story about the governance of cricket.

I was part of Lalit Modi's backroom team that planned the league in the early 1990s, before Zee or the BCCI dreamt of it, and much before it rolled out in 2008. Later, as chief operating officer for the Delhi Daredevils, I saw the IPL take off to become Indian cricket's greatest export, a hit formula that other countries have replicated.

The IPL is a dazzling spectacle, a cricket carnival with cheerleaders, vibrant crowds and celebrities waving cheerfully at television cameras. But behind the glitter simmer conflict and controversy, tension and turbulence, and friction between franchise and state associations. The IPL's spectacular success comes with challenges—and the suspicion that this golden goose is actually a greedy commercial crocodile devouring traditional cricket. And, more seriously, the question: what will happen if assertive team owners who have bought themselves expensive toys demand a role in governance?

This is the story of the IPL.

The Indian team is a tight-knit, exclusive group and the dressing room is sacred territory with restricted access. It remains out of bounds for commoners and non-cricketers; even retired stars are unwelcome. I got lucky because managers and administrative staff are granted temporary membership—visiting rights only—to this elite club.

In the time that I spent with them, I observed that the team followed an undeclared hierarchy; its social construct respected seniority and success as recorded in the score book. Sachin Tendulkar was the first among equals, for obvious reasons. The team's traditions were enforced by the seniors, who led by example and nudged the juniors in the right direction. There was a clear code of conduct with protocols for seating, dress and punctuality which were backed by penal action, including monetary fines.

As manager, I attended team meetings where the quality of discussion varied widely, from casual family dinner conversation to seriously insightful stuff. I saw players as tough professionals and, when their guard was down, as vulnerable individuals living life in an artificial bubble of celebrityhood. I saw young kids suddenly zooming up into an unfamiliar universe which they knew nothing about; ordinary blokes who suddenly landed in a world of glamour and grandeur. I witnessed their ambitions and aspirations, doubts and disappointments, spectacular successes and depressing failures. I saw players who attained iconic status due to their extraordinary skills. Some who worked incredibly hard to maximise their natural abilities and others who disrespected their god-given gifts.

I saw the monotony of long tours and the boring hotel–airport–gym– ground routine. A non-glamorous life that revolved around room-service dinners, constant packing and unpacking, the nuisance of organising passes and match tickets for friends, and the search for Indian food. I saw anxious players keeping a watchful eye on cricket statistics, tracking media reports, worrying about public perception and what was going on in the minds of selectors. I saw them in tense situations and in relaxed settings. Having informal dinners in a wayside restaurant, chilling in the pool, playing darts in the team room. Participating in casual (yet competitive) table-tennis tournaments and golf putting competitions in hotel corridors. I saw the strain brought on by an uncertain professional life and corrosive insecurity. Cricket is an unforgiving, one-ball game and nobody knows what the next ball will bring.

I saw an Indian team that cared for Indians and Indian cricket. Players desperate to win abroad and leave a legacy. Players with fire and ambition, swag and self-confidence, passion and pride. Players who shed silent tears after a poor game and players who sprayed expensive champagne in the dressing room to celebrate a win.

I saw players take their shirt off to make a statement and lose their shirt in a moment of madness.

This is the story of Indian players.

2

THE INNINGS BEGINS

Like most Indian kids, I grew up with a permanent cricket *bukhaar*. Which meant playing cricket with cousins and mohalla friends in parks, gullies and any open space that we could find. With makeshift bats, tennis and cork balls and 'local' rules by which a batsman was dismissed for hitting too far or too high. Creative rules that would have stumped the Marylebone Cricket Club (MCC).

A symptom of this cricket fever was clipping photos of cricketers from newspapers and pasting them in scrapbooks. Mine had photos of Tiger Pataudi, Salim Durani, Rusi Surti, Abid Ali, Ken Barrington, Tom Graveney, Ted Dexter, Bob Cowper, Tom Vievers, Graham McKenzie, Ian Redpath, Paul Sheahan, Barry Richards, Greame Pollock, Garry Sobers, Conrad Hunte, Basil Butcher, Dick Motz, John Reid and Bevan Congdon.

I followed the Indian cricket team's tour in Australia (1964–65) and England (1967). I remember waking up early to catch the action from Australia and staying up late to listen to BBC's Test match commentary on a transistor radio when Tiger Pataudi made that splendid 148 at Leeds.

My cricket yatra started in Jaipur where hopeful kids went to the St. Xavier's School nets to be coached by N.D. Marshall, who had toured England with the Indian team in 1932. Marshall sa'ab, a Parsi gentleman with a sola topi, was devoted to cricket and its old-school values. Every afternoon he'd drive up in his dilapidated red Morris Minor to coach us. For him, correct technique was as sacred and as important as oxygen is to

Mt Abu coaching camp, 1973.
Seated: Coaches Arjun Naidu, Mushtaq Ali, N.D. Marshall, Surinder Singh

life and he insisted that everyone should follow the basics. Batting was about staying sideways and obeying straight lines—go back if the ball was short, forward if full. Marshall sa'ab ensured everyone played correctly and also learnt the life lessons that cricket teaches.

At the Rajasthan state annual summer coaching camp in Mt Abu, Marshall sa'ab was assisted by Mushtaq Ali, a legendary cricketer with a powerful personality and an intimidating aura. Mushtaq sa'ab wore his India blazer and his trademark silk scarf to practice and insisted on certain ground rules. Punctuality was non-negotiable, reporting late even by two minutes was a major crime and long hair attracted capital punishment. I wonder what he would have made of Ishant Sharma.

Mushtaq sa'ab made his Test debut in 1934 and was the first Indian to score a Test hundred overseas. He would have been a valuable asset in the IPL given his natural flair and aggressive mindset. For him, the bat was a weapon of aggression and batting was about scoring runs and punishing the bowlers. One day, he gave us a batting demo. Playing with one stump and without pads, he took on medium pacers by meeting the ball yards down the track. What a master!

When Dilip Sardesai dropped in at the Mt Abu nets a few months after scoring two Test centuries in the West Indies, he knocked a few balls but Marshall sa'ab was not impressed and told him that his technique was in need of urgent repair. Sardesai, who, along with Sunny Gavaskar, was the hero of the Caribbean triumph in 1971, faded soon thereafter.

At school in Rajasthan, I remember our team losing each year to Uttar Pradesh because they had players who were over the age limit. Rumour had it that some were married and even had children. Gopal Sharma was one of the exceptions. As a fourteen-year-old, he bowled flighted off-breaks and could turn the ball even on flat tracks.

The first time I saw a turf wicket was when we travelled to Nagpur to play Vidarbha. Before the game, our paan-chewing coach Surinder Singh-ji gave us a quick batting lesson: on turf, always get forward; playing back is inviting leg-before. The coach imposed an 8 p.m. curfew and warned us not to stray into the town—a warning we collectively defied. Unfortunately, we were caught because we ran into the coach himself in OB (out of bound) territory, way beyond the curfew hour.

Years later, at the U-23 level, our Central Zone team played West, which had off-spinner Ashok Patel (who played one-day matches for India) while Kiran More was a reserve. Put into bat on a wettish track, we were all out 30 minutes before lunch on day one and were defeated by an innings.

Growing up in the 1960s, I watched Ranji games at different venues in Jaipur (Chowgan Stadium, Maharaja College and Railway Ground, Ganapati Nagar) and saw my childhood heroes all smartly dressed in silk shirts rolled up to the elbows, pleated flannels and polished white spikes. The most strikingly handsome was Salim Durani, the Prince. He would walk out of the players' shamiana with a swagger, his shirt collar turned up, looking super cool and stylish. He had the air of a bored genius, whether bowling his left-arm spin off a whippy action or batting. Graceful and unhurried, always threatening to create magic. Players on the circuit confirmed that, judged on talent and natural ability, he was in a league of his own. People came to watch him play and left once he got out.

In a Ranji game, Salim bhai was padded up, in next, and when a wicket fell, he got up to go. Except, he couldn't find his bat. The great man then casually picked one from a kitbag lying nearby and walked out to bat. In the middle, he was all style, elegance and class. Every ball middled with someone else's bat!

An interesting story about Salim bhai is narrated by my friend Arul Lal. Delhi was playing Rajasthan at the Kotla in the 1974–75 season and Salim bhai was playing a scratchy innings. He attempted to late cut leggie Rakesh Pappuji Shukla, missed, and a young Delhi fielder at slip passed a rude remark. There was no reaction from the aging master, who was by now at the end of his career. An interesting passage of play followed. Every time Pappuji bowled, Salim bhai stepped legside to cut late, even balls pitched up or close to the stumps. This went on for a while till he finally nicked one and was caught behind, just short of 50. Walking back, he stopped to have a polite word with the fielders around him. *Thoda cricket hame bhi khelna aata hai*, he said.

In a Ranji final where Bombay crushed Rajasthan, with Vijay Manjrekar scoring a big daddy hundred, I remember Salim bhai hitting a Ramakant Desai bouncer for a six—the monster hit sailed over square leg to land on the railway track behind the pavilion.

Interestingly, this was the famous 'Singhji' Rajasthan Ranji side which was dominated by members of the royalty. The joke was that the royals selected themselves and commoners filled the remaining slots. Leaders of this star parade were Hanumant Singh-ji and his cousin Suryaveer, the elegant opener, from the hilly state of Banswara. Raj Singh-ji from

St. Stephen's College cricket team, 1978.
Front row (L to R): Shubhro Sen, Ramchandra Guha, Amrit Mathur, Subhash Sharma, Piyush Pandey, Clement Rajkumar, Rajinder Amarnath, Arun Lal

neighbouring Dungarpur was another regular, who ran in from close to the sight screen to bowl gentle outswing. Arvind Singh-ji of Mewar and Mahipendra Singh-ji of Data Bhavnagar were also part of the playing eleven.

Rajasthan cricket was run and funded by Bhagwat Singh-ji, the Maharana of Udaipur, who was the president of the cricket association and captain of the Ranji team. It was he who hired Vinoo Mankad, Rusi Surti and Subhash Gupte to play for Rajasthan.

I have some wonderful memories of watching Ranji. In a match in the early 1960s, Tiger Pataudi was dismissed in both innings by the medium-pacer G.R. Sunderam, who played two Tests for India. In the Ranji final between Rajasthan and Karnataka in 1974, on an underprepared track, Prasanna and Chandra were too hot to handle but Hanumant Singh-ji produced a batting masterclass, scoring 83 of Rajasthan's 186. However, Salim bhai had a forgettable game, out for a pair, dismissed in both innings by Prasanna.

Parath Sharma was the local hero, Rajasthan's big hope. A gifted timer of the ball, he butchered spin and his languid cover drive was a delight to watch. The portly Parath had a razor-sharp cricketing mind and he later contributed to the progress of Rahul Dravid and Gautam Gambhir at the National Cricket Academy (NCA).

Kailash Gattani was the other hero, a swing bowler in the Glenn McGrath mould who relied on control and strict discipline. Laxman Singh, another star, toured England and Australia with the Indian Schools team and played Ranji for ten seasons (1967–77), the last of these when he was only twenty-five. Unfortunately, he passed away ten years later.

But the biggest name in Rajasthan was captain Hanumant Singh, the universally respected master strategist. An elegant player, he relied on touch and timing to work the ball into gaps with supple wrists. His other passion was golf and during Ranji games he could be spotted practising his swing. A technically correct golfer, he minimised risk by not using woods and teed off instead with a 4-iron.

I went to St. Stephen's College in Delhi where cricket was taken very seriously. The annual inter-college battle between St. Stephen's and Hindu College—once played over seven days—was the stuff of legends. And the final was something special: classes suspended in Delhi University, thousands of spectators at the university ground and live commentary on radio. The cricket was competitive and the hall of fame celebrated the superhuman feats of champions Mike Dalvi, Ashok Gandotra, S.S. Lee, and also Vinay Lamba (of Delhi and North Zone), who made four hundreds in four successive inter-college finals.

Praveen Oberoi was the reigning king at St. Stephen's. He took 50 wickets in five finals. His partner, Rajinder Singh Hans, played in the shadow of the greatest left-arm spin bowler, Bishan Singh Bedi. Hans started his first-class career after college, finished with 340 wickets for Uttar Pradesh (with 27 five-wicket hauls from 78 games) and became a national selector.

Our batting star was Arun Lal, from Mayo College. He was rejected by Rajasthan schools, but in college he immediately made a mark. A stubborn player intent on grinding the opposition into the dust, Lal scored big in university and U-22 cricket. His 99 against Kim Hughes's Australian team in Srinagar opened the door to the Indian dressing room.

St. Stephen's also had Kirti Azad, Rajinder Johnny Amarnath, Aamer Bin Jung, Piyush Pandey and Ramchandra Guha, the off-spinner best remembered for catching Deshpal Singh in a key game when a miscued on-drive found his right hand at short mid-wicket. Not to forget Deepak Sharma (called 'Bonnet' because he was from Sonnet Club), the off-spinner and opener who played 11 seasons for Haryana and scored 199 in the Ranji final where they beat Bombay by 2 runs.

On paper, Hindu College was the stronger team, with star players Karun Dube, the stylish opener who played with a Duncan Fearnley bat, Surinder Khanna, an aggressive player who loved playing on the up, and Sunil Valson, a seriously quick bowler. However, as a group, they choked when things got tense. In a final, when 340 were needed in the last innings, they were cruising with Hari Gidwani on 180 in the post-tea session on day 5, but collapsed dramatically to lose by a few runs.

Cricket in Delhi University was so intense that during Diwali, when the other students went home, the college team stayed back to play practice games. College cricket was top priority and players missed state games, even Ranji, if they clashed with inter-college cricket. Jimmy Amarnath was at Khalsa College and Randhir Singh and Raman Lamba, who both went on to play Test cricket, represented PGDAV College. Raman was a tough professional with an outstanding work ethic. He played professional club cricket in Ireland and Bangladesh, where he tragically passed away, hit on the head while fielding at short leg. He was a stalwart of Sonnet and Delhi cricket and was the first to spot Ashish Nehra. Pointing to him

Rohinton Baria winners, Delhi University. L to R : Kirti Azad, Sunil Valson, Amrit Mathur, Arun Lal, Piyush Pandey, Karun Dube, Randhir Singh

at the Delhi & District Cricket Association (DDCA) Kotla number 2 net, he predicted, 'Yeh ladka zaroor India khelega.' (This boy will definitely play for India.)

I barely made it to the Delhi University team which had Arun Lal, Raman Lamba, Kirti Azad, Randhir Singh, Surinder Khanna and Sunil Valson. Not to forget Piyush Pandey, now the don of a different field.

When Delhi won the Rohinton Baria Trophy, the national inter-university championship in 1978, a young Kapil Dev made 300 but his team still lost the game. In the same season, Deepak Sharma and Deepak Chopra, Delhi's number 10 and 11, made hundreds in the North Zone final and then repeated the feat in the All India final—still batting at 10 and 11.

I remember the time the Delhi team played in Aligarh in tough off-field conditions. Sixteen players crammed into one filthy college dormitory room which was visited by field rats every night. Dirty loos, freezing cold weather and no hot water. There was bun, makhan, omelette for lunch and dal, sabzi, kadak naan for dinner. The same menu for thirty days!

The cricket was pretty good though, marred only by minor accidents. One night, teammate Vinay Aggarwal accidentally set his bedding on fire, having forgotten to snuff out the agarbatti after puja. Another time, play was suspended when two hares—yes, hares!—strayed into the field and both teams, reserve players, umpires and scorers paused play to try and catch them.

The Rohinton Baria final between Delhi and Osmania was a tense affair. The Osmania team had Shivlal Yadav, who bowled loopy off-breaks with Prasanna's action and Shahid Akbar, the aggressive left-handed opener. And yet Delhi won, with Arun Lal, who had an ankle in plaster, and Sunil Valson adding 90 for the last wicket. Number eleven Valson contributed zero to this partnership.

College cricket wasn't always an unrelenting grind. We looked forward to the annual fun fixture at Roshanara Club with its English-style dressing rooms. The draw for us: beer with lunch. Another popular fixture was the match against the Air Force at the Race Course ground, Safdarjung, which is now a golf club. Services had Group Captain Ajay Jha and Wing Commander R.K. Ohri, both perfect gentlemen who captained their Ranji sides. There was also Subroto Porel, who bowled sharp inswing and Surinder Nath, former India pacer who had a great away delivery.

In a friendly one-day game between St. Stephen's and Bank of Baroda, Chetan Chauhan opened the batting against my classmate Shubhro Sen, a skiddy fast bowler who was all shoulder from a shortish run-up. Very early in his innings, Chetan misjudged a short ball which rushed on to him. Unable to get out of the way, he got hit flush on the jaw.

His jaw shattered and pieces of broken bone and teeth fell on the pitch. He walked off, clutching his face, and I rushed him to RML Hospital on my scooter, a 20-minute drive through Delhi's busy traffic. The doctors there wired the jaw, put him on a liquid diet and told him not to play in order to allow the wound to heal.

Chetan ignored the advice and within weeks of the injury travelled to play Duleep Trophy. A hundred in the final there put him on the flight to Australia with the Indian team—a comeback after a five-year gap. He scored 80-odd runs in the first Test at Perth and, as Gavaskar's opening partner, frustrated bowlers for years after that. A true fighter, Chetan the batsman was an advertisement for grit, unaffected by the balls he played and missed. Cricket for him was about the next ball; the previous delivery was just another entry in the score book.

The 1980s was the golden era for Delhi cricket because of the mighty team assembled by Bishan Bedi, who had recently returned from England. Bishan imported players (Madan Lal, Jimmy and Surinder Amarnath, Chetan Chauhan) from other states to stitch together a powerful team that rivalled Bombay. I spent many misty winter mornings at Kotla watching them play. Besides the imports, the team had leggie Rakesh Shukla and left-arm quick Suresh Luthra, who was an absolute terror on dodgy tracks.

I vividly remember Bishan's effortless excellence, and Ramesh Saxena hitting a brilliant hundred playing for Bihar, repeatedly stepping out to the spinners to ease the ball through cover. Also, the game between Delhi and Haryana where a forty-plus Rajinder Goel bowled more than forty overs in a day, the ball slanting in to cramp the batsmen. With Goel there were no free hits, only awkward questions.

Whereas, with Bishan, there were angles and stories. A master raconteur, he is capable of being hilarious and bitingly critical. He equates cricket with life and respects the spirit of fairness that is reflected in the phrase, 'It's not cricket'. The wily bowler celebrated for bounce and turn would urge everyone to play with a straight bat.

According to Bishan, Tiger Pataudi was the greatest Indian cricketer and Garry Sobers the next best cricketer of all time, after Bradman. One of his favourite stories, later in life, was about getting Barry Richards out by challenging his ego. Bishan bowled at him with a silly point and short leg. Richards, stung by the insult, attacked recklessly. And got caught at cover.

The first Test match I watched live was West Indies versus India in 1974 at the Feroz Shah Kotla stadium, sitting in the ₹28 season ticket stand on the south side directly opposite the Willingdon pavilion. We had to be seated by 8 a.m., two hours before play, to find a place on the concrete steps. And then baked in the sun all day without water or food, except for sandwiches carried from college.

All this, of course, was worth it because I got to see Clive Lloyd, Alvin Kallicharran, Keith Boyce and Andy Roberts play. India made a few with Rajasthan star Parath Sharma stroking a cultured 50 on his debut but West Indies piled up almost 500. Viv Richards, the then unknown number 3, hit 192 in less than five-and-a-half hours with six big sixes, some which sailed into the Ambedkar football stadium (behind the sight screen at the far end) and Kotla number 2 (behind square leg).

Watching India and England play at the same stadium was a far more pleasant experience. By then my father was the Delhi Police chief, so we sat on sofas near the boundary next to the fine leg fielder with plenty of food and drinks.

I followed cricket closely, especially because many of my friends were making their way through it and I was among the millions who kept track of what was going on. Then, against the run of play, things changed to bring me closer to the action. A career-changing moment happened, almost by accident.

After joining the civil service, I was with the Indian Railways in Delhi when Madhavrao Scindia became the minister of Railways. Scindia was keen on cricket and every weekend, social cricket matches were organised at the Karnail Singh stadium.

I was called to play and soon found myself opening the innings with the minister himself. Scindia was a determined, correct player who looked to drive from a pronounced forward trigger movement. Together we made some runs against some very friendly oppositions, but every time we played, my biggest fear was a mid-pitch mix-up resulting in him getting run out.

The interest of the minister, that too someone as fastidious as Scindia, ensured that these matches were held in style with top-class arrangements and excellent catering. The games were friendly, yet competitive, and participants included past players, members of parliament and business leaders. Tiger Pataudi turned up occasionally to umpire from both ends for a few overs.

Watching intently from the gallery were the Railway ministry top brass, chairman and other members of the board. I am sure they were miserable, having to land up on a holiday and sit through a game that did not interest them in the least. After a while, Scindia sensed their discomfort and a message was sent to let them know that as official business was not likely to be transacted, they could enjoy their weekends at home.

The presence of the Railway bosses, however, had a profound *cricket ka side effect* on my career. Word spread in Railway circles about my proximity to Scindia and, as happens in government, things changed subtly. Though I was only at step one of the bureaucracy, I noticed seniors starting to treat me differently. I was careful to play this correctly, but there was a marked change as others began to give me *bhaav*. Perception is everything, especially in *sarkar*.

One weekend I was on night duty in the Railway control room, tasked to ensure that the special train by which the minister was travelling to Delhi arrived on time. On its arrival on Sunday morning—very much on time—Scindia was met, as per standard protocol, by a large number of officials at the VIP platform. He walked past them but stopped when he spotted me at the end of the line. What are you doing here? he asked, somewhat confused. See you at the ground at ten, he added, getting into his car.

A few months later, returning home from an official tour one evening, I found a senior officer waiting outside my flat, carrying an order for my transfer. He informed me that I was being posted 'with immediate effect' as secretary, Railway Sports Board, and that the minister had instructed that I join work the next morning.

This was a surprising and unexpected break. The post was usually held by someone far more senior, so for me it was a double promotion of sorts. Not sure whether I could handle the responsibility or whether this was good for me professionally, I sought advice from close friends—only to be told that there was no choice.

From this point, my career in the Railways changed track. I was now part of the world of professional sports and the new job automatically placed me on every National Sports Federation in India.

Importantly, it was my passport to the BCCI. A massive stroke of luck, and the start of a new innings.

3

MAKING HISTORY: SOUTH AFRICA AND ZIMBABWE, 1992

In 1992, South Africa was readmitted to the International Cricket Council (ICC), ending twenty-one years of international sporting isolation. India did not have diplomatic relations with South Africa at the time and Indian passports had a warning stamped on them: *Not valid for travel to Israel and South Africa.*

South Africa was experiencing political instability and social turmoil. Apartheid had ended but its horrible scars continued to divide people. Nelson Mandela, released from jail after twenty-seven years in captivity, was looking to heal the wounds inflicted by the inhuman white regime. Cricket became an instrument to unite people and India was the first team to tour South Africa, stopping in Harare to play Zimbabwe's maiden Test.

This was the momentous 'Friendship Tour'. And I had the privilege of being the manager of the Indian team on tour.

A Rousing Start

September 1992. We were in Harare on the first leg of the tour. One evening, the phone rang and I had an alarmed Ali Bacher on the line from Johannesburg. Ali was the administrator of the United Cricket Board of South Africa and he spoke about plans for the mayor's reception for the Indian team in the Town Hall in Durban. After a quick update, Ali popped a question: *Who, from the Indian team, will respond to the mayor's welcome address?* He needed a name to print on the official programme.

I already knew I had landed myself in a difficult situation by taking on the role of team manager. I felt like an inexperienced opening batsman who was heading out to bat against quality bowling on an absolute green top. I thought of captain Mohammad Azharuddin, but he ducked the bouncer. Coach Ajit Wadekar came next to mind, but he too shouldered arms. I realised there was no way out, nowhere to hide—it had to be me, the manager of the team.

Public speaking was a challenge, even ordinarily, and this would be much worse. A big audience, a formal sit-down dinner, live television, the South African sports minister, cricket top brass and other guests seated at the high table. Definitely a frightening combination. The thought running through my head that night in Harare was that this wasn't a normal tour, and I wasn't the usual manager. South Africa was cricket's uncharted territory and a diplomatic minefield, and we had just taken a giant (careless?) leap into the unknown.

The tour was a follow-up to South Africa's visit in early 1992, which was put together to fill the gap created by the cancellation of Pakistan's visit to India. The South African team led by Clive Rice had taken a chartered flight to Calcutta at a week's notice and were amazed to find thousands lining the streets to greet them. The two cricket boards reached an agreement that India would be the first team to tour South Africa and end its cricket isolation. South Africa wanted to send out a message by inviting a non-white team; India wanted to send a signal about its leadership role in world cricket. The deal was struck between Madhavrao Scindia and Ali Bacher, two astute players who saw the larger picture.

There is an interesting side story here. Apparently, Asif Iqbal approached Ali Bacher with a proposal that cricket should resume in South Africa with India and Pakistan playing a series, proceeds from which would go to Imran Khan's cancer hospital project in Lahore. Ali, already committed to India, politely declined.

BCCI Makes Its First-ever Media Rights Sale

A few days before the start of South Africa's tour to India, Ali Bacher, otherwise so supremely composed, was in panic mode because the broadcast deal hadn't been closed yet. Considering the high interest among viewers back home, an anxious Ali asked BCCI to quote a price for the television rights. The request stumped the BCCI. They didn't know they owned the rights that Ali wanted to buy.

To understand the lay of the land, BCCI President Madhavrao Scindia asked me to do two things: one, check whether the BCCI owned the rights and two, in case the BCCI did own this valuable asset, to decide the price for the three-match series.

I approached Doordarshan because, in those days, they covered cricket and retained all on-air advertising revenue while the BCCI kept the in-stadia ground advertising income. I drew a blank with them. DD had no experience of selling cricket rights and were unhelpful when it came to putting a value to it. I only got vague advice: US$ 10,000 per game should be a good price.

I reached out to BCCI Secretary Jagmohan Dalmiya for a second opinion. He wasn't on the ball either and his advice was equally hit or miss: Ask South Africa for US$ 20,000 per game.

Unsure if this was the right thing to do, I played safe and asked Ali to make an offer for the BCCI to consider. Ali reverted promptly, quoting US$ 90,000 for the three-match series and then, sensing my hesitation, raised the figure to a quarter million rands, approximately US$ 120,000.

The BCCI and South Africa shook hands on that and that's how the first-ever deal for the television rights for cricket came through for India. During the 1992 Delhi ODI at the Jawaharlal Nehru Stadium, Ali handed a cheque to BCCI President Scindia.

PS: Thirty years later, the media value of each BCCI game was more than ₹100 crore.

Getting Started

The Friendship Tour saw cricket played against a backdrop of political turbulence. In the aftermath of Nelson Mandela's release from prison, there was uncertainty about how the transfer of power would play out. The South African Cricket Board led by Ali and Joe Pamensky united different cricket bodies under one banner and launched an inclusive programme. Ali ran the cricket but he looked up to Joe, an imposing man who exuded power and authority.

The Indian team included stalwarts (Azhar, Ravi Shastri, Kapil Dev, Sanjay Manjrekar) and rising stars (Sachin Tendulkar, Anil Kumble, Ajay Jadeja, Javagal Srinath). Ajit Wadekar had been pulled out of retirement and appointed coach and the only support staff was Dr Ali Irani, the all-rounder who wore multiple hats—of physio, trainer, doctor, assistant coach and manager—and gladly took on any additional duties assigned to him.

I understood soon enough that the manager was the boss on the tour. In a sense, he represented India and the BCCI, and was the leader of the delegation. According to settled protocol, the manager and the captain got suites in the hotel while all the others were allotted single rooms. The manager took all the calls when it came to admin: deciding which invitations and engagements (cricket or social) to accept, setting the departure time for the bus from the team hotel, laying down the policy for night curfew and media interaction and even issuing *firmaans* about the dress code. Blazer and tie for official engagements, smart casuals for social outings and, on other occasions, just about anything. But no jeans for any team function.

The manager also did some of the serious cricket stuff like convening selection committee meetings and maintaining minutes which were signed by the captain and the coach. He was the bridge between the BCCI and the host country for tickets, hotel, travel arrangements and finances. He coordinated with the match referee in the event of a dispute or a player hearing. Also, at the end of the tour, he was required to submit a confidential report on the players, reporting on their commitment, attitude and conduct.

Which I remember doing, feeling foolish—imagine a first-time, inexperienced team manager passing judgement on Azhar, Ravi Shastri and Kapil Dev! I wrote a general report which said nothing but I needn't have worried because, as I later learnt, nobody read the report anyway.

Among the less serious but painful duties of a team manager was distributing food allowances to players. This was a complicated exercise—receiving a large amount of cash, calculating the amount due to each player, keeping the accounts and maintaining a register where players signed for the money they received. Fortunately, Ali Bacher saved me from this misery, short-circuiting the process by instructing his office to work the numbers and place the exact amounts in separate envelopes. This made my job easy as I only had to call out the names of the players in the team bus and hand out the envelopes.

As team manager I met many important people, including Steve Tshwete, a staunch ally of Ali Bacher within the African National Congress (ANC) who later became the sports minister of South Africa. Steve was close to Thabo Mbeke, the future foreign minister who succeeded Mandela to become the president of South Africa. In Zimbabwe I met Justice Ibrahim, the cultured gentleman who headed Zimbabwe cricket.

India's influence could be seen everywhere in South Africa, especially in Durban, the city with more people of Indian origin than any other city outside of India. Local FM radio played Hindi film music round the clock even though the fourth- or fifth-generation Indians here did not understand the language and couldn't follow the lyrics. We were surprised to find samosas being served as starters and curry as the main dish at official banquets. The local people were warm and welcoming and, inevitably, the team was invited to the homes of Indians.

One bonus of this was that players got to eat homemade Indian food, something the vegetarians in particular looked forward to, as the local cuisine was more suited to those who ate meat. Srinath and Kumble, though, were prepared for any eventuality; they had brought along a small pressure cooker and prepared rice and sambar in their hotel room.

My task as the team manager was made easy by Ali Bacher, always so composed that he could have given tips to Mahendra Singh Dhoni. Ali, never shaken or stirred, was always one step ahead because of his extraordinary efficiency. His day started very early and he cleared his desk before going for a morning jog. A quick on-the-go breakfast and he would be back in his office by eight. During the tour, Ali and I established a routine. Every morning, we would speak and settle any issues that needed attention. Ali gave helpful suggestions about cricket and the political developments playing out in the background.

Ali self-deprecatingly described himself as a modest cricketer but he had played 15 years of first-class cricket and 12 Tests, four as captain. This was the 1967 series when South Africa whipped Australia 4-0 and Graham McKenzie got only one wicket — that of Bacher pulling a short ball, stepping on his wicket. Ali's greatest contribution, according to him, was that he kept the great Barry Richards out for a series.

Ali will be remembered especially for his contribution to social integration in post-apartheid South Africa. Mandela famously said that sports has the power to change society and when South Africa dismantled the policies of racial discrimination, Ali was among those who grasped which way the ball was running. He became an instrument of change and, as the head of a united cricket body, batted for social inclusion. He introduced programmes that supported talent from different ethnic backgrounds. He shaped change by building lasting relationships with players, sponsors, fans and broadcasters. A friend of Indian cricket, Ali is an example of a good player becoming a good administrator.

During a relaxed jog one morning around a Johannesburg golf course, Ali provided an insight about cricket administration that has stayed with me. *The job of every cricket official*, he said, *is to ensure three fundamental things: attract talent to play sport, create goodwill and organise funds.* He then asked a question: *India has these three in abundance. Every kid loves to swing a bat and there is no shortage of support or money. So how come India is not the best cricket team in the world?*

From a cricket standpoint this was not a memorable tour, unlike 1971 or 1983. India lost the Tests (0-1) and the one-dayers (2-5). What the statistics don't reveal is that South African cricket, despite twenty years of isolation and political lockdown, was robust and capable of taking on the best. It had great infrastructure, more floodlit venues than other countries, a good tournament structure, players with a professional attitude, and forward-looking cricket administrators. Hansie Cronje was a fringe player at the time and not yet established in the side, but his potential was there for all to see. Ali had no hesitation in declaring that Hansie would be their next captain.

There was also plenty of non-field action during the three-month tour. The team was granted a private audience with Nelson Mandela and the players were delighted when he made time to watch a match in Johannesburg. Shortly after Mandela's visit, I remember, I received a message that President Frederik Willem de Klerk would be at the Centurion game and wished to meet the team. I knew it would be bad optics for the Indian team to be seen with him. But how do you decline a request from a president? Ultimately, a solution was found whereby President de Klerk came to the dressing room, shook hands with the boys, chatted for a while and left. The visit lasted barely ten minutes.

Harare, October 1992

En route to South Africa, the Indian team stopped in Harare to play a Test match. Zimbabwe's entry into Test cricket was disappointingly low-key with very few spectators turning up for the inaugural game. The two captains went out to toss and the teams lined up for the formal pre-game introduction. The start, however, was delayed. The cause of the delay? The late arrival of President Mugabe, whose official residence was next door to the Harare

Cricket Club. He arrived after a longish wait, shook hands all around, wished both teams luck, and only after that did the umpires call play.

The Test nearly became an embarrassment for India—at one point, the team struggled to avoid a follow-on against a side comprising mostly of unknowns and nobodies. Zimbabwe made 456 and India limped to 307. In a way, the Harare hop was a practice net, a warm-up game before the tougher South Africa tour. Cricket was an amatuer sport in Zimbabwe, with players holding regular jobs and practising only on weekends. But even without money, motivation and a proper cricket structure, they gave India a mighty scare.

The only positive from India's perspective was the helicopter ride to see the spectacular Victoria falls on the Zambezi River on the Zimbabwe–Zambia border.

Highlights

- Sachin Tendulkar was dismissed for zero, caught and bowled by Traicos, age 45, who finished with 5/86 from 50 overs.
- Sanjay Manjrekar scored a century. He was at the crease for 500 minutes and faced 397 balls.
- Unmissable all through the tour were the loud, raucous Zimbabwe fans whose voices grew louder by late afternoon, once they were sun soaked and beer drenched.

A Leap in the Dark

The South Africa tour started without a formal sign-off on the playing conditions—which would be unthinkable today. All bilateral tours are now governed by an agreement that covers every minute detail. But this wasn't done on the 1992 tour and I was told by the BCCI to close the matter with Ali. When Ali requested a meeting, I asked Azhar and Ajit Wadekar to join the discussion. *Tu dekh le*, I was politely told by both. I then dragged vice-captain Ravi Shastri to the meeting where Ali tossed up some googlies. He wanted television cameras to decide line calls, run-outs and stumpings, a system South Africa had successfully trialled in domestic cricket. Neither Ravi nor I had clear views on this and there wasn't any real reason to object. We agreed—and soon found out its significance in the first Test at Durban.

With Nicky Openheimer,
Johannesburg

Ali also wanted three umpires instead of the customary two to stand in a game, so they could take a break after every two-hour session to avoid fatigue. We turned down this suggestion, with Ravi making the valid point that umpiring requires consistency in judging no-balls, wides and lbws.

Yeh Kepler Kaun Hai?

The first team meeting in Durban highlighted the shocking fact that the Indian team's preparation and knowledge about the opposition was almost zero. Coach Wadekar wasn't up to speed, which was not surprising considering he had been away from the game for a long while. Ravi Shastri knew some of the South African players from the English county circuit, but for the other players they were just names. Their knowledge of Zimbabwe was scant, though Ravi helpfully pointed out that it was a pretty country with lovely jacaranda trees.

The general ignorance was illustrated by the innocent question asked by a player about the South African skipper: *Yeh Kepler kaun hai?* This when Kepler Wessels had already played Tests for Australia. In hindsight, I feel this question captured the extent of India's readiness for the tough cricket tour.

The Tour Opener

Nicky Oppenheimer, the South African billionaire businessman, is a cricket fanatic. He owned a private cricket ground near Johannesburg and invited the Indian team to play a tour opener on the lines of the Arundel Castle cricket games in Sussex, England, where visiting teams play a friendly warm-up game. This was an exclusive, no-spectator affair with entry by invitation only. Personal guests arrived from across the world in private jets and were seated in plush marquees around the boundary. The newly constructed pavilion was a 5-star facility with top-end hospitality and catering by chefs

Durban Test. L to R: Mohammad Azharuddin, Ajit Wadekar, Clive Lloyd, Amrit Mathur, Colin Cowdrey, Ravi Shastri

especially flown in from Bombay. The quality of food wasn't great, but I guess it's the thought that matters.

Unfortunately, plans for the grand opening sprung a leak when it began to pour early in the morning. Frantic efforts were made to dry out the pitch and outfield by using super soppers, blowers and helicopters, but the slushy ground was clearly unplayable. By mid-afternoon the guests had begun to get restless with too much wine and no cricket. To prevent a complete washout, the players sportingly agreed to have a hit and provide some entertainment.

The gloomy afternoon was lit up by Sachin, who, much to everyone's delight, blazed to a hundred in no time. After the game the invited media asked for an unscheduled interaction with the players in a tent next to the new pavilion. Sachin handled the press conference and the excited gaggle of journalists like a champion celebrity. Ali, who knew a bit about the media, gasped in admiration: *This man is a genius, an absolute superstar!*

Firsts on the Tour

The first Test at Durban was historic in more ways than one. Before the start, ICC chief Colin Cowdrey inaugurated the new pavilion stand and the two captains, accompanied by Krish Mackerdhuj, the chief of the South African Cricket Board, released pigeons to signify peace and friendship.

Test Highlights

- The first ball produced a wicket—Jimmy Cook nicked Kapil Dev to Sachin Tendulkar at slip.
- Praveen Amre scored a hundred on his debut on a green top, coming in to bat with India on the ropes at 38/4. In the pre-match team meeting the previous evening, he had made a stirring *desh bhakti* speech in true Manoj Kumar style about the honour of playing for India.
- Sachin became Test cricket's first 'TV victim', caught short by the camera from a direct hit by Jonty Rhodes. Some of us who were sitting near the boundary thought he was safely in.

Long before India became familiar with it, the concept of 'player appearances' at commercial and social events was quite common in South Africa. In this arrangement, players had to show up, 'appear' at malls, showrooms and private dinners to sign autographs, pose for photographs, cut a ribbon or make a short speech—for a fee paid in advance. The Indian players found themselves in demand for such commercial events, especially with businesses run by Indians.

Durban Test, ceremonial opening.
L to R: Krish Mackerdhuj, Azharuddin, Kepler Wessels, Amrit Mathur

On one occasion, some of the Indian players visited a popular men's clothing store in Durban, called Casanova of all things. The money was good but snide (and unfair) remarks circulated later about some hidden, previously unknown skills of Indian cricketers.

Replay in Johannesburg

The fourth ODI was rained out, to the disappointment of a packed stadium. A worried Ali came to the Indian dressing room and took me aside to make a surprising suggestion. *See all these blokes waiting patiently for play to start? They paid good money to see the Indian stars play and for us the Johannesburg game is like Boxing Day at the Melbourne Cricket Ground.* Then he made a stunning offer: *Instead of scrapping the game—rained off—how about just rescheduling it for tomorrow? We play tomorrow,* he said in his characteristically cool manner. *Nothing changes.*

Surprised that he was so casually suggesting rescheduling an official international game, I replied that the team was due to travel the next morning and this would mean changing too many things. Ali was prepared for this pushback. *Leave that to me,* he said with the assurance of a person who knows what he is doing. *That's all sorted, I have handled that. Everything is in place; the broadcasters and the South African team are on board. You talk to your boys.*

Which I did. In one corner of the Wanderers dressing room, I put Ali's audacious proposal to Azhar, Ravi, Kapil and Sachin. After a brief chat they green-lighted the idea. The two teams played the next day at Johannesburg in bright sunshine in front of a happy, sold-out crowd.

In hindsight, the incident frightens me. How could we reschedule an international game as if it was a friendly weekend club match in some dusty maidan? Could this happen today? Such a change now would involve the ICC, the two boards, sponsors, broadcasters and other stakeholders. But those were simpler times and I could take that decision with the consent of the players because the BCCI wasn't breathing down my neck, giving instructions and demanding compliance. Forget seeking permission, I don't remember informing anyone back in India. We just went ahead and played the game.

Fitness Troubles

India was blown away by a superior, better prepared team. We found out that South Africa, despite years of isolation, was very much part of cricket's first world with its competitive domestic cricket and tough professional players. To cite one example, during practice ahead of an ODI, captain Wessels and Fanie de Villiers collided with each other while going for a high catch. Both suffered serious injuries which required multiple stitches on the face. I met

Wessels, his face heavily bandaged, in the hotel lift the same evening. He shrugged off the pain and said he would be fit to play the next day—and play he did. Same with Fanie, who was put through a tough fitness test the next morning. My guess: In a similar situation, most Indian players would have rested in the hotel.

Not Kapil Dev though, who pulled a hamstring before a game. Coach Wadekar thought it best that he take a break. But the champion all-rounder was determined not to miss out. Standard protocol in such situations demands a fitness test supervised by the physiotherapist. On the morning of the game, Kapil, in obvious pain, went through the drill, driven by willpower and bulldog determination. After a tough test, physiotherapist Ali Irani declared him good to go, shaking his head in amazement: *Kapil paaji ki himmat ka jawab nahin!*

In 1992, fitness was a choice players made. It was good to attain but not non-negotiable as it is today. But for Kapil, working on fitness was central to training and preparation. He knew his body and knew what worked for him, and his go-to strategy was long runs to build strength in his legs. Kapil and his fitness partner Ajay Jadeja would often jog back to the hotel after playing instead of hopping on to the team bus.

A Freak Injury

At a practice session, W.V. Raman was getting ready to bat. Slated to go in next, he was putting on his thigh pad. Just when he bent down to collect his gear before going in, Vijay Yadav, who was standing near him, picked a ball from the net and chucked it back to the bowler. The ball did not get that far, instead it hit Raman bang on his face, close to the left eye. He needed stitches and was out of action for a few games. He recovered later to score a sparkling hundred in the Centurion ODI which India won. Raman's other (and less painful) memory from the tour is Sachin's masterly century at the Wanderers and facing Brett Schultz, the tall left-arm quick sending thunderbolts from an awkward action.

Raman got limited chances for India but is a respected coach with an awe-inspiring track record. He has worked with Ranji teams (West Bengal and Tamil Nadu), IPL franchises (Kings XI Punjab and Kolkata Knight Riders), with junior players (India A and Emerging India teams) and has been head coach of the Indian women's team.

The End of a Career

The tour sadly also brought to a close Ravi Shastri's career as a cricket player. A knee injury had been troubling him for a while and he'd had an arthroscopy done earlier in Sydney on his left knee. In South Africa, the injury flared up with a tear in the posterior ligament. We contacted Dr Dave Pollock, an authority in this field, and Ravi and I went to Cape Town to meet him. After looking at the test results, Dr Pollock recommended surgery but before that he sat Ravi down to explain the situation in a manner that was brutally frank. He told Ravi that, despite surgery, the knee wouldn't mend enough for him to play competitive international sport. *You might want to look at other things to do.*

With vice-captain Ravi Shastri

I was with Ravi in the hospital during this difficult period. The surgery was satisfactory but the knee wasn't good enough despite extensive rehab. A few months after the South Africa tour, Ravi retired from all cricket. He was only 31. He still remembers the traumatic experience as if it was yesterday. The doctor's assessment of the impact of the injury on his career came as a shock to him at the time, but he now appreciates the fact that the doctor was upfront and didn't hold out any false hope.

Ravi transitioned from the dressing room to the commentary box and his new career took off—to use his trademark phrase—like a tracer bullet. His 11-year cricket career (80 Tests and 150 ODIs) was remarkable for his versatility and raw grit. Starting in Mumbai as a 17-year-old, he began playing for India within two years, taking three wickets in four balls in his Test debut. Later, success came more with the bat than with the ball. Ravi was often booed by fans for his slow batting but he smashed Tilak Raj for six sixes in an over, blazing to the quickest double hundred in Ranji (113

29

minutes/123 balls). For India, Ravi first batted at number ten but steadily climbed up the order to open the innings. He went on to become India's most successful opener overseas, scoring 5 of his 11 hundreds in England (including one at Lord's), West Indies, Pakistan and Australia against top bowlers who were fast and fierce.

The South Africa tour was clearly not a memorable one for Ravi, but he fondly remembers meeting Nelson Mandela. There is a reason why this was special. When he was playing county cricket in England for Glamorgan, Ravi was approached to join a rebel tour to South Africa with a you-name-your-price kind of offer. Ravi put away the juicy half-volley with disdain, saying he would happily play in South Africa—but only in official cricket as an India player. When the Indian team landed in Durban, Ravi ran into the person who had tried recruiting him. He shook hands with him politely, then pointed to the Indian team blazer and said: *Mate, I am here—in an official capacity, with the Indian team!*

Hunter on the Prowl

Early one morning, I was woken up by frantic callers enquiring whether I had seen the Manoj Prabhakar interview in a Durban tabloid. Apparently, in an exclusive to a young female reporter, Manoj had touched briefly upon his cricketing career and spoken at great length about his other skills, notably those which female fans found irresistible. He boasted about his charm and strike rate and described himself, rather interestingly, as a *hunter*.

Sensational stuff, but senseless distraction at the beginning of the tour. Exactly what the team did not need. A quick glance at the newspaper headline was enough to convince me this was bizarre bordering on crazy. Absolutely cringeworthy. Why would anyone shoot his mouth off and make wild statements—that too, on record, during a formal interview with a journalist?

The BCCI president was soon on the phone from India, screaming with rage and demanding an explanation. He wanted Prabhakar to be put on the first flight back. As the team manager, the ball was squarely in my court. The issues before me were:

- Check the story: Did it happen, did Manoj actually shoot his mouth off?
- Damage control: Negative publicity was the last thing the Indian team needed.
- Administrative response: Take action, set limits, prevent repeats.

Enquiries confirmed that the interview did take place and the news report wasn't an instance of journalistic creativity but the irrefutable truth. More damning was the fact that the interview took place not in the hotel lobby but in Manoj's room, apparently on his insistence. The contents were correct and there was no misreporting, no 'I have been misquoted' defence. The reporter offered to share the taped interview with me and said that what appeared in print was the tame stuff—she had already edited out the juicy bits.

That evening, in a team meeting, I informed the players that the BCCI president wanted Manoj to be sent home. Without passing any judgement on the matter, Manoj was asked to explain the what and why of the interview to his colleagues so that they could know first-hand what had happened. This he did with some embarrassment but little regret. He denied his role, but his defence was as weak as a number eleven's batting technique.

With that, the matter stood closed. The *hunter* got the message that this game was banned and another irresponsible strike would attract severe penalties. The players understood that it had to be cricket first—and last—because when it came to Team India you couldn't cross the line. I realised that the manager's job was more challenging than I had thought. Forget enemies, you had to watch out for friendly fire from your own side.

A Swinging Party

Of the hectic social side of the cricket tour, what stood out was the New Year's Eve party hosted in Cape Town by Sol Kerzner, the casino tycoon who had built Sun City and Lost City, South Africa's Las Vegas, along with the iconic Atlantis Hotel in Dubai. Sol was a flamboyant figure, a magnified Vijay Mallya-like showman known for his over-the-top lifestyle.

To bring in the New Year, guests reached his palatial residence on the top of a hill overlooking the sea after clearing many levels of security. The hospitality was of a level befitting a modern maharaja. Precisely at midnight, firecrackers lit up the sky above the ships anchored at sea and by the time the celebrations wound up many hours later, most of the guests were happy and some smashed by the excesses of the evening.

Before that I witnessed an interesting exchange between Kapil and a business tycoon, someone very high up in Rothmans who was apparently a keen student of the game. The gentleman, assisted by a generous amount of *daaru*, proceeded to explain the intricacies of swing bowling in great detail.

For a while Kapil played with a straight bat, giving him a patient hearing, nodding his head from time to time to indicate he was alert and attentive. Then, unable to hold back, he launched a strong counterattack by giving him a quick lesson in how to run his business! This was reverse swing, in 1992, long before Pakistani quicks invented the art.

Kepler vs Kapil

In 1992, Kapil Dev was Indian cricket's top star, a hero celebrated for his exploits with both the bat and the ball and admired for his *dabang* style. He played hard but his rugged face was never without a smile. He batted like a carefree millionaire and bowled lethal outswingers. A great entertainer, he enjoyed what he did and gave joy to those who watched. In South Africa, Kapil was expected to run through the batsmen and hold India's middle order together, but he was not at his best. Except for a spectacular performance in the third Test at Port Elizabeth where Allan Donald demolished India by taking 12 wickets.

In the second innings India was miserable at 27/5, then 31/6 before Paaji, the number 7, launched an astonishing counterattack. In an innings of extraordinary daring and defiance, Kapil Dev made 129 runs in a team total of 215 (the next highest score by a player in that innings was 17), savagely hitting Donald, Brett Schultz and Brian McMillan.

This stunning feat was eclipsed by controversy when Kapil ran out Peter Kirsten at the non-striker's end after warning him twice earlier. Kirsten stormed into the pavilion, red-faced and angry, projecting himself as the aggrieved party.

The facts of the run-out were quite different. Kirsten, the non-striker, was prone to going for a walk and taking an illegal start as the bowler ran in. Kapil, noticing this, warned him, not once but twice, and on the third occasion he took the bails off. The umpire, guided by the laws of cricket, ruled Kirsten run-out. The South African team thought this was 'unfair' and against the 'spirit of the game'. The Indian team thought this stand was rubbish because the 'spirit' was violated when Kirsten, the non-striker, kept leaving the crease despite being warned.

The run-out triggered a series of unpleasant events, starting with Kepler Wessels hitting Kapil on the ankle with his bat while taking a run. At first, this looked like a harmless accident, a case of a batsman colliding mid-pitch with a bowler. During tea, an incensed Kapil offered a different version of what had transpired in the middle. He was convinced Kepler hit him on purpose.

With tempers running high, an outraged Indian dressing room demanded action and it was decided that I, as the team manager, should lodge a complaint with the ICC match referee, Clive Lloyd. Based on Kapil's version, I wrote a complaint and handed it to Lloyd, who looked as if I had handed him a live hand grenade.

Deliberate physical assault and violence on the cricket field is a serious matter. Also, this was not a frivolous charge by just somebody against a nobody; it was Kapil Dev, a high-profile star, against Kepler Wessels, captain of a national team. Besides the 'spirit' of cricket and the code of conduct, it was a juicy media story worthy of front-page banner headlines.

That evening, at the post-play press conference, the media centre was understandably packed. When asked about the run-out and the subsequent incident, I stated the Indian team's position and mentioned the official complaint to the match referee. This ruffled my friend Ali Bacher, who thought it was inappropriate to prejudge the case and urged restraint in the matter. I understood Ali's concern — the last thing he wanted was controversy and negative publicity. He had worked incredibly hard to put this tour together and the Indian team's visit was to have a deep impact on the future direction of cricket and sport in South Africa. He feared the controversy could undo the good work of the cricket board.

ICC referee Clive Lloyd was caught in an equally difficult situation. He struggled to make up his mind, not sure what to do with the conflicting arguments presented before him during the inquiry. Kapil argued his case forcefully, convinced that Wessels did what he did on purpose. Wessels refuted the charge (with a very straight face). He claimed that it was an accident. Unable to decide, Lloyd said this was a case of one person's word against the other's. With that, he shrugged his massive shoulders and put the matter to rest.

Lloyd's inability to act decisively and his helplessness was partly due to a bizarre twist. The inquiry rested on evidence and the key to resolving the issue was TV footage, the visuals of what had happened on the field. But here Lloyd reached a dead end because the broadcaster, SABC, declined to supply the relevant match recording, claiming it had been inadvertently deleted due to a technical glitch. This convinced nobody and only strengthened the belief that the footage had been deliberately suppressed to hide an inconvenient truth.

Realising that the inquiry was going nowhere, I appealed to Lloyd, resting my case on the logic that Kapil Dev was not one to press imaginary charges. It was disrespectful to assume that a cricketer who was known for his integrity would make an insincere complaint. Lloyd knew who was in the wrong but hesitated to trust his conscience. I also got the sense, when I saw him agonising about what call to take, that he was worried about a racist angle in case he held Wessels guilty of misconduct.

Was Lloyd under pressure to close the matter? Did he lack the moral courage in a tricky situation which could have exposed him to criticism? Did he, after weighing different options, decide to play safe?

It's difficult to tell for sure, but I felt that the 'big cat', otherwise so decisive at the crease, had decided to let the ball go and not play a shot.

Meeting Nelson Mandela

Before the Indian team's departure for South Africa, BCCI President Madhavrao Scindia had given me one instruction: the first thing the team should do is call on Nelson Mandela. This directive put the tour to South Africa in perspective. From a cricket standpoint, this was a manned mission into the unknown, there being no intelligence about South African grounds, conditions, pitches or players. It was, however, apparent that forces other than cricket were also at play and that there was a political context to the trip. The Indian team's visit was to make a statement that went beyond cricket.

After the rousing reception that the team received in Durban, which involved a ride from the airport to the hotel in open cars and a civic reception, I spoke to Ali about meeting Mandela. An appointment was soon granted and a visibly excited team set out to meet the great man one afternoon in Johannesburg. With us were key officials of South African cricket and the ANC: Krish Mackerdhuj, Ali Bacher and Steve Tshwete. Anand Sharma, who was then working for political change with the ANC and later went on to become the minister of external affairs in the Government of India, also accompanied us.

Ahead of the meeting, two matters caused concern. The first was to do with a gift for the great man. Would it be proper to present him with a BCCI tie, a team shirt, a traditional Indian artefact or a silk scarf? After much debate, a safe option was chosen: a cricket bat signed by the team.

The other matter worried me directly as the team manager. On formal occasions, the standard drill is that the manager says a few words on behalf of the BCCI and the team. In routine circumstances, the usual polite words would have been enough, but this was no ordinary occasion. The Indian team was meeting an iconic world leader and it was my responsibility to say the right things. I worked hard on my speech, making sure it included Gandhi, peace, satyagraha, non-cooperation, and close ties between India and South Africa. I memorised it by heart, then rehearsed it many times.

The team was led into Mandela's office after passing through several layers of security, with metal doors that opened and shut with the press of buttons, iron grills and trained (and armed) personnel frisking everyone. Afterwards, we stood around in a hall waiting for him to arrive. A short while later, Mandela walked in, serene and gracious, a half-smile on his face, radiating warmth and goodness, exuding charm and humility. We looked at him, speechless with awe, thrilled at the opportunity to meet him, blessed to be in his presence.

Handshakes done and introductions made, it was time for business and my turn to speak. As everyone stood around in a semicircle, taking a deep breath and saying a silent prayer, I recited my practised piece, thankfully without stuttering or stammering. An awkward silence followed my speech. We were waiting to hear Mandela speak, but apparently, he was waiting for something. A little later, an aide rushed in with a piece of paper containing points for him to use in his speech. He glanced at the paper quickly and then spoke eloquently, his words simple, encouraging and deeply inspiring.

Mandela graciously accepted the signed bat and said he appreciated the thoughtful gesture of the team. Later, Krish Mackerdhuj told me that the bat was displayed prominently on the mantelpiece in his office.

Mandela came to the Wanderers and watched the Test match with interest. I sat with him, answering all the questions he asked about the players and the game. He believed that sport had the power to change the world and perhaps, in a tiny way, the Indian team made a difference in South Africa in 1992–93.

PS: My most treasured possession is a photograph with him, signed: To Emrit, Mandela.

Tour Wrap

The tour was a massive education for me, a priceless cricket tuition of the highest quality that gave me an inside view of the dynamics of the team, the role of the captain (Azhar) and the coach (Ajit Wadekar) and the relationship between the seniors (Kapil, Ravi) and the juniors (Sachin, Srinath, Kumble).

L to R: Krish Mackerdhuj, Amrit Mathur, Nelson Mandela, Ali Bacher

My appointment as manager on this sensitive mission had come as a surprise to me and a shock to others. When Madhavrao Scindia announced my nomination in a BCCI meeting, some thought it ill-advised to name someone so young and inexperienced, but no one had the courage to question his decision.

The doubts about my abilities were not altogether misplaced. Yes, I was inexperienced, relatively new to the BCCI, and hadn't been around the Indian team till then in any formal capacity. I had no clue what the manager was supposed to do. And yes, I was young for the job, didn't have any grey hair and was roughly the same age as Kapil Dev, the respected senior statesman of the touring squad. When the team landed in Harare and local officials came searching for an 'elderly' manager, it was Kapil who directed them to me. I learnt later that I was the youngest India manager since Fatesinghrao (Jackie) Gaekwad, the Maharaja of Baroda, who was 29 years old on the tour to England in 1959, and only 33 when he became the BCCI president in 1963.

This was a unique tour given the political context. The team depended on individual flair and brilliance, unsupported by planning or any strategic thinking, like students appearing for a tough examination without looking at the course material. Team meetings ahead of games were timepass, where everybody had tea and wished each other good luck. Practice sessions were unfocused, not very different from university or Ranji nets. Perhaps it's unfair to compare cricket then with cricket now—those were medieval times and the game has evolved rapidly since then.

Azhar was an old-school captain, relatively hands-off, distant at times. He thought players at this level should know what to do and shouldn't be treated like kids. If things went wrong, they ought to sort them out by themselves. When they didn't go right, Azhar's response was to shrug his shoulders, bite his nails and shake his head in disappointment. The Indian team in South Africa was an aircraft on autopilot, directionless and a touch out of control.

The tour didn't go well for the senior players. Azhar felt the heat but kept his sorrows to himself and, at a personal level, remained extremely pleasant and likeable. He lived in his own world, aloof and distant, seemingly

Game sanctuary visit on a day off. L to R: Vijay Yadav, Subroto Banerjee, Kapil Dev, Venkatapathy Raju, Kiran More, Anil Kumble, Amrit Mathur

unaffected by what was happening around him. I went shopping with him a few times and discovered he was fond of branded stuff and designer suits, described by him as 'class'. I also discovered he had an amazing memory: once, when filling a form at an airport, I was trying to remember my passport number when he rattled it off. Seeing my surprised look, he explained: *Passport pehle dekha tha ek baar, flight pe.*

All through the tour, Ravi Shastri struggled for runs at the top of the order and was hampered by a career-threatening knee injury. Sanjay Manjrekar was seriously tested by a new ball attack that was sharp and relentless.

Kapil Dev's performance fell short of his own high standards and, like any great champion used to uninterrupted success, he found this phase particularly stressful. And yet, he held himself together.

I had discovered early on that success and adulation sat easily on Paaji. He was a star without makeup or practiced lines, a living example of 'Sirji, we are like this only'. He had a natural flair for cricket, which is why the smile never left his face.

Hard work was his mantra, physical pain only a temporary nuisance. When young fast bowlers went to him for advice, Paaji told them to run, *bhaago, to build strong legs. Swing, pace apne aap aa jayegi.* What was his secret, I once asked him. His simple response: *Mehnat, aur pet mein aag honi chahiye.*

I realised soon enough that *mehnat* was indeed the basic building block and he never spared himself. He turned up for every optional practice session and often jogged back to the hotel after play instead of taking the bus.

During the tour, it became clear that Indian cricket was turning towards a new set of players. From now on, the batting would rely on Sachin and India's bowling would be in the capable hands of Kumble and Srinath.

India's performance disappointed fans who wanted the team to vanquish its hosts in order to shatter the repulsive white supremacy theory. Unfortunately, that did not happen and once, after a loss in Durban, the players faced angry fans who expressed their feelings freely.

From a political standpoint, the Friendship Tour was significant as it marked the cricket rebirth of a proud nation and India played a role in this. At times, the busy social side became a distraction and a burden for the players and for me because of the endless speeches I had to make on behalf of the team. But I found a way out by encouraging players to take on some off-field responsibilities. Kapil was always happy to speak a few entertaining words and young Ajay Jadeja was also surprisingly good.

Once, I was at the receiving end of a freak injury. During team practice, I was standing at the shortish square leg, behind the protective net, when Sanjay Manjrekar's on-drive ricocheted off the metal pole and struck me on my forehead. The impact split my sunglasses in two and left a deep gash near my left eye. I was rushed to the hospital with minor bleeding and required six stitches but was soon well.

For me, the manager thrown into the deep end, the tour was a success in the sense that I came out without doing anything foolish and navigated the difficult terrain without setting off a landmine. Not failing was in itself a victory and it was quite an experience shaking hands with Mugabe and Mandela.

I recall that *Sunday*, the popular weekly magazine, ran a special piece, 'Mathur Mania', on my role. And Sanjay Manjrekar wrote in Cricinfo, 'There were too many official functions and he handled them so well. He was such a good communicator and a guy who spoke on behalf of us and presented the Indian perspective. He was young and on the same wavelength. He did a brilliant job.'

Ali Bacher wrote to Madhavrao Scindia, thanking him for the Indian team's visit. In the letter, he noted, 'Amrit Mathur is a gem, BCCI should look after him!'

The Mathur mania

SILLY POINT

V GANGADHAR'S COLUMN

THE sports desks of most of the Indian newspapers are now confronted with a major problem. The Mathur mania of the cricket correspondents who are covering the Indian team's tour of South Africa.

Let me explain. Agency correspondents, special correspondents, syndicated correspondents, in fact, cricket writers of all hues seem to be obsessed with the activities of team manager Amrit Mathur. Everyday, millions of words are filed on what Mathur did, spoke, advised, instructed and so on, relegating even details of the actual game.

Let us now spend sometime at the sports desk of a national newspaper to find out how it deals with this torrent of material on Amrit Mathur. Those present on the scene are the sports editor, a couple of sub editors who are in charge of the layout.

Editor: The Test could take an interesting turn. Particularly on the last day, if the wicket takes some spin. Has our correspondent sent anything today?

Sub: Nothing has arrived on the state of the game. But he has already sent three columns on Amrit Mathur's encouraging words to the players and how the entire team looked rejuvenated after listening to Mathur.

Editor: That's okay. But we do have a lot of standing matter on Mathur, have we?

Sub: Certainly. I think around 60 columns of matter are pending on Mathur. This is after publishing 675 columns of material on Mathur ever since the begining of the South African tour. Today, Sunil Gavaskar has sent something on how the entire team and the accompanying journalists kneel down, pray and sing bhajans thanking Ishwar, Allah and Esu, for their good fortune in having Amrit Mathur as the manager of the team. Very moving.

Editor: Mathur is okay, but how can any paper carry so much on the manager? There should be some limit on the Mathur coverage. That is what I instructed our special correspondent. Has he replied to my fax?

Sub: Yes, the reply came last night. He explained he does not want to be left behind because every single correspondent is on the Mathur bandwagon. He says that the correspondents do not watch the game themselves. On the contrary, they make a circle around Mathur and then take down his comments and observations on the game.

Editor: I think that is going too far. Tell our chap he has to cover the game on his own. Here's something coming on the fax. Perhaps it is the curtain-raiser on the last day's play. Let's have a look.

Sub: No, this has nothing to do with the game. It is the medical reports of 22 doctors who attended to the wound received by Amrit Mathur, when he was supervising the net practice. Remember, he received a gash on his forehead. And then all the scribes gathered around Mathur offering him their blood.

Editor: This is rather unusual. But Mathur's injury was not serious at all. Why make such a fuss?

Sub: I don't know. But according to the 'Behind the Scenes' story put out by the Professional Management Group, the scribes were worried over Mathur's injury. Some of them offered to shave their heads, donate half their daily allowance and even give up drinks, if Mathur recovered quickly.

Editor: I don't know what is happening to cricket journalism.

Telephone rings. The editor has a long conversation with the man at the other end of the phone.

Editor: That was our man in Jo'burg. He says he is filing details of Mathur's meeting with Mandela, Mathur's visit to the Gandhi ashram, Mathur's gesture in handing over cricket kit to some black youngsters, the wonderful scene inside the AIR commentary box when Suresh Saraiya and Harsha Bhogle competed with each other in shining Mathur's shoes and the unusual sight of Sunil Gavaskar and Ayaz Memon carrying Mathur's laundry. He is also doing a story 'A Day in the Life of Amrit Mathur'. Do we need so much on Mathur?

Sub: Certainly, we must. Particularly when Mathur happens to be the favourite bureaucrat who was handpicked as manager by a popular cabinet minister. The right-hand man of a minister deserves special media attention. Here is something on the fax. An agency copy on Mathur's views on South African women. He says he has clarified Manoj Prabhakar's views on the same subject.

4

WILLS WORLD CUP, 1996

Can you come over? It was Madhavrao Scindia on the phone and the urgent tone suggested he wasn't actually asking. This was late one evening in January 1993, soon after I returned from the Indian team's tour of South Africa. I rushed to his 27, Safdarjung Road residence and was shown into his office.

Scindia told me India was bidding for the 1996 World Cup and this would be put to vote by the ICC. The crucial question in the election arithmetic was which way South Africa (Ali Bacher) and Zimbabwe (Peter Chingoka) would go. I briefed him about the two gentlemen based on my recent interactions with them.

After a long chat about the possible scenarios, he saw me to the door. As I waited for my car to arrive, he said abruptly, *I am going to London for the ICC meeting, why don't you come with me?* Taken by surprise, I muttered that I would need various government permissions (from my employers, the Railways) to travel abroad. He brushed aside my objections. *Don't worry*, he said. *I'll speak to your minister. You make your travel arrangements.* Within a week of that late-night meeting, I found myself in London, part of a small BCCI team that included Jagmohan Dalmiya and I.S. Bindra.

The right to host the World Cup was subject to a financial bid and, having done the maths, Dalmiya had persuaded Scindia to put the BCCI's hat in the ring. The financial numbers were important because the ICC split the guaranteed amount paid by the host among (the few) Test-playing nations and (the majority) associate members. Driven by self-interest, members voted for whoever promised more money. To secure support from the Test-playing nations, an alliance was formed by India with neighbours Pakistan and Sri Lanka. PILCOM (Pak–Indo–Lanka Joint Management Committee) was formed with Pakistan and India as equal partners while Sri Lanka de-risked itself and decided against any commercial stake in the project. (PILCOM later became a template for Test-playing nations from the subcontinent when they wished to push a common agenda and speak in one voice.)

To get the associate ICC members on board, Indian-style election strategies were used. First, various Indian- and Pakistani-origin people controlling cricket bodies were identified. This was followed by an emotional appeal that sought to give PILCOM's bid an anti-white (we need to teach the racist nations a lesson) angle.

But the critical bit was putting an attractive financial package on the table. In a clever move, PILCOM tweaked the commercial payout to offer a larger guarantee to each associate member by cutting back on the shares of the Test-playing nations. It also offered a larger piece of the financial cake to the ICC and sliced it in a manner that ensured the majority, i.e., the associates, got a bigger helping.

The political reverse swing worked. PILCOM secured a majority (the white nations opposed and South Africa abstained, not wanting to offend either group) but there was a hitch because two or three of the Test-playing members held an indirect veto on the decision. The outcome was a deadlock but when the associates unanimously supported PILCOM, the ICC was compelled to award the 1996 World Cup to the subcontinent, with India, Pakistan and Sri Lanka jointly hosting the matches.

PILCOM Wins the Bid

ICC meetings are traditionally held at Lord's, on the ground floor of the main pavilion. On the day of the meeting, delegates from different countries trickled in. As per procedure, two delegates from each Test-playing nation attended. Scindia and Dalmiya, president and secretary, represented the BCCI while Bindra and I waited outside in the Long Room. Keeping us company were our colleagues from Pakistan, among them General Zahid Ali Akbar, Ehsan Mani and Imran Khan.

For all of us, it was a long, frustrating wait. The meeting went on forever and we, the backroom support team, had little to do. Surprisingly, the meeting attracted little attention and the media gave it a miss. Neither was Lord's fussed about what was happening and although we waited all day, there was practically nothing to eat. The staff at Lord's placed a self-service trolley in a corner that had tea, coffee and some cookies. That was all.

Bored by the wait, Imran and I stepped out of the Long Room in the afternoon and walked through the famous gate to stretch our legs and get some fresh air. No sooner had we taken a few steps along the boundary than a steward showed up to hand out a polite warning. Stepping on the grass is not allowed, sir, we were sternly told.

Imagine! This was in January, with no cricket on the horizon for at least three months. Could we have damaged the Lord's turf in any way? Also, remember, this was Imran Khan, Pakistan captain and cricket legend, being told to take a walk for walking on the grass next to the boundary!

Wills World Cup mascot launch: Madhavrao Scindia, I.S. Bindra

The PILCOM Nomination

PILCOM had ten members—four each from India and Pakistan, and two from Sri Lanka. This construct triggered a scramble in the BCCI with members scurrying for a position on the committee. Pakistan and Sri Lanka chose their representatives and urged India to name theirs. To put a lid on the lobbying, Scindia summoned Jagmohan Dalmiya to Delhi. We met in his television room lined with crystal and silver, framed photographs on side tables, and antiques and paintings on the walls.

When asked to name four members, Scindia first proposed my name. This shocked everyone. There was a tense silence before Dalmiya collected himself to point out that I was the junior-most member of the BCCI and many seniors, including former presidents of the board, would be very upset.

Scindia heard him out patiently, then said in a firm voice: *Let us discuss the other three names.* Game, set and match! The discussion was closed. Finally, India's four PILCOM nominees were: Madhavrao Scindia, Jagmohan Dalmiya, I.S. Bindra and Amrit Mathur. Missing from the list was C. Nagaraj, secretary, BCCI.

When I brought this up later, Scindia suggested we speak to Pakistan about including a fifth member, but the proposal didn't go through. My nomination caused heartburn, yet no one spoke about it openly in the BCCI. Nor did I sense any overt antagonism or direct negativity. Instead, others looked at me with respect as someone who enjoyed the trust of the president.

Pakistan in PILCOM

PILCOM was led by India through Dalmiya, who was the secretary-convenor of the committee. Pakistan played second fiddle because Dalmiya was not a great advocate of participatory democracy, but they were happy to come along for the ride without having to do the heavy lifting.

PILCOM faced one peculiar problem: Pakistan's members kept changing with the successive changes in the country's government. Within a short span, people joined the committee and exited as if from a revolving door: Tahir Menon, Zafar Altaf, Ashiq Qureshi, Shahid Rafi, Javed Burki and his famous cousin Majid Khan—all nominated to serve but suddenly replaced.

One constant in the continuous churn from the Pakistani side was Ehsan Mani, the likeable London-based chartered accountant who assisted the

Pakistan Cricket Board (PCB). Ehsan, a brilliant professional, meticulously examined documents and offered sound advice, especially on financial matters. He had a healthy relationship with Dalmiya and many annual PILCOM meetings were held at his London office.

An urbane, balanced voice in the otherwise noisy world of cricket, Ehsan always spoke straight and sensibly.

Meeting Justice Shah

At the beginning, PILCOM encountered a roadblock over who would head the body. Technically, the honour belonged to Pakistan because the 1987 Wills World Cup Organising Committee was headed by N.K.P. Salve from India. But a concern arose this time because the PCB chief, Justice Nasim Hasan Shah, Hon'ble Chief Justice of the Pakistan Supreme Court, was not involved with cricket full-time.

The BCCI suggested a solution: Justice Shah would be the chairman and Scindia would be designated president of PILCOM with appropriate administrative powers. There was only one catch: someone had to take this to the PCB and get Justice Shah to sign off on it.

Ahead of a meeting in Lahore, India's PILCOM members discussed the matter at length. Dalmiya and Bindra were hesitant to lead the conversation and chose to drop this hot potato on my lap.

We took an evening flight from Delhi to Lahore and drove straight from the airport to Justice Shah's official residence for dinner. It was a large party with lots of guests and typically over-the-top hospitality. When I requested Justice Shah for a word in private, he led me into a room that looked like a library-cum-office and closed the door behind us. I nervously outlined the chairman-president arrangement for PILCOM and informed him that this was a personal request from Scindia sa'ab. The Justice took not more than a minute to give his verdict. *Bilkul manzoor hai*, he said without any hesitation. *Aap unhe ittla kar de (I am in full agreement. Please inform them)*.

PS: Justice Shah is best known for his verdict against Zulfiqar Ali Bhutto that led to the death penalty. He was also responsible for the restoration of Parliament, which had been dissolved earlier by President Ghulam Ishaq Khan, thus becoming instrumental in the reinstatement of the Nawaz Sharif government in 1993.

45

Perks of PILCOM

Besides the prestige and recognition, one perk of being a member of PILCOM was the opportunity to learn first-hand the complexity of putting together a global event. The experience (and exposure) was invaluable.

Another bonus was visiting Lahore, and the annual pilgrimage to London every summer to coincide with ICC meetings. In Lahore, meetings were held at the Pearl Continental hotel or at the Gaddafi Stadium. I also have fond memories of early morning runs in *Bagh e Jinnah*, the old Company Garden, next door to the hotel.

The Arrival of WorldTel

PILCOM's first challenge was to pay the ICC the first instalment of the guarantee money, or default and lose the right to hold the World Cup. A broke PILCOM looked to raise funds by negotiating a television and media rights deal. Bids were invited, potential partners sounded, and Saatchi and Saatchi commissioned to find a broadcast partner. Despite these strenuous efforts there was no money in sight.

With the ICC deadline nearing, Mark Mascarenhas of WorldTel met me. A common friend had made the introduction. Mark requested that he be allowed to make a bid for the rights. With the bidding process over and offers already received, it seemed improper to introduce a new player at this late stage. But Mark made a compelling case by agreeing to pay a higher guarantee amount and put down an advance payment in cash for PILCOM to pay off the ICC.

I took this difficult-to-refuse offer to Mr Scindia and Dalmiya-ji. It was decided that we would discuss the matter at PILCOM's next meeting in Lahore. The two-day meeting was turbulent, the drama heightened by the Pakistani members who were upset by the last-minute entry of a new player, especially one whose background and credentials were supposedly suspect.

Their fears were not unfounded. Mark was relatively unknown in the media rights business; he was a club cricketer wanting to audition for the national side. WorldTel, his company, had no previous experience of television production or of handling an event as important as the World Cup. All Mark had to show for himself were small football deals in Europe, making money by buying cheap media rights and reselling them to broadcasters. He worked out of the US and had an office in England with nothing more than a desk, a computer and a part-time secretary. Clearly, he was a one-man army, commander-in-chief and jawan rolled into one. What worked for him was his enthusiasm and a fierce desire to clinch the deal. He was large-hearted, loud-mouthed and friendly — never short of words or energy. Like a gambler, he was willing to stake his all to make it work.

PILCOM, however, didn't share his enthusiasm. The hard-nosed committee demanded tight guarantees and money on the table. On day one of the meeting, the discussion went back and forth with people who had bid earlier, to confirm whether they were willing to make payments upfront. With no firm assurances received, PILCOM turned to Mark.

On day two, PILCOM had two urgent deadlines: one, the immediate ask of the ICC for a financial guarantee, and two, India's delegates wanting closure because they were booked on the evening flight to Delhi.

There was hard bargaining all day with PILCOM seeking guarantees and Mark providing assurances from his lawyer in New York and an accountant in London, both connected over the telephone. It was fascinating to follow the negotiation, with faxes coming in, guarantees being produced and a memorandum of understanding being drafted, amended and redrafted many times.

What I learnt that day was that business discussions are not just about broad terms. The fine print in the clauses covering likely situations is equally important. PILCOM wanted guaranteed payments and an upfront advance as well as clear commitments about quality television production. All this took time and energy and, in the end, the paperwork concluded just in time for us to dash to the airport and fly back to Delhi.

Ultimately, the television deal was Mark's because he agreed to pay PILCOM a minimum guarantee of US$ 10 million. The rights for the 1992 World Cup in Australia had gone for less than half that amount. PILCOM also received US$ 3.6 million as a cash advance to meet its urgent financial commitments.

Ehsan remembers the sale of the 1992 World Cup media rights as a path-breaking development. The spike in the value of television rights made the ICC realise where the future of cricket lay. PILCOM's calculated punt with Mark succeeded. The worldwide media rights sales fetched more than the US$ 10 million guarantee, with total sales touching US$ 23 million. PILCOM's final share was US$ 18 million — the overflow beyond the minimum guarantee of US$ 10 million was split between India and Pakistan according to a pre-agreed formula.

In the aftermath of the success of PILCOM, several important developments took place. For one, Dalmiya leveraged the World Cup to become ICC chief, the first Indian to head cricket globally. His was a remarkable journey—a businessman from Kolkata who rapidly rose to power and controlled the game worldwide. In the 1999 World Cup held in England, it was he who handed the trophy to Steve Waugh, captain of the winning Australian team. In the audience that day at Lord's was the Queen of England, who had arrived to witness the final.

With Jaggu-da's rise, India's clout grew in international cricket. The champion strategist ensured that the subcontinent stayed united and voted together on key issues—an example of vote bank politics entering the corridors of the ICC.

L: With Ehsan Mani; R: Justice Nasim Hasan Shah

Starting 1999, the ICC (under Dalmiya) claimed the World Cup as its property and managed the event to retain the profits from broadcast and sponsorship revenue. Member countries were only granted rights to 'host' the event for which they were paid a fee.

For Ehsan Mani, PILCOM became a springboard to a distinguished career in cricket administration. He went on to head the ICC with great distinction, his calm and dignified conduct encouraging a sense of inclusion and teamwork among members. He also led the PCB, handpicked by Prime Minister Imran Khan to reboot Pakistani cricket.

Mark Mascarenhas went on to become a major player in the cricket broadcasting business. He kept chasing deals, pushing the envelope in his flamboyant style and raising the bar to stay one step ahead of the competition. He moved to a ground-floor flat in London's tony Holland Park and lived life king-sized. I recall spending a leisurely afternoon with him when Imran was also present, busy on the pool table in an adjoining room. The ball-tampering controversy was raging at the time, with Pakistan's bowlers having been accused of using bottle caps, nails and artificial surfaces to work the ball. Imran admitted to this publicly but others chose the route of denial, issuing statements declaring their innocence and feigning ignorance about the practice.

A prominent bowler dropped in to meet Mark and saw Imran, who had just gone public on the issue. Nothing was said, the ball-tampering topic was not mentioned, but the *mahaul* changed—there was a strained silence and dark clouds suddenly descended over a sunny London.

PS: In a private conversation after the WorldTel deal went through, Mark Mascarenhas admitted that he had made large financial commitments to PILCOM when he had no money. He had exposed himself to serious personal risk by borrowing money to make timely payments and would have been on a very sticky wicket had the media deal failed.

A Disastrous Opening

The World Cup kicked off at Eden Gardens, but what was to be a grand opening ceremony turned out to be a total dud. With the performers' costumes held up in the Calcutta traffic, the artistes went on stage in mismatched uniforms. Flags of participating countries were hoisted upside down. The emcee, apparently under the influence of alcohol to overcome stage fright, kept messing up his lines. And to make matters worse, it started raining and a strong breeze literally blew away the laser show and the screen that was to be its centrepiece.

The botched opening angered many, not least Ali Bacher, whose displeasure was over a protocol issue. Ali was miffed that Clyde Walcott, the president of the ICC, had been sidelined—he had not been given any role in the launch of the tournament. The omission did not go down well with ICC members.

The Presidential Banquet

The opening ceremony in Eden Gardens wasn't the only thing that went wrong. The lead up to the final in Lahore was equally forgettable. A day before the final, the president of Pakistan, Farooq Leghari (ace tennis and polo player, and a shooter who represented Pakistan at the Tehran Asian

Games), held a dinner on the lawns of the Pearl Continental. The president and other VIPs occupied the high table while the other invitees (officials, players and the media) sat facing them behind a rope.

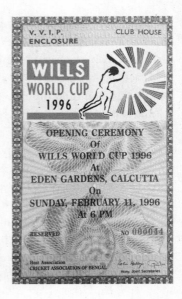

The function started late, which made everybody edgy and impatient. Aussie captain Mark Taylor was seated next to me. Thirsty and hungry, he had to curb the urge to get up and leave as long speeches caused a further delay.

What followed once the official formalities were over was pure anarchy. The main guests were served at the table but the service was annoyingly sloppy, making everyone all the more frustrated. Waiters plonked cold drinks in front of guests in a manner reminiscent of a community langar, not a presidential banquet.

While dinner dragged on in slow motion at the VIP high table, the pace was quicker for the others. As soon as the buffet was opened, there was a virtual stampede to attack the food and all the arrangements collapsed under this ugly assault. But the commotion ended as swiftly as it had begun because, having grabbed whatever food could be found, the guests trooped out, past the main table where the dignitaries were still waiting for the main course.

The president and his guests were the last to leave. By that time, the place looked like a disaster site.

The World Cup Final

The jinx on the tournament extended to the final in Lahore. The exits of India and Pakistan sapped public interest in the tournament, and the chartered flight from Chandigarh to Lahore had several last-minute cancellations. Tickets for the final, so much in demand earlier, were freely available as Indian fans changed their plans. Left with plenty of invites which nobody wanted, I offered my tickets to a grateful Sri Lanka Cricket (SLC), whose members were in need of them.

The Australia–Sri Lanka final left the fans cold. Without either India or Pakistan, it was just another cricket match, not the big, star-studded game that everyone had hoped for. A downpour ahead of the game literally washed away the VIP hospitality tent and caused traffic snarls around the Gaddafi Stadium. The chaos left many, including Imran Khan and Sharmila Tagore, fuming as they reached late.

Aravinda De Silva led Sri Lanka to a spectacular win before a disinterested crowd that stirred into action and found its voice only late in the evening. Unfortunately, it wasn't the cricket that moved them—their attention was caught by an announcement on the public address system about Prime Minister Benazir Bhutto's arrival. On hearing her name, the stadium erupted in an expression of collective displeasure. Later, during the prize distribution ceremony, she was booed as she handed the trophy to a beaming Arjuna Ranatunga. As the presentations went on, it started to rain, forcing the drenched dignitaries to run for cover.

Problems at DDCA

The Delhi District Cricket Association (DDCA) has a rich tradition of being in the news for the wrong reasons. For the BCCI, the DDCA has been a problem child in need of regular discipline, rehab and occasional punishment.

In 1996, when a key World Cup game was allotted to Delhi, the DDCA was caught up in a crisis regarding financial misappropriation. The BCCI stepped in to restore order: DDCA was suspended, president's rule imposed and a two-member ad hoc committee was constituted to organise the World Cup game. Former President P.M. Rungta was the chair and I was appointed secretary-convenor.

The most urgent task facing the committee was meeting the ICC's preconditions for holding matches. Chief among them was that the venues should have proper dressing rooms, a modern media centre, and a special stand and seating for sponsors as well as guests.

The DDCA had none of these.

There followed a race against time to construct the New Club House (NCH) with these facilities on the south side, next to the old Willingdon pavilion. Arun Loomba, the architect who had designed Punjab's Mohali Stadium, was appointed to oversee the project, which was mired in even more problems than the obvious constraint of time. For instance, the Archaeological Survey of India (ASI) was concerned that the new stand was close to the ruins of Ferozeshah Tughlaq's fourteenth-century Kotla and local authorities were worried about the design of the new block.

Despite these hiccups, the new block came up just in time. It was a photo finish on match day, 2 March 1996. Structural engineers signed the temporary safety certificate for the new construction a few days before the game and formal approvals were secured at the very last minute. The dressing rooms were still being painted as the teams arrived on match day. But the match took place as scheduled and the newly constructed stand stood firm.

It was the Indian team that collapsed, blown away by Sri Lanka, who chased down India's 271/3 (Tendulkar, 137). Openers Sanath Jayasuriya (79 runs from 76 balls) and Romesh Kaluwitharana (26 runs from 16 balls with 6 fours) rewrote the one-day batting playbook by attacking from the start. Manoj Prabhakar was smashed for 33 in his first two overs, after which he bowled two overs of off-spin.

PS: The NCH continues to be in the news, although it has been many years since its construction in 1996. Local authorities have yet to grant a final completion certificate to approve the stand and certify its safety. The ASI declared the construction illegal and a lower court ordered that it should be dismantled. However, modifications to the structure have since been carried out and it seems that a closure to this long-lasting saga is around the corner.

Cricket and controversy are old allies in Delhi. The DDCA was affiliated with the BCCI in 1928 and first held a Test match in 1948. DDCA controversies also stretch back to that time.

5

THE NATWEST SERIES, 2002

The NatWest triangular tournament has a special place in Indian cricket history. The win was particularly memorable because India triumphed at Lord's where, in 1983, Kapil Dev had stood on the balcony holding the World Cup. At one stage of the NatWest final, chasing England's 350, India was 145 for 6 with Sachin back in the dressing room. But Yuvraj and Kaif turned things around to seal a win which Sourav Ganguly famously celebrated by waving his shirt from the Lord's balcony.

Rajeev Shukla and I shared the administrative duties on this tour. He was the team manager while I was the media manager.

Arrival in London

India's English summer, including the NatWest one-day tournament and the Test series, begins with a cold reception at Heathrow Airport. The team is received by John Carr, the director of cricket operations, England and Wales Cricket Board (ECB), a few TV networks and even fewer fans.

Sachin Tendulkar, wearing his trademark dark shades and headphones, strides out briskly, pushing his luggage trolley. Captain Sourav Ganguly mumbles something into the waiting microphones before joining his sleepy wife, daughter and maid on the bus. The check-in process at St. James' Court, a popular Taj property just off Buckingham Palace, is smooth, and the players, weary after the long flight, order room service and crash for the day.

Urgent matters are handled over breakfast the next morning. For instance, the room tariff does not include laundry and is too expensive, so we need to find cheaper options. Match ticket allocation is sorted, with seventy-five match tickets split amongst the group—the captain and the manager are allotted five tickets per game while the rest receive four each. The mobile phone policy is communicated, with players allowed to use phones till they disembark from the bus. The team accepts an invitation to the opening show of the musical *Bombay Dreams* and the fines policy is also decided: a penalty of five pounds per minute will be imposed for arriving late for the bus or for team meetings. Rajeev Shukla agrees to be the official timekeeper, rule enforcer and fine collector. I am convinced the first-time manager is unaware of the thankless nature of this job he has taken upon himself.

Players crib about the ill-fitting clothes that the BCCI has provided. The shirts are clumsy, the ties rotten and the blazers poorly tailored—and the view on this is unanimous. Hearing their complaints, I am relieved that Azhar isn't around. Excessively fussy about clothes, he would have expressed himself freely in the choicest Hyderabadi.

Sachin talks about melatonin, which helps overcome jet lag by releasing certain hormones in the body. Sachin is well-informed about medicines and speaks knowledgeably on health issues—it obviously helps to have a wife who is a doctor!

A Practice Session

The team bus rolls into Lord's for the practice session and is parked next to the museum entrance close to the pavilion. Players look around, gaping with awe and curiosity at the Home of Cricket. Once past the smartly dressed main pavilion stewards (who wear white jackets compared to green for other areas) and up the winding staircase, they settle into the visitors' dressing room.

A bemused Virender Sehwag is not overly impressed and wonders why such a fuss is made about Lord's. Sachin, a learned teacher to the curious student, gives him a brief lesson in cricket history and the significance of the ground. He explains the famous slope of Lord's which runs from the north end to the south with a drop of almost 8 feet.

Unlike Sehwag, Sachin has been here earlier and he likes the atmosphere. Walking across the ground to the nursery end practice area, he notices the sight screens are too low. Alex Tudor and Andrew Caddick are part of the England team and Sachin is worried their bowling arm will go over the screen. It strikes me then that the great man is yet to get his name on the honours board, although he has a hundred here from a Lady Diana charity match.

At Lord's, everything is just right, and one can tell the ground has 200 years of experience in hosting cricket. It comes as no surprise that the lunch menu for the Indian team includes chicken curry, rice, dal, roti and even *nimbu achaar.*

Rahul Dravid issues a *janhit mein jaari* warning about the food in England. He asks everyone to be careful about low-fat labels because they don't mention calories. Exercise in the morning to burn fat instead of carbs, he tells the players. Health freak Dravid stays away from the

INDIA'S TOUR TO ENGLAND
June-July 2002
One Day Series

Sourav **Ganguly** (Captain) Anil **Kumble** Virender **Sehwag**

Rahul **Dravid** (Vice-Captain) VVS **Laxman** Harbhajan **Singh**

Ajit **Agarkar** Dinesh **Mongia** Yuvraj **Singh**

Mohd. **Kaif** Ashish **Nehra** Sachin **Tendulkar**

Zaheer **Khan** Ajay **Ratra** Tinu **Yohannan**

Sachin Tendulkar

INDIA TEAM

PLAYERS &
OFFICIALS PASS

2002

ECB

ACCESS ALL AREAS

breakfast buffet, fearing excess fat and oil in the preparations. He swears by protein drinks and fruits and loads up on carbs on playing days.

Food is not the only *gyaan* Dravid gives to players. He talks about the professional attitude a player must have. He believes players representing India should know their roles and responsibilities, and that the drive to succeed must come from within. Dravid's mantra is discipline: *When you stand in front of a chocolate cake, it's between you and the cake— nobody else matters.*

When Geoff Boycott pops in, looking for his Prince, a playful Sachin tells him that the captain has collapsed after a tough fitness test. Everyone has a laugh but there are indeed two serious concerns for the team at this point: Sourav is down with hay fever and has been ruled out for a few days. And a hit on his forehead during the practice session earlier has left Sehwag bleeding. The scans don't show anything serious but he needs stitches. *Bina baat ka jhanjhat ho gaya*, he says.

A security briefing by the ICC follows the practice session. After a crisp presentation in the conference hall at St. James', the Scotland Yard officers ask if anyone has any questions. No hands go up because most of the players have slept through the presentation and those who managed to stay awake struggled with the *angrez* accent. However, one line from the presentation stays with the players: *Everyone remembers a player. Nobody forgets a cheat!*

Dinner at Lord's

The team attends an official dinner hosted by the MCC at the Long Room of Lord's. With Sourav Ganguly indisposed, Rahul Dravid has to speak on behalf of the team. He prepares diligently, like a student preparing to crack an important exam. He invents funny lines to introduce his teammates (*Nehra speaks faster than he bowls*) and impresses guests with an entertaining, carefully constructed speech—very much like the technically correct player he is. After dinner, colleagues congratulate him on the excellent speech and the unanimous verdict is: *Ab tension khatam. Dravid will handle all the speeches on the tour!*

Former England captain Ted Dexter says that Dravid was excellent. *Sourav better get well soon*, he warns, *because there is another captain waiting to take over.* Anil Kumble finds the atmosphere at Lord's too stiff. Junior players think the food is disappointing—to the point where Mohammad Kaif goes looking for a McDonald's burger after the official banquet.

Sachin Takes Questions

To prepare for a media interaction, Sachin and I go over questions that may possibly be thrown at him. He is remarkably measured in his responses at the presser:

Q: *Looking forward to making runs?*
SRT: *Want India to do well. Hundreds are incidental.*
Q: *Want to captain again?*
SRT: *I don't rule it out. Will think about it.*
Q: *How tough is it to handle pressure?*
SRT: *Some pressure is good.*
Q: *Do you miss leading a normal life?*
SRT: *I miss playing with my kids in the park but value the good wishes of fans.*

It is past two in the afternoon and, back in the pavilion, a hungry Sachin tucks into prawn curry and says he likes Lord's. There is some good news: Sourav is feeling better. His fever is down and he is looking forward to the Brazil–England clash in the ongoing football World Cup. *Which side are you on?* I ask. *Always Brazil*, he says. *I hate England!* Brazil wins and an excited Sourav calls me to say: *I told you! Brazil is class.*

Resolving Contracts

Ahead of the 2003 World Cup, the ICC pushed all the participating countries to contract their players. This forced the BCCI to act, and Professor Ratnakar Shetty and I were asked to engage with the senior players (Sourav, Sachin, Kumble and Dravid) to put together a working document. There were several rounds of discussions, many versions of the contract were drafted, various experts consulted and contracts of other countries studied.

Dravid and Kumble led the discussion on behalf of the players, but progress was slow.

During the England tour matters came to a head with the ICC deadline nearing and no sign of agreement between the players and the BCCI. Captain Sourav Ganguly was caught in the crossfire, getting grief from his colleagues as well as from Jaggu-da and the BCCI. Ultimately, contracts were signed with the BCCI giving 26 per cent of its annual revenue to players, which, in the case of women's cricket, would be shared by international, domestic and junior cricketers in a 13, 10.4 and 2.6 per cent split.

Why 26 per cent? Jaggu-da hit upon this arbitrary number because he wanted to go one up on Australia, which shared 25 per cent with its players.

A Practice Game at Sussex

During the bus ride to Brighton, Dravid is immersed in *The Long Walk to Freedom*, Nelson Mandela's autobiography. V.V.S. Laxman, Ashish Nehra and Zaheer Khan are a noisy group at the back end—like backbenchers in school—and Harbhajan sleeps in the aisle between seats.

Sussex has a strong connection with India and with Ranjitsinh-ji (1895–1920), who played for the county. He was followed by his nephew Duleepsinh-ji (1924–32) and then by Tiger Pataudi (1957–70). It's bright and sunny here in Brighton, but the sea breeze is freezing. Experience comes in handy for Sachin—he wears tights under his track bottoms for protection. *Don't get fooled by the sun*, he advises the others.

This is typical of Sachin—always ready and neatly organised. His coffin box reflects his personality and approach to cricket. Bats, all in proper covers, helmets on one side, shoes stacked in the other corner. Gloves in separate plastic bags. Three things are stuck on the inside cover of the box: the Indian tricolour, a picture of Lord Ganesha and a good luck message from his kids.

The team management decides to include Sachin in the tour selection committee. When Rajeev Shukla and I inform him, he accepts the responsibility with humility, saying he is happy to contribute to the team.

A Team Meeting

Coach John Wright stumps everyone with a bouncer: *Do you guys like England?* Yes, the players respond, like hesitant students confronted by a stern tutor. Dinesh Mongia, Ajay Ratra and Virender Sehwag, who are touring England for the first time, say they think it is a great place. Someone whispers about good weather and *nice babes*.

Wright asks the players if England will still be a good place if they score no runs and take no wickets. The players sense what the coach is driving at. He speaks about performance, professional pride and the responsibility of representing India. The players listen to him in respectful silence, then get down to the business of planning strategy.

The key points for the batsmen are:

- Build the foundation and keep wickets in hand. According to Sachin, this formula works all over the world and the time for launching a final assault always depends on how many wickets the team has in hand. He quotes a 1999 World Cup game in Hove when India were only 2 down after 40 overs and should have attacked earlier.
- Avoid dot balls. Get something on the bat and run hard. No swing and miss.
- Aim for a run a ball in the last ten overs.

Sourav wants the players to look for boundaries, hit the gaps and play along the ground. Sehwag is advised to take time to settle down. Don't try to force the pace, he is told.

Wright sums up the discussion: *Once in, stay in. Carry the team along. Start the tour with a bang to send a positive signal to others. Our job is to win for our country. You need to be successful and prove others wrong.* He concludes the meeting on a positive note: *You guys are talented and great cricketers. Maximise your potential.*

The next day, however, all the carefully laid out plans collapse in the practice game. India barely scrapes through after a sloppy performance, with batsmen losing their wickets by playing poor shots. At the post-game meeting, Wright is furious. On the drive back to the hotel, Sachin and Sourav, both equally concerned about the listless performance, go into a huddle.

The Thing About Sachin

Sachin always sits in the front seat of the bus on the left side. Colleagues give him space and respect, and the senior pro is humble to a fault and disarmingly modest. But once he straps his lightweight Morrant pads on, Sachin is a dominant Bahubali—head held high, eyes looking confidently ahead, oozing power and authority with every stride. Crowds erupt on seeing him and opponents look at him with awe. Once he steps on the ground, the mild-mannered Sachin is the Don, he is cricket's Rajnikanth.

A brand ambassador for Fiat, Sachin is also a hardcore F1 fan. When I, a sceptic, once mentioned that it's difficult to even see the car as it zips by, or the driver, he is aghast. *You just have to hear the roar of the engine*, he says. *That itself is good enough. Cars are 30 yards away, going at 300 kmph and the sound is more than that of a MIG aircraft. Drivers take pit stops because tyres wear out because of the high speed. F1 is dangerous and exciting*, he says.

Focusing on Fitness

Physio Andrew Leipus and trainer Adrian Le Roux track the fitness of the players using the skinfold test which measures body fat. The ideal fat-to-muscle ratio, the skinfold, is 64—anything higher reflects additional weight that's slowing you down. Players like Sehwag and Mongia, who were over 100 when the tour started, have work to do. Kaif is just perfect and Sachin a touch above at 70.

There is healthy competition amongst the players to get fit. They are careful about food, count calories and are worried about the fitness tests. One player admits that as soon as he picks up a fork to eat, he invariably thinks of Andrew.

Another Practice Game

As we drive down to Kent, our next stop, the DVD of the movie *Chandni Bar* is playing, but it's a very bad copy. Manager Rajeev Shukla offers to arrange a special screening of *Devdas* by speaking to Shah Rukh Khan. The team stops for lunch at an Italian restaurant chosen by Dravid, who has played for Kent. Needless to say, Dravid is immensely respected here for his dignified conduct and professional attitude.

Kent is sleepy, relaxed and full of history. The team stays at the Falstaff, a heritage hotel that has served as an inn for travellers for almost five centuries. The Kent ground, voted the best in England, has the famous elm tree within the boundary. Local rules award 4 runs if a leaf is touched, whether from the bat or a throw from a fielder. The ground has stands named after Colin Cowdrey and Les Ames. Frank Woolley, another Kent hero, has scored 60,000 first-class runs and taken 2,000 wickets.

Despite the good conditions, the batting fails again and India lose the second practice game as well. The coach is very unhappy. Losing is bad and results matter, he reminds the team. There is more bad news in store. Sachin's shoulder requires serious attention—perhaps even a cortisone shot.

Tussles with the Referee

The customary meeting ahead of the one-day series with match referee Mike Procter is a disaster. He is abrasive and takes off on Sri Lankan captain Sanath Jayasuriya for coming late even as the latter defends himself saying that he wasn't informed about the meeting.

Procter then delivers a stern lecture telling captains to get on with play even when conditions are not perfect. This doesn't impress England skipper Nasser Hussain, who takes on Procter, first pointing out that everyone there has attended many referee meetings, so there is no need for him to repeat standard stuff, before disagreeing strongly about carrying on with the game even if the conditions are not good. Players should be treated with respect, Nasser tells Procter. He adds that they are all top athletes and it isn't right to mess around and risk their careers just because the ICC is feeling the heat from the media and TV sponsors.

Surprised by this strong pushback, Procter retreats, muttering meekly that he will revert to the ICC. Nasser repeats that he will stand up for his players and not expose them to any unnecessary risks.

The meeting is followed by a press conference and a launch function for the NatWest series. Right through the referee meeting, the press conference and the official launch, there are no refreshments and no tea. Not even a glass of water is served. And the press release that is handed out to the media has photographs of Sachin Tendulkar and Muttiah Muralitharan, not of captains Sourav Ganguly and Sanath Jayasuriya!

Asides

- Besides captaining the side, Sourav's biggest challenge is attending to his family. At hotels, he requires an adjoining room for his wife, daughter and maid, and sometimes this is difficult to arrange.
- Dravid finds Murali more difficult to read than Shane Warne. It was easy earlier because you played for the off-break but Murali's leg-break makes it more complicated.
- Kumble's epic response when asked if he wants to watch the Aamir Khan-starrer *Lagaan: I don't want to sit through an ODI.*
- Dravid's take on *Lagaan: Some bowlers have dicey actions, perhaps cleared by the ICC. Also, some dodgy lbw decisions.*

Match Day at Leicester

On the day of the match, Wright has a chat with the boys—he wants the younger players to contribute more. Sourav demands more from the middle order which, so far on the tour, has been wasting good starts.

The match is a run feast. Sourav and Sehwag take off like rockets, knocking 110 runs from the first 10 overs. Sachin is visibly pleased by the carnage. He reads Sourav's mind and predicts, *Dadi dega*, he will hit the next ball past point. His prediction comes true. When someone in the crowd loudly advises bowlers to bowl line and length, he laughs and says: *Kaunsi line, kaisi length!*

At Kumble's request, the team attends Jack Birkenshaw's testimonial dinner, a boring affair with the usual autograph and photograph session with fans. To get through the evening, the players opt for the handshake, smile into cameras, quick dinner, then exit routine. Dravid finds such events futile and wonders what one achieves with these appearances where the players end up having cricket conversations—and worse, receiving nuggets of wisdom based on technical analyses by non-cricketing people. It's nice to meet people, he says, but I would be happier if left alone to read two chapters of a book.

THE TOURNAMENT BEGINS

The next morning, the team takes a bus ride from Leicester to London and Sachin turns the conversation to motor racing and F1. He is a fan and a believer but the others on that bus are not so enthusiastic. One player puts Sachin's interest in perspective: *Others look out from the bus to spot girls but Sachin looks out for cars. Kamaal ka aadmi hai!*

29 June: India vs England

Lord's is packed by 9.30 in the morning for an 11 a.m. start. The strong Indian contingent includes Sunil Gavaskar, Farokh Engineer and Chandu Borde. Sachin gets out early, adjudged lbw. When he returns to the dressing room, not a word is said. He sits in his corner, grim-faced, watching the replay on the telly and working on his shoulder with an ice pack.

Sourav is caught by James Kirtley, an absolute stunner at long-on. India chase down the runs with Sehwag teeing off before getting dismissed trying a wild swing. The manner of Sehwag's dismissal annoys Wright. A calm Dravid takes India across the line, and the win at Lord's at the beginning of the tour is rightfully celebrated. Indians are notorious for being slow starters on overseas tours but this time, it seems, the ball is running for the team.

30 June: India vs Sri Lanka—and Wright vs Sehwag

An eventful game against Sri Lanka at the Oval. Sachin is caught behind in a low-scoring game. The master walks off the ground, although the umpire has not heard the ball being nicked on the way to the keeper. In the dressing room, a livid Wright confronts him: *Would Steve Waugh have walked?* Sachin's explanation: *Bahut bada edge laga tha!*

This incident is to become insignificant in comparison to what comes later. When Sehwag is dismissed playing a rash slog which fails to clear mid-off, Wright loses his shirt. In the heated exchange between player and coach, angry words are spoken and at one stage Wright apparently pushes Sehwag, who stumbles and falls to the dressing-room floor.

All hell breaks loose. Informed of the 'assault', I find a tense dressing room with an aggrieved Sehwag, sullen teammates and a stressed-out coach. When I ask around for information from witnesses, most confirm the incident but are hesitant to share details.

With John and Sachin at the Oval

Sourav is furious. He thinks Wright is treating junior players poorly and finds the physical altercation with Sehwag unacceptable. *The coach can't humiliate a player like this*, he says. Speaking for the team, he wants Wright to apologise to Sehwag in front of the players. The captain is so livid, he issues a warning—*If we have to, we will play without a coach!*

I inform Rajeev Shukla and the two of us meet Wright to understand his side of the story. Wright confirms that the scuffle did take place and says it was deliberate on his part. He wants to send out a message to the players, he wants them to realise that they can't be soft and unprofessional. *We almost lost a match we should have won easily*, he says.

He looks gaunt, sitting alone in the small cabin adjoining the main pavilion, beer can in one hand and a cigarette in the other. When I suggest that he have a private word with Sehwag and Sourav, he makes an alternate suggestion: *I will speak to Viru alone*, he says.

The players want nothing short of a public apology, which isn't a good idea. Public apologies often amount to public humiliation for the apologiser. My argument that the coach acted—overacted?—in the interest of the team doesn't impress the captain. There is no denying that Wright has crossed a line. But it is important to resolve the matter without either Sehwag or Wright losing face.

Rajeev Shukla and I decide it is best for the two of them to thrash it out without officials (meaning the both of us) or other players (including the captain) getting involved. With more people and more opinions, things would only get more complicated. I urge Wright to meet Sehwag. His thumbs-up gesture while walking past me to board the team bus as we leave the Oval indicates that Sehwag and he have made up. That Wright and Sourav sit next to each other in the bus is proof that all is well.

When I catch up with Sehwag over dinner at the hotel, he tells me about what transpired between him and the coach. *Sab theek hai*, he assures me. He has told Wright not to get physical because *agar maine bhi haath uthaya to kya hoga?*

At the next team meeting in Durham, Sachin raises a hand to draw everyone's attention. *I have something to say, a request to everyone*, he announces. *What happened at the Oval with Viru and John should remain in the dressing room. It should not go out and nobody should talk about it.* Wright echoes Sachin and reminds the players to fight for India and be tough and ruthless. Sourav, relieved that the storm has blown over, says,

Even I abuse you in the field because it is good for the team. Remember that we are a family.

The chapter is thus closed, with everyone involved showing maturity. *Aage badho, Munnabhai* — it is time to move on.

PS: The Wright–Sehwag *dangal* remained a secret for long, though Wright did mention it in his book. It surfaced during a live television commentary when V.V.S. Laxman brought it up with Sehwag, The latter confirmed the incident and also spoke of my role in defusing the situation.

Looking back, the incident illustrates how much things have changed. Earlier, it was possible to put a lid on things and maintain the privacy of the dressing room. In today's world of information overload, social media and intrusive press coverage, an incident of this kind would have been more explosive than the Pokharan blast. Television channels would have caught wind of the '*sansani*' breaking news and gone ballistic, with anchors screaming that the nation wanted revenge and that the player's *izzat* had to be restored! Players themselves would have gone to town on social media, giving the incident their own personal spin. Dressing-room 'sanctity' has become so yesteryear.

The Art of Ball Selection

What cricketers fuss about the most before a match are the pitch and the ball. Both affect play and the players constantly worry about how the two will behave during the match. Pitch preparation and reading its behaviour are part-science, part-mystery. Despite all kinds of theories, nobody has cracked it yet, and the pitch continues to defeat everyone.

Neither team can choose the pitch, but that is not the case with the ball. Before going in, umpires hand over a box containing twelve balls to the fielding team to choose the ones they want to use.

Selecting the right balls requires talent, skill and experience. Usually, bowlers collectively decide which one to pick. Pace bowlers look for one likely to swing, spinners choose one that fits well in their hands and has a pronounced seam. Each team has its experts, who have a knack for picking the ball that works for the bowlers.

It is fascinating to see how the ball is chosen. Sachin does the initial examination, shortlisting Kookaburra balls by tossing them in the air to check their flight and balance. He is very fussy — a slight wobble of the seam results in rejection. The balls are handed to Ajit Agarkar and then to Zaheer for a final nod. The ones that pass this multi-level scrutiny are offered to Harbhajan and Kumble for final approval.

At Lumley Castle

After a six-hour drive, the team checks into the 700-year-old Lumley Castle in Durham. The castle is an imposing structure with an impressive ambience, a river running by its side and a golf course next door.

The downside is that the place is spooky, with dark *bhoot bangla*—type rooms in different clusters. Some of the players say they feel like they are back in the past, personal guests of Maharana Pratap in Kumbhalgarh. It took ten minutes from the reception to reach my room, number 53, after walking through dimly lit corridors and climbing eighty steps up winding staircases filled with metal statues of warriors.

The players have a gentle stretching and jogging session to overcome stiffness after the long bus ride. The session ends when Dada works up a sweat after a twenty-minute jog around Lumley Castle.

We have dinner at a Bangladeshi restaurant discovered by our bus driver Tony (who is already down three pints of beer that evening). The owner of the restaurant, ignorant about cricket, thinks Sachin is a fast bowler. It is a lively evening with beer and wine and lots of food, but dessert is spurned because of the skinfold tests the next morning.

The players exchange cricket stories and anecdotes with Sachin holding court, recalling every detail from past games. He reels off scores and dismissals from previous tours, remembering catches dropped and good shots played from the time he first came to England as a kid with Kailash Gattani's Star Cricket Club.

At breakfast the next morning, Sourav, who is staying in the room directly opposite mine, tells me he was so scared that he kept the lights on all night and couldn't sleep. He wasn't the only one who lost sleep. Commentator Navjot Sidhu, who'd had a major makeover recently, turning philosophical and spiritual, also found his prayers for a restful night rejected by the ghosts at Lumley.

It's scary, boss, he admits. *Pata nahin raat ko kaun aa jaye.*

How can the Punjab ka sher be scared, I ask. *Arre Amrit bhai*, he replies, *I am a geedar from inside.*

The Indians were not the only ones who got a fright at Lumley. We were told that the Aussies, who were here the previous year, had fled after staying one night.

Asides

- Sachin's favourite expressions to describe class batting: *chabuk* and *tadi*.
- Sachin writes with his left hand, eats with the right hand and wears black/red leotards and reddish socks while batting.
- Sourav wears an impressive Omega Seamaster watch which costs a bomb. Sachin calls his kitbag, which contains many bats, a moving sports shop.

Sehwag's epic response during an interview with Channel 4 is the cause of much merriment. Asked about his similarity with Sachin, Sehwag answers: *We look different. Our batting style is different. Our bank balance is also different.*

Ahead of the next game, Sourav has one more headache to manage. He needs extra tickets for guests. When I tell him I have tickets for players' wives beyond the normal allocation, he asks for two. I agree on the condition that I get to tell the others that he has two wives. *Ok*, he agrees happily, *as long as you don't tell the real one!*

India vs England

The game starts under grey skies on a day so bitterly cold that the players wear three jumpers each. Umpire Peter Wiley comes to the dressing room and casually picks up bats lying around in kitbags. His surprise visit isn't entirely harmless—he is on a secret mission to check if the width of the bats is within legal limits.

Sourav is dismissed off the first ball, declared lbw when the ball is clearly too high and down leg. But the gloom is lifted by a master class in batting by Sachin, who smashes 105 and remains not out. His innings includes uncharacteristic reverse sweeps off Ashley Giles. Sachin returns to the pavilion showing no emotion, no high-fives, not even a smile. He goes straight to his corner, changes his clothes, puts his kit away, drinks Electral and lies down on the massage table.

Yuvraj admires Sachin's attitude and commitment. *Paaji* 32 *ho gaye par abhi bhi* 18 *lagte hain.* Sourav says Sachin is too big a player and there is no one even close to him.

When Wright remarks that Sachin will be the first to make 100 international hundreds, the Master replies: *Long way to go—38 more.*

Navjot Sidhu is happy with the Indian team's performance. According to him, *well-begun is half done because 'good lather is half the shave'*. Sidhu is living up to his reputation as an entertainer but complains that the network is squeezing him with too much work. If this continues any longer, *only khaara juice will come out together with the chilka.*

PS: When the match is abandoned midway due to rain, Anil Kumble poses difficult questions:

Will Sachin be Man of the Match for scoring a hundred?

Or will he be half Man of the Match?

Or is he only half man because there was only half match?

Nobody has satisfactory answers to these loaded questions. Beaten and bowled by Kumble!

When Sachin Met Schumacher

Sachin is excited about meeting Michael Schumacher at Silverstone and wants to know how the mind of a champion works.

He watches the F1 race (dressed fittingly in a bright red Adidas shirt) with his phone switched on so his wife, Anjali, can hear the sound in Mumbai. When he questions Schumacher about handling pressure, the champion driver says that it is best to ignore it. The trick is to build a wall around yourself, shut out the noise, remove negative thoughts and keep an uncluttered mind.

Wise words from one champ to another, but surely Sachin does not need to be told this. He handles stress and expectations each time he picks up his bat. And has done so all his life.

Birthday Celebrations

The team celebrates Harbhajan's birthday with dinner at a restaurant called Last Days of the Raj. It's difficult to organise because twenty-five people have fifty suggestions about the food they want and there will be complete chaos if everyone is allowed to order separately. What works best is discipline, not democracy; we settle the menu in advance and decide when it should be served. The deal that evening is £25 per head for food, with drinks on actuals.

At the restaurant, Sehwag plays a prank on Rajeev Shukla, thanking the manager for the dinner. Shukla-ji is aghast, but relieved when assured that everyone is going Dutch. After dinner, Harbhajan makes an entertaining speech and does a remarkable impersonation of the Punjab cricket chief, I.S. Bindra.

A few days later, the team has dinner together again to mark the captain's birthday. The Red Fort restaurant has great food (the spicy prawn curry is especially good) and loud Punjabi music. The players are in high spirits. Totally *balle balle!*

Fitness Again

The players follow a customised routine with sessions carefully logged and progress monitored. Skinfold tests are done every two weeks and it is not unusual to see players hit the gym after a game to lift weights and work out. Sehwag is the latest convert to the new fitness culture. Earlier, his training was running and squeezing *aata*; now it is cardio and weights for his shoulders.

Dravid puts his finger on the change. In 1999, in the West Indies, he went to the gym three times a week; now he goes every day. Earlier, the first question on reaching a new place was about the availability of Indian food. Now it is about how good the gym is.

There is no off-day for players on tour even when no fitness sessions are planned. On a day of optional practice, when many players turn up, Dada remarks that they have come to escape the tough gym session. Dada, a reluctant fitness person, describes himself as 'cricket-fit' as opposed to 'athletic-fit'. A voice from the back announces that Dada is not the fittest but the wealthiest.

The latest skinfold test results show that Sehwag is down to 100. He is delighted and says he feels lighter and quicker between wickets. The others are happy too. Kaif is supremely fit and Sachin pretty healthy at 71. An amazed Yuvraj tells him: *Paaji, tussi will soon disappear.*

Despite the positive news on his fitness, Sehwag is haunted by the memory of the poor shot he played—caught at mid-on trying to clear the circle. *The problem*, he explains in all seriousness, *is I can't play defensive. I think I can smash every ball that is pitched up.*

11 July: India vs Sri Lanka

India has already qualified for the final but the coach reminds the players to play and win for India, not for averages. He expects each player to rise to the occasion and raise his hand to say, *It is me, my day, I will do it.* Sourav, taking a more cautious line, warns against complacency. His message: Go out and fight. Kumble echoes the captain. His message: Stay focused. Don't relax or switch off.

Sourav visits the city centre, which has a statue of Raja Ram Mohan Roy. Photographer Pradeep Mandhani is with him to capture the 'historic' moment—Dada, modern Bengal's popular hero, with the Bengal renaissance giant.

Over dinner at Rajdoot Hotel, Sachin recalls meeting Sir Don Bradman and being greeted with a hard, firm handshake. Sachin compares Don's batting to book cricket where only fours and sixes are scored. He remembers the day Bradman passed away—26 February. Sachin's other hero is Garry Sobers, whose batting average he knows down to the last decimal point. And, of course, King Viv—because nobody gives better *tadi* than him.

Sachin speaks about unlikely turnarounds, and the 1993 Hero Cup semi-final against South Africa when India needed 6 to win in the last over. Sachin hadn't bowled in the innings till then, but conceded only 4 for India to win. *It just happened*, he says, explaining the miracle. Nobody in the world can guarantee a win from that position.

The game against Sri Lanka is India's sixth in twelve days and the physical strain is showing. Sachin looks like a soldier wounded in battle with a bad shoulder, strained calves and an aching hamstring because of the soft English outfields.

Despite the physical stress, Sachin scores a clinically brilliant hundred, once again getting the better of Murali, whom the others find difficult to read. Post-game, chatting with Wright, I ask what he would have done to get Sachin out. *Not easy*, the coach replies. *Best to keep him off strike to induce a high-risk shot through mid-wicket by leaving a gap and bowling very straight. But Sachin is so good he could adjust and convert the high-risk shot into a run-scoring option.*

Speaking of John Wright

While opinions are split in the debate about Indian versus foreign coaches, the players agree that John Wright is the right choice because the former New Zealand captain (who had scored three centuries against India) ticks all the boxes. Playing experience at the top level and coaching expertise? Tick. Professional attitude and good work ethic? Yes. Understanding of Indian cricket culture? Perfect.

John works silently and stays out of the frame, having learnt two essential lessons. One, don't fight the system, work within it. Two, in India, the captain is king. He calls the shots and, indirectly, appoints the coach.

The players respect John because he is fair and always puts the team first. It's not easy to manage a team of superstars but John, like a good batsman on a tricky wicket, has found a way to score. He has built a rapport with Sourav (Soorav to him), leaves Sachin (Sach to him) alone, is comfortable with Dravid (Rauul to him) and respects the professionalism of Kumble and Zak. Kaif is his favourite—John thinks he is a future leader.

The coach's job is extremely stressful but John is chilled out, except in tense match situations when he paces up and down the dressing room, muttering advice to the players under his breath. A good moment cheers him and a typical reaction to a good catch or a batting or bowling landmark is a pumped fist. After the end of play, he can be found in the gym; post dinner he plays the guitar to soothe his frayed nerves.

In a chat, John lists three key elements for success: a consistent selection policy, depth in pace bowling and a non-negotiable fitness culture. He makes an interesting observation about judging players. Selectors go by runs and stats but don't always factor in character, which is critical in team situations. He rates Dravid very high on commitment and toughness. Dravid thinks for the team, gets the best out of the youngsters, is straightforward and has integrity. Laxman, according to Wright, is tactically sound and is the link between the seniors and the juniors. Yuvraj is unbelievably talented but needs to direct his energy into cricket and not get distracted.

Before the NatWest Final

At the team meeting a day before the final, Sourav departs from routine to start the session with a spirited pep talk. He repeats the much-used line that this is just another game, *don't allow the pressure of the final to get to you. The team has done well till now*, he tells the players, *keep up the good work*.

The conversation turns to tackling Andrew Flintoff, the danger man, and there is agreement that he shouldn't get room to swing the bat. Focus instead on bowling straight to prevent him from hitting over the infield. Sachin points out that Flintoff is a striker who won't place the ball into gaps or nudge it for singles. Tempt him with a gap at mid-wicket—force him to play across the line. Dravid and Yuvraj make suggestions, as does young Ajay Ratra, who thinks Flintoff hangs back waiting for the cut. So bowl full, not short. Sachin supports this and says Kumble is the answer to Flintoff—he should be worried about the leg-spinner.

Dravid mentions Nasser's ability to play inside out and reverse sweep. This opens a discussion on field placings for Nasser, specially protecting third man and point. The team wants Zaheer to be aggressive and bowl fast. Batsmen are reminded about their roles and Sourav tells Sehwag to continue playing his natural game but adds a word of caution: *Keep the ball down.*

Strangely, the coach is bypassed in the meeting and the conversation is monopolised almost entirely by the players. But Wright rounds up the discussion to remind them to maintain intensity and, his favourite theme, fight for the country. Everyone must be up for it.

I wonder if something is the matter with Wright. The team is going into the final with a minor cold war between the captain and the coach. There had been the occasional flare-ups on the tour, but both handled these with maturity. Apparently, the trigger for the friction before the final was Sourav arriving late for nets, which angered Wright and led to an unpleasant public argument. Strong words were exchanged, which many heard. Wright maintains his dignity through it all but says later that he can't take it anymore. His position: *I am doing my job but if he wants to get rid of me, I am prepared to go.*

I find this disturbing, but seniors in the team who have witnessed such rows in the past tell me to chill. *Both are mad*, said one wise head, *and are on edge as nerves are frayed. Keep out of it—they are friends who fight but make up after some time.* Which is exactly what happened. When I check with Sourav whether things are sorted, he replies in the affirmative. *All ok*, he smiles. I can see the intensity and integrity on his face. He is doing his best for the team.

The Final

The bus ride to the ground is uneventful. The players are tense before the big game, silently looking out of the window or messaging on their mobiles. On reaching Lord's, Sourav dumps his bag in the dressing room, arranges his kit, chooses the right Oakley (from the dozens he has) and sticks Hero Honda stickers on his bats.

Battle-ready Sourav is the first out of the dressing room for his warm-up. A *match-fit player* (his description), he does not trouble the physio or trainer, nor does he require tapes, bandages or a massage before a game. He knocks

With Andrew Leipus and Rahul Dravid on the Lord's balcony

a few balls to get the reassuring feel of the ball hitting the bat, then goes to the middle to check the wicket with Michael Atherton.

Dravid has breakfast (the usual carbs, Weetabix, skimmed milk laced with honey) and prepares for another day of keeping wickets. Sachin, looking calm and determined, has deep heat treatment for his back and wears leotards. Yuvraj remarks that *Paaji is looking like Maurice Green*.

Others are also going through their pre-match routine and the dressing room looks like a dispensary on a busy day. Dinesh Mongia puts a red good-luck *teeka* on his forehead. Yuvraj looks for an ice pack. Kaif wants his fingers strapped. Kumble nurses his sprained calf. Zaheer has a shoulder rub. Nehra's left ankle requires multiple strappings.

England, meanwhile, is already done with training. Nasser stretches next to the stumps on the square. The television commentators walk around the pitch looking closely at the surface. Ravi Shastri, Michael Slater, Ian Botham and David Gower are happy that the weather forecast is good.

Back in the Indian dressing room, a nervous coach is trying to calm nervous players. *Don't bother about the big final at Lord's, just stick to the game plan and FIGHT*. Before the toss, the issue of Kumble's fitness has to be resolved. Andrew Leipus puts him through the usual warm-up drills. Kumble bowls a few balls but isn't sure. When Andrew suggests that, as a senior player, Kumble should decide for himself,

Sachin steps in to close the debate. Kumble should play even if 75 per cent fit because *woh dus over karke match jitayega*.

The other debate is about what to do with the four players—Wasim Jaffer, Sanjay Bangar, Parthiv Patel and Shiv Sundar Dass—who have arrived to join the team for the Test series. After much discussion, it is decided they should not sit in the dressing room so as to maintain the intensity of the NatWest squad. All four, wearing India ties and blazers, watch the match from the members' enclosure next to the pavilion.

When play starts, England seem to run away with the game as edges fall in gaps and players play and miss many times. Nasser makes a scratchy hundred and directs rude gestures at the press box, which appears unnecessary. Why behave in an undignified manner in a moment of celebration and personal triumph?

With 325 on the board, does England have too many? The mood in the dressing room is solemn and Laxman notices that the body language is not the best. The team eats in silence but Sehwag is positive. *Ab hamari bari hai, hamara jalwa bhi dekho, hum bhi maarenge*, he says. A sceptical Sourav wonders, *Kitna marenge?* Laxman advises Sehwag to play cricket shots, arguing it's not possible to get 325 with desperate hitting.

Dada chooses a bat from the seven lined up next to his kitbag, each with multiple grips sticking out on top beyond the handle. He changes bats often, sometimes even after hitting two boundaries in an over. Agarkar says that with Dada at the crease, the 12th man is tested as much as the opposition bowlers. When the innings starts, Sourav is off like a rocket, but is out after a rapid 50 and is furious with himself.

A stressed-out John sits in a corner, muttering instructions nobody can hear and talking to himself. The tension increases as Sachin makes his way back, bowled by Giles. Sachin sits with pads on, disappointed with the shot, but points out that he was looking for the gap in the offside. At 5 down for 146, it looks pretty hopeless.

Despite this crushing blow, the mood at 40 overs is positive, with Agarkar convinced India will win. This is the time when all the *tashan* starts. Instructions are issued for everyone not to move — it is lockdown time, a dressing-room curfew with all movement prohibited. Dravid and Sachin are marooned on Leipus's massage table for the rest of the game.

Sourav sends out silent appeals to all the gods he has on a personal hotline and offers them an interesting deal. *This is what I want more than anything,* he pleads, and promises not to ask for anything else in the future. Divine connections established by the captain, Kaif (87 not out) and Yuvraj (69) add 121 to take India to an unlikely win. Sourav takes off his shirt and zips down the stairs, shouting with delight, as surprised members in the Long Room applaud politely. He is leaping over the wicket gate before the steward can open it and runs on to the field to congratulate Kaif.

During the presentation, Jaggu-da calls to announce a cash award of one crore rupees for the team. Kaif, surprisingly composed despite the huge achievement, hands me his helmet and a stump (match souvenirs) before taking off for a victory lap. Harbhajan, more expressive, breaks into peppy *bhangra*. Sachin shares his *josh*.

The players are in no hurry to leave and decide *aaj sab tight ho kar jayenge*. In the dressing room, celebrations are in full swing and Ravi Shastri is one of the first to pop in. He unloads a magnum of expensive champagne (thoughtfully provided by Pete Lowe, the super-efficient dressing-room attendant) on Kaif and Yuvraj.

Sachin, meanwhile, is slyly hiding behind the door waiting for Harbhajan and pounces on the unsuspecting off-spinner when he arrives, to give him the full treatment. With mobiles ringing crazily and players screaming and shouting with joy, anarchy prevails in the Lord's dressing room. Pictures are taken and souvenirs collected, the most coveted being the black-coloured NatWest match stumps.

In the middle of the chaos, Dada announces that it's time for dinner (*It's on me*, he says) even as famished players attack lamb chops and pasta, the

A match stump from the final and its replica

post-match refreshments served by the Lord's kitchen. Match highlights are playing on the telly and every blow by Kaif and Yuvraj as India gets close to the target is greeted with whoops of delight.

On the bus ride back to the hotel, an emotionally drained Sourav rises from his designated seat (window, second row on the left, behind Sachin) to thank his teammates, a gracious leader addressing his victorious troops. The players are delighted that they have won at Lord's, beaten the *goras* and given them good *bamboo*.

Sourav's telephone keeps buzzing because the whole world is calling or messaging, but he can't get through to wife Dona. *I don't know why she has a mobile*, he cribs. *If I tell her, she says she was busy with our daughter.* Which proves that you may vanquish England at Lord's but winning an argument with the spouse is a tougher ball game.

PS: Sourav had wanted the entire team to participate in the shirt-waving Salman Khan routine but the proposal was shot down by Dravid.

At St. James' Court, hotel staff greet the players with laddoos and champagne. Sachin's wife Anjali is amongst those waiting in the lobby. A celebratory dinner at Four Seasons is hosted by Rashmi Mehta, the diamond merchant from Belgium who is a keen supporter of Indian cricket.

Kaif wants a tape of his innings. Mongia, going back to India after the ODIs, remarks that the work put in at the gym will be useful when he plays for Chemplast. *I cycled so much*, he says, *I reached Chandigarh from Delhi—soon I will have enough miles to go to and fro!*

Sachin, wearing a silver bracelet on his right wrist, is messaging friends and making plans for the break before the Tests. On the to-do list: watching *Bombay Dreams* followed by *Devdas*, courtesy of Shah Rukh Khan.

Dravid announces his retirement from wicket-keeping duties and asks Ratra to take over. *Don't want to see these gloves again, boss. Just leave me out now.* Kumble agrees. Rahul had a rough day because the ball was not coming in at an even pace. Dravid thinks about the bonus announced by the BCCI and feels that it should be distributed amongst all 18—the players and the coaching staff. Typical Dravid, selfless and considerate.

A little known fact: Yuvraj played the final with a broken bone. The very first ball of the match from Marcus Trescothick had chipped his little finger. *I knew straight away it was gone*, he said after consulting a doctor the next day. Out for at least three weeks.

A Typical Meeting

At team meetings, coach John Wright is like a college lecturer who has come prepared with notes to take a class. Mostly it is a one-sided conversation where he first does the talking and then extracts responses from the players. He presents a plan backed by stats, charts, diagrams and video footage. After that Sourav steps in to outline what is expected from each player. The team's batting, bowling and fielding groups also share their views.

Kaif, the designated fielding captain, makes a brilliant presentation about stopping singles in the ring and the importance of standing close to cut the angle. Dravid, the leader of the batting unit, says that the first 15 overs are tricky, so bowlers should try yorkers if confident. During this period, batsmen are expected to have a go; therefore, bowlers should be steady and not try too hard.

Kumble thinks team meetings should focus more on its strengths, plans and strategy for each batsman and bowler instead of concentrating on what the other side will do. The role of each batsman against each bowler should be defined. He makes interesting observations about the coach's role. He thinks there is excessive emphasis on physical fitness and less on skills. In the nets, players try to develop new shots and new ways to bowl. Look at how Nasser hits reverse sweeps because he can't hit over the top. In his opinion, coaching should be less theoretical. *Kids are taught grip, action, position of right arm, follow through—which is fine, but how do you get wickets? Batsmen are dismissed by setting them up, by working on weaknesses, by identifying faults and exposing errors. How is that done? What weaknesses should one watch out for?*

PS: Players think many coaches are net organisers without any cricket inputs. One Test opener went to the coach looking for help in handling the moving ball. All he got was, *Dil se khelo. That's great*, the player replied, *but what do I do to prevent edging Donald to slip?*

Practice at Arundel

After the NatWest campaign the team travels to Arundel and stays at a golf resort where Dravid and I try our hand at putting. Dravid, a quick learner, sorts out the technique and starts dropping short putts consistently. According to him, technique should be instinctive, not mechanical.

Conversation over dinner is about cricket and Dravid's own journey. Dravid feels strongly about having a professional attitude and admires the first-class set-up in England. County cricket is tough, players won't take nonsense from anyone and even a junior guy will tick you off, he says.

Dravid supports the practice of hiring foreign support staff as they bring superior knowledge and more experience. Outsiders treat everyone equally and pay attention to juniors who otherwise feel unwanted. Remove them from the scene and see how things decline, he says.

Dravid is intelligent, articulate and thoughtful. Cricket is all-consuming but he finds time to read and look beyond the 75-yard boundary of his professional career. Once done with cricket, he hopes to find fresh challenges that are fulfilling and competitive.

- Dravid's ideal future life: A flat in London, stay there in summer, then go back home to Bangalore.
- Dravid has simple tastes and doesn't chase designer cars, watches or clothes. What about designer women? I ask to provoke him. *Not a bad idea—worth considering*, he replies wickedly. It's not easy to disturb Dravid's focus—always plays with a straight bat, won't hit across the line!

After practice Sehwag and I stay back for a media interaction. Travelling back with Trevor, our luggage man, Sehwag says he is looking forward to opening the innings in Tests. His optimism stems from self-belief. *If I play well, I will score from any position*, he says.

Sehwag started cricket late and was twice rejected by Delhi at the U-19 trials—once given just 4 balls to bat in a net. *I was asked to get out*, he remembers the bitter experience. When he smashed 170 in a club game (with 14 sixes) the selectors woke up, and after that there was no looking back. He scored a hundred in his Ranji debut, playing at number 8 on a wicket so uneven it was a 'speedbreaker'.

Sehwag entertains no self-doubt, is aware of his abilities and cares little for the reputation of bowlers. His approach to batting remains unchanged though he is a recent convert to training and 'visualising', thinking about bowlers and match situations. *It is better to be prepared*, he says, but he is not fussed about the surface or the conditions. *I don't over analyse*, he says. *It's better to go with an open mind.*

Sachin joins the team again after a few days' break in London. He thanks me for allowing him to take a break and says he is refreshed and fully recharged for the Test series. It's like the first day of the tour all over again.

When I ask him to join us for dinner at India Gate restaurant, he excuses himself. *I want to get ready*, he says, *and get into the pre-match routine.*

But he changes his mind and turns up to eat crispy bhindi, dal, rice and his favourite prawn curry. It is a relaxed evening and Sachin speaks about his meeting with F1 superstar Michael Schumacher. Harbhajan's reaction on hearing that Schumacher's helmet cost a few crores: *Arre, usme to hamara ghar ban jaaye!*

When the conversation turns to cricket, Sourav is keen to know about past Indian greats. He knows and respects Polly ('Kaka') Umrigar, who scored 12 Test hundreds, quite a feat in those days because of the limited opportunities.

When it is pointed out that Tiger Pataudi had a (relatively) modest record, Sachin rises to his defence, saying cricket is tough even with two eyes. After an animated debate, a consensus is reached—Vijay Manjrekar and Jimmy Amarnath were India's best two BG (before Gavaskar) batsmen. Huge respect also for Padmakar Shivalkar and Rajinder Goel. Dravid decries the tendency of glorifying the past and wallowing in nostalgia and the romance of history. He thinks the 'in-our-good-old-days' narrative is annoying. *Who knows, I too might behave the same way, but the problem is, someone will pull out a video and expose me. Dad, the kids will say, don't give us goli or gyaan.*

PS: A question that keeps coming up: Why do past greats resent the success—fame, name, money—of present-day stars?

Sachin is shooting for a television programme where he breaks down his batting technique:

- Low grip on the bat: *It's natural, doesn't hinder me in any way.*
- Key to batting: *Still head, good balance and decisive foot movement. Hands close to the body, always under the head, not flying away.*
- Head position: *Leaning forward a shade even when the body (foot) is moving back—just in case you have to move forward again.*

After the shoot I rescue him from a mob of eager fans and remark that he handled the subject nicely. *It is easy to go out in the middle and play*, he says. *Khelne mein itna sochna nahin padta, bas ho jata hai. Here there is too much analysis!*

Danger in Hampshire

After the sensational NatWest final, attention shifts to the Test matches coming up. The practice game against Hampshire has run into an unexpected problem. Before the start, the umpires judged the wicket too dangerous, unfit for play. The captains agree with the assessment but are not able to make up their minds about what to do.

Option 1: Carry on and play despite the poor condition of the wicket. But what if someone gets hurt? Sachin is clear he won't bat on this surface.

Option 2: Abandon the game. *But that would be a disaster for Hampshire,* pleads former captain Robin Smith, because they hope to host an ODI and ECB inspectors are due for an inspection shortly. It would also be terrible publicity for the ECB.

Finally, it is decided that if the wicket is too dangerous, India will declare and invite the opposition to bat. Sehwag is happy to go out and give *tadi* and coach Wright is fine with carrying on. *So what if the wicket is bad?* he asks. Kumble, keen to bowl ahead of the Tests, agrees.

The match goes ahead as a 'fixed' game with both sides reaching a farcical arrangement: seam bowlers will bowl at half pace and pitch the ball up; spinners will bowl long spells. Players and officials agree not to reveal this secret understanding to avoid negative publicity. As far as the public is concerned, this will be another low intensity warm-up game, no better than a glorified net session.

After the game Sourav says it was a write-off and rues the absence of good practice before the first Test. A larger question remains unanswered. Why did we go through this drama and save Hampshire from potential embarrassment? Had this happened in India, would the ECB have been as understanding? No chance. They would have gone to town slamming India.

The Wisden Awards

The team attends a function at Wembley in London to celebrate the Wisden Indian Cricket Awards of the Century. Since it is an official BCCI-approved function, players wear formals and set off for a long bus ride on a wet and depressing London evening.

The event is bubbling with history and nostalgia with many past greats (Bishan Bedi, Farokh Engineer, Polly Umrigar) present but the function starts on a false note. The team is received by cheerleaders and, after a frustrating wait, taken backstage and then escorted into the main hall. The seats allotted to them are too far back and the players, clearly unhappy with the poor arrangements, threaten to walk out.

The sullen mood changes somewhat once the ceremony starts. Dravid says he will be surprised if Laxman and Kumble don't get awards. He is half-right, half-wrong—right about Laxman's monumental 281 at Eden Gardens, wrong about Kumble's 10 out of 10 at Kotla. Laxman makes a sober acceptance speech, speaking from the heart, and later asks, *Achha bola na?* The others are happy for him; Laxman is popular with his colleagues.

To everyone's surprise, Kumble is passed over in the bowlers category, the award going instead to Chandrasekhar's match-winning 6/38 at the Oval in 1971. Sunny Gavaskar, who reads out the name on opening the envelope, appears stunned not to see Kumble's name.

Kapil narrowly goes past Gavaskar to bag the (popular choice) best cricketer of the century award and Sachin, expectedly, wins a special award. In his acceptance speech, he humbly thanks the whole world: *Mr Gavaskar for gifting him lightweight Morrant pads, which was a special gesture; Kapil paaji for inspiring him to play cricket after the 1983 win; teammates for the home-away-from-home feeling and creating a family atmosphere in the dressing room.*

Sachin is accomplished with both the bat and the microphone. After the event I ask his wife Anjali if their new house has enough storage for the awards he has won. She smiles.

- Sachin on Kumble missing out on the bowling award: *Is taking 10 wickets in an innings not good enough? Do they want Anil to take 11 next time?*
- What did Kumble get for his 10/74? His name is on a road in Bangalore. Ten free tickets from Air India. One car. Some land 50 km outside city limits and minor cash. Almost nothing from sponsors.
- A comment on the quality of trophies handed out: *They look like what Rotary Club hands out!*

The Museum at Lord's

The Lord's museum contains valuable memorabilia but little of consequence from India is on display. Among the interesting items are the boots and spikes of past legends: Sir Don Bradman's is a small size 7, W.G. Grace's is somewhat bigger and Alec Bedser's is huge—almost one foot long. Sachin takes one look and remarks that both his feet would fit into one of those. On spotting Jack Hobbs's bat (a slim stick compared to the massive weapons used now), he points out that the great man made 197 first-class hundreds, 100 of them scored after he turned 40.

The Pre-match Meeting

Team morale is high and players are keen to maintain the winning momentum after the one-day games. The coach urges them to maintain intensity and reminds them that they are better than England, man for man. Winning is important for prestige, personal pride and a place in history.

There is also a strong feeling that we should give the Poms the thrashing of their lives. The players are warned to maintain focus because a Test match is a slow fight where sessions of play are similar to rounds in a boxing contest.

Three key decisions are taken:

- Each player to target one England player and unsettle him (Graham Thorpe, a prime target).
- Team to come together before every session even if it's for 15 seconds.
- Reserve players to help three or four players in the playing eleven to keep up the intensity.

The players watch images of India's famous past victories. This is followed by a brief discussion to decide the team motto for the series. The unanimous choice: FIGHT.

Sourav reminds Sachin to get his name on the honours board. The master batsman replies that he has been trying for the past twelve years.

A Fitness Update

Adrian and Andrew are satisfied with the players' state of fitness, now that they have embraced the new culture of systematic preparation and training. As they face different physical challenges, each player is given a customised routine. Sachin is given leg-strengthening exercises and advised to cycle because he is recovering from an ankle injury sustained in New Zealand. He also has a routine for his stiff back and instability in the shoulder. Sehwag does gym work and weights. Laxman exercises to increase the explosive power in his legs. Nehra needs constant attention for a weak ankle.

Andrew and Adrian rate Dravid the ideal pro in the team by a mile—he works very hard and follows every routine. He scores 10/10 on dedication and discipline.

The Magic of Lord's

It is amazing how well organised Lord's is on match day. Members wearing red and yellow MCC colours come through the turnstiles holding hampers of food. Even in the rush of day one of the Test, everything is in place. The hushed expectation of play and unmistakable respect for cricket make Lord's special.

The Test match track is marked out in advance and meticulously prepared. No cricket is allowed on this pitch to ensure the grass remains fresh. When I ask the head groundsman if skipper Nasser Hussain has a say in pitch preparations, he is horrified. *It is my job to prepare the pitch*, he replies frostily. *And it is his job to play.*

I do not tell him that this is not how it works in India.

The Lord's dressing room for the visiting team is supervised by the incredibly efficient Pete Lowe. He single-handedly does everything—arranges food, produces a typed team sheet before the toss, sorts out practice balls, puts extra grips on bats, delivers match passes to guests and receives the players' wives at the Grace gate. When Laxman's batting spikes need repair, Pete has them fixed by Brian and Brenda, the studding experts in Harrow. Pete is a magician, a fixer of all problems.

Before the game, it is interesting to see Sourav go through his batting routine. He pulls a bat from the kitbag and takes his stance, waiting for the bowler to run in. Taps the bat on the floor but does not play a shot, body poised in full readiness—bat raised, head still and eyes focused. Satisfied after 'keeping shape' a few times, he knocks his bat with an old ball to check its sound. Pleased with the result, he announces that the bat is good—*bilkul chabuk!*

Ahead of the game, Dada faces the usual headache of deciding the playing eleven. *I ask everyone but nobody is clear*, he complains. *So it all comes back on me.* Not easy. Sourav has to handle the perennial problem of team composition: extra quick or additional spinner? 3/1 or 2/2? If 3/1 then which one? Kumble or Harbhajan?

It's always a tough call. Wright wants 2/2 but the seniors want to go with 3/1, a view Sourav favours. The spinners don't have a great record overseas and he dreads a situation where, if one quick has a bad day, both spinners could be operating before first drinks on a flat wicket. In the end, after much debate and much back and forth, it's 3/1 with Kumble.

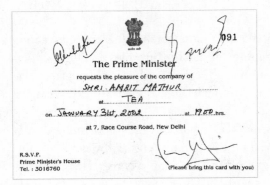

The Prime Minister

requests the pleasure of the company of

SHRI AMRIT MATHUR

at TEA

on JANUARY 31st, 2002 at 19.00 hrs.

at 7, Race Course Road, New Delhi

R.S.V.P.
Prime Minister's House
Tel. : 3016760
(Please bring this card with you)

After the day's play, there is a commotion as match referee Mike Procter drops in to measure bats to check whether their width is within legal limits. Procter puts on a fake show of appearing apologetic about the search, mumbling that he is merely following up on complaints. But he is obviously looking for something, like a cop suspecting a crime has been committed. He inspects some bats but finds nothing wrong. *Just doing my duty*, he says, stepping out. *All ok*. Seeing him disappear down the steps, at least two players heave a sigh of relief!

The team is informed about an informal 'get to know each other' meeting with the match referee and umpires after day two of the Test. Neither Sourav nor Nasser is keen (*the discussion is always only about umpiring decisions, so what is the point?*) but they reluctantly agree to attend.

The meeting is pretty routine except when umpire Nigel Lloyd brings up slow over rates. Reacting to the suggestion that captains should speed up play and get more overs in, Nasser, always ready with a sharp response, makes an interesting point. *It isn't easy at Lord's*, he says, *because it takes a long time to come down the many steps from the dressing room, then walk carefully through the Long Room past all the doddering members.*

Dilip Vengsarkar is also here as a guest of the ICC. Dilip scored three hundreds at Lord's and narrowly missed a fourth. *It was bad luck*, he laments the missed opportunity. *I cut Graham Dilley hard—straight to point!*

Dinner with Sunny

One bonus on cricket tours (if you are lucky) is you get time with Sunny Gavaskar, the sharpest cricket brain on the circuit. Sunny is cricket's Google—there is nothing about the game that he does not know. His alert mind picks up things that others are unable to see or understand.

Dinner with him is always delightful. Over crispy fried duck (one of his favourites) and red Columbian wine (about which he has deep knowledge), he tells me how Sidhu temporarily made him give up meat and become a vegetarian. But that decision has since been overturned—Gavaskar resumed his normal diet and gave up on Sidhu.

Sunny shares a strange love–hate relationship with English cricket. He respects the tradition and culture but his questioning mind resents the sense of superiority and underlying arrogance that is part of the system.

This trait of critical examination helps Sunny detect minor changes in Sachin's batting. *At stance he is balanced and nicely sideways*, he says, *with the right shoulder not visible to the bowler. But at the point of playing, he opens a shade so the bat goes away and can't come down straight.*

According to Sunny, Yuvraj's technical issue is about pushing forward and going across. *As a result, the bat gets in the way and he has to play around his pad. Yuvraj plays the short ball well: if it is very short, he can easily swing it away. If it gets to the rib area, then it becomes a problem.*

Net–net: Nobody does technique better than Sunny.

The Trouble with Logistics

Unlike other countries, in England, visiting teams travel in a coach and there is no air travel, no bother of queuing up for clearing security or a last-minute rush to board a flight. Most times it is a few hours' drive, except to Durham up north or to Manchester, which takes longer. Usually the team leaves for the next venue as soon as play ends at the earlier one; change and shower at the ground, grab some food and hit the road.

The team bus is a temporary home where players have designated seats. Someone puts on random music and, occasionally, a movie plays on the DVD player. Tired players sleep on the floor and leave behind stuff they don't need, rather than carry it to their hotel rooms.

The players' luggage and kitbags are moved separately in a van, which is a major logistics exercise. The Indian team doesn't travel light and the group has about 125 pieces of baggage which are transported by road ahead of its arrival at the next destination.

Handling this is the responsibility of Trevor Crouch, ECB's baggage person with the Indian team. Trevor is cheerful and extremely efficient, very hard-working and incredibly resourceful. Before every luggage move he sets a deadline, asking players to leave their bags outside their hotel rooms at a specific time. He picks them up himself—all alone—and loads them in his luggage van and sets off.

Trevor, the one-man army, reaches the next venue and personally places each of the 125 bags in the players' rooms before they arrive. It is an extremely complicated exercise but not once was a bag deposited in the wrong room. Besides handling luggage, Trevor is my go-to man for anything anyone needs. He buys SIM cards and medicines, receives guests, fixes bat grips, repairs bowling spikes, handles laundry and is useful in a million ways. Remarkably, he does all this without a complaint or a hint of impatience.

Once, Trevor and I got into a tricky situation when a leather pouch containing cash and receipts of expenses got misplaced. We spent two tense days searching everywhere (the hotel, the ground and the team bus) and checked with the players, but nobody knew anything. We considered lodging a police complaint but were hesitant because of the negative publicity this could attract.

Just when all seemed lost, we were saved by a lucky stroke. While sorting out his stuff in the Lord's dressing room, Kumble found something that didn't belong to him—the leather bag containing almost £5,000! People are known to experience life-changing moments. For Trevor and me, this was a life-saving one!

I returned home after the Lord's game with two large kitbags loaded with stuff players wanted sent back to India. The kitbags had been magically produced from somewhere by the ever reliable Pete.

Besides the loaded kitbags, I carried with me rich memories of the tour, the historic and improbable NatWest win, and the daily grind of an overseas tour. Every tour has its high points but not everything is as glamorous as it appears from the outside. The players live in a bubble of privilege and publicity but are burdened by expectations and corroded by doubt, uncertainty and tension. Inevitably, tragedy accompanies triumph, and after every tour some careers take off while others crash. There are moments of fun and frustration, occasional celebrations and constant challenges.

Pulling Together

The Indian team has set traditions which are carefully protected and handed down by the seniors, who are excellent role models. Mostly, it is informal tuition and stray advice. The youngsters know that *money can't buy such education*, as they watch Sachin arrange his gear in his favourite corner in the dressing room, observe Dravid go through his routine, note the calm determination of Kumble and the positive energy of Yuvraj and Sehwag.

Among all the cricket nations, England is special because of its rich cricketing tradition and culture. At Hove one can see the scorebooks of old games, including those played by Ranji, Duleep and Pataudi, and the Committee Room has pictures of county captains from 1839. Contrast this with some state associations in India that find it difficult to figure out who captained the side the previous season.

I was also amazed by the flourishing autograph industry, which worked at two levels. One, through the post, with people sending requests along with prepaid stamped envelopes asking for the team autograph sheet. At every venue, these were handed to the manager by the ground staff. The other was in the form of personal requests by young fans and elderly collectors, who stood near the dressing room or team bus, sometimes for hours, waiting for players to stop and sign their books. I helped as often as I could by collecting autograph books and getting them signed and distributing team autograph sheets. The practice matches didn't attract crowds but when the sun was out elderly couples could be seen sitting in the stands reading newspapers and keeping score, ball by ball, on a piece of paper.

Team officials remained busy working closely with the ECB, the match referees, umpires and ground staff. Looking after the needs of the players was a challenge, with arrangements to be made for travel and stay, team practice, net bowlers, food during matches, team room set-up, wiring for the video analyst, medicines and equipment needed by the physio and the trainer. On a long tour, bats had to be fixed, extra grips procured, bowling spikes repaired and sponsor stickers pasted on equipment or taped over.

Invariably, there were issues to do with players' fitness and official functions to attend where hands were shaken, toasts raised and speeches made. Also, the less serious stuff like arranging hospitality tickets for wives of players and knotting ties for those struggling to get it right.

In England, Sourav's team was focused on a higher goal—winning abroad. The seniors realised that true respect was to be earned (individually) by doing well in England and (collectively) by succeeding away from home. Both captain Sourav Ganguly and coach John Wright spoke about this regularly, reminding players about building reputations and leaving a legacy.

Sourav was a skilful leader who understood his players and earned their trust. Which wasn't easy considering he walked a tightrope with the BCCI breathing down his neck and his colleagues expecting him to do the best for them. But Dada played it well—he backed those he considered 'match winners' and gave them freedom, a licence to grow. For younger players, he was less captain, more an affectionate uncle willing them to do well. Sehwag became a different player when allowed to open the innings and Yuvraj, Kaif, Harbhajan and Zaheer enjoyed the full support of their captain.

Working with the team, I discovered two contradictory strands. One, the seniors, the so-called leadership group, had tremendous respect for one another. Each player felt the others were world-beaters and they genuinely rejoiced in their success. Dada spoke glowingly about the others and gave them space. This created harmony in the dressing room and his job became easier because he had wonderful players—Sachin, Dravid, Laxman and Kumble—to lean on. Two, although all the seniors were on the same page, there were times when Dada seemed to drive the others up the wall. More than once, spurred by instinct, he took last-minute decisions and overturned what had been collectively agreed on in team meetings. He would change his mind about the playing eleven and decide something different at the toss. But these flip-flops never created a crisis because everyone realised the final call rested with the captain.

In all this, coach John Wright was the captain's ally and co-conspirator. He kept a low profile, preferring to work quietly in the background, making sure all the pieces were in the right place for the team to succeed. From the outside, he and Sourav were so unlike each other: John, with every bone in his body totally professional; Sourav, relatively old-fashioned and laidback. John worked incredibly hard for every team meeting, Dada chose to be spontaneous and went with the flow. John swore by fitness and tough practice, Dada had a different understanding of what it means to be match-fit. John was almost annoyingly punctual, Dada's watch was set neither by GMT nor IST—he kept his own time.

Occasionally, this caused friction and for a while the two had a rocky relationship. No dressing-room blow-ups, only a case of two adults taking time to adjust to each other. Sourav wanted Fannie de Villiers as a bowling coach, an idea John wasn't excited about. John was sometimes exasperated by Sourav's stately attitude. But both pulled in the same direction and developed a strong partnership based on trust and respect.

6

ICC CRICKET WORLD CUP, 2003

One outcome of India winning the 2002 NatWest series in England was the unprecedented expectation from the team for another spectacular triumph—this time at the Cricket World Cup in South Africa. On this tour, I was the media director while BCCI treasurer Jyoti Bajpai served as the manager.

28 January

En route to Mumbai to join the team for the World Cup, I spot Kapil Dev seated in a row towards the front. When I go up to do the traditional *dua salaam*, Paaji gives me strict instructions: *Tell the boys to focus on cricket and win the World Cup*.

It's a busy day in Mumbai. Players collect their clothing, attend a UNICEF anti-polio event and rush to the Taj business centre for the team photograph. Those seated in the front row keep their hands on their knees for uniformity and all the players smile brightly for the camera.

The mandatory pre-departure press conference by Captain Sourav Ganguly is streamed live on TV channels. He handles it well but his admirable composure is almost breached when a young reporter wants him to assess each of the fourteen participating teams. He takes a deep breath to calm himself and asks: *Which paper do you work for?*

Sahara, the team sponsor, want the players to visit the Siddhi Vinayak temple. It's Tuesday, an auspicious day, and a temple visit would make for a great photo. Wise heads question the wisdom of visiting a temple, pointing out that the cricket team representes a secular India. *Is it, therefore, proper? Do you want to go?* Sachin Tendulkar is asked. *I have already done my prayers*, he responds. The temple visit is vetoed.

When the bus leaves for the airport, Sachin's customary seat—front row, left side, window seat—is vacant. He is to be picked up on the way. The bus stops for him near the Leela Hotel and Sachin jumps out of his car, parked next to a police escort with flashing lights, bids a quick farewell to brother Ajit and hops on. It is past midnight when we reach the airport, yet fans are waiting for the team. A player remarks that if the team were to come back with the trophy after 23 March (the date for the World Cup final), there would be more than one lakh people at the airport.

In the departure lounge, boarding cards are handed out for Flight 277 to Johannesburg. Soon, the ties are off and the blazers given to the air hostesses to stow away—it's an eight-hour flight and the players need to catch some sleep.

Like on the bus, Sachin Tendulkar's seat on the aircraft is 1A. Naturally.

31 January

We are in Durban, two weeks in advance, to train and prepare. Sourav is pleased. *It is madness in India*, he says, *people think we will win even before the tournament starts.*

I have dinner with Sourav and Rahul at Butcher Boys, a Sachin recommendation for its ambience and terrific food. The place is booked solid but a table is found and Diet Coke ordered—Diet Coke because Pepsi, the World Cup's official sponsor, has no product in the market. No beef for Rahul, only salad and chicken. Sourav opts for grilled calamari and lamb chops.

Sourav announces that captaincy is the worst job in the world. *Why?* I ask. *Because I hate going to functions and answering silly questions.* Dravid counters in amusement, *But Dada, there are also benefits, no?*

1 February

Another day of training, starting with a 30-minute run on the Durban seafront, its Golden Mile, along the Bay of Plenty, North Beach and Sea World. Then it's time for some fielding practice at Kingsmead, where Sourav wants coach John Wright to use his new bat to hit high catches. Wright tries but gives up, the bat is too heavy. Sourav practises with plastic balls being hurled at him from 15 yards, refusing to use the bowling machine because he can't spot the ball coming out of the slot. Sachin has a similar problem but decides to have a go anyway, instructing the person operating the machine to call 'ok' loudly to alert him before inserting the ball.

PS: Sachin's advice to a nine-year-old kid who had been accidentally hit while batting: *Don't worry, injuries bring luck. Next time, hit the ball instead of letting the ball hit you.*

2 February

According to the ICC guidelines, each team holds a mandatory 'open' media session where players are seated in small groups and are available for questions. Before starting, Javagal Srinath makes an excellent suggestion to condole the death of Kalpana Chawla, the astronaut of Indian origin who lost her life in the Columbia spaceship crash.

In the evening the team attends a civic reception by the Mayor of Thekwani at the Durban Town Hall. Dressed in our smart tour suits, we first wait for the mayor, who is busy elsewhere, and then are embarrassed as His Worship does not know which team he is meeting. In his speech, the mayor condemns England's political stance on Zimbabwe. The players, visibly bored, make calls on their cell phones and wait for food to be served.

With Shahryar Khan, Cape Town

Practice at Kingsmead

It's high catches at Kingsmead as the ball goes up miles in the sky— high enough, as 'Sherry' Sidhu describes it, to bring down an air hostess—but hardly any catch is dropped. During the fielding drill for run-outs, Sehwag hits the stumps more often than the others and reveals his secret. *Yeh doodh ka kamal hai*, he explains with a smile. When a reporter asks Sehwag the inevitable question about comparisons between him and Sachin, he invents a new line:

Purana (old) answer: *He is different, I am different, and our bank balances are different.*
Naya (new) answer: *I am small, he is big. Main tara, woh sitara.*

The team conducts a coaching clinic for kids of colour in Umlazi, a 30-minute drive from Durban, as part of a cricket development programme for underprivileged children run by the United Cricket Board (now known as Cricket South Africa). Each player is assigned a net and Sachin is the roving coach who drifts from net to net. After a while, Sachin zeroes in on where Sourav is coaching and starts bowling to kids and to Sourav, a gentle short ball that the captain unkindly smashes over cover. This displeases the Master, who changes gear to release a sharp bouncer that would have pleased Brett Lee.

Hours later, in the team room, it is Sourav versus Sachin again, a similar competitive streak surfacing in a friendly game of table tennis. Sachin tests his captain's patience by keeping the ball in play and returning everything that crosses the net. Annoyed by this tactic, Sourav forces the pace but hits long and wide. Sachin's reaction is not a fist pump but a wicked smile that says: *It is not easy to beat me.*

Rahul and I have dinner at Something Fishy, a modest café on the beachfront opposite our hotel. We have kingklip and grilled prawns. It is the kind of meal that the cricketers are not able to indulge in when at home in India. Rahul's pet dread: *talkative strangers on flights who want to prove they know more cricket than Bradman.* His clever game plan is to put on headphones and read a book. If he finds someone interesting, he drops the book and removes the headphones. A few minutes in, if he finds it was a case of false signalling, he reverts to the headphones and book routine.

Asides

- Dravid's wishlist if he had time: travel to Egypt and Rajasthan. Also to Agra, to see the Taj Mahal. Sit on the bench there and have a photograph taken, like Bill Clinton.
- Jonty Rhodes's magic mantra for fielding: *To save one run you have to practise one hour extra every day.*

Ali and I, Paarl

4 February

The first of the two practice matches is against KwaZulu-Natal at Maritzburg, a 45-minute drive. The 7 a.m. departure is too early for Yuvraj. Sehwag, though, is up at 6.40 a.m. to board the bus on time to escape the 50 rands per minute fine that Sanjay Bangar is authorised to impose. That day, everything is early for Sehwag—he boards the bus early and gets dismissed early too. *Cricket is tough*, he says glumly, sitting under a tree near the boundary. *It is not possible to just go out in the middle and swing a carefree bat.*

Ali Bacher drops in to discuss arrangements, but when I invite him to the dressing room, he expresses his inability to do so because his accreditation does not provide access. Astonishingly, the CEO of the 2003 Cricket World Cup can't move around freely at venues. This is so unlike India, especially Delhi, where the scorer's aunt and the driver of the Daryaganj Station House Officer (SHO) can march into the pavilion and demand lunch.

Asides

- Parthiv Patel's perennial problem: *When I go home, people think I have become thin. When I come back, Adrian says I have put on weight.*
- Food allowance for players: US$ 50 daily. Adrian is watching.

Keeping a watchful eye on the team's fitness is trainer Adrian Le Roux, a stern, no-nonsense professional. At the end of every week, players get a report card wherein they have been assessed and marked on their fitness criteria. The results are on one page for everyone to see.

Adrian goes for a long jog every morning, irrespective of Cape Town's blustery breeze or Durban's sapping humidity. He eats almost nothing, and most of his meals comprise fruit, a piece of meat and some salad. In Cape Town, he finished a half-marathon in 90 minutes. *It is nothing*, he says modestly. *I have done many full marathons and even run a 56-km race.*

Which Indian players would survive a half-marathon? I ask. *Quite a few*, he answers, *if you don't put a time limit. Kaif would.*

At practice, Sachin refuses a net and instead has balls chucked at him from 16 yards. When one ball leaps nastily at him to fly past his helmet, the youngster throwing the ball holds up a hand to apologise. *Don't worry*, Sachin reassures him, *it's ok. Make me uncomfortable — that is what I want.*

Aside

- What is the secret of John Wright's fitness?
  He trains with the boys, does regular workouts on the cross trainer in the gym and eats sparingly. Lunch is several glasses of cold water and some salad.

Dinner with Dada

I committed a serious mistake today. I invited Dada to dinner on a Tuesday, when he is vegetarian. We go to the Great Fish Company (next to the Durban harbour, with ships coming in and going past diners) which is famous for its seafood. Sourav studies the menu and contemplates moving his Tuesday fast to some other day. But this is the World Cup and every piece of providence must be called upon to assist the stars above us. God-fearing Dada refuses to risk fate and opts for a vegetarian pasta.

The evening is not a total write-off. Captaincy sits well on Sourav and after four years on the job he has earned the solid support of his team members, which points to two things: one, he is good with the players and the dressing room is happy; two, he is backed by an exceptional bunch of seniors who ensure he is happy.

We talk about his multiple personal contracts, each worth serious money, which give him luxuries like the red sports Mercedes he owns and a princely lifestyle. Yet he craves an ordinary life and says his famous car is an unused toy that remains parked in his Behala driveway and has covered

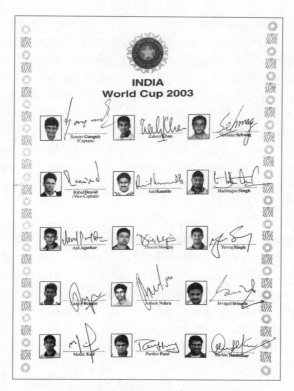

only 1,000 km in eight months. Sourav's take on life is that you don't need money beyond a point. *What do I spend money on? I have no expenses and no great desires. All you need is a cup of chai, some friends and your family next to you. What matters is mental satisfaction.*

He then asks about my role, whether it is a professional assignment with the BCCI. I reply in the negative. Honorary assignment, zero money. *That is foolish*, Sourav responds.

At the Shooting Range

Departing from routine, the team is taken to a shooting range where real weapons are handed out (semi-automatic machine guns and pistols) along with expert instructions (*wear earplugs to cut the noise and do keep the barrel pointing down*). The setting is like a Hollywood Western and one expects John Wayne to canter up on his horse any minute.

The players, or 'boys' as they are called, are excited to become commandos, squeezing the trigger of fully kosher weapons, firing *real* ammunition. The machine guns are easy to operate but pistols are a bit more complicated. Sachin and Sehwag, natural shot makers, are happy. Another player is shaken by the experience. He goes in, wears earplugs and picks up the weapon, then changes his mind. *I can't do it*, he says. Later, with nerves settled, he questions the purpose of the exercise. *What was this for? Why did we do this? To make us tough? Help concentration and improve the killer instinct?*

There are many answers to his many questions: Maybe all of the above. Maybe none. Maybe it was just a group activity to break the monotony of training.

6 February

The team plays a practice game against another KwaZulu-Natal side at Chatsworth, an 'Indian' suburb of Durban. By now the players have perfected the art of time management to avoid fines for turning up late: Open eyes at 7.30 a.m., breakfast at 7.40 a.m. and in the bus by 7.45 a.m. Every player glances at the clock as he enters the bus. Harbhajan, the undisputed master of this game, rushes in carrying brown toast and fruit. His late entry—by one minute—raises a loud cheer and Bangar, whose cash in hand ran out once his teammates started being on time, finally has a reason to smile.

The Chatsworth ground has been remodelled and has a new grandstand but the Indians are far from grand. They are dismissed for a disappointing 158 and dealt a shocking defeat. The ride back to the hotel is deathly quiet.

Rahul and I attend the launch of *Blacks in Whites*, a book about cricket in the apartheid era which graphically documents the plight of non-white cricketers with a pen dipped in acid. Logan Naidoo, the president of Durban Cricket, makes a stirring speech detailing the awful atrocities committed on the black population. One interested guest at the book launch is Shamila Batohi, the lawyer who made Hansie Cronje weep during the match-fixing inquiry.

There is a team dinner at Butcher Boys despite the protests from the vegetarians, who lose their appetite at the prospect of eating green salad and cheese. The food habits of the players vary: Dravid is 90 per cent vegetarian at home because of a strict grandmother; Kumble won't eat meat, only eggs; Srinath prefers Indian vegetarian food. Kaif decides to be adventurous, orders grilled calamari with garlic, and loves it. Sourav and Sachin opt for lamb chop steak, well done. The players spend quality time together, chatting about things of common interest (cars, films, music—in that order). Kaif takes pictures with his new digital camera; Kumble, a keen photographer, uses more sophisticated equipment.

The cost of dinner? Approximately 4,000 rands, paid using Sachin's credit card but split equally.

7 February

We fly to Cape Town for the opening ceremony. On the flight, Harbhajan tells his teammates about the importance of body language: *Be positive in the way you walk, talk and conduct yourself; let other teams be scared.*

Cape Town's Holiday Inn, Waterfront and the neighbouring Cullinan Hotel are buzzing. The Indians are in good spirits despite Chatsworth and the only dark cloud on the horizon is the vexed issue of ambush marketing which refuses to disappear. The ICC, keen to deliver value to its official partners, is concerned because LG is complaining about violations by competing brands featuring Indian players. They want the players to tell their sponsors to lay off. The letters from the ICC have a threatening tone and this worries the players. One confused soul asks: *I have agreed in the new Player's Terms about not having conflicting advertising during the event. But what can I do if a sponsor refuses to pull down a hoarding somewhere in Jhumritalaiya?*

Cape Town is breathtakingly beautiful but has unpredictable weather. Residents say the city can experience four seasons in four hours—and we experience it. The Cape Doctor, a blustery breeze, comes rocketing in as the official World Cup photo is being taken on the South African Navy's battleship *Outeniqua* in the harbour. The teams are lined up in alphabetical order but by the time it's done, the Cape Doctor is giving everyone a stiff dose, ties are flying and one has to clutch a railing for support.

The ceremony around the group photo is shifted indoors, to a cramped hall in Table Bay Hotel. The premier of the Western Cape welcomes the players, followed by a short, impressive speech by South Africa captain Shaun Pollock. While this is on, players turn down champagne to sip orange juice and take photographs, and Harbhajan and Yuvraj chat with Yousuf Youhana and Saqlain Mushtaq. Saeed Anwar, who is nursing an injured elbow after being hit by Shoaib Akhtar in the net, is wearing an eight-inch beard and looks like a maulvi from a Multan madrasa. Social niceties aside,

At the Cape Town seafront

the promised lunch is absent. There is no food in sight. Instead, everyone is handed a small gift bag containing tourism brochures.

This should have been prep for the evening letdown. The teams leave for the spectacular, multimillion-dollar opening ceremony at 7.15 p.m. and are promptly escorted into a hall and served canned fruit juice and chips. The show commences outside and the players watch it on a TV screen. For a while, everyone waits patiently. The Aussies down beers and Sachin huddles with Brian Lara in a corner, joined by Muralitharan after a while. The wait seems endless; it's been almost two hours. Picture the situation: all fourteen teams stuck in a hall with practically nothing to eat, denied a chance to witness the opening ceremony of an event they are going to be a key part of. When the announcement is finally made for them to march into the arena, the Indian team lines up quickly, Sourav in front.

But the ceremonial entry into Newlands is worth the wait. Sourav, holding aloft the tricolour, is overwhelmed. Later, he says nothing can beat the high this moment gave him. Except for the brief march into the stadium, the teams have little to do. They hear President Thabo Mbeki speak impressively about sports uniting people and South Africa's many attractions for tourists.

After the opening ceremony, the tired team boards a special train from Newlands station. Kaif is taking photos, Sourav rests his head against the window to get some sleep. Sachin says he can't remember the last time he saw the interior of a train; he used to take trains to get to Ranji matches, but that was many years ago.

The English players, sharing the compartment with the Indians, talk and joke loudly, and Matthew Hoggard and Michael Vaughan lead a noisy chorus we don't understand. But it must have been sufficiently funny because Alec Stewart is wearing a big smile on his wizened face. As the *angrez bahadur* create a racket, the normally talkative Indians sit in complete silence. Sehwag, not one to be suppressed easily, has a comment to offer: *Inki awaaz ground par band karni hogi (We have to stop their noise on the ground).*

9 February

For the first match, we travel to Paarl. It is located in the middle of the wine-growing town of Stellenbosch with the Drakensberg mountain in the background. The team stays at the Spier, a plush resort with rooms so large that the television in the far corner looks like a miniature model. The rooms have verandas overlooking large lawns. There is a golf course, a horse-riding area and a cheetah park in the vicinity. It's the start of a high-tension campaign, but there's a relaxed air about the place with players across teams chilling and chatting around the swimming pools. John Wright occasionally joins a group, playing his guitar.

A Session with Sandy Gordon

At Spier, the players have a session with sports psychologist Sandy Gordon. In India, anyone seeing a psychologist is immediately presumed unwell, but in modern sport it is accepted that sports persons need mental conditioning.

When John Wright suggested that Sandy Gordon, an experienced professional who had worked with the Aussies, speak to the boys, BCCI President Jagmohan Dalmiya had readily agreed. Sandy is already in Paarl for a conference and meets the boys in a group and also conducts individual sessions with whoever wants to chat with him.

At one point, he asks the players to choose a theme for the World Cup. Players opt for *Now or Never* over *Chak de Phatte* and *Teri Toh*. Sandy stresses strict compliance with 'team culture' and his other focus is on remaining positive at all times and being aggressive—with what he calls a *Fuck You* attitude—that goes down well with the group.

Gordon is useful, but once we are done, he spends a lot of time with the media, giving interviews to anyone who wants a quote. Whether you are a player, a priest, a politician or a psychologist, publicity clearly does not hurt.

The Point of Meetings

The first team meeting before the game against the Netherlands lasts forever. *What is the point of these team meetings*, asks a visibly irritated Srinath over dinner at an Indian restaurant. *Everyone is switched off and I have heard the same things for the last twelve years. Scrap meetings*, he says. Kumble takes a more reasoned approach. *If meetings don't work, fix them; abandoning them is no solution.*

After much discussion and food, a consensus is reached on what needs to be done: Lay down a law that everyone must speak. Everyone. Encourage guys to speak in Hindi. To get started, each person should say something nice about the guy on his left, even if it means manufacturing lies—this had worked well on the tour of New Zealand before the World Cup, despite the horrible outcome of the games themselves. One of the seniors says that while the players have lots to contribute, they are petrified when speaking to a large group. Sehwag knows what is what and is very smart, and if a conversation between Nehra, Harbhajan and Yuvraj were to be secretly taped, you would realise they are brilliant.

We are served by Krishna, a young Indian girl working as a part-time waitress to fund her PhD in microbiology at Stellenbosch University. Krishna keeps 18-hour days, lives alone and knows nobody in this part of the world. She knows nothing about cricket either, but that does not prevent her from throwing bouncers at Dravid.

How does it feel to play Pakistan? Do you hate them?
Why should I hate anybody? But when they play, I support the other team.
The next day, the team trains under a fierce sun and Sriram Bhargava, the computer wizard, digs up an interesting stat: the highest individual score in one-day internationals for the Netherlands is 68.

10 February

The Indian media is in Paarl in full force—there are almost a hundred of them. The team feels that the media is negative, lacks understanding of the game and is focused on sensationalising the least thing.

There are some ground rules for the team's interactions with the media:

- The team understands the media's need for information but players need to focus on the game.
- Because of a large number of requests, one-to-one exclusives are not possible and there is to be no direct approach to players.
- The captain will meet the media before and after every game.
- Star performers (Man of the Match, for instance) will be available for interviews.

Captain Sourav Ganguly digs his batting spike into the Paarl wicket and pronounces it damp. *If someone were to grant him one wish around his World Cup team, what would he want?* I ask. *Kapil Dev at number 7. With him, we would win the tournament hanste hanste.*

Later, I find Sourav in the Spier lobby, furiously making notes on a piece of paper. Is he writing his column, his message to the nation, his autobiography? No, Sourav shakes his head, *something more important. Points for the team meeting.*

The team dinner at Bukhara has an Indian spread this time, a concession to the vegetarians in the squad. Harbhajan, between mouthfuls of dal makhani and bhuna gosht, recounts his brush with the authorities at the NCA when, bowing to popular pressure, he, no more than eighteen, led a protest against sub-standard food. The authorities took a dim view of this rebellion and suspended him, even though he submitted a written apology. But here he is now—an NCA rebel at a World Cup!

12 February

In the first game, India is up against the Netherlands, a team as good as Himachal in Ranji. But then, this is the World Cup and *kuchh bhi ho sakta hai*. Anything can happen.

Sachin opens and Sehwag, the number 3, cleans his bat, puts new stickers on it, sings a song and waves to Indian fans as he waits for his turn. When Dada departs early, Sehwag goes in, but does not make much and returns. And starts cleaning his bat all over again. India wins the match.

Aside

- Sourav's comment when Pakistan is fined for slow over rate:
  The run-up of Shoaib Akhtar, the Rawalpindi Express, should be reduced to save time.

During the game, Percy Sonn, who later became president of the ICC, is accused of drunken and disorderly behaviour. Apparently, a sozzled Sonn had strong words for David Morgan, the ECB chief, and an inquiry is held. But Percy, a feisty character and a lawyer by profession, defends himself, claiming he did nothing wrong. His response to the charge of improper behaviour under the influence of liquor is classic: *The language used by me was appropriate to the occasion.*

India vs Australia

Important things to do before play:

- Final eleven, duly signed by the captain, to be intimated to the ICC by 9 a.m., one hour ahead of the scheduled start.
- ICC to randomly pick names of players for a dope test at 9 a.m.
- Captain to go for the toss at 9.30 a.m.

Australia start as favourites but Dravid puts the match in perspective: *Forget about winning and losing; it is important to have a good match and come up with a solid performance.*

Ravi Shastri (dapper, Oakleys in place) is near the main square for the pre-match analysis. The pitch is subjected to intense scrutiny and Sourav, Sachin and Dravid hold a war council to make an assessment. Ponting takes one quick look at the track and joins his team for fielding practice — obviously, he has no doubts about its behaviour.

Interestingly, both teams follow a similar pre-match routine. The same warm-up with the trainers, the same fielding routine (underarm throws at stumps for runouts, gentle skiers, some slip catching) and the same mandatory knocking for batsmen. All the international teams do the same things, but the Aussies have an air of arrogance and *akad* about them. They walk out of the dressing room looking as if they have already defeated the opposition. In terms of positive body language and confidence, they are leagues ahead of the others.

Sachin hits a few, then climbs the 65 steps and sits on a chair facing the ground. What is he doing, I wonder. Visualising? Psyching himself up? Calming his jumpy nerves?

During the game, Clive Lloyd checks the players' bats, which he says is part of his match referee duties, and discovers one that is wider than permitted by law. Manager Jyoti Bajpai and I go across to have a chat. Lloyd says the bat is just a shade wider (11 cm instead of the permitted 10.8 cm) close to the handle though the blade is fine. *Tell the player to fix it and also inform the others*, Lloyd says. We do so, and everyone checks their bats by passing them through the measure installed in the dressing room.

There is tremendous support for India in Pretoria. The tricolour is everywhere and fans, many with faces painted (for 20 rands), chant slogans and hold up banners invoking the blessings of Ganapati.

The match turns out to be a total disaster. More than the margin, it is the manner of defeat that comes as a shock. Sourav's face is dark with disappointment as he handles uncomfortable questions about the team's performance in the post-match presser.

What went wrong?

I don't know.

What next?

Now it is time for individuals to come up with the answers. Hopefully, we will be up for it by the next game.

Would you consider dropping down the order?

I have a decent record as an opener.

This will be a very long World Cup.

16 February

The mood is sombre as the team flies out to Harare because news has filtered in about the violent reactions at home following the Centurion collapse. The press accuses players of concentrating on contracts and cash instead of cricket, which is a convenient and quite *thakaa-hua* argument. But it always works.

Former players contribute liberally to this collective bashing in the media and angry fans protest outside Sourav, Kaif and Dravid's homes. India's defeat is also discussed in Parliament where the considered opinion of members is that India lost because of Dalmiya, the BCCI president. This is preposterous. If Sehwag chases a wide ball to be caught behind, how is that connected to the contracts issue? Similarly, when a fielder drops a sitter in the deep or India is dismissed for 125, how is the BCCI president to blame?

At the airport, Harbhajan tries to lift the spirits of his teammates. *Has someone died?* he asks. *Fight, show dum, show josh. Aur bhi match hain*, he reminds his mates.

President Dalmiya is on the phone, concerned by the shrill reaction at home, and speaks to John, Sourav, Sachin and Dravid. He assures them of the support of the board and urges the team to get its act together. His call indicates the gravity of the situation and Sourav spends a tense afternoon in the hotel business centre checking his email. I ask him if he is fine. *I am ok*, he replies, *this is part of the game. Except, this is the biggest part of the biggest game in India.*

Dravid is not okay. *Not really*, he says, as we jog around the Zimbabwe Cricket Academy ground where coach Geoff Marsh is chucking balls in the net to his eight-year-old son. *There is a limit to how far this can go. Why should fans threaten our families and write us off after one bad game?* I ask, *What is the way out?* The 30-minute run has me gasping for breath (Harare is approximately 5,500 feet above sea level) but Dravid has hardly broken a sweat. *Each one must introspect and find the answers*, he says. *Now every game is a final and it is not just cricket but a test of character.*

An angry Srinath favours direct action against past cricketers for trashing the team. Let others know the team can also give *bamboo* in return. Criticism must be constructive and balanced. Kaif, whose house was attacked by miscreants, thinks it is best to keep a low profile. *Why make a noise? Patthar or praise, baat to ek hi hai*, he says. *Chhodo and carry on.*

Frankly, there is no other way.

Harare

Looking at the league standings, John tells the players to wake up and perform as this is a must-win game. John is normally calm but during matches he gets hyper and starts muttering to himself, scribbling notes in his diary and giving non-stop instructions to the 12th man.

The previous evening, he had got a rude scare when he went to check the practice facilities at the Harare Sports Club, located next to Mugabe's presidential palace. John walked across to the middle to take a look at the wicket, but was stopped by an armed guard. *Disappear*, he told John. *Nobody is allowed here*. A startled John disappeared.

When I speak to Sachin about reassuring the Indian fans and appealing to them for support, he says he won't apologise but can explain that the team is trying its best. After practice, he faces the media and before the cameras roll, I announce that he won't be taking questions, merely making a statement. Sachin speaks with conviction and sincerity about meeting the expectations of the country. In Delhi, the prime minister makes a statement in Parliament, urging fans to be calm.

Sourav's press conference is along the expected lines.

What number will you bat at?

You will find out tomorrow.

Afterwards, I stay back with Sourav as he works on his *Outlook* column with Manu Joseph and poses for Atul Loke in the dressing room. No transport is available when they wind up, but after a wait, Manu finds a creaky cab. I protest that the Indian captain, used to travelling in a swanky Mercedes, is being treated badly by the media.

Asides

- Television commentator Ravi Shastri's suggestions for turning things around:
  Sourav to bat at number 4, Sehwag to open. Play 6 batsmen and 5 bowlers.
  Team should display *akad* while playing.
- Sachin's choice of *khaana*: Seafood and prawns. No snails. Won't touch snakes but has tried crocodile.
- Sourav Ganguly on captaining India: *It matters but also shatters.*

At the Indian High Commission

The players get weary of attending receptions and functions because they involve boring autograph and photograph sessions and distract them from the cricket. Today, when they reach India House, the residence of the High Commissioner, they are told by a sleepy *santri* that the High Commissioner has been transferred and the reception is at the Acting High Commissioner's house somewhere in the neighbourhood. It takes them a while to find the place and by then there is a drizzle and guests are huddled under a *shamiana*.

When the host speaks (too many) kind words profusely praising the players, Anil Kumble smiles and says we don't need Sandy Gordon—*this man is good enough to raise our spirits.*

The next evening, Justice Ibrahim, Zimbabwe Cricket Union (ZCU) chief, hosts a dinner for Malcolm Speed, the ICC CEO who is seen as anti-India and anti-Dalmiya. But Speed, a keen golfer, is surprisingly friendly and remembers the tight fairways of the Delhi Golf Club, particularly the narrow 9th next to the clubhouse. He confirms that the ICC will control the commercial side of the World Cup, a move which gives a larger role to ICC lawyers like Clifford Green, the gentleman seated to my right, who is in the news for demanding personal guarantees on ambush marketing from Indian players. He backed off when Dalmiya sent a rocket to the ICC, telling them sternly that players should not be disturbed during the tournament and that all communication on the subject should only be addressed to the BCCI.

Clifford, a fitness freak who participated in the Comrades Race run of over 90 km, says ambush marketing is a criminal offence in South Africa. To protect Pepsi, the official sponsors, he has employed 'spotters' at matches to look out for spectators wearing Coke shirts!

Another guest, the South African policeman who is in charge of World Cup security, says England screwed up by not playing in Zimbabwe and relying on wild assumptions. First, they projected Zimbabwe as a political issue (concerning democracy), then it became a moral issue (involving freedom in a repressive regime) and finally they discovered a security threat from an unknown group. By jumping in different directions, they lost friends both in South Africa and Zimbabwe.

Aside

- How does SA protect its wildlife and eliminate poaching?
  By treating it as a treasured heritage, like the Taj Mahal in India.

The Forest Rangers carry rifles with night vision and if an elephant is poached, they make sure the killers don't escape the tough provisions of the law.

The next day, a minor stir is caused when Clive Lloyd decides to inspect bats. He arrives armed with the rulebook and a measuring tape to find some bats too wide and says that the boys should shave the blade and sandpaper the sides. The matter should have rested there but the media get a whiff and the news is prominently splashed in Indian papers as a negative story hinting that Indian players are getting an unfair advantage. Lloyd shoots this down by confirming that bat inspections are routine and some Zimbabwe bats too had to be adjusted.

Going into the critical match against Zimbabwe, Sourav reminds everyone that all the teams in the World Cup receive *jhatkas*. Very reassuring that we aren't alone in our misery.

19 February

It is a tense morning because India must win to remain in the tournament. Referee Lloyd is at the ground at 8 a.m. but looks unwell. *I had a scare yesterday*, he tells me, clutching his stomach. *Severe pain, and I passed out.* I comfort him by saying he will live to be 100 and the big man protests. *I don't want that, man. Not 100, only 99.*

To everyone's relief, India wins in style, John Wright breathes easy after many days and the players are smiling. Captain Sourav Ganguly is surprised that his wife has sent him a congratulatory SMS. *I don't know what has happened. All these years she did not talk to me about cricket but now she follows the game and is on the button!*

Sidelights

- Percy Sonn is dazed by the amount of cricket going on. It is too much, he says with a disapproving shake of his head. I see bats and balls in my dreams.
- One surprise: Ashish Nehra registered 147 kmph on the speed radar.

Moving on

Ask a player what tires him out the most on a tour and he'll promptly tell you it's travel. How tough it can be is best illustrated by the fact that the team has to take a 6 a.m. flight the next morning from Harare and their luggage will be collected soon after the game. With travel every other day, players realise it's smart not to unpack. Experience dictates that you only pull out what is needed from the suitcase.

As handling luggage is a major job on a cricket tour, a 'baggage man' is attached to each team. With us is Achmat, the one-man army who ensures our bags reach intact and nothing is misplaced or lost. Besides moving luggage, Achmat is the go-to person for running errands. He gets things from the market, buys phone cards, fetches guests from the airport, drops players at restaurants and organises the laundry. The last is of vital importance as players receive a fixed daily allowance of US$ 15 for laundry but hotel charges are steep, so it has to be done elsewhere. The multitasking superman is also a useful net bowler who bowls decent medium-pace outswing off a smooth action.

After Harare, the next stop for the team is Pietermaritzburg's Golden Horse Hotel, which is a casino. Weird that in South Africa (the land of the match-fixing scandal and the King Commission) teams are being put up in a casino. *Log kya kahenge aur kya sochenge!*

Sidelight

- Herschelle Gibbs releases his autobiography but admits he has never read a book in his life. He adds, to protect his personal record: I don't think I will read my book either.

21 February

Distrust between current and past players has been simmering over critical comments on television and in the press. The team wants television experts to be balanced, that nobody should be offensive or ridicule the Indian team. They are angered by Srikkanth's sarcastic remark that Sourav should bat at number 14. Srinath speaks for his teammates when he says, *We know what these people did when they played and what their records are.*

What it boils down to is this: Each television channel has to decide its stance and it might well choose the 'blast-the-buggers' route for TRPs and instruct commentators to take that line. But this would invite a strong pushback from the team, and if any channel were to take this position, players would be justified in denying access. So, the network has to make up its mind about being friend or foe and decide to bat or bowl. If if doesn't cut down

Train ride to Pietermaritzburg with Sourav Ganguly and Rahul Dravid

the criticism, the players would refuse to talk to them and impose an informal ban.

Aside

- Sourav Ganguly's views on the media: *They can never be your friend. Nowadays, if they don't write bad things about me, I am surprised.*

Amid this controversy, the Indian High Commission and the Municipal Corporation organise a ceremonial train ride to Pietermaritzburg station where, on 7 June 1893, Mahatma Gandhi was ejected from a whites-only first-class compartment. Satyagraha started from here and the Mahatma has been quoted as saying he was born in India but made in South Africa.

The team (and the media) ride in a train pulled by a steam engine and it is an emotional experience to relive an event that shaped India's freedom struggle. During the 15-minute ride, Srinath masquerades as a ticket collector, playfully threatening to throw players out of the compartment. As the train pulls into the station, coming to a halt exactly where Gandhiji was thrown out, manager Bajpai reminds players in a stern, non-Gandhian manner that this is a solemn occasion, not a school outing, and decorum must be maintained.

A brief ceremony is held on the platform, a plaque is unveiled, speeches made and photos taken. One player, obviously not a student of history, wonders what Gandhiji was doing in South Africa. Another, obviously no fan of Gandhiji nor particularly reverent, says the team should have practised for two extra hours instead of making this trip. *Match mein kya Gandhiji pad pehen kar jayenge?*

India vs Namibia

Little is known about Namibia except that they field exceedingly well. Sourav and Sachin score big hundreds. Dada is hit in the face trying a slog and Leipus runs in with ice, but the captain waves him away because he wants to slog some more. The doctor who inspects the wound later decides it does not require stitches. This is a relief because Sourav, otherwise a superman, is terrified of syringes and stitches.

Asides

- Did Sourav's luck change because he changed his shirt number from 99 to 24? Initially he wore 1, but when India lost many finals, moved to 99 and then to 24.
- The reason why a young player agreed to be interviewed by women journalists: *This is to encourage women in the virgin field of cricket reporting. History will remember me and my statue will be erected in press clubs and cricket grounds.*
- How did Dravid's perspective change during the World Cup? Earlier he discussed the finer points of batting. Now he asks wicketkeepers for tips.
- Nehra twisted his ankle after bowling two balls and took no further part in the match. Sourav explained why Nehra was picked: *We wanted to know what he could do with the new ball. We found out that he falls down.*

Sachin, happy to score a hundred after a long gap, sits in an ice bath to ease muscle fatigue. As Leipus keeps time to ensure that he clocks 3 minutes in the tub, Sachin pleads for mercy: Only a minute and a half. After that, I'll freeze.

After Zimbabwe, the team is back in Durban for the big week with key matches against England and Pakistan before the end of the league stage.

The hotel is busy with the English team and their supporters who are staying there. It takes ten minutes to get the lift.

India's top headache is Nehra's wrenched ankle. Andrew shakes his head uncertainly, not sure if he will be fit, but Nehra announces he will play even if it is on one leg.

In the World Cup, each match is a final, but the England game ahead of the clash with Pakistan has added significance. Losing to England will mean having to beat Pakistan at all costs to make the Super 6 stage. *Woh tension kyun lena?*

Meanwhile, Bacher is happy with the World Cup. The cricket is good and the fans' response has been great. Bacher had studied the Sydney Olympics and was so impressed by the common signage at venues that he copied the format and gave all the grounds identical zebra-stripe branding. The influence of the Olympics was also visible in the opening ceremony and in the role of the volunteers. If the World Cup remains free of administrative glitches, the credit is due to Bacher, who has picked competent people and decentralised decision-making.

Asides

- Ravi Shastri on Bacher: *Ali is a master, never ruffled, always in control.*
- Bacher on Sachin: *Sachin is a genius like Bradman. But Sachin is universally liked.*

India vs England

Surprise! The final 11 is decided without much debate and a blazered Sourav is ready for the toss five minutes before time. When play starts, Sachin strides out to bat and David Morgan, the chairman of the ECB, settles down to watch in the presidential suite. *My wife and I have come specially to see him*, he says.

Sachin does not disappoint. When Andrew Caddick pitches short, Sachin's pull clears the old pavilion at square leg to land in the parking lot. *Never seen a shot go that far*, says Cassim Docrat, who has spent a lifetime at Kingsmead.

Mike Atherton, on the Sky commentary team, thinks India's 250 is inadequate, but England is blown away by Nehra's 6 for nothing from ten overs. Srinath raises a cheer for Nehra and others thank Leipus for keeping him standing on his feet. John Wright allows himself a rare smile. *It's always great to thrash the Poms.*

Aside

- Srinath on Nehra: *Greatest spell of fast bowling in Indian cricket history.*

The Indian team has come a long way from 15 February to 26 February — written off then, and written about now. At the post-match press conference, Nehra answers questions about his injury (he thanks Leipus and Adrian), his spell (Vaughan was the big wicket) and Wasim Akram (his hero and inspiration). Sourav is thrilled to answer critics who slammed the team after one poor game. This is a personal triumph, a stinging response to people who thought he should drop down the order and drop himself from the team.

What does a team do after a great win? Is there a big party to celebrate? Far from it. Nobody has the time or the energy. By the time the players return to the hotel after the customary post-match presentations and the media conference, it is close to midnight. Drained, they retire to their rooms to grab a quick room-service dinner. Vaughan and Stewart are in the lift, carrying their bags down, because England is leaving for Port Elizabeth at 7 a.m. the next morning. *Good luck*, they say. *Beat Pakistan.*

Beating England provides momentum to the team. Sehwag feels international cricket is not as tough as it is made out to be, *it is television that complicates cricket and creates drama. Replays show the ball swinging and the fielders appealing dramatically from twelve angles. But in the middle, the players just play normally.*

27 February

Departure for Johannesburg in the morning. Sourav carries a heavy handbag (*I can never travel light*, he moans) and looks for a trolley. Sachin has his trademark Adidas bag over his left shoulder and, besides his Oakleys, he is wearing a happy look.

I was striking the ball well, he describes his cracking half-century against England, *but couldn't sleep before the game due to tension.*

You are not serious, I say. *I am*, he replies. *For two–three days I kept getting up in the middle of the night.* This is what tension can do even to Tendulkar, after more than 400 matches, 65 international hundreds and 20,000 runs!

28 February

With England out of the way, the focus is on Pakistan. During the bus ride to Centurion for practice, Sourav fiddles with his mobiles (two connections, the India number known to all of India and the more private South Africa connection), sending text messages and making calls. For him, Pakistan is a must-win match because (a) it is Pakistan and (b) because teams carry points forward to the Super 6 stage.

He also understands there is another side to it. Not jihad or dharmyudh, as some rabid elements would have it, but pure pressure. It makes sense to downplay the match and treat it as just one more World Cup fixture.

The media, however, is already caught up in the hysteria. Many journalists seek interviews on the 'special' feeling of playing Pakistan and are intent on focusing on past battles. The players decide they won't add to the tension and Dravid tells the media that *it is a game and we prepare for it the same way we do for other matches, be it against Australia or Zimbabwe.*

But the media persists:

Isn't this game different because of the history associated with India–Pakistan?

We see it as an important World Cup game played with bat and ball, played over 21 yards by 22 players.

What would you like to tell India's cricket fans before the Pakistan match?

It is not for us to make a statement or a gesture. We are here to play cricket and it is a tremendous challenge to compete and succeed against the best.

Dravid's consistent stonewalling draws this response from a journalist: *He is right but we would have preferred masala—someone saying we will beat the hell out of them.*

Masala is served up by the Pakistani camp. Shoaib Akhtar, used to chucking bouncers (with a defective action), now hurls verbal no-balls (with a defective tongue) at Indian batsmen, going into detail on who he will target and in what fashion. When the media wants a reaction to this outburst, Sachin refuses to comment, but his smile and the cold ignore are expressive enough.

Asides

Sehwag's thoughts on batting:
- *Concentrate on the ball, not the bowler.*

- *Don't bother about reputations. If you think too much about who you are facing, you will be back in the dressing room.*
- *If struggling for runs in one-dayers, play positive. Otherwise both you and the team will struggle.*
- *Wickets are getting slower. In the West Indies, some were worse than Delhi's Kotla.*
- *On bouncy wickets like Durban, don't play the backfoot punch because the shot will go to gully. Better to cut hard or go over third slip to third man.*

India vs Pakistan

At a lunch hosted by Indian businessman Pawan Munjal a day before the match, Sourav behaves like an indulgent elder brother as Yuvraj and Sehwag joke with him. He complains good-humouredly that youngsters don't respect their seniors and adds that nobody would have dared to behave so freely with Azhar. Yuvraj promptly offers to be more proper, but Sourav responds with an expansive wave of his hand, saying it doesn't matter. *All I want is, you keep performing and winning matches for India.*

Wright understands India–Pakistan is a big match whose outcome could have a huge bearing on the World Cup. A win would inject enormous self-belief in the players but a loss would be a crippling setback. The key, he thinks, is discipline and the best way to confront an instinctive but unfocused Pakistan is through controlled cricket. *Stick to the basics, be tight and professional, and allow them to self-destruct. Meet them and beat them, not with passion alone but precision.*

By now the team selects itself, but there is still uncertainty about the spinner's slot.

At every press conference, Sourav says keeping Kumble out is a big and painful decision because he has won several matches for India. But tough decisions have to be taken and, in these circumstances, it is the captain alone who sticks his neck out. Others give advice but the captain must take a call, use his judgement, trust his instinct and then nod his head.

Will Harbhajan get the nod again? The spirited off-spinner appeals to his teammates to not worry about the pressure. *Bas dil se khelna.*

The team is up early and at breakfast well before the 7.50 a.m. departure (another sign that this isn't just one more game). The venue for breakfast has been shifted from the hotel coffee shop to the team room to keep

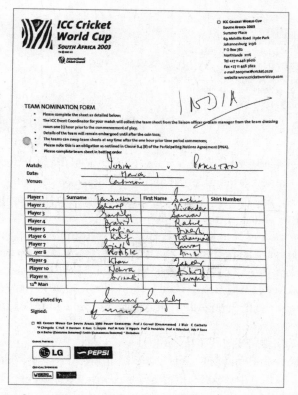

fans at bay. Kaif routs the computer expert Sriram in a table-tennis game with aggressive forehand shots and announces he is ready to take on the favourite, the number 1 seed Sachin Tendulkar, who meanwhile is eating fruit and cereal.

Soon the players find their way to the waiting bus through a side exit to escape the crowd in the lobby. Sachin, Sourav, Dravid, Kaif and Sehwag are carrying their match bats. What do they do with them in their hotel rooms? Play shadow shots, practise imaginary drives or just keep them, like soldiers keeping their weapons by their side.

The Pakistani team is already at Centurion, ahead of the Indians, loud music blaring from their dressing room. Wasim Akram spots the Indians getting off the bus and waves a friendly hand. Manager Shahryar Khan enquires about first cousin Tiger Pataudi and is surprised to know that Tiger is in Cape Town for a cricket show anchored by Mandira Bedi. Shahryar sa'ab does not know Mandira Bedi, nor does Tiger I presume, but he promises to get in touch with his relative after the match.

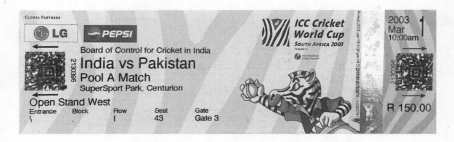

The teams take the 65 steps from the pavilion and, as directed by their respective trainers, embark on identical physical conditioning and fielding drills. The Indians are not the most athletic team in the competition but, compared to Pakistan, they are definitely fitter and faster. Saeed Anwar, Wasim Akram and Waqar Younis are players from the slow-motion era of cricket, all great players but not the type to be made fielding captains, even of a first-class side. I congratulate Wasim for taking 500 one-day wickets and add jokingly that his next target should be 1,000 international wickets. Wasim laughs at the suggestion and says it's impossible. *As it is, I need a stretcher nowadays.*

Referee Mike Procter drops in to have a chat, ostensibly to issue some important reminders. Get overs done in time, make sure batsmen cross on the field when a wicket falls. But his motive is different. This becomes obvious when he mentions how this game (India versus Pakistan) is a huge opportunity to perform—and also a great responsibility.

Basically, the referee is saying, cool it folks, don't do anything silly that may provoke the charged fans and cause ugly incidents. *This is an important contest,* he goes on in a roundabout manner, *a big advertisement for cricket, lots of attention is focused on the match.* Clever, I thought. Good point to make to keep everyone in line.

Before the start, there is one more reminder that this is a special occasion. The teams are asked to meet on the ground, shake hands and exchange souvenirs before the batsmen go in. When the idea was mooted, Pakistan agreed instantly and an announcement was made for the press. Now photographers and cameramen line up near the steps of the dressing room to record the event. At the last minute, a player questions the wisdom of doing something special for the Pakistan match. *If this is just another game, why deviate from the norm and make a statement? Why is the ICC suddenly behaving like the UN?*

Shahryar says he is fine either way, but the ceremony goes through because a sudden cancellation would have attracted flak for India for snubbing Pakistan. The players eventually go down and shake hands, Waqar and Sourav exchange ties and the brief ceremony is over in a minute.

Whatever the players' reservations, the gesture is well received by everyone. It sends out a positive signal to fans (at the stadium and those watching around the world) that this is a cricket contest played in a civilised manner. Who could possibly fault a handshake?

When play starts, Saeed Anwar speeds off like Schumacher's Ferrari, working the ball away fluidly like only he can. This causes a complete collapse of the body language in the presidential suite. Raj Singh Dungarpur, in a state of deep despair, thinks the boys look tired and jaded. *Our players are not strong, they need rest, not nets before a match*, he says. Raj bhai marches off to the dressing room to tell John Wright he should ease up and not try to make the Indian cricketers Olympic athletes. *Yeh ladke nahin kar sakte.*

National selector Kirti Azad is worried, he feels the Indian bowlers are not penetrative and need helpful tracks to deliver. Shyam Bhatia, who lives in Dubai and is the author of a book on the stars of one-day cricket, can't hide his grief. *We must win against Pakistan*, he says, confirming the common view that, whatever else may happen in the World Cup, it is necessary to beat Pakistan.

With Pakistan reaching 273, most think a win is going to be very tough to achieve. At lunch the *charcha is kya hoga*, is the Pakistan total too much or just a little too much because of Waqar and Wasim? There are many theories and majority opinion favours Pakistan for no reason other than a pessimistic feeling that India will collapse under pressure. There is that plaintive question again: *Pakistan ke against kya ho jaata hai?* One guest wants to catch an early flight back because he does not want to witness another defeat; someone else, more militant, suggests the team should be thrown off Vijay Mallya's jet. Mallya himself refrains from expressing an opinion. Dapper in a white linen suit, diamond ear studs gleaming, mobile phones in hand, he is flamboyant, filmy and totally flash.

But real style and sheer class are revealed after lunch by Sachin Tendulkar, the Master himself. He launches his innings like a batsman at a net after the coach has announced a last round. Ordinary players play according to the merit of the ball, but Tendulkar plays according to his will. He hits, others watch (Waqar and Wasim have the best view, privileged to be so close), stunned by the ferocity and audacious strokeplay. Here is a champion player at the top of his game, mistreating top bowlers—completely riveting stuff.

Shoaib Akhtar runs in from a mile, but when the ball disappears quickly off Sachin's bat, he takes really long to get back to his run-up. Waqar, punished severely, can only stare helplessly. Akram? He cannot believe what is happening. He bowls a perfect ball, the right length, the right line, swinging in just a shade. Sachin punches it through the offside, giving mid-off and cover no chance. Bacher rubs his eyes in disbelief. *This is genius*, he exclaims.

Dada perishes on the first ball, but with Sachin in commanding form, India is rolling towards victory. Cricket, however, is never without tension and drama; Sourav watches tensely, claps excitedly for each run scored, holds his special tabeez, recites his prayers and goes through every *tashan* routine he knows.

Sachin, stricken with cramps, is in obvious pain. Leipus gives him a rehydrating drink, stretches the hamstring, but the pain persists. He loses his wicket on 98, fending a short ball, unable to move quickly, and makes the long walk (climb, really) back to the Centurion dressing room. He is limping and while the entire stadium cheers an outstanding innings, he sits down on a stool to rest, drained physically and emotionally, sweating profusely, head hanging with disappointment.

Normally, after a match-winning innings, players celebrate, shout, scream with delight and rejoice when the batsman returns. But not a word is said as Sachin watches his dismissal on TV. John goes across to pat him on the back but says nothing. Someone helps Sachin take off his pads. Sourav claps silently to acknowledge a great knock and the brave effort.

After a few hiccups, India wins—and only then does the dressing room erupt. There are high-fives all round, much clapping and shouting, *jhappies* and handshakes. Sourav sprints down to greet Yuvraj and Dravid. The Pakistanis reach across to congratulate the Indians, Abdul Razzaq and Saeed Anwar come into the Indian dressing room to wish the players. Sourav wants the entire team out for the presentation, a gesture aimed at the Pakistani and Indian fans. There is one voice that favours caution (why change *tashan, kahin aage latak jayein*) but barring a tired Dravid, the boys go down to the field. Before that, Harbhajan grabs the Indian flag and waves it proudly throughout the ceremony.

Sachin, recovered but still walking with a limp, is greeted with a cheer so loud it could have been heard in Pretoria, half an hour away. He is moved by the response of the fans but when someone commiserates with him for missing out on a hundred, he says the team comes first, that winning matters and the hundreds will come.

––

Joke Received via SMS

Pakistan's major worry: Players want to return but no seats are available on the Rawalpindi Express.

––

The players celebrate, hanging around at the ground to enjoy the moment, as John says, and to be with each other. Amstel cans are passed around and refused by most. Some brave ones have a swig, grimace and shift to Diet Pepsi. Bangar and Sehwag, both strictly no-alcohol types, are chided by a senior who asks: *Kab tak buttermilk aur doodh piyoge?*

While the others are over the moon, John is typically underplayed. But even he can't mask his joy—this is a big, big win. A huge mountain has been overcome for the team and for him.

Sachin calls home and his wife, Anjali, takes the phone near the window so that he can hear the crackers bursting outside. *There is more noise than Diwali*, she says. Sourav receives a similar report from his wife in Kolkata. *People have gone crazy in India*, he says and adds that it is a great feeling to be able to put smiles on their faces. Kaif, usually calm and collected, is in a daze but reports of wild celebrations and rejoicing in India leave him a bit cold. Extreme behaviour is not good, he says. *Yeh kya, kabhi gaali aur kabhi khushi.*

This, however, is not the time for deep reflection as the players are on a high, and not merely from beating Pakistan. The Indian team has been criticised for lacking the killer instinct, for crumbling under pressure, for snatching defeat from the jaws of victory, but today these cliches have been disproved. The team won not by fluke or because of chancy umpiring but through ruthless, professional play.

Asides

- Why did Sachin refuse a runner till very late?

I like to take my runs. I know how hard I have hit a ball—the same message does not go to a runner.
- How important was the Pakistan match for Sachin?
  I have been thinking about this for more than one year.

Sachin rates his blistering innings as one of the best. *This was my day,* he explains, typically modest. *Right from the beginning, I picked the ball up early and was confident of playing shots.*

I am curious and ask: *Does an inner rhythm determine your style of play? Batting is instinctive,* he replies. *Sometimes you feel good from the start. Sometimes you struggle. Today there were so many times that balls close to 150 looked like 130.*

Dressing-room Quotes
- Comment on Shoaib Akhtar's action: *Kuchh to sharam honi chahiye.*
- Comment on Saeed Anwar: *He has a rule that you don't field after making a century.*
- Comment on Shahid Afridi: *Can't bat or bowl but is good at fighting and creating problems.*
- Sourav on tension in an India versus Pakistan match: *One of these days someone will have a heart attack.*
- First call from India after victory: BCCI President Jagmohan Dalmiya, even before the post-match presentation started.
- Former India captain to make a call: Tiger Pataudi.
- Three cheers raised by Srinath and Harbhajan: For Sachin, then Yuvraj and Dravid, then Bharat Mata.

After Pakistan
Having got through the league stage with five wins out of six, India finishes second behind Australia and carries points into the Super 6 stage. Another plus is that matches in the Super 6 stage will be played at venues better than dreary Bloemfontein.

For two days after the Pakistan match, cricket is temporarily paused and players get a break to recover and prepare afresh for the next battle. They go shopping, one group with Anil Kumble to a mall an hour outside Johannesburg that is owned by his friend Mohammad. They buy shoes, Oakleys and clothes—all at huge discounts.

Mohammad, a generous host, lays out an elaborate lunch at a farmhouse next to a river, in a breathtakingly beautiful spot. Those with more energy (Kaif and Parthiv Patel) ride a water scooter on the river. Initially they are careful, trying to get the hang of it, like uncertain batsmen judging a fresh pitch or reading a wrist spinner. But after coming to grips with the machine, they zip along at high speed.

In a tournament that stretches for so long, maintaining momentum is a prime concern. When the players are on a roll and the team is winning, problems get automatically sorted out. But keeping the players focused and their confidence up is a major task. Sensing that complacency could arrive uninvited, Wright cautions the players when they return to Newlands. *This is a reality check*, he says. *The good work is over, past us, gone—the harder exam starts now.*

Wright wants the players to maintain intensity and, once again, plays the emotional card. *Be true to yourself, your mates in the team and the country,* he says. *We are all part of a family and can't let anyone down.* Which shows that a coach is not just a coach who straightens the backlift and corrects the position of the wrist while bowling outswingers. He is a teacher, an elder brother, a school master, an understanding uncle.

6 March

On a morning jog around the Waterfront, you can see the place is full of kids and old folks, all working out seriously. Now I understand what Adrian means when he says sports and fitness are part of South African culture. Achmat was supposed to run too, but changed his mind. *I need to conserve energy to bowl in the nets*, he said.

Newlands, Cape Town has to be one of the prettiest cricket centres in the world. The setting is majestic: Table Mountain on one side, neat hospitality boxes and an imposing grandstand on the other. The cricket facilities are outstanding, the dressing rooms so large they could accommodate three teams. There is a board in a lobby with the names of all the captains of the Western Province since 1864. Sachin and Rahul stand near the players' balcony on the first floor and gaze at Table Mountain with its inevitable cloud cover. *I saw the best batting of my life here,* recalls Rahul, *when Sachin and Azhar made centuries and scored almost 180 in two hours between lunch and tea. The batting was so spectacular that Vikram Rathour and I went inside to watch it on TV, not wanting to miss the replays.*

Sachin dismisses this praise with a modest comment (*we were striking the ball well*) but remembers that India lost because Lance Klusener hammered the bowling. Sachin's other memory from the game is being caught by Adam Bacher. He pulled Brian McMillan and thought it was a six but Bacher leaped up at the square leg boundary and held the ball in his right hand while stretching to his left.

Cape Town's Waterfront is abuzz with activity, coming alive after sunset, filling up with people. It offers hundreds of eating options and the seafood is truly 'class', as the Indian players put it. With us is Arun Lal, part of the Sony commentary team which includes Mandira Bedi, the latest sensation on the Indian cricket scene. Apparently, commentators are queuing up to volunteer for extra sessions on the Extraaa Innings programme because of Mandira's irresistible personality.

Tiger Pataudi has flown in from Delhi for television commentary but got less than ten minutes in two stints on the show. Fellow studio-guest Kapil Dev thought this was ridiculous. People might want to see Mandira but Tiger deserved better, having made the trip after great persuasion, for he hates flying.

7 March

The pre-match press conference is dominated by an issue unrelated to Kenya. A website report has floated a wild theory that the BCCI is engaged in discussions with Bob Woolmer to replace John Wright. The story is ludicrous (who would sack a successful coach?) and ill-timed (immediately after a win over Pakistan?) and has to be scotched. Sourav wants to make a statement but Manager Bajpai puts out an official denial which kills the silly speculation.

It's a lacklustre day in the field, the players appear a step slow and the fielding is sloppy. Nehra is luckless, catches are dropped off his bowling and Kenya makes a respectable total. India loses quick wickets, causing Dr Prannoy Roy, NDTV boss and a staunch cricket fan, to wince. Prannoy often travels abroad to watch the Indians play but has a 100 per cent record of failure—whenever he is present at a venue, India loses. Today, with wickets tumbling (3/26), it seems he is all set to extend his sorry record, that too against Kenya.

As the head of an influential TV channel, Prannoy supports the players' stand on unfair criticism in the media. When all of India was jumping on the team, he issued written instructions to ensure NDTV's cricket coverage was balanced.

Before going in to bat, Sourav flips through a book on the stars of one-day cricket and is startled to find an interview with him about a memorable innings. *I never spoke to anybody*, he protests. *Did not do any interview of this kind.*

As Yuvraj and Sourav rebuild India's innings against Kenya, Parthiv Patel sits in the players' balcony holding bats for Sourav, including the one he used in the NatWest final last year in England. Sachin and Sehwag, both dismissed early, carry on a hilarious commentary—in Hindi—on the game for more than one hour. Sehwag the commentator is entertaining, while Sachin is the brutally frank expert.

John Wright is happy that Sourav with twenty-one one-day hundreds (and eight misses in the nineties, including four against Pakistan) is second only to Sachin in the number of centuries scored. While Sourav goes for the post-match press conference, the rest of the players watch Gilchrist, Hayden and Ponting slaughter the Sri Lankans and make mental notes. The general assessment: *what tadi*!

When the team leaves the ground a noisy group of fans shouts the usual slogans about India winning the World Cup. What is surprising, however, is the sight of a young, attractive girl holding up a banner for Ashish Nehra, the new star after the England game.

The players reach their hotel around midnight and Sourav, still to complete his press interviews, goes up to his room and orders room service for the Kolkata journalists, all wanting exclusive quotes on his latest hundred.

Asides

- Sachin's name for Yuvraj Singh: Young
- Sourav Ganguly's room number at the Cullinan: 420

Departure for Johannesburg is at nine in the morning. Sourav arrives for breakfast and orders tea, as usual, but eats nothing. *Too early?* I ask. *No, still sleeping*, he replies. In the bus, Srinath takes the commentary forward and another episode of the Ekta Kapoor-style soap unfolds. Television networks are now telling experts to be constructive and not go ballistic when criticising players. Srinath feels the team should either confront the experts or ignore the channels and dissociate from them. The latter option is more powerful because channels want access, interviews and news about Indian players for their Indian audience.

This time, the team is staying at the Sandton Sun, conveniently located adjacent to a big shopping mall and the famous Sandton square, which offers a wide choice of food. The gym is well appointed and I see Steve Buckner going from machine to machine to complete the full circuit.

The team attends a black-tie dinner at the Sandton Convention Centre to celebrate Joe Pamensky's fifty years of service to South African cricket. Joe is their father (maybe grandfather) figure, a respected chartered accountant and financial expert by profession. The function to honour him is a slick corporate affair with tables taken by sponsors and over 500 business barons and cricket celebrities present, including Clive Lloyd and Barry Richards.

Function over, I rush to Bombay Blues, the restaurant where Sourav is dining with friends Anshu Jain (top gun of Deutsche Bank, who has cricket in his system) and Arun Lal. Between juicy kebabs and dal, Sourav talks of the upcoming match with Sri Lanka. He says Chaminda Vaas is a good friend and a good bowler but underrated.

9 March

Parthiv Patel's eighteenth birthday is celebrated at Ghazal restaurant, with the highlight of the evening being an entertaining speech by Sehwag. *Aapka swagat hai*, Sehwag starts, sounding formal, but then goes on to make a profound and highly original point about Parthiv becoming an adult.

One precondition of the birthday dinner was that Parthiv would give a speech. This almost caused the young keeper to cancel the celebration but, having given the matter mature thought befitting his eighteen years, he delivers his memorised speech. Short and sweet. While driving back to the hotel, he confesses, *Mike se dar lagta hai, batting se nahin*.

Parthiv looks like a schoolboy but is an experienced cricketer. Having toured the cricket globe with junior India teams, he knows his way around. This babyface can also give *tagdi gaalis* in Punjabi and English.

10 March

The Indian openers put on 150, their best start in the competition. Sachin keeps hitting into the gaps, making one wonder why all the fielders are placed wrong for him. Sehwag begins well but is dismissed slogging Muralitharan.

When teammates question his poor shot selection, his defence is disarming: *Main kya karun, haath apne aap chal gaye.*

Sachin steps out to Muralitharan, trying a risky sweep, and misses a hundred. *Bad luck*, someone comforts him. *Centuries are made by muqaddar*, responds the Master.

Srinath destroys Sri Lanka, which gladdens Ali Bacher because, with South Africa out of the competition, India is crucial for the commercial success of the World Cup.

Brijesh Patel, chairman of the selection committee, calls to congratulate Srinath and one irreverent voice jokes that the bowler is at his best close to retirement. Muralitharan pops in to shake hands and wants an Indian shirt as a souvenir. Nehra, meanwhile, is screaming in pain as the tape strapping is removed from his ankle. Seeing my alarmed look, Andrew says, *There is just no other way, mate.*

A little later, Ashish Nehra is smiling, his pain forgotten, as adoring fans mob him. *Cup jeetne ka chance hai*, he says. *Bahut badi baat hogi.*

11 March

The team has optional practice, a break from the nets, but the players are in the Sandton Towers gym. I watch Nehra and Zaheer work out. They begin with half an hour of leg strengthening on the cycle, and follow it up with speed work on the treadmill, running at 13 kmph, then weights, and finally, stretches to relax strained muscles. Serious stuff. Harbhajan, going through his routine, marvels at South Africa's fitness culture and observes that the gyms are so busy, you have to book in advance.

12 March

Practice today is at Centurion, a half-hour drive from the hotel. The Wanderers Stadium is only a stone's throw (or a big hit) away, but John wants to stay with the winning pattern. Same reason for playing volleyball, batsmen versus bowlers; the latter win hands down.

There is plenty of slip catching. Sachin and Sourav chuck balls (both careful not to strain their shoulders) which Sehwag tries to edge to a waiting slip cordon. When Harbhajan joins the group, the captain tells him to be careful and not hurt his spinning finger.

News about Kenya beating Zimbabwe to become India's opponent in the semi-final is greeted with silent smiles. This is a lottery. All we need now is one good day. Sponsors Sahara are already planning for it. They are bringing a charter load of VIPs for the match and announcing gifts for players if they win the Cup.

Meanwhile, Dravid meets journalists and fields questions with technically correct answers. Nothing breaches his solid defence.

- On the mystery of batting: *Nobody knows the formula for success. It is a rhythm game. Sometimes you are flowing and everything is good. Other times, nothing works.*
- On discussions in team meetings: *There is a healthy difference of opinion which gives strength. Expressing a frank opinion is good provided what is said is reasoned and with team interest at heart. The team does not need eleven yes-men. It needs strong individuals.*

Asides

- Sourav's comment on his fit appearance: *This is due to tension. I can't sleep, have lost weight and my hair has turned grey.*
- Sachin on tension: *Some tension is good because it helps concentrate. But when it becomes too much, you can't sleep. I was cramping against Pakistan because of nervousness.*

In a media session, Sehwag hits through the line in his signature style. One example: How does Sachin's presence help you? *I play my game, he plays his game.*

John Wright's method of handling the media is in complete contrast to that of Sehwag. It is difficult to get a word out of him. Some gems from an encounter:

Can India beat the Aussies? *We will try and put them under pressure.*

Is New Zealand a grudge match? *We would like to keep our winning momentum going.*

Is this India's best ever pace attack? *The boys are exciting.*

What is your contribution to the Indian team? *I am privileged to work with immensely talented cricketers.*

Your team is in the semi-final, say something to show you are excited. *That is not my style.*

14 March

Departure from the hotel is delayed and a head count reveals one player is missing. The wait is for Ashish Nehra, who rushes in five minutes late (a fine of 250 rands) complaining that *the wake-up call did not come ... nobody woke me up ... could not even wash my face ... had no breakfast ...*

The match is one-sided, with the seamers slicing through the New Zealand top order. The person most delighted, obviously, is John Wright because this emphatic *badla* has erased the depressing memories of India in New Zealand when it was presented with terrible tracks.

Richard Hadlee, master of swing and control, watches New Zealand's demolition from the presidential suite and takes notes on a pad for his newspaper column. *This is great stuff from Zaheer*, he says with admiration. The union of fast bowlers knows no boundaries. Man of the Match Zaheer explains the strategy behind India's pace attack. *We bowl as a team and have a clear role. Srinath bowls length and line, Nehra swings the ball in and I hit the deck.*

Against New Zealand the plan succeeds, and the match ends ahead of schedule, which is terrific cricket but a commercial disaster for the broadcaster. According to Harish Thawani, boss of Nimbus, and Digvijay Singh, the CEO: *When India wins like this, we cry. The main reason is the steep price of the World Cup rights. Forget profits, for accounts to square up we must generate about 7 crore of advertising per game.*

Aside

- Sourav's surprised reaction on seeing Zaheer going to the gym after the match against New Zealand: *Kya ho gaya hai players ko?*

16 March

Breakfast with Sandip Patil, team manager of Kenya, the surprise semi-finalists. Sandip coached India for five matches in the mid-1990s, and having worked with Kenya for four years, he now wants to change jobs and start afresh in India. Kenya's success is astonishing considering that cricket is confined to Nairobi where 14 clubs play 50-over games on weekends. The cricket structure is pretty basic but Kenya has 11 selectors (a committee of eight plus manager, coach and captain).

The Aussies are in Durban for their next match and appear to be a happy lot at breakfast. Andrew Symonds, carrying a towel, is headed for the beach. Ponting, in shorts and slippers and wearing a cap, is straight out of bed. Former players (Ian Healy, Mark Taylor) sit at the same table and all the players, past and present, share a friendly relationship without the kind of barriers that exist in other teams.

Could this happen with Indian players? *No chance*, says one. *Our seniors won't come and sit with us because they feel guilty having said strange things about us as commentators and experts.*

The boys are on their own today but many land up in the gym. Among them is Anil Kumble, who has had only a marginal role to play in the World Cup but conducts himself in a dignified, professional manner. He doesn't allow personal disappointment to surface, never throws a tantrum and always remains switched on to help the team.

Kumble receives a rude shock in the gym when the electricity trips and the treadmill comes to a sudden halt. He is almost knocked to the ground but escapes getting hurt. Roger Knight, secretary of the MCC, witnesses the accident and raises one eyebrow to express concern. Later, he speaks about the changes at Lord's, the re-turfing of the outfield done for the first time in 200 years to improve drainage. The cost of refurbishment? A minor amount of £1.3 million.

Before the semi-final, the team has one eye on Kenya and the other on the big game after that. Players know they are close to making history because VIPs are coming to share their glory and get a slice of free publicity.

Some players take a dim view of this and raise valid questions. One: *We don't play cricket for politicians and film stars, so why allow them this chance to promote themselves?* Two: *Where were these well-wishers of Indian cricket when stones were thrown at our houses?*

Of course, not everyone is here for publicity. N.K.P. Salve, former president of the BCCI, turned 82 on 18 March and a small celebration was held in his hotel suite with French champagne and exquisite *khajoor* mithai brought by Kanak Khimji from Muscat. Raj Singh-ji says Salve sa'ab's zest for life is such that he is ready to go shopping after sitting through a full day's play watching the Netherlands take on Namibia.

Over dinner at the Jewel of India restaurant, Dilip Doshi recounts horror stories from his playing days—about a divided Indian team and players distrustful of each other. Sourav is aghast and says he is thankful his team is united and has outstanding seniors.

It is Tuesday, so the food is vegetarian and the chef has strict instructions to go easy on the chilli. Sourav is in a relaxed mood but is disturbed by his mobile phones which beep constantly. He looks at the screen before responding and remarks that it is impossible to keep his numbers secret. *The whole world keeps calling me*, he says.

This, however, is only one of Sourav's worries. He is hassled by other minor irritants—the intrusive media (*they won't let you do anything in peace, not even go to the loo*), the VIPs descending on the team (*this is for personal publicity*) and the unending scrutiny (*everyone has a strong opinion and passes instant judgement*).

Yet, there is nothing he enjoys more than playing cricket. *Had I been a normal kid in Kolkata, or someone doing a routine job, I would have learnt little. But as India captain my life has changed. I have gone through the whole 360 degrees, that too, more than once.*

Despite these rich rewards, including the unique honour of captaining India in 100 one-dayers, Sourav hungers for more. *I have just one more wish*, he says. *I want to win on 23 March. After that I will not ask for anything. Never.*

Asides

- Sourav's all-time favourite cricketer: Garry Sobers
- Greatest Indian cricketer ever: Sachin Tendulkar
- Greatest *tadi* batsman: Viv Richards

19 March

Rain, lots of it. Practice is shifted indoors but as team *tashan* is a prime consideration, the schedule remains unchanged. A game of volleyball is played in the cramped space next to the indoor nets. On the bus, while returning to the hotel, players are shocked to see Sachin Tendulkar going around getting a bat signed by teammates. With a straight face, he offers a valid reason for this unprecedented act. *This is for Nelson Mandela*, he says. Everybody signs.

Srinath contemplates his uncertain future beyond the World Cup. He is encouraged to carry on because he is bowling better than ever. But he is past 30, fitness is a major issue, and after 13 years on the circuit, his body is complaining.

Later in the evening, Dalmiya meets the team and after congratulating them, offers one piece of advice: *Play to potential, and fight.* Everyone, expectedly, nods their heads.

20 March: The Semi-final

The morning is exceedingly bleak, dark clouds cover the Durban skyline and most observers rule out play. But not Cassim Docrat from Kingsmead, who is confident play will commence on schedule provided it does not rain any more.

By mid-afternoon the threatening clouds drift away and the team is held back not by rain but a malfunctioning lift. The 12.30 p.m. departure is delayed because vice-captain Dravid is trapped in the hotel lift for close to ten minutes, an experience he describes as exceedingly scary. *The lift just stopped midway*, said a shaken Dravid. *I felt completely helpless.*

The players appear less tense because they know that Kenya, despite its impressive showing so far, won't push them too much. When the match begins, Sachin is off to a flying start but misses what could have been his fourth hundred in the tournament. *Aaj muqaddar mein nahin tha*, he says, emerging from the shower. *Centuries make you feel good but I am happy if the team wins.*

The Indian captain ensures this, scoring his 22nd one-day hundred. As the innings draws to a close, Dinesh Mongia and Harbhajan start a running commentary like Sachin and Sehwag in Cape Town, the only difference being that their account ignores the on-field action to concentrate on what they consider 'talent' in the crowd.

Anil Kumble takes pictures from the dressing-room balcony, adding to his collection from each tour since 1991, all kept neatly catalogued in his Bangalore home. Kumble prefers to work with a traditional still camera but is experimenting these days with digital equipment.

India's 270 score could have been bigger but Kaif is run out by miles. Someone observes that he would have made his ground if the pitch was shortened to 18 yards. India wins and the boys are thrilled about making the World Cup final exactly twenty years after the win at Lord's in 1983. There are smiles all around and everyone is busy getting souvenirs signed.

These joyous scenes are in sharp contrast to the sad memories from Kingsmead a decade ago. In 1992, during the first-ever tour to South Africa, the poor performance of the Indian team had so incensed the crowd that the police were summoned to keep order. Sachin, Srinath and Kumble were on that trip and the irony of the changed circumstances is not lost on them. But that is how the dice rolls in sport—the players know they can go from zero to hero, or the other way round, in no time.

When the team returns to the Elangeni, the lobby is packed with India supporters and the bar resembles Churchgate station during rush hour. What did the Indian team do to celebrate? Well, nothing! They sneaked into the hotel through a side entrance and packed their bags in readiness for the early morning flight to Johannesburg.

21 March

The Indian media on the flight badgers Dravid for a reaction on an AFP story about his marriage plans. The eminently suitable boy looks suitably shocked but refuses to confirm or deny the news and wonders why his marriage plans should interest others. *How does it matter,* he asks naively, completely missing (or choosing to ignore) the point that his countless (female) fans are keenly interested in knowing whether his wicket is intact or has fallen to some deadly swing.

On reaching Johannesburg around midday, the team gets a shock as the hotel has no electricity and the elevators are not working. Climbing up to the team room leaves even the fittest among them panting for breath. *This is like a training session,* says Sourav, unamused.

The night before the 2003 World Cup final, an official banquet is held at the Sandton Sun hotel and Wes Hall makes a long and eloquent speech. *Cricket,* says Hall, *is a super glue which holds people (as in India) and nations (as in the West Indies) together.* Hall praises cricket, glorifies it, celebrates its power, and also points to the challenges confronting it, ranging from match-fixing to player contracts and the shape and colour of the Kookaburra ball.

Change is essential, he says and cautions administrators about the grave consequences of failing to move with the times. Coming from the tourism minister, a preacher and former president of the West Indies Cricket Board (WICB), each word has to be taken seriously. *Dinosaurs became extinct,* according to Hall, *because they could not adjust.* Basic message: *Recognise reality, be flexible. Or perish.*

Hall praises India and Australia for reaching the final, and makes a subtle distinction between playing well and knowing the trick of winning. He congratulates South Africa for a wonderful World Cup but is unimpressed with its policy of quotas for players of colour. Improve quality by teaching kids, he says, give them equal opportunity, not a free ticket.

From the Oration

- On Ali Bacher: *I love him as much as a man can love a man and still be a man.* (Not something one might say now!)
- On quotas for coloured players: *Don't pick people because they look like me.*
- On himself: *At my age, the abdomen guard is used for keeping my cufflinks.*
- On the decline of West Indies cricket: *Youngsters think the 3 Ws stand for the World Wide Web.*

22 March

It's exam time. Something the players have prepared for and looked forward to with fear and anxiety. The wait is nerve-wracking and leaves a tense, tight feeling in the stomach. Yet, strangely, the pressure is accompanied by a sense of release because there is little now that can be done. As the moment of reckoning draws close, events unfold on their own. The only thing the players can do is stay calm, remain focused and go into the match with a positive frame of mind.

Practice is a formality, a quick last-minute revision of essentials. Once again, like they have done all through the tournament, the team plays volleyball on the main ground, a noisy contest followed by a relaxed net. Sachin refuses a hit, choosing to work with the bowlers on one side of the ground. Later, he says he had just one regular net in the entire tournament, before the match against Zimbabwe in Harare. For him, nets and practice are useful for fine-tuning his batting mechanics and working on minor adjustments. Is this complex preparation or a superstitious repeat?

The rest of the team does its drills: Yuvraj smashes several balls into the Wanderers hospitality area, causing Sourav to admiringly comment that he has 'too much' talent. When informed of Kent's interest in signing Yuvraj, Sourav thinks it will do him good. *County cricket is tough*, says Sourav, *it*

*teaches you discipline because you are on your own and still have to deliver.
In India, there are so many people to help you out.*

Later, Sourav meets the media and answers the usual questions about
plans for stopping Australia, countering Brett Lee, and the team composition
(the inevitable question about Kumble or Harbhajan). By early afternoon
everyone is back at the hotel. Sourav has half an hour to grab a bite in the
Sandton food court before meeting the Indian sports minister, who has come
carrying a good-luck message from the prime minister.

The 1.30 p.m. appointment is delayed because the team room in
Jacaranda Hall is occupied—physio Andrew Leipus is giving a tired Virender
Sehwag a rub-down. When they are done, the room is cleared out quickly
enough. Minister Sahib Singh Verma arrives accompanied by TV cameras
to read out the prime minister's message. Like a seasoned diplomat, Sourav
responds by saying that this wonderful gesture will inspire the team.

Sahib Singh Verma distributes special barfi brought from Delhi, which
Sehwag accepts gleefully, but only after a quick look to make sure Leipus
has left. Sourav and Dravid bite into the sweets in the *mooh mitha* ceremony
for the benefit of the TV cameras and the boxes of sweets are passed around
to the media persons in attendance.

India has reached the final after being beaten once by Australia. Australia
survived a few hiccups, barely scraping through against England and Sri
Lanka. But the odds favour them, experts say. Australia is too strong and
too confident. But are they unbeatable? No, says Sachin. He recalls India
halting them in Tests after 16 successive wins. Now, when they have won
16 straight one-dayers, it is time to break their streak again.

Sidelights

- When Sehwag and Kaif leave the Bombay Blues restaurant after
  dinner the night before the final, others guests stand up, clap and
  wish them luck.
- G.R. Vishwanath's advice to Sourav: *Don't be tense, just relax.*

With India in the final, guests descend on Johannesburg to witness the
game, which creates a problem as hotel rooms and match tickets aren't
available, both sold out much in advance. The BCCI has asked for help but
Ali refuses, citing a technicality that the BCCI did not exercise its option of
buying tickets in time. There is another angle to this: relations between Ali

and Dalmiya have soured and a miffed Ali is unwilling to play ball. Dalmiya asks me to speak to Ali and when I make the request, he offers a diplomatic, win-win solution: *Can't give tickets to BCCI because I have officially said no. But I can give tickets to you, my friend.*

Problem solved!

23 March: The Final

Breakfast is so routine this could be a game against Namibia or the Netherlands. Players rush in carrying bags (and match bats), mumble good mornings all around and settle down to eat. Sachin is having cereal and fruit, Dravid opts for cereal topped with a dash of honey, Sourav asks for tea, Yuvraj sticks to croissants, fruit and guava juice.

The bus ride is no different, as players beat the 8 a.m. departure deadline and occupy their regular seats. Sachin first left, behind him Sourav, then Yuvraj followed by Ajit Agarkar. On the right are Bangar, Dravid, Kaif and Kumble. The short drive to the ground is completed in silence and by 8.15 a.m. the team is at the ground, settling down in the visitors' dressing room.

But this is no ordinary game, this is the final, and its significance is unmistakable. It's scheduled to start at 9.30 a.m. but the ground is already filling up, the Indian tricolour is visible around the ground. Security is tight because President Thabo Mbeki is expected.

As the boys go down for their stretching routine, an urgent message is delivered from the Rashtrapati Bhavan, Delhi. The president of India has sent his best wishes. A fax from Deputy Prime Minister L.K. Advani conveys similar sentiments. By this time Sourav is already out in the centre, looking at the wicket, but the others have 30 minutes before reporting to Adrian Le Roux for training. The players check their gear, change clothes, flip through the match brochure, read a newspaper, drink tea to calm the nerves before slipping into the high-pressure contest.

After the formalities it's time for the game. How do the players get ready? Some (Sachin, Dravid) get into tights, some (Sehwag, Mongia) eat bananas and apples, others clean their sunglasses and apply sunblock cream. Harbhajan and Nehra choose the match ball from the box brought by the third umpire.

The last thing done by the Indian team before going onto the field? They sign a paper on which is printed the slogan 'I CAN, WE CAN'. It is an old ritual that began in Zimbabwe, before the match that turned the tide for India.

Unfortunately, the final is a disaster from the very first over. The bowlers hit the wrong length and the Aussie batsmen hit the right shots. Ponting plays out of his skin, a dream innings where he can do no wrong, even hitting a one-handed six off Srinath. The last ten overs produce 109 runs and India go for 359, which is a decent day's score in a Test match. During the break the dressing room is silent, the gloomy atmosphere broken only once, when Zaheer Khan comes looking for food in the dining area. Someone jokes, *Itna khayaa ground mein phir bhi bhook baaki hai? (You're still hungry, after getting stuffed in the field?).*

While the Indians collect their thoughts, the Australians give them a little more to think about. Just outside the change rooms at the Wanderers is a tiny patch of grass, next to the passage used by the players to walk down to the middle. During the innings break, the Aussie pacemen (Lee, McGrath, Andy Bichel) decide to loosen up right in front of the Indian dressing room. They bowl from two-step run-ups, pitching short, the ball thudding into Jimmy Maher's baseball glove. A routine drill or a ploy to unnerve the Indians?

How does a team approach a seemingly unattainable total? Waiting for his turn, Sourav weighs his options and concludes there is nothing to do except whack it and hope for the best. Realistically, a score of 359 cannot be chased, not against Bangladesh and certainly not against Australia.

Sachin tries and perishes, his first-over dismissal caused more by pressure than by McGrath. There is stunned silence as he returns. No words are spoken, but the dull sound of a bat being flung into the coffin conveys the hopelessness of the situation.

The final is a huge missed opportunity. Sachin Tendulkar, the game's greatest star, came to it after sizzling, match-winning innings, one after another, each effort brilliantly crafted. He has every reason to be proud of what he has done, but he is not. Sachin's cricket is fuelled by a fierce rage from within and his grim expression today, as Sehwag scatters the bowlers, advertises an internal grief. There is nothing he would have loved more than to perform on this wonderful stage and win the World Cup for India. But even true champions have their offdays, and Sachin will have to wait and continue his search for his version of nirvana.

Hope is not extinguished with Sachin's dismissal. Though wickets tumble, Sehwag attacks fearlessly and Yuvraj, not one to quit easily, says there is a chance if they somehow get two twenty-run overs. There is no sign of these good overs but threatening clouds and stray drops of rain provide a glimmer of hope. Dravid carries the Duckworth-Lewis calculation sheets to the crease and when rain interrupts play, some see a lifeline, but it is only a passing shower.

As the dream of winning the World Cup fades, the rosy optimism of the morning is replaced by grim reality and a terrible feeling of emptiness. Sourav rues the missed chance. The sombre look on John Wright's face says all that has to be said. For months he worked like a man possessed, driving himself and all around him, determined to win despite the sniggering doubts from sceptics. In true professional fashion, Andrew and Adrian conceal their emotions but Harbhajan, Yuvraj, Srinath and Kumble are visibly gutted.

As always, nothing dramatic happens after the defeat—there is no finger pointing, no arguments, no injuries caused by spiked shoes flung across the dressing room. Just a dull sense of loss and deep, deep despair. At times like this, reason is usually the first casualty and it is difficult to weigh matters sensibly.

Should Sourav be happy India made the final, played like champions and lost to a superior side who had an outstanding day? Or should he be in mourning and shed tears? Should Sachin be satisfied with the Player of the Tournament award or grieve about not making a sizable contribution in the final? (During the press conference afterwards, he said individual performances did not matter, he would have been far happier had India won.) Should Srinath, Zaheer and Nehra be lauded for winning matches through the tournament or criticised for an ordinary performance against Australia? Basically, should India cry or should they hold their heads high? Is reaching the final an achievement or is losing to a superpower a disgrace?

There are no clear answers. When the match ends, nobody thinks about them anyway because there are more urgent, practical matters to attend to. Bats and shirts are signed, kitbags packed one final time. Sourav decides to declutter his coffin and gift stuff—spikes to someone, a glove and thigh pad to someone else. The team leaves the ground cheered by fans and receives a similarly warm reception at the hotel. The players gather in the team room for a debrief session. John makes an emotional speech, congratulating them for their great effort and, on a more personal note, says it is a privilege to work with such a talented bunch of cricketers.

Sourav, like a general addressing his officers after a failed campaign, tells the boys to hold their heads high. He makes a stirring speech — congratulates Sachin, thanks the bowlers (who were hammered in the final) for bringing the team this far, praises others for playing outstanding cricket and makes a special reference to Anil Kumble's support. Kumble played only three of the team's 11 matches, with Harbhajan being picked as the frontline spinner, but was a rock through all the ups and downs. Sourav speaks from the heart and, overcoming the disappointment of a dreadful day, looks ahead with optimism. He wants to carry on, keep the team united and take Indian cricket forward.

The team raises three cheers for Srinath, who will soon make a formal announcement of retiring from cricket. In his farewell speech, Srinath says he is sorry for letting the team down in the final. He thanks Sourav (for having faith in him and calling him out of retirement a year ago) and Andrew and Adrian (for keeping his body together). He praises Zaheer and Nehra for their fantastic contribution and predicts a bright future for them.

Aside

- Srinath's regret: *The current team is so good I wish I had started my career later and carried on longer.*

The post-final debrief makes the players feel better. By talking to each other and exchanging reassuring words, the pain of defeat eases a little. *Karod nahin mile to koi baat nahin, kam se kam joote to nahin padenge (So what if we missed out on the crores, at least we're not going to have shoes flung at us)*, observes one disappointed but optimistic individual. The players know they missed out but are proud of what they have achieved, and satisfied that they didn't fail for lack of effort.

24 March

The players want to return immediately after the final but South African Airways, the official carrier for the World Cup, have no seats available on any flight to India until two days later. Sehwag gets everyone to pack in one hour to make the Air India flight leaving early in the evening. Dravid and Srinath stay back in South Africa and the BCCI approves the travel plan change (overlooking the protests of South African Airways) provided the players travel economy because the business-class seats are all taken.

Sourav readily agrees, saying he is willing to sit in the aisle if needed, but Sachin points out one problem: *other passengers in economy won't leave us alone.*

At the airport, there is a mad rush at the check-in counters because of the VIPs (Arun Jaitley, Sharad Pawar, Vikram Verma) on the flight.

Sourav's attempt to get a VAT refund is turned down as he can't produce for inspection his expensive Versace clothes which he had packed into the checked-in suitcase. He argues and pleads but the lady at the counter doesn't budge. Unhappy about the substantial financial hit, Sourav moans that he has no influence. *I don't count.*

AI flight 5224 is packed and, even before the seat belt signs come on, Sachin's misery begins. He is in seat 38B (with Harbhajan, Nehra and Zaheer around him as a security shield) but his efforts to put his head down and hide fail. Here he is, a day after a crushing defeat, surrounded by a planeload of fans who paid serious money to make the trip to South Africa. Each one sees this as a golden opportunity to click a photo and get something signed.

For almost three hours—even through dinner—Sachin does precisely this. He pushes some food into his mouth with his left hand, drops the fork to sign, then calmly resumes eating. Strangers pat him on the shoulder, put an arm around him, grab his hand and do everything short of tearing him to bits.

Not for a moment does Sachin show the slightest hint of irritation. No autograph is refused, no request for a photo turned down, no tantrum thrown. Sachin Tendulkar is an exhibit on display with no escape. He greets everyone politely and does what is asked of him with grace, humility and amazing poise.

With everyone drawn towards Sachin (armed with miniature bats and shirts for his signature) normal activity on the aircraft goes for a toss. The stewards can't take two steps without colliding with passengers who should have been sitting with their seat belts on. But some of them don't mind the turbulence and feel this is fun because normal flights are boring, at least today there is some *raunaq.*

With the cricketers providing entertainment, the in-flight movie is ignored. It's the usual mindless action thriller anyway, for which you don't need the audio to understand what is going on. Once the movie ends and the screens have gone blank, singer Abhijeet gives a live performance. After that, the air hostesses put away the coffee and liqueur trays, the lights are dimmed and the passengers prepare for sleep.

Sachin is still busy signing autographs and looking into cameras for one last photo for one more fan. Seated two rows away, Anil Kumble says, *Just imagine what would have happened if we had won the cup!*

When I congratulate Sachin on his extraordinary patience, his reply is revealing. *Kya fayda. Patience wicket par honi chahiye thi.*

Obviously, cricket dominates conversations on the flight. Dalmiya huddles with Sourav while some of the VIPs talk about the mood in India and the overwhelming feeling of disappointment. Anil Kumble says Indians don't understand the hard work that goes into sport and that's why, instead of looking at the positives, there is a tendency to find fault. *People don't love sport and don't respect sportsmen.*

Meanwhile, Sehwag sleeps soundly, unmindful of the gadar around him. Mongia reads cyclist Lance Armstrong's epic about battling cancer. Sanjay Bangar and his wife try to calm their two-year-old son, Aryan. Parthiv Patel wonders about his class 12 exam in Ahmedabad the following day. Are you prepared? I ask. Parthiv smiles. *I don't even know kya paper hai.*

25 March

Back after almost two months, the team is met by a large crowd inside the airport terminal and there is plenty of jostling and pushing. As the players seek refuge in the customs officer's room, photographs are taken and cold drinks passed around. Sachin, Agarkar and Zaheer say quick goodbyes and depart while others check their flight connections. Kumble finds one for Bangalore immediately but the Delhi boys (Sehwag, Nehra and Harbhajan) have a two-hour wait. Sourav will fly out in the evening.

Everyone goes to the Leela Hotel where the media is waiting for the post-tournament press conference. Sourav looks at the assembled reporters and winces, a why-must-I-endure-this look on his face. *Give me 15 minutes*, he says, and disappears for breakfast in the coffee shop. He returns after stopping in the hotel lobby to remind the other players to come to Mumbai in three days' time for a charity match to raise funds for a hospital supported by Lata Mangeshkar.

Cricket never stops, the circus keeps rolling.

Fans at Work

Watching the sea of Indian flags at SuperSport Park, Centurion, Zaheer thought it was like playing at home. Ali Bacher was happy the Indian fans added colour and character to the World Cup. Some fans had travelled from America and England despite not having match tickets. They boarded a flight hoping to get in somehow. Others came in groups, their trips planned by tour operators who offered comforts (including specially catered Indian food) at a stiff price. And there were the lucky ones who got a free ride courtesy the tournament sponsors.

Indian fans were driven by passion for cricket and a sense of patriotism for Bharat Mata. Sensing this, the Indian High Commission distributed flags at the grounds and Air India handed out replicas of Indian team shirts and caps. When Air India's special flight took off from Mumbai, its well-heeled passengers couldn't stop themselves from shouting *Jeetega, jeetega*! During the matches, they shouted, yelled, beat the dhol, chanted slogans and sang film songs. They encouraged the Indians (naturally) and denounced Pakistan (why?), maintaining an impressive level of noise all the while.

In contrast to this rowdy set was the sober VIP contingent consisting of influential politicians, corporate czars and celebrities who hopped in and out of South Africa for the key India matches. The Lok Sabha Speaker was accompanied by a few MPs. Later, Praful Patel and Saleem Sherwani dropped in, as did Jyotiraditya Scindia, Lalit Suri and ministers Vikram Verma and Sahib Singh Verma. Also Rammohan Rao, the Governor of Tamil Nadu, and Jayant Advani.

Film-maker Rajeev Menon (fresh from a shoot with Aishwarya Rai) and media top guns Shobhana Bhartiya, Aroon Purie and M.J. Akbar put in an appearance. Rajiv Bakshi (of Pepsi) and Pawan Munjal (of Hero Honda) cheered India. So did Moni Verma (of Veetee Rice, England) and Kanak Khimji (from Muscat).

Perhaps the most visible visitor was business tycoon Vijay Mallya, who made several trips in his private jet, bringing with him celebs Shilpa Shetty and Shobhaa De.

BCCI officials Sharad Pawar and Raj Singh Dungarpur spent a considerable amount of time in South Africa. Other cricket personalities following the fortunes of the team were BCCI officials S.K. Nair and Kishore Rungta, and selectors Kirti Azad, Pronob Roy and Kiran More.

The Team Room

There was a time when teams met in the manager's suite before a match to have tea and dispersed after wishing each other luck. A lot has changed since. Now players meet in a boardroom situation, and at the World Cup, each team was allotted a dedicated room in their hotel. The team room essentially belonged to the coach, who used it to run meetings with charts, computers and a projector. Motivational posters (We Are for India, Win for India) and the Indian flag were prominently placed in our team room.

Sriram Bhargava, the computer analyst, was the chief ally of the coach and dug up relevant information about individual players and the opposition. Most afternoons, with the team away at practice, Sriram was on his computer crunching data and creating video clips for the players.

The team room was used a lot by physio Leipus. His portable massage table, placed in a corner, was seldom unoccupied as he worked on Srinath's shoulder, Zaheer's hamstring, Nehra's ankle, Sachin's back, or gave someone a relaxing rub-down. The team room was also a convenient place to store odd items—medical equipment, plastic stumps, baseball glov—es, health drinks, extra boxes of Carbo Plus and Gatorade, luggage and laundry.

The players used the room to relax. The pool table was always busy and many epic table-tennis battles were fought there. Yuvraj, Kaif, Mongia, Sehwag and Agarkar made rapid strides as the tour progressed but all of them struggled to get past Sachin, an expert in defensive play.

Considering the interest in table tennis, a suggestion was floated about a team tournament, but the idea was abandoned. The official reason for the cancellation was lack of time (and preoccupation with cricket) but some had a sneaking suspicion that it was a sinister conspiracy to sabotage Sachin's chances of winning.

The Way Things Work

The manager was the boss—he represented the board and headed protocol. Jyoti-ji, calm and collected, handled matters efficiently. He distributed tour allowances (the standard ICC rate of US$ 50) and match passes (five per player because the team got 100) and convened the tour selection committee for which (apart from Sourav, Dravid and John) Sachin was co-opted as a senior pro.

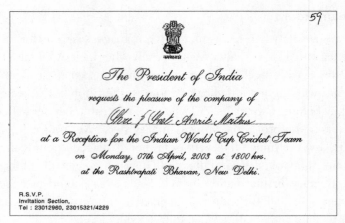

59

The President of India
requests the pleasure of the company of
_____Shri / Smt Amrit Mathur_____
at a Reception for the Indian World Cup Cricket Team
on Monday, 07th April, 2003 at 1800 hrs.
at the Rashtrapati Bhavan, New Delhi.

R.S.V.P.
Invitation Section,
Tel : 23012960, 23015321/4229

On cricket matters the captain's word was final—he picked the 11 from the shortlisted 12. Coach Wright, Andrew and Adrian ensured the players were fit and ready. The captain, the face of the team, had extensive media responsibilities. According to the ICC guidelines, he had to meet the press before and after every match and was to be available for comments on important issues.

Sourav's team was cohesive and united and operated in a democratic manner. At meetings, debate was encouraged and players freely expressed their opinions. Sehwag, Yuvraj and Kaif didn't hesitate to tick off seniors for moving slowly in the field or missing a chance for a run-out. But the criticism was constructive and controlled, the players knew how far to go and where to draw the line.

Everyone was immensely proud of belonging to the Indian team, they respected each other and were comfortable with the success of their colleagues. Contrary to what people suspected, there were no cliques, no fights, no ego clashes, no tension between individuals. This was a happy, well-adjusted team.

The cordial relationship among the players erased the usual gulf between seniors and juniors. Parthiv Patel was respectful towards Anil bhai and Sri bhai but comfortable in their company. Sachin was Paaji to half the team, Sachin to the rest. Sourav was Dada or Dadi.

Some thought the Indian team was boring, lacking masala and spice. Sehwag observed that India was the only team that did not harass umpires or curse other players. Patrick, the security chief, said he never had any problems with the Indians—they followed instructions without a fuss.

During the World Cup, Shane Warne was caught doping, Chris Cairns brawled with night-club bouncers, Shoaib Akhtar and Andrew Caddick chucked silly verbal bouncers at Sachin, Henry Olonga and Andy Flower created a big stir. Not to forget the Pakistani players who attacked each other during a football practice game.

India did nothing even remotely sensational. No controversy, no scandal. Nobody abused anybody, nobody fought, and nobody had exciting partnerships with women. The media had little to report apart from the usual net and match routine. For people searching for interesting *khabar*, this was very disappointing—India was too proper, too correct, too well behaved.

Mantras to Improve Indian Cricket

- John Wright: Cricket culture must change with more emphasis on athleticism.
- Dinesh Mongia: First-class players need security. They need jobs.
- An unnamed player: Female personal trainers should be appointed. The players will become fit.
- Srinath: Improve wickets. This should be first on the agenda. Get professionals from outside, change the soil, do whatever.
- Dravid: Decide on your goal, make a detailed plan, provide inputs. Then work towards that systematically.
- Ravi Shastri: Stop all honorary business. Appoint professionals who are accountable.
- Consensus: Treat domestic cricket seriously. Which means more money, more competition and better wickets.

At Rashtrapati Bhavan

Soon after the World Cup, the team was invited by President A.P.J. Abdul Kalam for a reception at the Mughul Gardens in Rashtrapati Bhavan, a rare honour.

The players assembled in the lobby of the Taj Palace hotel with a palpable sense of excitement and anticipation. Though accustomed to celebrity lives and adulation, an invite from the president of India was a thrill. The players were smartly turned out for this special occasion; the dress code was the official blazer and India tie.

From the hotel to Rashtrapati Bhavan was a short ride and the players occupied their usual positions in the bus, though some seats were vacant.

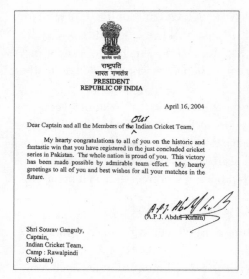

Coach John Wright was away in New Zealand due to his father's illness and Harbhajan was missing, nobody knew why. His Punjab colleague, Yuvraj Singh, couldn't hide his delight as the team bus rolled up the Rashtrapati Bhavan forecourt. Climbing the steps to the entrance, which was dominated by a Mauryan-era Nandi statue, he was awed by the magnificence and grandeur of the majestic building. Anil Kumble, surprisingly without his camera, wondered if it would have been okay to take pictures.

Captain Sourav led the team into the Mughal Gardens where a host of cricket celebrities had already gathered. Among the A-listers present were Tiger Pataudi, Bishan Singh Bedi, Arun Jaitley, and the BCCI top brass led by Jagmohan Dalmiya and P.M. Rungta.

When the arrival of President Kalam was announced, the team lined up to be introduced to him. Sourav and Dalmiya greeted the president, after which the customary handshakes began. The president greeted everyone warmly and paused to have a special word with Sachin.

As he walked towards the other guests, Rahul Dravid stumped him with a special request. Pulling out a copy of Dr Kalam's book, *Ignited Minds*, he asked him to sign it. The president obliged, and scribbled a message (*You will Win*) with a flourish.

After the formalities concluded, Dr Kalam had a quiet chat with the players. They sat round him in a semi-circle and he spoke to them like a teacher in a classroom. His message, almost a lecture to attentive children, was simple yet inspirational. Citing Vikram Sarabhai as his guru, he said science is useful for different purposes, it creates missiles and also advances healthcare, which promotes happiness and wellness. Likewise, he said, sports should be used as a trigger to improve the health of the nation.

He also had some advice for the players. He stressed the need to stay determined and to train the mind. He appealed to the players to work with children because they held the key to the future.

The president hailed the achievement of the team in the World Cup, then posed a question that caught everyone by surprise. What made Australia better, he asked in his soft, straightforward manner. An uneasy silence followed as the players looked at each other, not sure what to say. After a longish pause, Sachin responded with a short answer about their first-class cricket being more competitive.

Interaction over, it was time for photographs. Prime Minister Vajpayee and L.K. Advani joined the group and smiled for the cameras. Sachin presented the president with a bat signed by the team. With that a memorable evening came to a close, made special by the simplicity and humility of President Kalam.

7

VICTORY IN PAKISTAN, 2004

I first visited Pakistan in 1987 as a journalist to cover the Reliance World Cup. I flew from Delhi to Karachi, then travelled three hours by road to reach Hyderabad, Sindh, the evening before the first game. That left me with little time to write the pre-game 'curtain-raiser'. While I struggled to string together the words, other Indian journalists had no such worry. The clever pros had written their reports before leaving Delhi—they simply filed them from Pakistan.

The World Cup was a great cricket mela and Pakistan was an eye-opener. The country was so similar, yet so different from India. It looked modern, with swanky imported cars on the road, bottled water and an electronic telephone exchange that allowed you to instantly connect STD calls.

Two years later, I returned to Lahore for the Super Wills Trophy, which had two strong teams playing a 50-over match. Delhi, the winners from India, were playing against United Bank, who were the champions in Pakistan. Saeed Anwar and Mansoor Akhtar, a favourite of Imran's, made half-centuries against a good Delhi attack of Madan Lal, Manoj Prabhakar, Sanjeev Sharma, Maninder Singh and Kirti Azad. Delhi chased down 243 with Manu Nayyar and Raman Lamba putting up plenty for the first wicket. Bhaskar Pillai built on the strong start by making a stylish 74 and was adjudged Man of the Match.

The match was a rare instance of cricket contact between India and Pakistan but it is remembered more for the arrival of a player who went on to become a superstar. Waqar Younis, largely unknown at that point, bowled ten wicketless overs for 37, but his talent was unmistakable. Opener Raman Lamba and Bhaskar Pillai said the team knew about Salim Jaffer and Sikander Bakht but lightning-quick Younis came as a surprise.

Imran watched Younis bowl and liked what he saw. A month later, in November 1989, Waqar was fast-tracked into Test cricket and made his debut against England in Karachi.

When PILCOM was formed in 1993 for the 1996 World Cup and I was selected as a member of the committee, it gave me an opportunity to visit Pakistan often and work closely with the PCB. Later, in 1999, Pakistan toured India and Shahryar Khan, a senior career diplomat and former foreign secretary, was appointed as the team manager. When the Indian government asked the BCCI to attach a senior official with him, the role came to me. And so, I had the unique experience of working with a visiting team in India. Initially, it felt weird to stay in the same hotel as the Pakistan team, travel in their bus and head for the visiting team's dressing room at the cricket grounds. But it wasn't terribly difficult because the cricket routines and team culture of India and Pakistan were quite similar.

The small differences, though, were interesting. Shahryar sa'ab focused on the larger political context of the tour and stayed away from direct interference in cricket matters. He was a man of letters and the players respected him for his deep knowledge of India's history, which wasn't surprising since his mother was the Begum of Bhopal in pre-Partition India and Tiger Pataudi was a close relative: their mothers were sisters.

It was fascinating to witness first-hand the internal dynamics of the Pakistan team. It lived up to its popular image of being a splintered unit comprising brilliant individuals who were always one step short of declaring civil war. The team was a creaky coalition of individuals who, given half a chance, would head in different directions.

To say that the captain, Wasim Akram, and the coach, Javed Miandad, were not on the same page would be an understatement. The divide was obvious—they wouldn't even share a biryani. Miandad wasn't the most popular coach. At times I was asked to convey messages to them, but in the Wasim–Miandad sideshow, I adopted a strict non-aligned policy. The last thing I wanted as the BCCI's representative was to get dragged into the politics of the dysfunctional Pakistan team.

Interestingly, the fractured team disproved the notion that good cricket can only be played if eleven players are united and agree on a common minimum programme. Throughout the tour, the players made sure that personal differences did not come in the way of the team's performance. On the contrary, they were always strongly motivated to give their best and it was country first, always.

The captain led from the front, setting an example for the others to follow. During the Calcutta Test match, Wasim was unwell and unfit. A diabetic, he was suffering from a severe sugar spike and running a high temperature. Yet, he bowled 48 overs and scored 38 runs while batting at number nine, willing himself to carry on despite acute discomfort. During lunch and tea he would stagger into the dressing room and collapse on the massage table, only to magically rise as the umpires walked out.

The Calcutta Test match was memorable on three counts. One, Shoaib Akhtar dismissed Dravid and Sachin off successive deliveries. The two toe-crushing in-swinging yorkers were simply sensational. Two, there was a controversy around Sachin's run-out in the second innings, which led to the game being concluded without fans. Three, Saeed Anwar's phenomenal second innings, where he scored 188 runs and remained not out, contributing massively to Pakistan's total of 316.

Surprisingly, when Saeed Anwar returned to the pavilion after that masterly hundred, he received a cold reception. He sat in the dressing room like a stranger to the others, alone and unwanted. He was clearly peeved because the coach did not acknowledge his effort, let alone praise his innings. When play ended, before returning to the hotel, he presented me with the bat with which he had scored the hundred. Inscribed on the blade was the following message:

> *Dear Amrit Mathur*
> *Thank you for taking such good care of us. May God give you all that you may want in your life. With love. Saeed Anwar.*

I didn't ask for his bat and have no idea why he gave it to me. But it is a treasured part of my cricket memorabilia collection.

When the team went to Jaipur for the ODI, it turned out that Shahryar sa'ab had accepted a dinner invitation from Rajmata Gayatri Devi. One evening I received a telephone call from the Rajmata. She crisply introduced herself and wanted to know about cricket-related people in Jaipur whom she could invite to dinner.

I suggested a few names but sensed instant disapproval from the other side. *I don't want such people at my house for dinner.* She sounded appalled and her tone conveyed a rebuke for making silly suggestions.

It turned out that not many people met with her royal approval. The guest list for the private dinner at her Moti Dungri Palace was limited to a few close friends and family. Amongst them was Maharaj Jai Singh, the polo player who was with Shahryar sa'ab at Cambridge.

The First Visit

All overseas tours require political and security clearance from the Indian government. In 2004, opinion was sharply divided on the team's proposed visit to Pakistan. The government was more anti- than pro-tour and the BCCI was undecided on the issue. The board was like a batsman at the crease, unsure whether to go forward or back.

Initially, it decided to test the waters by sending a security delegation to Pakistan to assess the situation on the ground. I was a member of this security team, along with Professor Ratnakar Shetty of the BCCI and

KHUSHAMDEED!: Pakistan cricketer Shahid Afridi (left) greets Amrit Mathur, BCCI media manager, at the National Stadium, Karachi, on Thursday.

Yashovardhan Azad, a top man from the Ministry of Home Affairs (MHA), Government of India.

We landed in Lahore in a blaze of publicity, with media and television networks tracking our every move. Our luggage was collected by the airline staff and delivered directly to the hotel, while we were taken from the airport to meet the secretary of the Ministry of Interior.

The ministry downplayed the security issue, calling it a *mamooli masla*, a trivial issue, that had been hyped by the media. We were told that the Pakistani people and politicians were in favour of the tour and the authorities supported the plan to hold matches in Karachi and Peshawar. Senior officials assured us that Pakistan was ready to host the Indian team and intelligence agencies were keeping a close watch on various terror groups. There is no threat, they told us with extraordinary confidence. One officer provided additional perspective to convince us that the Indian team would be safe. A *white-skinned American in Anarkali is under a bigger threat*, he said.

It was obvious that Pakistan desperately wanted the tour. The PCB needed the money that the sale of television rights would bring. Also, Pakistan's reputation was at stake. A military regime unable to provide security to a visiting cricket team would make for awful optics—it would destroy the image of the army generals in power.

Irrespective of Pakistan's position, India couldn't ignore the hard facts. Pakistan was unsafe, if not dangerous, territory. The recent incident of a bomb explosion shattering the windows of the hotel where the New Zealand team was staying and causing injury to some of the players was fresh in everyone's mind. New Zealand abandoned the tour midway and this only added to the narrative of Pakistan not being tour-ready.

During meetings, hardliner Yashovardhan was uncompromising, outlining concerns and insisting on certain requirements from the standpoint of security. Surprised by his tough stance and serious tone, the Pakistanis could only scribble notes and offer assurances.

The formal response came early the next morning and the message was brief. The Indian security wish list had been approved at the highest level. Instructions had already been given from the top to—as they say in sarkari language—'do the needful'. They had a request too: *If anything else is needed, please tell us.*

Reassured by the positive response, we set off to visit the venues for an on-ground assessment and to meet with local authorities. It was the most comprehensive Pakistan darshan that a tourist could hope for. The itinerary covered Lahore, Rawalpindi, Islamabad, Multan, Gujranwala and the two security hotspots, Peshawar and Karachi.

We first went to Rawalpindi, where General Pervez Musharraf had recently survived an assassination attempt. The incident had taken place not far from the office of the police chief, who admitted that he had feared dismissal, even arrest, and hadn't been sure at the time whether he would survive. He took us through the arrangements for the tour, covering all the points flagged by Yashovardhan in the meeting with the ministry.

We realised that the police officers were using the same security playbook while making presentations to us. The same assurances were repeated at every venue, the message being: *Hamare bhai from Hindustan are most welcome.*

In Multan, the meeting started with a short recitation from the Quran by a maulvi. We had been informed that this southern Punjab city was a land of docile, God-fearing, peace-loving people and Sufi saints. There had not been any terrorist activity in the last three years and all possible threats had been eliminated. Also, in a proactive move, the police had rounded up all persons capable of creating trouble and put them in jail!

In Lahore, our next stop, the police briefing was conducted at the Pearl Continental hotel, which was decked up for Basant, the equivalent of Diwali, with colourful kites decorating the lobby. Ali Zafar's popular number 'Channo' was blaring full blast in the background, adding to the festive spirit.

DIG Tariq promised 'foolproof security' with all systems fully cranked up for action. *We are preparing for the worst but not anticipating it*, he said, and held out a thinly veiled threat to miscreants: *Lahoris are aware of our capability.*

After Lahore, our next stop was Faisalabad. A textile hub, it was known as Lyallpur till the mid-1970s. The city is linked to Bhagat Singh and Sir Ganga Ram, and the cricket stadium was named after the poet Iqbal. Here too, local authorities had made extensive arrangements for hosting us. During the breakfast meeting, pizzas, sandwiches and gulab jamuns were served in a show of Pakistani hospitality. The security plan was equally elaborate.

The two-hour drive from Lahore to Faisalabad was a pleasant one. We went by the modern motorway, past the Sargodha Air Force base, the Ravi river and Gujranwala, escorted by a small contingent of Punjab Police commandos wearing black tracksuits.

Next on our itinerary was the frontier city of Peshawar (pronounced 'Peshaaar'). Here, the writ of the government didn't run beyond the city limits, guns were sold on thelas at street corners and rockets could be home delivered. This posed a major security challenge for the tour.

We met the governor of the North West Frontier Province (NWFP) at his official residence, an imposing colonial bungalow with a long driveway through vast manicured gardens where we saw herds of deer grazing peacefully. This tranquillity, however, couldn't mask the turbulence in the neighbourhood.

In Karachi, which was next on our itinerary, we met General Javed Zia, the director general of Rangers, Sindh. As the head of the elite force, the general was responsible for law and order in the province. He confirmed that his crack troops were prepared to meet any situation and all threats had been analysed and responses readied.

After declaring that peace prevailed in Karachi, he outlined a security plan which was similar to a slick military operation. Its main features were:

Transit roads: Closed to traffic, entire route lined with sharpshooters and Rapid Action Force. Snipers to be deployed on terraces of buildings.

Hotel: Players to stay on a security-sanitised floor. No visitors allowed, all calls to be monitored. Security personnel in and around the hotel.

Stadium: Control room set up, Rangers in the stands, which would have CCTV coverage. Mobile patrolling in the vicinity of the National Stadium.

Total security cover: 1,300 Rangers on duty. Additional 50 for team escort purposes.

The security recce confirmed that the Pakistan government was willing to do whatever it took for the tour to go ahead. That it was ready to deploy the extra beat constables and commandoes, the bomb disposable unit and the Rapid Action Force to make the guests from India feel safe. When top guns show intent, the wheels move.

Of course, none of this made Pakistan as safe as Switzerland. A newspaper reported that the sports minister of Punjab had been abducted and released after 23 days, after paying a hefty ransom. Surprisingly, neither the abduction nor the news of his resuming office made it to the front pages. Both items were buried on the inside pages of local dailies—a confirmation of sorts that security dhamakas were routine—*koi bada masla nahin hai.* To borrow SRK's famous line: *Bade bade shehron mein chhoti chhoti batein hoti hain!*

Back in India, the security delegation submitted its report. The Indian government decided it was fine, politically, to send the team to Pakistan and that security concerns about Peshawar and Karachi could be overcome by limiting the duration of the team's stay in the two cities. Ironically, political biggies who had initially opposed the tour executed a neat somersault and insisted on Karachi hosting a game. These flexible politicians, as expected, were quick to take credit for the statesman-like breakthrough to improve Indo–Pak relations.

TOUR DIARY: PAKISTAN, 2004

I shared administrative duties on the Pakistan tour with Professor Shetty.

A Meeting with the Prime Minister

On arrival at the prime minister's official residence at 7 Race Course Road, players are greeted by children waving the tricolour and shouting *Bharat mata ki jai*. They are escorted to a hall and shortly afterwards Prime Minister Vajpayee arrives, taking small steps in a laboured manner but exuding warmth like a caring uncle. He shakes hands with the players, laughs and smiles. The message that comes through clearly in his short speech: *Match bhi jeeto aur dil bhi*.

Refreshments are served (laddoos, barfis and fruit juice) and the Delhi Police band fittingly plays 'Hum honge kamyab' in the background. The media wants soundbites from the prime minister but he deflects the political questions like a skilled batsman.

An example:

With your popularity, you can win an election in Pakistan. Aapka comment?

Yahan jeetna zyada mushkil hai.

From 7, Race Course Road the team drives to Palam for the Air India flight to Lahore. Players make last-minute calls from the bus and, when they arrive at the airport, are surprised to see a large crowd waiting for them.

Arrival in Lahore

The team is welcomed on the tarmac by the PCB with shiny garlands and an impressive security presence. Amid the usual chaos (of fans, cameramen and other passengers), the players are escorted from the airport to the waiting bus.

Arrival in Lahore, with Professor Shetty and Sourav Ganguly

The ride into town to the Pearl Continental hotel is smooth, with roads blocked for the general traffic, and the team gets its first taste of tight security. Punjab Police commandoes carrying automatic weapons accompany us on the bus and there is also a cavalcade of motorcycle outriders and shrieking patrol cars.

The hotel staff are friendly and the players receive a warm welcome as they check in at the reception. After a quick media interaction where only cricket-related questions are allowed, they assemble for the first team meeting.

John Wright sets the agenda and asks the players to choose a theme for the tour. After a healthy debate (meaning loud arguments and a lot of confusion) a decision is reached. The chosen theme: Pride and passion — be the first. It is appropriate, as India has not yet won a series in Pakistan.

A barbecue dinner is set up for the players in the hotel's courtyard. Hotel guests approach Sachin, Yuvraj and Murali Kartik for autographs as they feast on Lahore's famous kebabs. Sachin handles the intrusion with remarkable calm. Before leaving Delhi, the players had been apprehensive about what to expect but they have quickly adjusted to Pakistan. Someone observes: *It is India only—same to same. Even the singer in the lobby sang old Mohammad Rafi songs, though in a slightly besura manner!*

The tour opens with a one-day practice game against the Pakistan A side. At breakfast in the Dum Pukht restaurant of the Pearl Continental, Dada has some fruit and disapproves of the tea. *It's bad, thank God I brought my stock from Calcutta,* he says. The elite Punjab Police commandoes (with 'No Fear' printed on their black t-shirts) surround the team bus. Dada notices their alert eyes which keep darting around. *Wait till you see the Karachi Rangers,* I tell him. *They are special.*

Driving past the governor's house, down Canal Road and Gulbarga, it takes us ten minutes to reach Gaddafi Stadium. Security is tight with lots of police (some in crisp uniform and others in loose salwar kameez), bomb detection units and sniffer dogs.

Before the game, there is the usual activity in the spacious dressing room. Players choose their spots and the video analyst sets up his system. The support staff get down to business: massage tables are laid out and carbon-plus drinks are prepared.

Sachin wants a drill to fix something and Yuvraj suddenly remembers that he had left some money in the hotel lobby. Dada's announcement that he had left ₹4,000 on the luggage trolley at Palam receives no sympathy. *It is no loss, just a drop in the ocean,* someone remarks.

When I meet Sultan Rana, the Pakistan team selector (once an ace 3-handicap golfer), he tells me that the Pakistan A team has good youngsters, so it should be a decent practice game. India bats first and Sehwag smashes the first ball over extra cover for four runs. The Indians score more than 300, with most batsmen performing well on the dead track except Dada, who, suffering a minor cold, retreats to a corner of the dressing room and sleeps.

Arun Jaitley calls to confirm the arrangements for his trip and asks whether he should carry a formal jacket. Rajeev Shukla is on the telephone to coordinate the visit of Priyanka and Rahul Gandhi.

The practice game is a disaster as Imran Nazir and Taufeeq Umar, both in extraordinary form, slaughter the Indian bowling. A furious coach reads out the riot act: *With bowling like this we won't win any game.*

Back in the hotel, the players are summoned for an urgent team meeting at 8 p.m. The captain cautions against panic but warns that against Pakistan there is only one option—*win. Otherwise careers end. Wake up and raise your game.* John repeats the captain's words and demands greater commitment. He feels that the players are too soft and the team culture must change.

Ahead of the ODIs, players discuss individual Pakistani batsmen. When Yasir Hameed's name comes up, there is silence. Nobody has a clue. Players look at each other, at the video analyst and the coach. I think it's strange that the basic homework hasn't been done before such an important tour.

The First ODI

The team is greeted by Karachi's Nazir (mayor), who presents everyone with traditional Sindhi caps and shawls in the airport lounge. After a brief ceremony the team leaves for the hotel amidst tight security, with armoured escort cars and commandoes carrying automatic weapons.

The security is supervised by Lt Gen. Javed Zia, head of the Rangers in Karachi, who has planned the entire drill of snipers, rapid action units, elite commandoes, electronic jammers, CCTVs in each stand and surveillance by helicopters along the team's route. Kaif is impressed by the elaborate bandobast: *Lagta hai raja ya PM ki sawari ja rahi hai.*

But the security is only a show of strength, a deterrent and a bit of a *shosha.* Despite the strict cover, the players are jostled by fans and a worrying incident occurs in Karachi where, in a serious breach, two unidentified persons hop on to the bus and request the players for autographs. Nobody noticed them, not the hundreds of policemen on duty, not the two armed commandoes present in the bus. Another time, a commando in the bus hands his automatic weapon to a player. *Ek minute pakadna*, he says, *main Tendulkar sa'ab ke saath photo le loon!*

It is a busy afternoon with a Samsung shoot followed by a press conference and a meeting with the match referee. Nets after that.

Karachi is of special interest to Sachin, who started his cricket journey here in 1989 as a 16-year-old. Now the seniormost Test cricketer, he possibly has another ten years in the game. *It will be difficult*, he says, *because one has to be fit and maintain enthusiasm for the game.*

Sachin soaks in the atmosphere of Karachi's National Stadium before going out to the middle to chat with the groundsman. But the crusty curator is tight-lipped about the pitch. *Kuchh nahi bola. Kya turn karegi? Nahin maloom. Ball nikalti hai? Pata nahin.*

Chameli Hall, Indian Team Room

I send two commandoes to escort Jagmohan Dalmiya from his suite to have a word with the boys. Before the meeting he asks for 'talking points' and my inputs are simple: 1) players should not worry about security, they are safe, and 2) they should play good cricket and be happy.

Dalmiya speaks encouraging words in his brief speech. After his departure, the players discuss strategy and note that Pakistan is under pressure to win at home. Dada makes the following key points:

- Maintain intensity even if things are not working out.
- Batsmen must fire—anyone who is in has to make it big.
- Bowlers to focus on yorkers, slower balls and angle deliveries across right-handers.

I accompany Arun Jaitley to dinner at a palatial house made of Jodhpur sandstone in Clifton, close to the Teen Talwar monument that commemorates Quaid-e-Azam's slogan of dignity and pride. The host is obviously well-connected (Imran Khan drops in late, making a grand entry) and affluent; the place is opulent, crammed with antiques, paintings and exotic carpets. In this privileged world of the powerful Pakistani elite, guests drink expensive whiskey and feast on kebabs, tikkas and raan. Vegetarians are served idlis (for dinner!) and Karachi kulfa, the delicious dessert.

Jaitley observes that Pakistan has only rich and poor, no middle class. He had gone to a mall earlier in the morning and found it surprisingly deserted. *Nothing compared to our Gurgaon malls*, he says. Jaitley is a man who wears many hats—politician, cricket lover, and a person of refined taste who shops for clothes in London's Old Bond Street.

Jaitley sa'ab's family is originally from Lahore and he is in Karachi not only as the minister for commerce and industry but as someone who follows the game closely and can recall events and player stats quicker than a computer. He speaks about making the BCCI more professional and warns against the danger of having too many politicians in the board. There can be a situation in the future, he cautions, when cricket is swamped by politics.

Match Day at Karachi

7.45 a.m. departure for the ground. Dada, wearing all kinds of threads, charms and lockets, is the last to board the bus. The drive to the National Stadium takes us only 17 minutes as traffic has been blocked and the team bus, accompanied by motorbike outriders, police vehicles with flashing lights and screaming sirens, sails through the empty Shahrah-e-Faisal, past Quaid Museum, the naval commander's house and Pir Pagaro's residence.

Dada is the last to alight from the bus (one of his many *tashans*) and as the players climb the steps to the dressing room, they are greeted warmly by Moin Khan and Saqlain Mushtaq, the latter sporting a Saeed Anwar–style beard.

John gives the players 20 minutes to settle in. Sachin chooses a corner in the dressing room to place his kitbag and unpacks carefully, arranging his gear. He sandpapers his match bat, tries out his batting gloves and checks his helmet. Sehwag puts fresh stickers on his bat. Dravid has had his special pre-match breakfast: fruit and cereal laced with honey, and a protein drink. Andrew Leipus sets up the massage table and pulls out tapes, ice packs and other equipment.

The National Stadium is packed and the game has attracted high-profile guests from India. Among them are Vikram Verma, India's sports minister, and Priyanka and Rahul Gandhi, who are treated like visiting royalty. The two watch the game from the chairman's box for a while before moving to the general stand and proudly wave the Indian flag. Priyanka is curious about how the players have trained and handled pressure. Rahul is focused on the cricket.

Ian Chappell is surprised that Nehra is playing ahead of Irfan Pathan. When asked about the wicket, he gives an honest answer: *Mate, that is one thing I don't understand.* Imran, looking fit and athletic, is part of the PTV commentary team. He says that India–Pakistan games test character more than skills and the team that handles pressure better wins.

There is bad news for India as VVS complains of a sprained left knee and pulls out at the last minute. India lose the toss and are put in, which is fine because Sourav is looking to bat anyway. When Shoaib Akhtar steams in, a tense next-in Sourav watchs intently. *Too much pressure in India–Pak games*, he says. *One of these days someone will die of stress.*

Nehra, ankle heavily strapped by Andrew, is catching up on sleep. A relaxed Dravid checks his gloves and places a plastic ball cut in half inside the right glove to deaden the impact of the ball hitting the bat. In the middle, Sachin lacks rhythm and is surprisingly scratchy. He plays and misses, edges fly into gaps and, like Sehwag, is once caught off a no-ball. Luckily, his top edge off a Shoaib bouncer sails over fine leg for a six.

The Pakistani bowlers are all over the place and Imran comments sarcastically that they are being nice hosts. Sehwag gives *tadi*, on the up drives through cover and a strange cross-batted tennis forehand (so described

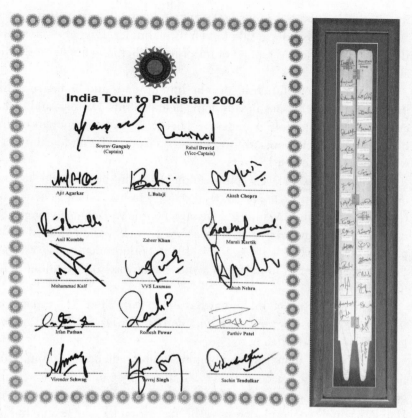

by Murali Kartik), fetching a ball from outside off and hitting it to the sight screen.

He gets out at the wrong time and is disappointed by his shot. *Main koot raha tha*, he says, *to take pressure off Paaji but woh slow ball miss ho gaya.* Jaitley sa'ab defends Sehwag, saying that's the way he bats. Sehwag thinks that the team has missed ten runs in the end and wonders, *Kahin yeh bhaari nahin pad jaye.*

When Mohammad Sami clocks in at 150 kmph, a doubtful Sachin remarks that the machine must be wrong because Shoaib is definitely quicker. An impressed Imran says Sami's fluid run-up and action remind him of Malcolm Marshall.

Dravid falls for 99 after a typically controlled knock, getting out to the first crude shot he attempts. The team feels bad for him as he walks back dejected. No words are said and there is no demonstration of emotion in the dressing room. Just a silent congratulatory clap from teammates, a nod of the head and a gentle tap on the shoulder. Drenched in sweat, Dravid looks at the TV replays of his dismissal before going for a shower and change.

The players have lunch before the innings ends and by the time the umpires walk out they are already doing fielding drills. Dalmiya and Jaitley are in the dressing room, wondering whether India have enough on the board. VVS, the cautious pro who knows cricket is difficult to call, says it will depend on the first 15 overs.

During the break players comment that Pakistan should be docked two overs for a slow over rate and allowed only 48 to bat. When I check with match referee Ranjan Madugalle, he says the rule was changed long back; now there are financial penalties for a slow over rate, as mentioned in the playing conditions. It is strange that this important change has escaped the attention of coach John Wright, who is otherwise so meticulous in his preparations.

Before the players go in, Sourav has a chat with them. *Make noise and support the bowlers—if they go for runs, don't drop your shoulders. Runs are gettable*, he warns the team.

After 35 overs, it appears that Sourav's grim prediction is coming true. Seventy-five runs are needed from the last 15 deliveries and it's touch and go. Pakistan's chase is anchored by a magnificent effort from Inzamam-ul-Haq. Amazingly cool under pressure, he cleverly nudges singles and hits big shots when required. But the match swings India's way with Kaif's stunning catch to dismiss Shoaib Malik. He runs in several yards from long-off to hold it under Hemang Badani's nose at long-on.

By that time the atmosphere is electrifying, as the game swings crazily. The Pakistan dressing room is already in celebration mode, confident of victory, and the noise is deafening—so loud that you wouldn't have heard a bomb explode.

Finally, India prevails thanks to an amazing spell from Nehra, who defends eight in the last over. Great bowling, and inspired captaincy from Sourav who would have been roasted had the result gone the other way. Yuvraj agrees: *The match was very exciting but hamare gale mein aa gayi thi.*

Dada leads the team in, shaking his head in disbelief, wondering how they pulled it off. He slumps into a chair, drained physically and emotionally, while the dressing room shrieks with happiness. *Khushi* and *jhappies*, happiness and hugs all around. Laxman hands out drinks to tired teammates. No one is more wired than Wright. As if in a trance, he yells with joy, pumps his fists and talks to himself till he loses all vocabulary and keeps repeating *fuck, fuck, fuck* …

The prime minister calls, but Sourav has already gone down for media interviews. At the prize distribution, when I mention that Priyanka Gandhi wants to meet the team, Sourav asks me to invite her to the dressing room. Sehwag gets the award for the fastest 50, but he rues missing the opportunity to score a hundred. He does a quick calculation to arrive at his 25 per cent share of the US$ 1,500 prize money and notes that it is enough to pay for dinner.

I fetch Priyanka Gandhi from the chairman's box after warning the players to get appropriately dressed. Sourav puts on his most pleasing smile and greets her warmly. Excited and happy, Priyanka walks shyly into the dressing room (which is otherwise out of bounds for women) to shake hands with the players and have pictures clicked with Sourav, Sachin and Dravid, who beam happily into the camera. She congratulates the players and, a bit embarrassed, says that she knows she is not supposed to be in the dressing room. She is clearly thrilled and the players are impressed with her effortless grace and regal aura.

Sourav Ganguly at the Press Conference

- *What instructions did you give Nehra before the last over?*
  Don't concede ten.
- *Were you scared of history and Miandad's last-ball six?*
  I don't know history and Miandad wasn't in the middle.
- *What do you think of the tight security?*
  We are thrilled to be escorted like the president.

The players pack their stuff—they have an 8 p.m. flight to catch. The television is playing 'It's the Time to Disco', a song from the SRK-starrer *Kal Ho Naa Ho*. Irfan admires Preity Zinta's nimble footwork but Yuvraj is not so impressed. It is ordinary, he feels, and he could do better.

Sachin assesses the game philosophically: *You need muqaddar to win even after 350. Agar nahin likha to nahin hoga.* After 15 years on the circuit, with more highs than lows, he knows there is a powerful umpire up there who ultimately decides the game. Nehra, more practical than philosophical, describes his thoughts going into the final over. *Meri bilkul phati thi, kahin Chetan Sharma nahin ho jaoon!*

Kaif describes his stunning, match-winning catch off Malik: *I knew it was crucial and started running as soon as it went up. I didn't notice what Badani was doing. I just wanted to take it.*

The team rushes back to the hotel for a quick pit stop before proceeding to the airport. Dravid, seated next to me in the bus, clutches a stump, his prized souvenir from the game. Totally knackered, he calls home, then dozes off.

Asides

- Dravid's bats are covered with cloth and wool covers to prevent them from getting scratched.
- Players have different coloured grips on their bats: Sachin (red), Dada (yellow), Dravid (blue).

The Pakistan team has already boarded as they had come straight from the ground. Their mood is sombre, having lost a game they had controlled for the most part. During the flight, Moin Khan says Pakistan cricket is a one-man show and the president of the PCB is a badshah. Players don't have contracts, only seniority-based graded match fees. Domestic cricket is poorly organised, so nobody wants to play. But Moin praises General Musharraf, a former commando, who occasionally drops in at practice and shares fitness tips with the players.

Inzamam, understandably disappointed, remembers matches in Sharjah where anything above 250 was a winning score. *Lekin ab koi 400 bhi bana dega.* For today's match Pakistan's game plan was 250 from 40 because 100 in the last ten isn't difficult. Dravid *achha khela, lekin hamari shuru mein* bowling *loose thi,* the big man feels.

Inzamam is bothered by the excessive media noise surrounding the tour and complains that the Indian press is hounding him. *I have changed my mobile and told them only coach Miandad will talk,* he says. The excessive media attention, though annoying, has an upside because each of Inzamam's ghosted columns fetches him US$ 1,200.

He admits to a frosty relationship with Miandad but says, *Pehle banti nahin thi par ab theek hai.* Unlike Miandad, who is known to be a street-smart battler, Inzamam is chilled out, a pleasant individual and a terrific player. Not the most articulate, but warm, likeable and dignified.

Sidelights

- Banner at Karachi airport: Welcome Indian guests and Indian cricketers.
- BCCI President Dalmiya signed autographs for fans and did multiple interviews with the media. After the game he declared cricket a winner, proclaiming that *Dostana aur dil jeetna bhi zaroori hai.* To which a player responded: *Dil aur koi jeete, hamein match jeetna hai.*

At Rawalpindi airport, while Sourav speaks to the press, Sehwag playfully carries on a funny word-by-word translation in Hindi. During the 20-minute ride to the Marriott, Dravid complains of a splitting headache and decides to take a Paracetamol. *One-day matches are usually a blur and you forget them,* he says, *but this is one game I will remember.*

Irfan is thrilled to know that Ian Chappell was surprised he wasn't picked for the game. He takes the exclusion in his stride and promises to work harder. *Bas, mujhe aur mehnat karni hai.*

When Sourav informs the others that General Musharraf has survived two recent assassination attempts in Rawalpindi, a nervous voice from the rear of the bus thanks him for reminding them. Before getting off the bus, John praises the team for taking the first step towards winning the series. His speech is well received, but not the short message that follows. Groans are heard when he announces a stretching session in the morning and practice in the afternoon for those who didn't play today.

At the Rawalpindi Marriott, hotel staff bring out a cake to celebrate the Indian win. Dravid breaks the security cordon to sign autographs, ignoring protests from police officials. It is almost midnight now, and what a day it has been for the team—an incredible win when all seemed lost.

The Second ODI

In the middle of an interview with PTV, Irfan is suddenly asked loaded questions about Indo–Pak relations and the experience of being a Muslim in an Indian team. He handles these bouncers with great skill and presence of mind. *I don't understand non-cricket matters,* he responds. *I am proud to be representing India,* he adds.

Later, he asks me what should be said on these issues. I advise him not to comment and ask the media to direct such questions to the team management.

Dravid and Kartik visit Taxila, an hour's drive from Rawalpindi. Dravid comes back with stories of Ashoka, who ruled over a kingdom bigger than modern India. He is impressed that Ashoka spoke about the duties of a king and about protecting the environment and wildlife. Remarkably, Ashoka practised religious secularism and supported inclusion and tolerance, values that have shaped India.

In the evening the team drives up Margalla Hills, which has a spectacular view of Islamabad, including the Faisal Mosque and the mazaar of President Zia-ul-Haq. Chai and pakoras are had at a roadside restaurant which has photos of Benazir Bhutto, Dev Anand and Lady Diana.

After dinner, which consists of excellent dal gosht, the players have a putting competition in the hotel corridor. Sachin, all concentration, aims for a glass 10 yards away on a wobbly carpet. Head still, conscious not to 'break' his wrist, he putts with a fluid stroke but—much to the delight of his teammates—misses.

Disturbed by the commotion outside his room, a sleepy Yuvraj emerges to try his hand and makes a perfect putt in his first attempt. He raises his arms in triumph and immediately announces his retirement from competitive golf. *You should know when to go*, he says, retiring to his room.

Dada, running a low fever, misses practice but comes to the ground anyway. Worried by the small outfield, he has a quick chat with the groundsman and the umpires about extending the boundary by 5 yards. *On a small ground they can just tonk the ball, now dar to lagega aur Inzy ko bhaagna padega for runs*, he explains.

Sidelights

- Sachin and Laxman shoot a short promotional film for UNICEF's polio eradication programme in the hotel's business centre. VVS has come after an extended pool session to loosen his strained knee. In front of the camera, he is far from fluent—he fumbles his lines and looks stiff. Sachin, a pro at this game, tells him the trick is to relax and not look too hard at the camera.
- Sachin gets it right in the first attempt. Learns his lines quickly and delivers a perfect shot.

Takeaways from the Pre-match Meeting

- Sourav's response when John congratulates him, tongue-in-cheek, for running three in the last game: *Now you know why I am running a fever.*

- Nehra's plan for Inzamam: *Samajh kar khelta hai, lappe nahin marega. Bowl straight and give no room, otherwise he works the angles.*
- Handling Shoaib Akhtar in the death overs: *Not easy to attack him because of pace. Try 6 singles and hope for the boundary. Also, look for byes because keeper Moin is too deep.*
- Debate about Kaif's position at short cover: Sehwag suggests he should stay a bit deep to stop the boundary. *No point standing close because nobody will take a single from you anyway.*

While going for breakfast, Pakistan player Yasir Hameed rushes into the lift just as the doors are about to close. He sees Dravid and greets him respectfully. Dravid mistakes him for the young off-spinner who bowled with Saqlain's action. Yasir, deeply embarrassed, mumbles that he is a batsman. Dravid, even more embarrassed, realises that he is the new opener and apologises profusely.

In the game, Pakistan is on fire and Abdul Razzaq and Shoaib Malik plunder 51 from the last five overs. Trying to take a caught and bowled chance, Nehra splits the webbing on his bowling hand. He is in great pain and requires stitches. President Musharraf, who is present at the ground (which, incidentally, was inaugurated by his political opponent Mian Nawaz Sharif, a cricket supporter, in 1992), is mighty pleased that Pakistan is winning.

When it is India's turn to bat, Shoaib sprints from behind the Samsung 30-yard ground logo. *What wouldn't we give to have someone like him*, John says, watching him run in. When Sehwag takes a huge swing at him and misses, John exclaims that the shot would have landed in Lahore had he connected. Yuvraj feels that Sami is as quick—*ball tej aata hai, bat uthne ke pehle hi gayab.*

Sachin scores a stunning hundred but is disappointed that the team is losing. In the dressing room, he sits with pads on, chewing his nails nervously. Dravid is seated next to him and both stare vacantly ahead. Not a word is spoken. Sehwag lightens the gloom by delivering a ball-by-ball commentary ('*aankhon dekha haal*') in Hindi.

Dada spots Miandad on the Pakistan team balcony and says only he can control their players. Sehwag agrees: *Gadbad hone par pant utar deta hai.*

The match is effectively over but Romesh Powar fights hard despite being fazed by a beamer from Shoaib. When Powar and Lakshmipathy Balaji swing their bats players make fun of Sami and Shoaib steaming in and getting hit for boundaries. Before the next match they will have a team meeting to discuss Balaji!

India fall short by just 12 runs. Two tight games in Karachi and Rawalpindi have produced four consecutive scores over 300. When the match ends, a happy and relieved Pakistan team comes to the Indian dressing room to shake hands.

I discuss likely questions for the press briefing with Sachin, who is adjudged Man of the Match. I advise him to be positive about Pakistan, refrain from commenting on security and, if asked about the invitation to Musharraf's reception, say the team is honoured. Dravid overhears the conversation and asks: *But are we?*

Questions from Sachin's press conference

- Why don't you finish matches?
  Please check the score cards.
- How do you cope with reverse swing?
  This wasn't discovered yesterday and I have been around 15 years.
- How do you feel in Pakistan?
  Bahut khushi hai, sab hamara khayal rakh rahe hain.

There is a growing feeling that Shoaib is getting away with a very suspicious action and players wonder why the umpires allow him to bowl. Shoaib is under no pressure, he just runs in and chucks. Let him bowl at 175 kmph—but with a legal action.

During play, when Moin casually says *well bowled* to Shoaib, the Indian batsman in the middle questions whether it can be called bowling. Shoaib overhears the exchange and wants to know what has been said. The Indian batsman responds: *You really want me to spell it out?*

President Musharraf's Reception

It is a short five-minute hop from the team hotel to the president's palace. The bus is stopped at the gate before the security staff wave it forward. The players are told to leave their mobiles in the bus and names are tallied with a list and ticked off. Gifts for the president (BCCI mementos and a bat signed by the players, with the names written by Laxman, who has neat handwriting) are taken away for security screening and will be delivered inside.

A short walk through a corridor leads to lifts with copper-coloured doors. The team is ushered into a hall with a high ceiling, bare except for a random sculpture in the centre, some paintings and a few sofas. A large chandelier dominates the hall, its white walls in contrast to the dark brown doors with brass fittings. Decorating the walls are various swords gifted to General Zia-ul-Haq by King Faisal, and others from Saudi Arabia and Qatar. My impression of the place: not a patch on the regal splendour of Rashtrapati Bhavan on Raisina Hill, New Delhi.

Among the guests waiting are Foreign Minister Khurshid Mahmud Kasuri, High Commissioners Shiv Shankar Menon and Riaz Khokhar, and PCB chief Shahryar Khan along with CEO Ramiz Raja.

After a brief wait, the president strides in, impeccable in his crisp khaki uniform and black military boots. He appears taller than he looks on TV and wears his trousers high, which makes his legs look disproportionately long.

The players line up for introductions and the president gives Sachin a long and vigorous handshake. After desultory yet polite conversation with the assembled guests, he walks to the centre of the hall and everyone gathers in a semicircle around him. Gifts are presented and the General thanks the team profusely. He proceeds to give a surprisingly accurate recap of the last two games.

He mentions Sachin's batting, Kaif's great catch that turned the game in India's favour and Afridi's performance with the bat and ball. He is knowledgeable and well-informed about cricket—he points out that the teams have been scoring big, 300 isn't a safe score anymore, and batting and bowling plans have to change.

He goes on to make a statesman-like speech, saying cricket brings people together, Pakistan and India should engage with each other more often and move forward towards peace and progress. *I want the Indian PM and Sonia Gandhi to come,* he announces, and asks his staff whether Priyanka Gandhi has returned to India.

The soldier in the General measures performances in terms of victory and defeat. For him a cricket match is a battle, it's about the fighting spirit, not giving up, showing commitment and executing impactful action. He appreciates the challenge and the excitement of a sporting contest and is happy that both sides have displayed exemplary courage.

The General makes flattering references to Inzamam, clearly a personal favourite, but doesn't spare him for his extra weight and slow movement on the field. Tense games are not good for the Pakistan captain, he says. *Inzamam was forced to dive and the ground shook when 200 pounds suddenly fell down.*

But Musharraf's best is reserved for Balaji, whom he hails as a great soldier, fighting bravely for his team even in a lost cause. *As a soldier*, he announces, not without a touch of drama, *I salute his spirit.*

Musharraf's charm offensive continues through the chai ceremony. In what appears to be a carefully thought-through act, he mingles with the players, breaking protocol to make informal conversation. He requests Sachin for a photo, pats Balaji on the back and has a longish conversation with a beaming Parthiv Patel.

Clearly, the General is a master communicator with a knack for holding the attention of audiences. He comes across as a grounded, witty person. When waiters appear with fruit juice, he directs them towards the Indian team. As refreshments are served, he announces that WMDs (weapons of mass destruction) in the form of gulab jamuns and pedas have been specially sourced for the Indian guests from Karachi.

He jokes that cricket has overtaken Pakistan and all work has ceased in offices. *Even I am wasting government money, only watching TV and doing daak. I don't know what I am writing or signing*, he says. The hour-long meeting ends with Musharraf shaking hands once again with everyone. He exits with a dramatic military salute.

At the Indian High Commission

The reception hosted by Indian High Commissioner Shiv Shankar Menon in Islamabad is different from the other official functions because wine and beer are served. Menon gives a brief update on Indo–Pak relations, making the point that people want peace but this doesn't suit the Pakistan Army which needs an enemy to justify its existence. The only way to escape from this circle is to exert pressure on the government and reach out to the people. Like water flowing down a slope, India must go around an obstacle that it can't remove—and somehow find a way.

Away from the pitch, players from both teams mix and chat in a relaxed atmosphere. When Shoaib complains of stiffness and feeling tired, a concerned Sehwag gives him friendly advice: *Right haath ki massage kara, tu bahut effort lagata hai.* The hidden message behind these comforting words isn't lost on the others.

The Third ODI

A local holiday is declared on match day and when tickets are put on sale, the demand is so great that the police resort to a lathi charge to restore order.

The match is played in the backdrop of fierce gun battles in neighbouring Wana, South Waziristan, with Pakistan's security agencies battling 'high value' Al Qaeda targets in the mountain ranges.

At the pre-match press conference Dada is asked about Shoaib Akhtar's bowling action.

Does he chuck?

Dada smiles. *We have all seen it on TV. We know the answer.*

A masterly deflection, neatly flicked off his legs. But also a spark to ignite a raging controversy!

India lose the match as the top order is blown away by Shabbir Ahmad on a damp wicket. Sachin gets out without scoring, a stark contrast to his 141 at Rawalindi. Yet, there is no change in his attitude. He remains undemonstrative, betraying no emotion—the mask never drops.

Sami clocks 100 mph on the machine but players insist that Shoaib is quicker. So fast that slips can't catch edges and the keeper stands behind the 30-yard circle.

Returning to Lahore, John has words of encouragement for the players: *We are not dead yet, boys. Hold your heads high and fight. We have done this before.*

Asides

- Yuvi's elaborate pre-match routine: Fingers are taped, elbow protected, zinc cream applied on face. Right ankle and left knee strapped. After that a 5–7 minute ice bath to ease muscles and plenty of hydration to avoid cramps.
- A habit both Sourav and Sachin have: Chewing their nails when tense.

Carpet Shopping in Peshawar

Sadar Bazaar closes at 8 p.m. but today the shops have been kept open beyond the scheduled time. The bazaar is full of people cheering and waving, all eager to catch a glimpse of the cricketers. In the general rush, fans block the narrow road. The police escort tries to find a way past the crowd but the team bus can't move. The security team decides to abandon shopping plans and with great difficulty, with fans banging on the bus window, the bus exits the busy shopping area.

The team is taken to a carpet showroom a little distance away, a three-storey building stacked with exquisite carpets from Iran, Bukhara, Afghanistan and Samarkhand.

The owner (a cricket fan) pulls out the best silk and wool pieces for Sachin, ranging from small bedside pieces to bigger ones costing US$ 7,000 to US$ 10,000, but nothing interests the master. *I don't know carpets*, he says. *Shauk hi nahin hai.* It is amazing to see the popularity and mass hysteria triggered by Sachin in a remote part of a foreign country. It speaks volumes about the power of sport to connect with people.

After looking at hundreds of carpets, dhurries and rugs, Dravid and I find a strikingly beautiful Afghani kilim. Dravid makes a quick call home to seek approval before going ahead with the purchase.

Back at the hotel, a chappalwala brings a vast collection of Peshawar's famous jootis. Players buy the stuff in bulk because *yeh hamari range mein hai*. Carpets for US$ 7,000, jootis for 700 Pakistani rupees!

Lahore

The players have been given time off for R and R (rest and recovery). Sachin uses the break to shop at Bareeze, the upmarket women's fashion store specialising in hand-embroidered garments. *Great stuff*, he says on coming back with a bagful of clothes, *but prices are steep*. This is a useful tip because if something is expensive for Sachin, the others might as well strike it off their shopping list.

Some of the players visit the famous Lahore Museum which contains priceless antiquities from the Indus Valley sites of Mohenjodaro and Harappa, as well as Gandhara art, Buddha sculptures, miniature portraits of Mughal kings, notably Akbar, and objects pertaining to Maharaja Ranjit Singh. Fabulous items, though many are stacked in shabby wooden almirahs with poor lighting and scant information.

More satisfying is the short detour to Biddon Road to taste Lahore's famous dry-fruit ice cream.

Asides

- John Wright's mantra for fighting tension: *Go for a jog, play the guitar.*
- Sidhu's comment on poor shot selection while batting: *Bad shots are like soft beds, easy to get in, difficult to get out of.*

VVS on a Horse

When VVS was persuaded by photographer Pradeep Mandhani to do an offbeat, non-cricket exclusive photo shoot, he didn't know what he was signing up for. He is made to sit on a horse and pose in his training gear. The shoot takes place just outside the hotel lobby and attracts the attention of guests, passers-by, drivers and the security staff.

VVS's embarrassment increases when Mandhani, a fussy pro looking for the perfect frame, is not impressed by the look of the horse and asks for a replacement. In the end, Mandhani gets two priceless photographs—cricket warrior VVS on a black horse and cricket warrior VVS on a white one.

Dinner at Lahore Fort

The chief minister of Punjab hosts a dinner for the Indian team at Lahore Fort, which is the venue for official banquets (like Hyderabad House is in Delhi). The setting is truly majestic. The sixteenth-century Mughal fort is tastefully lit and has soldiers in traditional court uniforms holding decorated

Punjab chief minister's reception at Lahore fort

spears. The notes of a shehnai floating down its ramparts enhance the grandeur of the fort.

The host makes a brief welcome speech. This is followed by an entertainment programme. Celebrated comedian Moin Akhtar cracks jokes about Amitabh Bachchan and SRK, and Ghulam Ali sings a few of his popular ghazals.

The Indian players and guests (including Rajmata Gayatri Devi of Jaipur) are seated in a cordoned-off area managed by young architecture students who are part of an event management company. Dravid is introduced to the Rajmata, who speaks about the polo team's defeat in some recent exhibition matches and wants the cricketers to avenge the loss.

The function is poorly organised, the service slow and the speeches long. The players, tired and bored, eat quickly and exit even as other guests wait for their food.

Dada, impressed by the fort and its ambience, wonders about the lavish lifestyle of the Mughal kings and raises a practical point: *How did they run their empires and manage so many wives? Isn't it difficult to handle even one?*

ODIs, Lahore

India is 2–1 down and the last two ODIs are day-and-night games to be played in Lahore. In the pre-match team meeting, there is a difference of opinion on the team's decision should it win the toss. Batting first would mean handling a fresh wicket but chasing would add pressure. The debate is inconclusive and the captain confused.

India draws level in the first game, chasing down Pakistan's 293 (Inzamam makes a superb 123). After an initial stutter, Dravid and Kaif, the two calmest heads in the team, add 132.

The final game sees VVS hit a hundred his Hyderabad colleague Azhar would have called 'pure class'. Irfan dismisses three top-order batsmen (Yousuf, Younus and Taufeeq Umar) to set India on the path to an emphatic victory. A standout memory from the game is of Sachin catching Inzy's flat hit off Murali Kartik on the long-on fence. The other highlight is Balaji smashing Shoaib for a six, a front foot strike that sails over long-on.

Despite India winning the game, there is some bad news. Dada's back had packed up midway through the innings and he had to be stretchered into the pavilion. Though in great pain, he was desperate to return to the middle and asked for a painkiller injection. Andrew, professional and unemotional, ruled him out of the game and warned him that this could be serious.

Dada's *zidd* to get back on the ground was understandable. He wanted to be out there in the middle and not on the physio's massage table. He was distraught—overcome by pain, anger, helplessness and frustration.

When congratulatory messages are delivered from the president, the prime minister and the deputy prime minister, the players realise the enormity of this historic win. The reaction back home has shattered the official line that India versus Pakistan is just another bat-ball contest played by 11 players. The players know it's much more, it's a huge challenge and an opportunity to become a hero.

Even before play ends, the crowd thins out, and by the time the post-match presentation concludes, the stadium is almost empty. When the team poses for the customary victory photograph, some Indian politicians try to get into the frame. Their efforts are thwarted by shouts of *team only* from photographers. Players mutter that the publicity-thirsty political leaders are shamelessly thick-skinned.

Dada's back continues to cause concern and Andrew advises that he return to India to consult an expert. High Commissioner Menon tries locating one in Pakistan but, in the end, Dada has to fly back.

With the one-dayers done, attention shifts to the Test series and the first match in Multan.

Multan

A sleepy Punjab town famous for its *mitti* and *malta*, cotton textiles, blue pottery, camel leather products and a vibrant Sufi tradition, Multan has a modern cricket stadium with the main pavilion named after the local cricket icon, Inzamam. After practice some players visit the main shrine in the city centre, which is packed for Friday prayers. This results in a visit from the Police Special Branch, who want to know (most politely) the purpose of this unscheduled visit.

Dada is ruled out of the Test because of his back. He sees a doctor and gets an MRI done, but the swelling and discomfort persist. The morning practice session is routine, with only a minor flutter of excitement when the security unit arrives with sniffer dogs to check the dressing room for explosives.

The team has an Open Press Day in the late afternoon. Journalists in small groups circulate from table to table to speak with the players. Sachin, understandably, is very busy, as are Balaji and Irfan. But it is Sehwag who steals the show with his answers.

Who is the favourite to win the series?

India, because I am playing for India.

What will you take from Pakistan for your wedding?

Nothing except runs.

Does John Wright tear his hair out because of your batting?

Many times.

John tells the boys that India can beat Pakistan. *All we need is discipline, discipline and discipline.* He feels that India is more intelligent and the better team, but *we have to defeat the Pakistan team with our minds, intellect, superior planning and thinking.* In his opinion, Pakistan is an undisciplined side which could self-destruct.

He reminds the players about the team motto: Pride and passion—be the first. *And make a name for yourself.* He also makes the point that a Test match goes session by session, unlike an ODI which is one big bang and out.

Captain Dravid warns against complacency because Pakistan is known to come back hard when you think they are down. He speaks about the importance of beginning well to set the tone. VVS is tasked with checking that the players maintain intensity during play.

In the evening, Imran holds a durbar in the hotel lobby with Miandad, Shoaib and Moin. Khan sa'ab wants Pakistan to prepare quick wickets and play to its strength. Always animated and forthright, he says he is surprised that India's bowling has been so ordinary.

Match Day at Multan

On the first day of the Test series, the team leaves at 8 a.m. Captain Dravid carries his India blazer on a hanger and his bats in Reebok wool covers. The players are tense and the 15-minute drive is steeped in silence.

Some radical political groups have called for a strike to protest the Indian team's visit but the security staff have confirmed—*koi masla nahin hai*. Multan is a city of peace, saints and Inzamam, but has also recently become a recruiting ground for jihadis because of the lack of education, widespread poverty and unemployment. The main traffic island or roundabout leading to the stadium features Shaheen, Pakistan's missile, but alongside it are banners that announce, 'Cricket for peace and dignity'.

At the ground, both teams go through their pre-match warm-up routine. Everyone is apprehensive about the wicket. Rules allow only the captain, coach and manager to inspect the track, and the inspection must be done without spikes. The rule, however, is openly flouted. Dravid has a close look at the track. He feels the surface with his fingers to check the moisture and scratches it with his spiked shoe to judge its firmness.

When Inzamam tosses the coin, it goes straight up, without spinning. It doesn't tumble or turn on landing either; it just lands flat on the wicket. Ian Chappell is surprised that the coin hasn't 'toppled over' and so is Dravid. He has correctly called 'heads' and has no hesitation in batting first.

The Pakistan team goes into a huddle before play. Dada observes that this practice, started by India at the 2003 World Cup based on advice from sports psychologist Sandy Gordon, has been adopted by other teams as well.

India gets off to a rapid start. Sehwag is in imperious form and slashes a short ball for six over point. Imran, between his commentary stints, thinks Pakistan is overdoing the hospitality by preparing flat tracks that help India.

It's simple common sense, thunders Khan sa'ab, *that you first decide your strategy to win—and everything follows from that. Removing grass is cowardice and the only consequence of that is death*, he says, and recites an Urdu couplet to support his view. Imran is very critical of Miandad, who he thinks contributes nothing. *He only flaps his hands and acts busy*, he says.

Imran is delightful company because he has firm views which he expresses in fearless Pathan fashion. He detests captains who play safe

175

and feels the focus should always be on winning. He cites the example of India's previous visit when Pakistan captain Mushtaq Mohammad was scared of India's spinners and thought they would turn the ball even on green tracks.

Imran only has harsh words for Pakistan's domestic cricket structure. Denouncing it as an utter waste of time, he reveals that he had prevented Inzamam from wasting himself in meaningless matches and that's what he would advise Imran Nazir, a great talent, to do too.

Imran Khan has charm, charisma, and an aura of power and authority. He pushed hard for introducing neutral umpires in Tests and played cricket on his own terms. He refused to play domestic cricket after 1981 because it didn't help him become a better player. He didn't bowl much towards the end of his career; he focused instead on batting and went up the order.

Dada misses most of the pre-lunch action as he falls asleep on the massage table while getting a rub-down. Waking up, he asks whether Sehwag has given *tadi* to Shoaib Akhtar.

With India in a comfortable place, the mood in the dressing room is upbeat. Supervised by the trainer, Greg King, Parthiv Patel does crunches. VVS and Irfan search for the best hotel deals as they both have to make arrangements for visiting parents. Sachin carefully tests his bat, knocking it with his knuckles to check the sound of the willow. Dravid flips through a local English newspaper and is appalled by the quality of writing. Irked by words like 'unneeded', he wonders whether the journalists had access to Microsoft Word.

Players are shocked when Sehwag, batting at 199, plays out a maiden over off Sami. A wise voice (that of captain Dravid) says it's the best over he has ever played in his life but others are certain that Sehwag will go wild after scoring 200. *Uske baad dekhna.*

At stumps, Sehwag, now batting at 220, gets a stern lecture from VVS, who urges him to go past Hayden's 380. Only 160 to go, and tomorrow is a fresh day, a fresh start. Later that day, Andrew Leipus works on Sehwag's back to relax his sore muscles.

Dada is also tired. *It is very difficult to watch a match*, he says, but admires Sehwag's brilliance. He predicts that Sehwag will go on to score at least 20 Test hundreds and VVS will make 12 or 13 centuries in the next 50 matches. Dada is confident that he, Dravid, Kumble and Sehwag will end up playing more than 100 Tests. When I ask him about Sachin, he says, at least 150.

Reflecting on the day's play, he questions Shoaib's strategy of running in to clock miles on the machine—he got hit for two boundaries in each over.

Refreshed after a rub-down and a shower, Sehwag prepares for the post-game press conference. Some interesting bits from the conference:

How do you feel about your double hundred?

This is the first time I batted six hours. Never played 90 overs before. My 275 in Duleep was scored in five hours.

What keeps you going?

Master Sachin was at the other end. He kept talking to me.

What was your exchange with Shoaib?

Nothing. Chutkule ho rahe the.

On the way back to the hotel, Sehwag says a cheerful *thank you, boys* to his teammates. Dada navigates his way past fans in the hotel lobby to go to his room. In the coffee shop Khan sa'ab is holding his usual adda, with Sami and Shoaib, taking their 'class'. Imran is critical of the defensive mindset of Miandad and Inzamam. *Imagine*, he says, *they are scared of Zaheer and Irfan!*

Speaking of Miandad

One player narrated this interesting story about the coach, Javed Miandad. Abdul Razzaq was batting and, for some reason, Miandad was gesturing desperately from the pavilion to catch his attention. The player pointed out to Razzaq that the coach was signalling. *Chutiya*, Razzak said, ignoring Miandad.

Balaji on Hitting Shoaib Akhtar for a Six

- *I can't believe it. Before this, I never hit a six even in club cricket.*

The Declaration

While the teams are going through their pre-match warm-up drills, I jog around the ground with Miandad. Umpire Simon Taufel joins us but, unable to match our (slow) pace, decides to sprint. Later, stretching his hamstring near the advertising boards, Taufel says that fitness keeps him alert and he does at least three serious gym sessions a week.

Miandad has a different fitness routine. Mindful of his strained back, he follows a programme designed by a yoga expert from Bangalore. Miandad tells players to be sensible about weights and work more on their cricket muscles.

When play starts, Sehwag goes past VVS's 281, the highest score by an Indian in Tests. VVS, happy for Sehwag, announces that Hayden's 380, the highest score in Test history, is under threat. At lunch Sehwag has *dahi* (after carefully removing *malai*), Alphonso mangoes (brought by Raj Singh-ji from Mumbai), and a piece of cake and ice cream because *aaj sab maaf hai*.

Soon after lunch, Sehwag reaches 300, the first Indian in 72 years to reach the magical figure, a statistic Yuvraj didn't know. He loses his wicket a little later, edging Sami to slip, his outstanding innings doubly special because he had reached 100 and 300 by hitting huge sixes. In the dressing room, Sehwag receives a warm hug from Sachin and a big, friendly danda from VVS for not going past Hayden.

As India grinds Pakistan into submission, Dada notices their poor body language—heads down and shoulders drooping. He is surprised when Saqlain bowls into Sachin's pads with six fielders on the leg side. *He will never get out like that.* Dada speaks glowingly about Sachin, calling him India's greatest ever *khiladi* and wonders about the many records he will leave behind.

Post-tea, Dravid waves from the balcony to call the batsmen back, with India at 675/5 and Sachin stranded on 194. The great man climbs the stairs to the dressing room slowly, face red with simmering emotion and not just from the searing Multan heat.

He sits there in silence, wearing the India cap and a dark expression. Is he angry, disappointed or just tired? With Sachin one can never tell. He conceals his emotions like bowlers hide the shiny side of the ball while trying to reverse.

He changes, gets an ice-pack on his left ankle, has his toes taped, and asks Greg King to check for dehydration. By this time the dressing room is vacant—the team is in the field for the few overs before stumps and the other players stand silently on the balcony outside, deciding wisely to keep a safe distance from Sachin.

The coach is doing stomach exercises in a corner of the large dressing room and after a while I hesitantly suggest to Sachin that he should go out to field, otherwise his absence might be misunderstood. He hears me, says nothing, but after a while he gets up and goes out to join the team.

At the end of play, one can tell that Sachin is still seething. While walking across the ground for the press conference (the Multan media centre is located directly opposite the pavilion), I ask him to gather his thoughts and decide what he wants to say. He nods his head and replies that he will say he was surprised and disappointed by the declaration.

In the media room he says exactly that: *I was surprised and disappointed.*

The controversy about the declaration has people in different corners. Those who are sympathetic to Sachin feel that waiting a few more overs wouldn't have mattered because time wasn't an issue in the game. At tea India was 588 from 148 overs (Sachin, 165). The team batted for 13 overs more before closing the innings and eventually bowled 16 overs at the tired Pakistani openers.

Some believe Sachin deserved consideration. Others think the team comes first, individual milestones are irrelevant and Sachin had already consumed too much time.

Imran backs Dravid and recalls the time when he called Miandad back when he was on 280 against India during the 1982–83 series.

Someone says that this is azaadi, liberation day for Indian cricket. Dada sees it differently. *Such things happen, disagreements will take place*, he says philosophically.

Dada gets dragged into the controversy. Apparently, when Dravid called the batsmen back, Dada was standing in the balcony, which led to speculation that he was party to the decision.

My understanding is that it was captain Dravid's call and he played it off his own bat. The declaration, however, did raise questions about communication within the team: Was Sachin given sufficient notice? Was he clearly told when the innings would close? At one stage, Kartik conveyed Dravid's message that he wanted the team to bowl one hour before close of play. Romesh Powar also went in (carrying gloves) and said there was only one more over to go—and then the declaration happened.

Postscript

Prof. Shetty and I were present in the dressing room when this played out, but both were far removed from the call that was taken. It emerged later that, to achieve closure on the controversy, Sachin and Dravid had a private chat.

Dravid hasn't publicly commented on the matter, but Sachin, in his autobiography, described how things unfolded. The decision at teatime was to give Pakistan 15 overs that day and he planned his innings accordingly. But Romesh Pawar came rushing up with a message, first to ask him to hurry and then a second time to say that Rahul wanted to declare—with 12 balls still remaining. Sachin didn't get strike the next over, and the declaration was made with 16 overs still to go.

He came back to the pavilion fuming because that wasn't what had been discussed and decided. Coach John Wright apologised to him, and that evening Sachin went to the gym to work out his frustration and get the episode out of his system. When Rahul met him the next morning, an upset Sachin told him they had agreed on a plan at tea but that wasn't how things happened. But he also assured him that this wouldn't have any bearing on his involvement in the field.

Sachin mentioned that despite this incident, Rahul and he remained good friends and neither their cricket nor their friendship was affected.

At the end of the match, Dravid and I have a short discussion ahead of the post-match presser and decide to make a firm statement that the team is united and there are no differences. Our approach is to downplay the incident and move on to the positives: the historic win and Sehwag's 300.

Dravid handles the tricky press conference brilliantly, focusing on team effort instead of individual performances. He makes the important point that the performance of 11 players is linked to many things (cricket structure and support staff) and the failure of 11 players shows deficiencies down the line.

Dravid carries himself with remarkable poise, dignity and self-confidence. He wears the India cap with pride and is a great ambassador for Indian cricket. He also wears a mask that hides the emotions surging inside him. Despite the stoic exterior and brave front, the declaration controversy has bruised him—he is disappointed that others looked for conspiracies in what had been a cricket decision made in the team's best interest. But Dravid always plays with the bat close to his body, which is why he refrains from fuelling the debate by reacting to the wild reports that have been circulating.

Virender Dabang Sehwag

Triple centurion Sehwag recalls his early years when he would leave home every day at 5 a.m. and his days as a ball boy at the Ferozshah Kotla grounds in 1992. He moved the sight screen for three days but fell ill after that and the DDCA didn't pay him because he didn't turn up on day 4. He nurses an even bigger grouse: *While I sat in the sun near the boundary, team mate Aakaash Chopra, assisting the Australian team, sat in the dressing room drinking coffee.*

Soon after this unpleasant experience, Sehwag's career took off due to a defining innings in a club game. Playing for Jamia Millia against Bantoo Singh's Central Bank, he blasted 150 with many hits that sailed into the stands. This got him into the Delhi U-19 team and soon word spread about a hard-hitting lower order batsman who also bowled useful off-breaks. On his Ranji debut, Sehwag scored a hundred batting at number eight. His international debut against Pakistan at Mohali was equally sensational. This is how he described it: *I went for a big shot against Shoaib Akhtar and was bowled before the bat could come down.*

Sehwag admits his aggressive DNA causes problems. He rues the occasional missed opportunity (the possible hundred at Lord's, dismissed at 86 trying a crude slog) but he trusts his own game and his judgement. Sometimes his self-belief causes harm because *mujhe lagta hai har* ball *ko maar sakta hoon.*

Sidelights

- Sehwag cut a cake with 309 written on it and retired early to bed.
- Sehwag's reply when asked whether his parents encouraged him to play: *They realised 'padhai mein kuchh nahin hoga isliye cricket khelne do'.*
- Sehwag's ambition in cricket: A five-wicket haul in a Test match.
- What surprised VVS most about Sehwag's innings: He told Saqlain before the game that Pakistan would field for two days.

After play ended on day 2, Shoaib ran around the ground, cooling down after a tough day. This drew an admiring comment from Sehwag, who said no batsmen could relax against him. He kept running in and the ball hit the bat at the same pace—from the first ball on day 1 to the last ball on day 2.

The next day, India makes early inroads but suffers a blow when Zaheer limps off with a pulled hamstring. Pakistan follows on and John asks the players to be hard on themselves and not reduce the intensity of play.

Dada spreads a towel on the dressing-room floor and sleeps, only to wake up with a start when Imran Farhat is caught and bowled by Kumble. When Inzamam is spectacularly run out by Yuvraj, Dada screams with delight and predicts that the match will end on day 4.

Pakistan caves in, but Yousuf (formerly Youhana) helps himself to a free hit, an easy Test hundred, so described by an unimpressed Indian player.

Watching the Pakistan team in disarray, Ian Chappell blames ordinary leadership and even more ordinary bowling for their plight.

On day 5, with India one wicket away from victory, Kumble is worried by stray clouds in the sky but is reassured by an old hand who confirms that Multan has rain only two days in a year. Once the last wicket falls in the second over, the celebrations begin. Sachin, however, advises restraint because there are two more matches to go. *Kuchh series ke liye bhi rakho.*

Dada leaves for India—carrying only hand baggage—to get his back fixed, hopeful of returning soon. Kumble also heads home because his wife is pregnant. Overheard in the dressing room a few days later, when news comes of the birth of his son: *Kumble has produced a perfect delivery!*

——

The team makes a brief visit to an SOS children's orphanage village before returning to the hotel. Surprisingly, the orphanage turns out to be a fancy five-star facility run by the wives of VIPs. The 'village' has modern classrooms and auditoriums and is no less fancy than Gurgaon's private schools. The players play tennis-ball cricket with the kids and when Balaji bowls a slow short ball, a young kid smashes it out of the ground.

——

The Indian team receives an interesting message from Chief of Army Staff General N.C. Vij: Congratulations and compliments from the Indian Army to the cricket team.

The message sparks a thought: *What happened to the idea of keeping sport and politics separate?* If there was any illusion that India–Pakistan cricket was only a sporting contest, the army chief's message dispelled it.

Dinner with the Team

In Lahore, the team has dinner at the hotel poolside to celebrate the Multan win. The significance of India's first Test win in Pakistan in 50 years is yet to sink in.

The players talk shop and the conversation is mercilessly frank; nobody is spared and nothing goes unnoticed. They believe the ultimate test of batting is fast bowling *ko jhelna* and to perform when West Indies is telling their quicks to *Get him, maan.* Reputations are shredded in minutes and there is talk of players who suddenly develop upset stomachs on seeing grass on the pitch. Stories of scared batsmen touching the surface in the hope of detecting some non-existent moisture (saying *isme kuchh hai*) so they could avoid batting. Others saying, *tu ja, tu ja*, to escape a tough examination.

Fans go by statistics and the opinion of pundits but players have their own way of determining who is good, bad and very bad. They know each other, and in their private rating system, things are pretty straightforward: it's black or white, pass or fail, nothing in between. There's respect for those who stand up to pace and anyone giving *tadi*, like Viv Richards.

By now there is general outrage in Pakistan over the Multan Test and different reasons are put forward to explain the crushing defeat. Inzamam has been quoted as saying that the Pakistan bowlers are far from world-class. Curator Andy Atkinson has been accused of being pro-India. Most extraordinary is a statement from a government official rejecting the rumour that the defeat was arranged to please Prime Minister Vajpayee!

The final word on India's win in Multan comes from Imran Khan: *Before the series Indians were worried about security. After Multan the Pakistani team needs security.*

Ian Chappell agrees with Imran that India has been the better side and has had multiple captaincy options besides Dada and Dravid, including VVS, Kumble and Sachin. India is spoilt for choice. Pakistan, on the other hand, is spoilt because it has no choice.

Jab They Met: Imran and Sourav

During a casual conversation, when I mention Imran's dominant role in Pakistan cricket, Sourav expresses a desire to meet him. Imran is only too happy to have a chat and they meet in Multan in the PCB chairman's box adjacent to the Indian dressing room.

Top performers usually respect each other and this is clearly evident as the two speak. In Imran, Dada sees a charismatic captain with such authority that nobody dares to cross his path or question his methods. Imran is impressed that Dada leads with the intent to win and backs match-winning players.

Imran speaks about leadership and stresses the importance of creating loyalty by picking the right players and trusting them. Dada listens attentively, an alert student in the presence of a senior, and asks pertinent questions.

Sourav is intrigued by the fact that Imran did not play first-class cricket for many years and gave domestic matches a royal miss. Imran's explanation is typically blunt: *Pakistan domestic cricket does nothing for quality and you don't learn anything.*

The conversation ends when Imran has to get on air to resume commentary. As we climb the steps to the Indian dressing room, Dada says: *Kya cheez hai!*

Sidelights

- Assessment of Inzamam, the batsman: Has a sharp cricket head and good hands. Not sure about his legs though—he is dangerous for teammates while running between the wickets.
- Inzamam gifted shirts made in his factory in Multan to each member of the Indian team.
- Reasons for Inzamam's popularity: He is laidback and pleasant. Even his *gaalis* are given *'pyaar se'*.
- Despite intense on-field rivalry, players from both teams got along with each other. They laughed and chatted, and Shoaib was a frequent visitor to the Indian dressing room.
- On the flight back from Multan, Indian players joked with Moin, who was penalised by the match referee for showing dissent and using 'bad' language. A smiling Moin pleaded innocence: *Arre, mujhe to gaali aati hi nahin.*

A Coaching Masterclass

In one corner of the Holiday Inn coffee shop, Imran is holding court. Waiters hover around to serve Khan sa'ab his simple dinner of gosht and roti. Kids patiently wait for autographs and players from both teams hang on to his words of wisdom.

Today, Khan sa'ab's focus is Irfan Pathan, who he considers a match winner, a *tagda ghoda*. Talking to him as an interested tutor and a fond *chacha*, Imran delivers a masterclass in fast bowling, which a wide-eyed Irfan absorbs gratefully.

Khan sa'ab's core message to Irfan is that he must make his legs strong because strong legs are the foundation of fast bowling. *Do sprints but no jogging. Do weights for upper body strength, not for bulk, because bodybuilder nahin banna hai.*

Imran thinks that Irfan's action and wrist movement are good. No need to change anything, especially if things are working. But minor

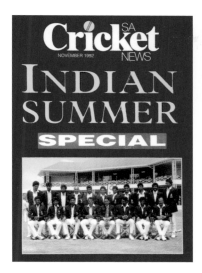

Indian team tour to South Africa,
Johannesburg, 1992

Reception for the Indian team,
Durban, 1992

INDIAN CRICKET TEAM
ZIMBABWE & SOUTH AFRICA TOURS 1992—1993

SITTING L TO R — CHETAN SHARMA, W. RAMAN, RAVI SHASTRI (V. Captain), M. AZHARUDDIN (Captain) AJIT WADEKAR (Manager Cricket), KAPIL DEV, KIRAN MORE, SANJAY MANJREKAR. ABSENT–M. PRABHAKAR

STANDING L TO R — SACHIN TENDULKAR, VENKATAPATHI RAJU, S. BANERJEE, ANIL KUMBLE, J. SRINATH PRAVIN AMRE, AJAY JADEJA, VIJAY YADAV, AMRIT MATHUR (Manager)

GOPAL PHOTOS BOMBAY

Nelson Mandela, Johannesburg, 1992

President Kalam's reception at
Rashtrapati Bhavan after the 2003
Cricket World Cup

Prime Minister Vajpayee's
reception in Delhi before
India's tour to Pakistan, 2004

General Parvez Musharraf,
Islamabad, 2004

Madhavrao and Jyotiraditya Scindia
at a Wills World Cup game,
Gwalior, 1996

Sourav Ganguly,
Sachin Tendulkar,
Arun Jaitley at
Prime Minister
Vajpayee's reception,
2004

PILCOM meeting,
London, 1994

Front row:
Thilanga Sumathipala,
Madhavrao Scindia,
Zulfikar Ali Shah
Bukhari, Jagmohan
Dalmiya, Majid Khan

Back row:
Ehsan Mani,
Javed Burki, I.S. Bindra

Procession at IPL opening, Cape Town, 2009

IPL team owners Preity Zinta of
Kings XI Punjab and S. Bommidala
of Delhi Daredevils

With Virender Sehwag, captain,
Delhi Daredevils, Delhi, 2008

Victory in Lahore, 2004

Virender Sehwag, Sachin Tendulkar at Lahore Fort, 2004

BCCI AGM.
Front row: Ranbir Singh Mahindra, Kishore Rungta, Jagmohan Dalmiya, Arun Jaitley, Kamal Morarka, N. Srinivasan, P.M. Rungta
Back row: Rajeev Shukla, Sanjay Jagdale

Below: The Delhi Daredevils, Capetown, South Africa, 2009

Seated: Daniel Vettori, Gautam Gambhir, T. A. Sekar, S. Bommidala, B. Vanchi, Virender Sehwag, Paul Collingwood, Greg Shipperd

Standing: Aashish Kapoor, Tillakaratne Dilshan, David Warner, Ashish Nehra, A.B. de Villiers, Dinesh Karthik, Umesh Yadav, Manoj Tiwary

Mohammad Kaif, Sourav Ganguly, Sachin Tendulkar, Rahul Dravid at the opening ceremony of the Cricket World Cup, Cape Town, 2003

NatWest triumph, Lord's, 2002

With family at the Cricket World Cup final, Lord's, 2019

tweaks are suggested: *Run-up tej bhago, right hand upar karo and panja khulla rakho.*

He tells Irfan to be smart about practice and to bowl with concentration and focus. *Net mein fizool ball nahin daalna. Not more than five overs with full run-up. After that preserve your energy for the match.*

Imran compares Irfan to a young, raw Wasim Akram who didn't understand how the ball swung. He thinks Irfan could be as good as Akram with more experience and more body strength.

Visit to Wagah

After a 30-minute drive from Lahore, on narrow, dusty roads past sleepy villages, we reach the Wagah border. The team is met by the Rangers and escorted towards Mile Zero, a line drawn across the road by Cyril Radcliffe to separate India and Pakistan. Every evening, the Pakistani Rangers and Indian Border Security Force (BSF) jawans face each other during the flag lowering ceremony—a spectacle that draws crowds of almost 10,000 on weekends. The atmosphere is festive and patriotic—national flags are waved and from the Indian side Mahendra Kapoor's stirring '*Mere desh ki dharti*' from Manoj Kumar's epic *Upkar* is played at top volume. Rangers on horseback in smart grey uniforms keep a close watch on the barbed wire fence.

Ironically, the Indian team is sitting on the *wrong* side, like a visiting team occupying the home dressing room, surrounded by a large, noisy group screaming *Jiyo Jiyo Pakistan*. But there is no tension or discomfort because the Pakistani crowd happily greet the players. Soon, spectators on the Indian side spot the players among the Pakistanis. The loudest cheer from Lahore—and Amritsar—is reserved for Balaji, the latest superstar.

The flag-lowering ceremony is dramatic, as if inspired by Bollywood choreographer Farah Khan. In a synchronised move, jawans on either side of Mile Zero lower the flags ceremonially. The Pakistan Rangers, each one seven feet tall, slim and erect, dressed in black, march with stiff steps, raising their legs so high they almost touch their colourful turbans. This raises gasps from the spectators and concern from trainer Greg King, who disapproves of heavy military boots stomping on the concrete road. *Bad for the knees*, he mutters.

The solemn ceremony has become a crowd-pleasing event which plays to the gallery. It is an entertaining show with jawans marching in a synchronised manner, snorting and snarling at each other in mock anger

Indian team with Rangers at Wagah

while the audience on both sides encourages them with whistles and patriotic chants. Spectators enjoy the drama of two nations separated by a line that divides people and separates time. At Wagah, it's 6 p.m. on an Indian watch, while it's 5.30 p.m. in Pakistan.

The Rangers serve warm cups of tea to the team. Dravid signs the visitors' book which is neatly placed on a green table covered with green felt, with a pen that has green ink.

Driving back to Lahore, the discussion in the bus is about Pakistan, with players agreeing that youngsters on this side of the border are cool. They are not burdened by the baggage of history and are disinterested in fighting their grandfathers' war. Everyone wants peace and a better life.

The players are overwhelmed by the genuine warmth and all-round affection. The consensus about Pakistan is that it feels like playing at home.

Asides

- Balaji's reaction when cheered by girls at Wagah: *I didn't know what to do. I wanted to hide.*
- Sachin posed for a photograph with one leg on either side of Mile Zero. *Bada achha photo nikala.*

The Second Test, Lahore

Following an old tradition, Test debutants Irfan and Romesh Powar make a short speech each, at the team meeting. Both try to wriggle out and do *hazaar nakhra* till strict seniors put their foot down and insist that the team *parampara* can't be disregarded. Sensing that there is no room for escape, a nervous Powar gathers courage and finds his voice to promise his best. Irfan, more skilled at this game, thanks his teammates for their support. Captain Dravid wishes Sehwag another great game, after reminding him about the dreaded law of averages. His wise words: *Next innings you start from zero, not 300.*

The next morning, the supremely organised Dravid forgets to carry his India blazer to the ground. Masood, the team liaison officer, rushes back to the hotel to fetch it, but it's 9.40 a.m. by the time he returns, too late for the toss. A non-blazered Dravid wins the toss and, to Inzamam's surprise, decides to bat first on a greenish surface.

The Indian batting collapses, but Yuvraj and Irfan pull things back from 120/7. An aggressive Yuvraj attacks the ball and the bowler (Sami) and as the partnership flourishes, the team *tashan* kicks in. Sachin and Sehwag are reduced to statues, glued to their seats. Even toilet breaks are not permitted.

Day 2 is miserable. Play is marred by poor umpiring, especially from Bucknor. Sehwag and Dravid request him to remain alert, not a diplomatic thing to do, and a visibly angry John Wright storms into match referee Ranjan Madugalle's room to register an official protest. The players wonder why umpires are not dropped on account of poor performance, as they are. Most are convinced that Bucknor *bahut kharab hai*, he doesn't want India to win. This sentiment is reinforced when Kumble is given out stumped. But there is nothing to be done because poor decisions, as they say, are part of the game. When Inzamam hears about it, his reaction is: *Arre, just play cricket yaar!*

Parthiv Patel is fined 60 per cent of his match fee for uttering an audible obscenity ('fucking hell!') after a caught behind decision is disallowed. But the players are more amused than angry, they declare (in villainous Ajit-style) that Parthiv is a naughty 'boooy' who has to be disciplined. Despite the bad day at office, the team is in a happy space. John announces early pack up and orders a pool session at the hotel.

The next day, the Pakistan tail wags to stretch the lead beyond 200 and the match seems lost. Sachin gets an iffy lbw decision, Laxman is bowled by a beauty from Umar Gul and Dravid is run out in Inzamam style — short of the crease when he doesn't dive to save himself. A defiant Sehwag keeps hope alive and Ramiz Raja can't stop praising him.

The beauty about Sehwag, he says, is that he isn't bothered about looking beautiful, about keeping elbow up or head down. All that matters is where the ball has gone. Sehwag's great quality is that he likes to keep things simple. Batting is about making runs. Dilip Vengsarkar, like Ramiz, is a Sehwag fan. He says Sehwag's square cut is as good as (Gundappa Viswanath) Vishy's.

At lunch, Pakistan needs just 30 to win. Dravid asks the players to maintain intensity and not give Pakistan extra confidence. Entering the field, he repeats the message in a loud voice: *Body language, boys, body language.*

Pakistan wins comfortably by nine wickets, with hundreds from the dependable Inzamam and the hugely talented Imran Farhat. Earlier, Sehwag blazed to 90 and Yuvraj (standing in for Dada) made 112, his first Test century.

After the game I ask Dravid to pick four players to go to Lahore University Management Studies (LUMS) to interact with the students. *Spare me, boss*, Dravid laughs. *I have made decisions that have backfired these last two weeks — first Multan and then batting first at Lahore to lose four wickets before lunch. No more decisions now. I will only do what others tell me.*

Dravid is being flippant, but handling stress is an important part of competitive sport. Even the sturdiest wall can develop a crack under pressure.

On the last day of the game, Dada returns after a week in India. He looks fit, rested and refreshed. He trains in the gym in his easygoing manner and has a hit in the nets to get back into the groove.

Meeting Students at Lahore University

On an invitation from Amber Rehman, president of the LUMS Culture Society, I accompany Dravid, Irfan, Agarkar and Balaji for an 'apolitical cross cultural interactive exchange' with students. As we arrive at the impressive building and walk up to the auditorium on the first floor, a surprise awaits us.

The place is packed to capacity, with students sitting in the aisles and standing at the back. When we are ushered in, the hall breaks into shouts of

Balaji Balaji, not dissimilar to the *Sachin Sachin* chant at Indian grounds. Hearing this noisy reception, you'd imagine Balaji was a rockstar or the Big B himself, the reigning king of Hindi cinema.

The Balaji cult started when General Musharraf praised him for his fighting qualities in an ODI which India lost. Musharraf saw a soldier in Balaji and fans connected with this handsome young dude with a dazzling smile. In Pakistan, Balaji is cool—and hot.

The LUMS students, representing the modern face of Pakistan, are welcoming and extremely understanding. They listen to Dravid with respect, go crazy when Balaji smiles and present an altogether different side when Irfan speaks.

Irfan is navigating the questions about cricket and the experience of touring Pakistan when, suddenly, one student stands up to lob a live grenade about Hindu–Muslim relations. Even as Irfan gathers his thoughts, others in the auditorium gave the mischief-maker a fitting reply. He is shouted down and evicted from the hall.

Asides

- LUMS students on why Balaji is such a hit: *He has the X factor.*
- Balaji's epic comment about his cult status in Pakistan: *It is ok, but who will recognise me in Chennai?*

The team has dinner at Lahore's famous Asif Jah Haveli, a red-brick building deep inside the walled city, near Masti Gate, Chuna Mandi. Built by Nur Jahan's brother, the haveli has a great ambience with Radha-Krishna frescoes and majestic architecture. Traditional Mughlai cuisine is followed by Sufi qawwalis sung by a group from Karachi. We learned that Cooco's Den, in Heeramandi, is another popular eating place because of the majestic view of the Badshahi mosque, and the unique experience of food (cooked on the ground floor) pulled up in rope baskets to be served on the rooftop.

Aside

- Miandad on coaching: *Cricket is played with bat and ball, not computers and books. Test cricket is not a training school or a classroom. Players must come ready to perform.*

The Difference Between Bats

- Sachin's bat: Weighs 2 pounds and 10–11 ounces and has narrow grains. It is thick at the bottom and has a stiff handle with no spring to prevent give. Sachin likes to knock the willow with his knuckles to check the sound.
- Dravid's bat: Light, weighs 2.8 pounds. It has a thin blade and a thin handle for a better grip.
- Sourav's bat: Wide blade, flat at the bottom, not rounded. It has different coloured multiple grips extending a few inches beyond the top. Sourav uses bats according to the pitch and match situation.

Most players deny this, but they track statistics and keep a close eye on averages and strike rates. Their recall is sharp and they remember seemingly minor details with astonishing clarity.

Equally impressive is their ability to look at old pictures and place them for date and place. Dada takes one look at an old photo, which shows him square-cutting a ball, and recognises that it is Brisbane because of the coloured seats in the background. Another photo of him playing an elegant cover drive in England is identified by the shirt he is wearing. Sachin's memory is even sharper: Given a bunch of photos to identify, he is on the ball, literally, each time.

The Final Test, Rawalpindi

On the day before the last Test, the players are looking forward to returning home after a tense tour. Sachin wants to fly back directly from Rawalpindi after day 5. Sehwag, too, is in a hurry to get back because of his impending wedding.

At the team meeting before the game, Dada asks players to stay switched on because there is lots to play for and it's critical to finish the tour on a high. Sachin, like Dada, puts the Test in perspective, saying that this is the most important game of his career because there is nothing bigger than winning against Pakistan. Sehwag announces that he will bat at number two and not face the first ball.

John plays a tape of the team celebrating after Multan and tells the players that they have another opportunity to create magic. He then challenges each player, setting individual goals:

Dada:	*You have to get back to Tests.*
Sachin:	*The greatest batsman in the world must make this one count.*
Sehwag:	*The last two games are gone, forget what happened.*
Dravid:	*Make up for missing out in the series.*
VVS:	*You won us the ODI final, let's see you do it in a Test.*
Yuvi:	*Two hundreds in two Tests would be great.*

Match Day

Watching Pakistan playing football during warm-up, John Wright shakes his head in disapproval. *This is crazy,* he says, *players can get injured. Also, all of them are wearing similar shirts — how do they know who is in which team?*

Departing from the set routine, Dada chooses to field on winning the toss but feels uneasy about the decision. A firm believer in the 'putting runs on the board' theory, he prefers batting first, but this time he has been persuaded otherwise.

The scene on the morning before play: Dravid, all concentration, focuses on his pre-game routine, VVS is ready for battle, and a surprisingly relaxed Dada is sipping tea. Sachin takes high catches in the middle. When I enquire if he remembers dropping skiers in the deep, he replies, *Bahut chhode hain par bolo mat, kahin aaj ho jaye.*

The first session (two-and-a-half hours to accommodate the mid-afternoon break for Friday prayers) is a nightmare, with sloppy ground fielding and dropped catches. During the break Sachin recalls our chat about fielding and has a good laugh. *Cricket mein kuchh nahin pata.* He dropped one today at point, a fielding position he isn't familiar with.

A furious John gives the players hell for low intensity and horrible body language. His sharpest rebuke: *It appears you guys are already in Delhi.*

VVS Laxman

If Dravid is model pro number one, VVS occupies a slot close to him. He is from the same school — self-driven, on automatic mode, always striving to improve.

On off days, when others are catching up on sleep, he is in the gym doing weights or working the cycle. When the coach announces optional practice, he knows VVS will surely turn up. When batsmen return to the dressing room after a session, VVS is the first to offer them drinks. He gets autographs signed on bats and team sheets, motivates the fielders during play and leads the batting group to sort out strategy.

It's not just cricket where he presents a straight bat—VVS is the sincere, earnest, dependable guy in the group. A mature adult among excitable youngsters, he is immensely respected for his dignified conduct. Always positive, ever willing to help others.

He is also very, very fussy about his clothes and appearance. A god-fearing man, a firm believer in traditional values, cricket is almost saadhna to VVS. He loves playing in England but finds county cricket too demanding and prefers club cricket with its easier pace. On this tour, VVS is frustrated that he hasn't made big scores. When the media want to interview him, he refuses politely: *Pehle mujhe kuchh karne do.*

Irfan Pathan

Though only 19, Irfan is a cricket veteran with 100 first-class wickets who has been on the international circuit with junior Indian teams for years. Irfan, like VVS, is a pleasant person and a hardworking professional with a wonderful work ethic, always keen to learn. *Bahut mehnat karni hai,* he says after a rigorous gym session.

Dravid is his role model and, like him, Irfan respects the history and traditions of the game. *Yeh game kisi ke liye nahin rukta,* he says and recalls a visit to Lord's when, after checking that no one was looking, he picked a blade of grass and put it in his blazer pocket.

Asides

- Name given to Kaif: Bhai sa'ab.
- Most popular expression: *Koi masla nahin.*
- Little-known facts: Kumble and Sachin were ball boys during the 1987 World Cup. Parthiv Patel is yet to play Ranji.

The Rawalpindi Test

Dravid makes it count, scoring a big double hundred—extracting runs through strong technique and a steely will. He bats for two days with monumental concentration to score 270, the second highest score ever by an Indian abroad. When dismissed, Inzamam runs (in itself no mean feat) from mid-wicket to shake his hand.

It's fashionable to talk of processes and preparation and trusting routine, but Dravid practises this philosophy—he is a high-quality machine equipped with AI who has broken down batting into small parts to understand it better. Training is one part, match day execution quite another, and Dravid leaves very little to chance. He is fussy about his kit and pays special attention to what and when he eats and how much he drinks. Given Dravid's history of cramping due to loss of fluids, the support staff carefully monitor his hydration levels during breaks.

PLAYERS DRESSING ROOM & MATCH OFFICIAL AREA

Pakistan Vs India

PLAYER

Name: Rahul Dravid

Issuing Authority

In the dressing room, teammates applaud his innings. Dravid is universally liked and is everyone's favourite. Irfan is the happiest of the lot as he remembers Dravid telling him at LUMS before the Test that he was *due a big one. Kya khiladi hai*, he says, *main to fida ho gaya.*

Sidelights

- Dravid's *tashan* during the epic Lahore innings: Didn't shave for two days.
- Dravid's recovery plan after three days in the field: Ice bath for 3–4 minutes followed by a hot shower (for contracting and loosening muscles) and a pool session. Plenty of Gatorade to replenish body fluids and prevent dehydration.

Dada, padded up, is edgy waiting for his turn. When he finally goes in (his first hit since 24 March), he flows elegantly to 77 before getting lazily run out. He is miserable about missing out on a hundred but relieved that he had a decent hit. On the massage table, with the physio rubbing his back, he says batting is the best part of cricket. The rest he does, he admits frankly, because he has to. *Nahin to doosre maar denge.*

There is a discussion about declaring the Indian innings an hour after tea because John and Dada want to bowl 15 overs. Players insist that Balaji be given a chance to have a go with the bat—which he does in splendid style. One monster hit clearing mid-wicket leads to loud celebrations in the dressing room. Eventually India crosses 600, leaving a 'leg and leg' Pakistan a big mountain to climb.

Dinner with Imran

When the players reach Imran's house for dinner, the host greets them warmly, singling out Dravid, the hero of the Rawalpindi match. *He is my favourite player*, declares Khan sa'ab, speaking with an authority you wouldn't want to question. Dravid's innings was about the art of batting that others have forgotten, he says. To Inzamam, another favourite, Imran offers condolences. *Yeh hota hai Test mein — kabhi nothing goes right in a game.*

The evening, however, is just right. Great ambience, outdoor seating in the lawn, soft shehnai playing in the background. Imran and his wife Jemima play gracious hosts to the smallish guest list. No pushy kids scrambling for autographs. No requests for photo-*shoto*. As it is a private event and not an official function, the players have been released from the tour dress code. Dada has chosen to don a fashionable brown jacket. Sachin wears trendy black.

Both Indian and Pakistani players chat and joke without any trace of tension. But when Shoaib gives a detailed account of his physical condition — wrenched wrist, left rib strain which could put him out for 2–3 months — Dravid hears him out with a doubtful smirk and remarks, *With him one must discount the drama. Don't we know him?*

Aside

- Sidhu's comment on Sachin being the centre of attention at Imran's dinner: *People crowd around him like shehad par makhi.*

The UNICEF Anti-Polio/AIDS Programme

The Indian and Pakistani teams collaborate on a UNICEF initiative to fight polio and AIDS. Sachin, UNICEF's brand ambassador, makes a moving speech about players uniting to fight a bigger cause. The federal health minister says the same thing but takes 20 minutes more to do so. He profusely thanks General Musharraf, Prime Minister Vajpayee and Sachin for the campaign to 'bowl out polio' and 'prevent it from scoring any runs'.

All good stuff, but the minister's factually inaccurate reference to Sachin ('captain of India') greatly embarrasses the master. *I think you are mistaken*, he interrupts the minister after a while. *I captained the side only for two overs when Dada left the field.*

Inzamam pledges support to the noble cause but expresses a minor crib: *Do din ki fielding ke baad bhi rest nahin karne dete.*

A Historic Win

India wins by an innings and 131 runs—the first series win in Pakistan, a moment to cherish, savour and celebrate.

The arrival of six bottles of champagne (courtesy High Commissioner Shiv Shankar Menon) sparks a dressing-room debate: Is it appropriate to celebrate at the ground, or should the *jashan* shift to the hotel? After a mini team meeting, consensus is reached following a strong intervention by Dada: *We don't win abroad too often. Let's celebrate here.*

At the end of the game, it is Holi in the dressing room with players spraying champagne on each other and depositing most of it on the floor. No pretence of even trying to drink the expensive stuff. The mood is of joy and *josh*, so different from the tense situation in Multan not long back. The team is united, the players respect each other, and any misunderstandings or differences are a thing of the past.

At the prize distribution ceremony, Dada is detached and distant. He says he was disappointed to have to go home after Multan and wanted to return quickly. The Calcutta doctor wasn't of much help. Dada played the Rawalpindi game after taking painkillers.

The celebrations in the hotel continue late into the afternoon. Emotional speeches are made, Sachin holds centre stage to congratulate the team for correcting the impression that they were tigers only at home. Striking a personal note, he expresses satisfaction at the win because his own cricket journey started in Pakistan.

Kumble, the elder statesman, applauds youngsters Balaji and Irfan and wishes them many more victories overseas. *You are lucky*, he says, *compared to us seniors who waited so long for anything like this.*

John praises the collective effort of the boys and has a special word for those who didn't play (Murali, Kaif and Powar) but contributed to the team effort. *The win is your achievement*, he says. *The coach is only a vehicle to take players to a destination.* Dada thanks the team and declares that this is the happiest day of his life. He thanks Dravid for the Multan win which set up the series.

The day winds down with dinner at Hotspot, the popular restaurant owned by Shahryar Khan's son, where John, of all people, recommends everyone try the Mississippi Mud Pie, the mouth-watering dessert with at least a million calories in each spoonful.

More on Fitness

Andrew Leipus and Greg King worked behind the scenes to ensure the players were fit and took the field in the best physical shape. Their task was far from easy given the history of injuries and niggles.

Sample the list: Laxman (knee), Agarkar (calf), Kumble (shoulder), Dravid (knees), Yuvi (shoulder, knee), Zaheer (right hamstring and much more), Sachin (left ankle).

Add to this the challenges posed by the sapping heat and humidity of Pakistan. The players wore cooling vests in the dressing room—a useful recovery tool because it contained gel that helped lower body temperature. During play, they used the Arctic Cool Collar around their necks for short durations.

The players were monitored closely for dehydration, especially Sachin and Dravid, who had a history of cramping. Their urine samples were checked using a spectrometer during breaks. A reading of 10 was considered normal but anything near 30 indicated a severe shortage of essential fluids. Left unmanaged, this could impair concentration, affect eye judgement and cause severe fatigue, thus impacting performance.

Andrew felt that the fitness culture was well established in the team, with players embracing scientific training to enhance performance. The change was evident; the players had regular gym-pool sessions and knew what to do to stay in good physical shape.

The Master and the Blaster

Sachin and Sehwag share a special bond: Sachin admires Sehwag's talent, his self-belief and fearless attitude. Sehwag admires everything about Sachin, the 'God of cricket'.

In Lahore, Sachin gave Sehwag a lesson in opening a champagne bottle, giving instructions as a coach would to a newbie wanting to learn how to hold a bat. *Learn this now that you are getting married*, says master Sachin to student Sehwag. *Remove the wrapper, hold the bottle in your left hand and turn the screw exactly six times. Then shake the bottle and pop the cork with the right thumb with your other hand on top to prevent it from flying off and hurting someone.*

Sehwag catches every word hungrily, looking a bit puzzled—a confused student getting a difficult maths tuition. Sachin also teaches him how to check crystal for quality by knocking on the wine glass with his index finger. A sharp, distinct sound indicates purity.

And It's a Wrap

In the end, to use a cliché, it was a historic tour. India beat Pakistan in the Tests and the one-dayers. The standout memories from the tour are: Kaif's stunning catch at Karachi, Sehwag's triple hundred, the controversial declaration in Multan and Dravid's monumental innings in Rawalpindi.

Initially, the players were apprehensive of their reception in Pakistan and concerned about security. But these concerns vanished quickly and the tour was proof that sport can ease tension, heal wounds and create goodwill. At every stage in Pakistan, for the players and the visiting fans, there was nothing but warmth, goodwill and *dosti*.

Shopkeepers in Gulbarga and Lahore gave discounts to *hamare mehmaan* from Hindustan. At the Gaddafi Stadium, students from Delhi were surprised when a Pakistani family sitting next to them offered to wave the *tiranga* because *aap thak gaye honge*. Another visitor, looking for refreshments, was escorted to the parking lot where chilled beer cans were pulled out from a car's boot.

My own experience confirmed this sense of brotherhood. In Multan, a restaurant owner politely informed me they would only serve chicken because meat was not served on Tuesdays. Another time, in Lahore, when I asked for the bill, the waiter pointed to a guest sitting in the far corner— who I did not know—and said it was already settled. In Rawalpindi, in a crowded hotel gym, I was waiting to use the treadmill when others insisted I jump the queue.

Sehwag Trivia

- Best shot: Slashed square cut. Safe because edge will go over slip and, if well-connected, will beat the point fielder.
- Pull shot: Too risky with fast bowlers, can get hit if you miss the line. Why take *faltu panga* when it's possible to play other shots?

- Slowest innings: 30 runs in one session in a county game. *Aage* beat, *peeche* pad *par*. Just could not connect.
- Tuesday *tashan*: Does not shave. Keeps a fast for Bajrang Bali. Turns vegetarian for the day.
- Admires: Sachin for technique. Dravid for patience. VVS for timing.

The high-profile series was a challenge for the PCB but they handled the tour with remarkable competence. PCB President Shahryar Khan (even more laidback than his cousin Tiger Pataudi) was assisted by the super-efficient Asad Mustafa Subhan Ahmad and Sami Burney, the media head who went out of his way to ensure all went well.

Through it all, CEO Ramiz Raja remained in the background, making sure that all the pieces were in place. It was a tribute to his multitasking skills that he could, in the middle of a busy tour, find time to also fulfil his television commentary commitments.

Of course, not everything was smooth and occasionally, the cracks surfaced. When BCCI officials and Indian guests arrived in Lahore towards the end of the tour, hotel rooms were in short supply. My requests to the PCB for assistance proved fruitless, and on making enquiries, I found out why—hotels were unwilling to extend credit to the PCB and said they'd release rooms only if full payment was made in advance.

Sachin Trivia

- Special batting sessions: Sachin had plastic balls chucked at him from 10 yards to practise against short bowling. The plastic balls bounced high and swung, and he ducked to get out of the way.
- Unusual sight: Sachin going around the dressing room getting a miniature bat signed for Moin Khan.
- Miandad gave Sachin a picture taken earlier, when he had presented his book to him. Signed: Best wishes, Secheen! Sachin accepted the gift, noticed his misspelt name and said with a smile, *I will keep this*.
- Pakistan's all-time great, Fazal Mehmood, dropped in to chat with Sachin. Hanif Mohammad, another legend, presented his book to Sachin.

When the tour ended, there was a rush to return, with visitors from India wanting to get on the special Air India flight from Lahore. Under an agreement with the airline, I had the authority to release extra seats (after accommodating players, BCCI officials and guests) on the flight. There was pressure for bookings but commentators Sanjay Manjrekar and Navjot Sidhu were put on the flight. Then Sidhu called at the last minute to inform us about a change. *I have been told to contest the Lok Sabha elections*, he said, *and file my nomination in Amritsar. So, I will go by road through Wagah.*

Looking back, my final thoughts on the memorable tour are about the Indian team and its mature leadership group. The senior players were not just professional athletes but sensible adults who understood their responsibilities, conducted themselves with dignity and wore the India colours with pride.

Imran noticed this and said India was a better side due to the 'intellectual capacity' of its players. A valid observation because, had the Multan declaration happened on the Pakistan side, with one batsman just short of 200, the dressing room would probably have become a war zone and the police called in to quell the riot.

The Indian team handled the tricky situation with maturity and understanding. Sachin and Dravid met behind closed doors to have a chat to sort things out. And the team moved on, unscarred by the controversy.

Some Years Later: Mumbai, 2015

In 2015, PCB's interim president, Najam Sethi, and former chief, Shahryar Khan, arrived in Mumbai to discuss the resumption of cricket ties with the BCCI. They weren't exactly close friends but renewing cricket with India was a priority for both.

That morning, Shashank Manohar (president, BCCI) Dr M.V. Sridhar (general manager—operations, BCCI) and I (general manager—coordination, BCCI) had breakfast at Mumbai's Trident hotel and left for the office after reminding Shahryar sa'ab about the 11 a.m. meeting at Cricket Centre, Wankhede Stadium.

For us, it was another busy day at work. Whenever Shashank, who was based in Nagpur, came to Mumbai, several meetings were crammed into the daily schedule. The Pakistani delegation's visit was one more important appointment in the diary.

Unlike weather bulletins that warn of approaching cyclones, we had no prior intimation of the storm that was about to hit the BCCI. Within minutes of reaching the office, as if on cue, there was a loud commotion and an excited mob invaded the BCCI headquarters. Quickly past the solitary security guard at the reception, people ran up the steps to barge into the president's second-floor office.

Emerging from my office (next door to the president's) I saw 20-odd persons surrounding Shashank, shouting slogans denouncing Pakistan and holding placards opposing any cricket contact with them. Seeing this, I called Shahryar sa'ab and advised him to stay put at the hotel.

Shashank sat through the gadar with extraordinary calm, realising the mayhem was about Pakistan, not him or the BCCI. He sensed this was not a spontaneous protest by an incensed fringe group but a carefully choreographed publicity event executed with precision and planning. The protesters were accompanied by reporters and displayed admirable presence of mind by screaming their protests looking directly into television cameras. Within minutes 'BCCI under attack' was breaking news on television channels.

With their job done, the protesters retreated. The *tamasha* lasted not more than 20 minutes. In true Hindi film style, the police arrived after the mob had left. They assured protection to the Pakistani delegation and promised the meeting would be held without any disturbance.

The meeting never happened. The BCCI decided not to engage with Pakistan in this charged atmosphere and the day passed without the two boards sitting across the table. The rebuffed PCB members remained at the Trident, waiting for word from the BCCI, but there was no call all day.

8

IPL: SEASON ONE

In late 2007, Lalit Modi called over some of his friends and family for what film folk would call a narration. To them he rolled out a seductive dream, the story of a made-for-television cricket tournament spiced with Bollywood masala. The Indian Premier League (IPL)—twenty-over cricket matches played by the best in the business for privately owned teams—promised quality cricket, exciting entertainment and, importantly, loads of cash.

For the 'target audience' that had come over at his invitation, Lalit offered a deal that was too good to miss out on. Everyone present there knew that cricket couldn't go wrong in India, such was its appeal. Yet, there were doubts because cricket had never before partnered with private enterprise. Lalit's experiment would take them into uncharted territory, a leap in the dark that made many apprehensive.

Sceptics asked awkward questions but Lalit was ready with the answers. Would world-class players show up for India's domestic tournament? Lalit told everyone they had already agreed. Would broadcasters pay top dollar for media rights? Lalit pulled out a signed contract to confirm the deal. Would private ownership work? Lalit presented the BCCI's approval.

With all their doubts cleared, the group exchanged high-fives and warm hugs. To support Lalit's idea, which was still only on paper, they collectively put US$ 723.59 million on the table.

The business model of the IPL broke the mould. This was cricket's first-ever handshake with private investment which resulted in actual ownership, not just sponsorship. Bruised from an earlier botched attempt in the mid-1990s when a similar proposal was struck down by the BCCI, Lalit knew that private investment had to sit with official sanction. That cricket couldn't survive without the approval of its governing body had been proved by Packer's push in Australia and the collapse of Subhash Chandra's renegade Indian Cricket League (ICL).

With the IPL owned and operated by the BCCI, the private sector got skin in the game. This wasn't the government exiting a failed business or offloading stake in a broke Public Sector Undertaking (PSU). Rather, it was a case of visionary economic *bhagidari* for generating wealth.

It was a game-changing moment for the BCCI. By creating a commercial vertical (while retaining its monopoly control), it gifted corporate India access to Indian cricket's dressing room. Team owners were assured of positive returns by creating an artificial scarcity, the number of teams limited to ten to ensure demand always outstripped supply, thus translating into a rise in value. Also, the side benefits of owning an IPL team (social status, image-building and networking) were good for business and priceless for bragging rights.

The IPL aligned this philosophy to a creative business model which ensured the BCCI was a guaranteed winner with assured revenue from media rights, central sponsorships and franchise fees. The BCCI de-risked itself financially and deflected potential danger to the teams.

Starting Up with the Delhi Daredevils and GMR

After a quick get-to-know-each-other process, I was hired as head of operations of the Delhi Daredevils (DD) by the GMR group. Apparently, GMR had heard about me from people in cricket's ecosystem and I presume my 20-year association with the BCCI and familiarity with Delhi cricket worked in my favour. Strangely, I didn't know anything about GMR despite their presence in Delhi as the operators of the new international airport.

GMR, like other team owners, had good reason to invest in cricket. Despite its substantial presence in Andhra Pradesh, the company was largely unknown in Delhi. The IPL, therefore, was the right instrument, the best entry strategy to make a splash and get noticed. Cricket would guarantee mileage, build their brand, open the right bureaucratic doors—and also make money.

The IPL was a fresh start for both GMR and me. I resigned from my secure government job of 28 years to start a new innings with new challenges in the corporate world. This was cricket and commerce in equal parts and I knew that the balance sheet was as vital as the score book.

Getting Ready

In the first year of the IPL, it was a mad scramble to get things rolling and the teams literally hit the pitch running. It was like the umpires had gone in and the opening batsmen were still scurrying to put their pads on. Everything moved in fast-forward mode because a million things had to be sorted before play could begin.

One problem was the absence of a precedent that would help navigate this journey. The IPL was an unknown beast without a previous reference point—no different from a *teen patti* game played blind. More error than trial, more miss than hit.

On the commercial side, there were many questions: Would people buy tickets to watch seven games in six weeks, that too in peak summer? How could one fix ticket rates for a 4 p.m. game for the East Stand which was exposed to direct sunlight? Should there be a concession for students, a separate enclosure for women, a premium on tickets for the popular weekend night games? Would the status-conscious Delhi elite pay ₹20,000 for sitting next to the players' dressing room? Should we charge extra for the KKR game by spreading the rumour that Shah Rukh Khan would turn up to wave to his loyal subjects? What would happen to ticket sales if DD lost three games in a row? There were many questions but very few answers.

The teams had to find sponsors but selling assets was a classic case of 'a swing and a miss'. Nobody knew what the main property (logo across the chest) on the team jersey was worth. There were no media tracking agencies to suggest whether the value was ₹10 crore or ₹20 crore or somewhere in between. HERO paid Delhi ₹18 crore for each of the first three years—the highest figure in the IPL—but neither they nor DD knew if that was the correct number. We found out later that the GMR–DD sponsorship deal was the highest in the IPL. HERO found out—and were horrified—that they had overpaid for the asset.

All commercial issues were discussed in boardrooms (with impressive PowerPoint presentations and complicated spreadsheets) and in the DDCA

IPL match, Delhi

with Arun Jaitley, the president, giving his inputs over sugary tea and oily pakoras. In the end, it boiled down to one person's opinion against the other's gut feeling. Most decisions were based on guesswork, goli and gyaan.

Putting things together was particularly challenging because nothing in Delhi is easy. It is a city with a flourishing VIP culture where everyone is a heavyweight ready to throw their weight around. Delhi is about power and entitlement; it is about government regulations and people who must be 'obliged'. Holding a commercial cricket tournament in such an environment tested the notion of the ease of doing business.

Also, working with the DDCA wasn't easy. It had a well-earned reputation as a divided house constantly in a state of civil war and internal insurgency. The silver lining in the otherwise dark scenario was Arun Jaitley, the one-man DRS (dispute resolution system) who, whenever there was a disagreement, heard your appeal for relief and fair play and passed a nuanced judgement.

Jaitley's intervention was needed often because the IPL disturbed the power equation within state associations. During the IPL, control of stadium facilities shifted from association officials to team owners, a change resented by the local cricket dons because it meant the tenants were calling the shots instead of the landlords.

That the IPL demanded 'world-class' standards and a good 'fan experience' on the ground was another reason for franchise teams to sweat. The IPL small print included designer invites, a consistent 'look and feel', and fine dining with customised crockery and branded napkins. The league was positioned as the big fat Indian wedding: grand in scale, full of glitter and glamour, noisy and garish. The IPL matches were pitched as events, a concept that was very different from the ordinary BCCI games where it was enough to mark the wicket and get 22 players on the ground.

The Kotla infrastructure was not even remotely world-class. The ground didn't have floodlights or essential facilities for spectators. The Delhi Daredevils hired a cleaning agency a month before Kotla's first IPL match in 2008 to get the stadium spruced up in time. We discovered, not to our surprise, that there were parts of the ground that had not met a brush or a bottle of cleaning liquid for years.'

Securing permissions to stage the event was also sheer torture. Several government agencies had to be satisfied (police, entertainment tax, electricity and water, fire, disaster management) and getting the paperwork done eventually boiled down to delicate negotiations over free tickets and passes. In Delhi, managing the distribution of freebies is a highly valued skill.

From an operations standpoint, besides the standard drill, one had to be mindful of the anti-dew treatment before an 8 a.m. game and fogging the playing area to keep mosquitos away. Generators had to be hired to guard against power failure and security guards were hired to guard the generators and prevent sabotage.

The Delhi Police deployed almost 2,000 personnel for overall security, background checks of people and sanitising the stadium. On match days, sniffer dogs checked the premises and scanners, metal detectors and CCTVs were installed at strategic points. Security was strict to the point where spectators were not allowed to bring pens or coins into the stadium.

Despite frantic efforts to tie up all the loose ends we came close to breaking point on many occasions. The accreditation system collapsed just before the first home game, leading to extreme panic because, without proper IDs, the police refused to allow players, umpires and the ground staff in. When the ticket box office opened at Dr Ambedkar Stadium, the rush was such that the police had to be called to restore order. Some scalpers were arrested for selling tickets in 'black', a development which led to an investigation to determine whether franchise insiders were involved.

Imagine also the horror when we were left with unsold tickets for lower-end seats for some games. As empty stands look bad on television, schoolchildren were bussed into the stadium and given free drinks.

The chaos in the exclusive hospitality areas was even more troubling. The high-end corporate boxes were marketed as a khaana-peena-daaru deal that promised five-star catering and premium liquor. The strategy worked. However, an unexpected snag developed when hordes of gatecrashers invaded the hospitality boxes. Security broke down, drunken brawls took place and the Delhi Police registered a case of public disorder, unruly behaviour and hooliganism. A concerned senior officer gave me friendly advice: *Free daaru ko roko. Yeh Dilli culture mein nahi chalta.*

Arun Jaitley supported the liquor ban for a similar reason. During the matches, his box was full of uninvited guests who raided the food counter and polished off the drinks. Unable to control this, he switched to a strict 'no alcohol, only soft drinks' policy in his box. This worked: the number of gate crashers dropped and order was restored.

By the end of the first IPL season four FIRs had been filed against me, the Daredevils' chief operating officer, for black marketing of tickets, overcharging for food items in the stadium, betting on games, and for the 'indecent behaviour' of cheerleaders.

Lesson learnt about the golden rule for successful match-day operations: It doesn't matter which big shot you have on speed dial in Delhi, just ensure that two key people are on your side—the local SHO and the entertainment tax officer. Without these two in your corner it is not possible to organise matches in Delhi.

Auction Time

If 2008 was operationally a mixed bag for DD, so was the cricket.

GMR secured the rights to operate the Delhi franchise in perpetuity by writing a cheque for US$ 84 million. The process of finding eight team owners was an open auction with interested parties submitting financial bids. However, Lalit Modi did the backroom work and pushed the right buttons to ensure that the right people got the right teams. The IPL team auction attracted ten bids, two of which were rejected on technical grounds. With eight valid bids for eight cities, it was easy to decide who got what.

Having bagged Delhi, GMR's first challenge was to put the playing squad together. T.A. Sekar and Aashish Kapoor, former India players, consulted Dennis Lillee. He recommended Greg Shipperd (Shippy), the highly respected T20 coach of Victoria. Shippy recruited DD's support staff, including bowling coach David Sekar and video analyst Trent Woodhill.

DD's playing squad was stitched together by Sekar and Aashish. The IPL allotted Sehwag to DD as its 'icon' player and 'uncapped' domestic players (Shikhar Dhawan, Amit Mishra, Rajat Bhatia, Mithun Manhas) were signed up to form the core of the team ahead of the auction.

The remaining players had to be purchased in the mega auction where each team had a US$ 5 million player purse. Identifying the right players was tricky because nobody was familiar with the dynamics of bidding, nor was data available on the T20 skills of players.

Sekar recalls that the players were picked on hope, instinct and reputation. We wanted Delhi players and so we went big for Gautam Gambhir. We wanted Indian talent, so we went for Dinesh Karthik and Manoj Tiwary. We wanted multi-skilled players, so we went for Shoaib Malik (specialist all-rounder), A.B. de Villiers (who could keep wickets) and Tillakaratne Dilshan (who could bat up the order and also play lower down).

DD built a formidable squad with good Indian players and impressive foreign talent, notably Pakistan's Mohammad Asif (a crafty exponent of seam and swing), Glenn McGrath, Daniel Vettori and all-rounder Farveez Maharoof. Interestingly, Sekar and Aashish kept the coach out of the auction. Shippy was consulted on team composition based on skill sets but not on individual players to fill the slots.

According to Aashish, the teams faced a problem because the IPL allowed non-capped players ('anyone who hadn't played for his country in the last three years') to be signed outside the auction. Their wages were not offset against the US$ 5 million purse. This led to a mad scramble with teams approaching players with all kinds of offers. In the crazy rush, DD approached Ashish Nehra and Praveen Kumar but lost out because they got calls from the 'high command' of other teams.

As it happened, DD's on-field performance was satisfactory, not spectacular. Sehwag, Gambhir and Shikhar made runs. Yo Mahesh and Maharoof were the top wicket takers. McGrath struggled on the slow Kotla track and de Villiers couldn't keep his place after a few games. With seven wins from 14 games, DD made the knockouts by the skin of their teeth. They sneaked in because the Mumbai Indians lost a close game to the Rajasthan Royals (RR) when a win would have taken them past Delhi.

But luck deserted DD in the semi-final at the Wankhede Stadium. Put in on a wicket that had plenty for the bowlers, RR got 192 with contributions from Shane Watson at the top and Yusuf Pathan at the back end. DD was never in the game and collapsed in a heap—all out for 87 in 16.1 overs, thrashed by 105 runs.

Rebuilding the Team

The DD squad needed urgent 'denting and painting' after season one, more so as the Pakistani players were banished from the IPL following an informal nudge from the Indian government. This meant DD would lose Shoaib Malik and Mohammad Asif. Also, captain Sehwag wanted more firepower in bowling, an express 140 kmph bowler. The search for this ended with Dirk Nannes of Victoria, Australia, a skier and adventurer who was creating waves in the Sheffield Shield.

The First Year of DD

Failing to make the IPL final was not the only setback for DD. Its ordinary off-field performance was the other crushing disappointment. The first-year financial results were a shocker. DD took a severe hit and the balance sheet was a disastrous red, mainly due to reckless marketing and promotional expenses to create brand awareness.

DD wasn't alone in suffering big losses; the other teams too were bleeding. After the first year, franchise teams realised that the IPL wasn't the money-spinning dream that Lalit Modi had sold to them. A strict fact check exposed his rosy numbers as unrealistic and it dawned on the teams that it would take the league some time to turn the commercial corner. They also learnt that the IPL was a valuation, not a balance sheet game and sustained investment was required to build the brand. There was light at the end of the multimillion-dollar investment tunnel, but the journey was going to be long and hard.

A chance remark by Ness Wadia, co-owner of Kings XI Punjab, summed up the general sentiment: *We thought, given our business background, that if you take the right steps, you achieve the desired objective. But sport does not work to plan. You can do all the right things and still have wrong results.*

In this gloom, the one bright spot was that the fans kept faith and ticket revenue was independent of the Delhi Daredevils' performance. In most leagues fan loyalty depends on match results, and poor team performance depresses ticket sales. Delhi faced no such threat and, in a twisted way, the absence of team loyalty became an asset instead of a disadvantage. It didn't matter whether Delhi won or lost; tickets got sold regardless. This confirmed that T20 cricket and Sehwag were more loved than the Daredevils.

But the overall financial *jhatka* did have repercussions and the internal season-end debrief was a tense affair. When the top brass of GMR assembled in the Bannerghatta office in Bengaluru to make sense of what had gone wrong, searching questions were asked. The answers offered precedents from other leagues to explain the loss. The owners were informed that the IPL was a start-up and it would take time for the business to stabilise.

Contrary to our deepest fears, the review ended on a surprisingly positive note with DD's board members showing the understanding that sport, especially cricket, is unpredictable and there is no guarantee of success. This was a relief because other team owners, when denied the financial lottery they had hoped for, read out the riot act.

A lasting memory from the meeting is of Group Chairman G.M. Rao expressing faith in the new business venture. His son-in-law, S. Bommidala, captain of DD's cricket business, was a progressive leader who refrained from direct interference in routine matters. Yet, on policy matters he was pragmatic, decisive and very much on the ball. Classic advice from him: (1) Be financially prudent, but remember that cheap is expensive. (2) Be open and transparent in business, but not naked.

The first year's substantial financial hit caused concern and the negative balance sheet triggered a serious discussion on risk-mitigating strategies. Austerity was the new buzzword and the clear policy directive was: cut flab, go on a strict diet.

During the get-fit discussion, one radical but impractical option was casually floated by a senior finance person. His point was that when a team wins, commercial success and profit are guaranteed. But winning is not in anyone's control—cost is. So, just focus on depressing expense (by reducing player salaries, marketing costs and other overheads) and delivering a profit. Simply put, teams can win commercially even when they lose on the cricket field.

Swapping Shikhar

In IPL's first-ever trade, DD and MI swapped players—Shikhar went to the Mumbai Indians and Nehra moved to the Delhi Daredevils. Delhi sold Shikhar for US$ 4,00,000 per year for the remaining two years of his contract, against his annual auction price of US$ 65,000. Under an arrangement with Shikhar, the upside of the new contract was shared on a 50-50 basis between him and Delhi Daredevils. Both made an additional US$ 3,35,000 from the deal over two years.

As a part of the deal between DD and MI, Ashish Nehra moved to Delhi at his original price of ₹1.6 crore/US$ 400,000.

The Daredevil Ambassador

When Bollywood superstar Akshay Kumar was appointed DD's brand ambassador to create a buzz around the team, it seemed a perfect fit: Akshay was a Dilli person who connected with the youth because he was athletic, super fit and a sports lover. Moreover, as pointed out by the marketing wizards, the film star had a well-earned reputation for playing off the front foot. He was a filmi daredevil who enjoyed *khatra* and *khel*.

DD wasn't the only IPL team to appoint a brand ambassador to catch the attention of fans. Some of the teams had co-founders who, with their charm and their existing fan base from the world of cinema, added to the glamour and the frenzy of the IPL. Rajasthan Royals had Shilpa Shetty to sing and dance to '*Halla Bol*', Kings XI Punjab had Preity Zinta, real PZ, to attract eyeballs. KKR did not need any help in brand building—King Khan had only to arch his back and stretch a romantic arm to ensure the franchise remained in the news.

Akshay signed a three-year deal with Delhi Daredevils to shoot promotional films, attend meet-and-greet events and make appearances at corporate events. On one occasion, he performed daring stunts at the Kotla during the short pre-toss window. The gig received mixed reviews: some liked it but the majority thought it was *thanda* and lacked *dhamaka*.

Apart from the Kotla act, nothing much happened because Akshay was busy and DD didn't know how to leverage him. At the end of the season, during the elaborate post-mortem held against the backdrop of serious financial losses, DD decided to cancel or renegotiate the contract.

This was easier said than done. Akshay's contract provided no exit; on the contrary, it gave him solid guarantees for a period of three years. DD's lawyers approached Akshay's staff, wanting to revisit the contract, but they made no headway. The (legally correct) response from his side was that the contract did not factor in early termination and it had to run its course with full monetary compensation.

Seen from the perspective of DD, Akshay's multi-crore contract could be equated to a self-goal or a hit-wicket dismissal. Considering the disastrous financial results and the need for austerity, the star had become an avoidable expense. Knowing there was no legal lifeline available, DD appealed to Akshay for mercy.

My request for a meeting was promptly agreed to, and Akshay's secretary reverted with a date and time to meet the star at Mehboob Studio in

Mumbai. I rehearsed the meeting in my head, going over every argument from every angle and listing reasons for requesting an early closure. I had a feeling it would be unpleasant because DD didn't have a case.

On the morning of the meeting, Akshay's office called to shift the venue to Andheri, where he was shooting for his latest film, *Chandni Chowk to China*. His staff met me there and I waited in his vanity van for a while before deciding to watch the shooting. A complicated comic scene was being filmed, where a goofy Akshay, doing puja, had to light an incense stick that accidentally sparks a fire.

For a seasoned artist like Akshay, this was child's play. After the shot, we returned to his vanity van and I, very hesitantly, explained the reason for my visit and outlined DD's financial troubles.

Akshay grasped the situation quicker than Sachin spotting a googly from Shane Warne. *No problem ji*, he said, in a sympathetic manner. *If it is not working out, let's close it.*

I thought I hadn't heard him right. Seeing my confused look, he clarified slowly: *Isko khatam kar dete hain. No problem.* When I mumbled incoherently about the stringent contract clauses, he reassured me: *Koi baat nahin, main lawyer ko bol doonga.*

I figured I should make a quick exit in case he changed his mind. But Akshay was waiting for his next shot to be ready and started chatting about his love for sport and his personal commitment to fitness. He was extremely disciplined and stuck to a daily routine that would have impressed the fitness-conscious Virat Kohli: non-negotiable gym sessions, a healthy vegetarian diet and strict avoidance of smoking, alcohol and late nights.

Even after so many years I am surprised that Akshay waived off such a large amount of money. Just like that—a snap decision when he could have easily thrown the contract at us. What also remains with me is his parting shot. As I prepared to leave, he said, *I am from Delhi and my heart is with the Daredevils. Our contract is over but I will come for DD whenever you call me.*

This, I thought, was the usual make-you-feel-good goodbye delivered by a seasoned performer. But next year, when the IPL was played in South Africa, we got a message that Akshay, who was shooting for the television series, *Khatron ke Khiladi*, wanted to watch a Daredevils match. He requested match tickets and DD's match jersey.

Years later, when I heard that Akshay was making Airlift, a film about a rescue mission out of Kuwait, my thoughts went back to 2009, when he had come to the rescue of the Delhi Daredevils.

IPL in South Africa, 2009

When Lalit Modi moved the IPL to South Africa, Daniel Vettori said the tournament didn't look the same because he missed the noise and the *raunaq* of Indian fans. Straight after the India–New Zealand series, Vettori flew three hours to Sydney, then another 14 hours to join the Delhi Daredevils in Johannesburg. He praised Mahendra Singh Dhoni, whom we met accidentally in the airport lounge. When informed that Vettori had said nice things about him, Dhoni smiled his trademark pleasant smile. *Good bowler, Vettori*, he said, *but Yuvraj and Raina know how to deal with him.*

MSD asked about Sehwag and was told that he would arrive two days before the first game. He smiled once again: *Chalo, toss ke pehle to aa jayega*!

A few days later, Sehwag arrived, flying Delhi–Dubai–Cape Town, looking drained but glad he had gone home for a few days. *Sab sponsor promotions aur appearances kar diye*, he said.

Before the grand IPL opening ceremony, the Cullinan Hotel was very busy since five of the teams were staying there. SRK held court near the pool and discussed team plans. KKR had leadership issues with uncertainty about Dada's role. When I asked Joy Bhattacharjya what was brewing, he avoided a direct answer. *It's a clever marketing strategy to generate interest*, he said with a wicked smile. *A Buchanan-inspired 'predict the captain' contest.*

Even before the tournament started, bad news trickled in. Pujara had bust his knee during practice. Kaif was distraught because he had been told by the Rajasthan Royals that he must go back to India as the squad had been trimmed to 18 to cut costs. This was hugely disrespectful because Kaif, centrally contracted by the BCCI, was not a fringe player and should have been informed in advance. Kaif wanted to meet Lalit Modi to protest but that would have been of little use because, in the IPL, the market is the third umpire who decides merit and value. Kaif wasn't the only one to be treated shabbily. The Royal Challengers Bangalore (RCB) decided to travel with 18 players and 11 others were put in a camp in Johannesburg. The Deccan Chargers (DC) also sent players home after deciding to work with a leaner squad. So did KKR.

Besides the players, the teams carried a large coaching staff whose sole purpose, it seemed, was to create work to justify their existence. *Where is the time to train or practice*, questioned a senior Indian player. *We are playing or travelling and there is hardly any practice. Coaches, support staff and experts only complicate matters. T20 is about the top four or five batters exploiting the powerplay and bowlers nailing yorkers in the end; if that doesn't happen, you are gone.* There was also an undercurrent, the feeling that the league was foreign-dominated in terms of support staff. Teams hired foreign coaches who brought their own people with them and the system worked as a convenient employment agency for overseas experts.

But even without them, there was an abundance of talent in the Delhi Daredevils dressing room with Sehwag, Gambhir, de Villiers, Dilshan, Collingwood, Vettori, McGrath and Warner. Was there anything they didn't collectively know about T20 cricket?

I met Sehwag, who was recovering from a fever, at breakfast. He repeated his views about having Indian staff in the IPL because they knew the Indian players and understood their mindset. His position on foreign coaches and numerous coaching staff: *Coaches kitna karenge. Players know everything.* He made a valid point: If top playing professionals can't sort out strategy, nobody can.

The pre-tournament meeting was held at One and Only, the super luxury hotel (and temporary home of Lalit Modi) with a breathtaking view of Table Mountain. All the stakeholders were present and there was plenty on the agenda. But Lalit, IPL czar and commissioner, rushed through the meeting as only he could. He ticked off points quickly, disallowed discussion and announced decisions. It was like a five-day match had ended in 20 overs. Typically Lalit—decisive and autocratic. Certainly, he couldn't be accused of wasting time.

Cape Town Carnival

The IPL kicked off in South Africa with a grand parade through Cape Town. The teams assembled at the hotel in a holding area where star owners Preity Zinta and Shilpa Shetty were present along with a chain-smoking Lalit. Only KKR's King Khan gave the public parade a royal miss. Players climbed into separate team floats and the cricket circus rolled through the busy Cape Town streets accompanied by singing, dancing, waving, cheering and whistling. Bemused locals wondered what all the fuss was about. The players enjoyed their moment of publicity in the Cape Town sun. A peppy Warner swayed to the bhangra beat and Collingwood (normally so proper) was a surprise packet, waving to everyone enthusiastically. Sri Lanka's Maharoof raised a pertinent point: Would the Delhi Police have allowed such a parade given the security considerations?

The IPL in South Africa had the appearance of a family holiday; this was Indian cricket's annual *chhutti* with players accompanied by their partners and children. Sehwag's cute son was everyone's favourite. Asked to signal a boundary, he promptly raised his hands to indicate a six. *This is fine*, said Dilshan (who had with him his seven-month-old daughter) *because Daddy Viru only hits sixes*. Sachin's kids came, but headed back after a few days because schools in Mumbai were reopening.

Opening Ceremony

The bus parade was followed by a glittering ceremony with impressive fireworks and speeches. The speeches, too long and too many, tested everyone's patience. The teams lined up on the ground with Sachin, dapper in a smartly tailored Mumbai Indians jacket, leading the captains group. But the real star was SRK, who arrived in a black BMW accompanied by bodyguards, to be greeted by screaming fans. He sat in box 311 dressed in his trademark formal clothing: black suit, black tie, crisp white shirt and shiny black laced shoes.

Aside

- Change of roles: Sachin Tendulkar and Pravin Amre toured South Africa with the Indian team in 1992 and Amre made his Test debut in Durban. Now, in the IPL in 2009, Sachin is captain of Mumbai Indians and Amre is part of the coaching staff.

Durban: Kingsmead Double Header

I met Harsh Shringla, fellow Stephanian and India's Consul General over coffee. He told me that Durban had the largest Indian-origin community in the world outside of India and they were very excited about the IPL. Shringla had made special efforts to ensure that schoolchildren were invited to the games.

Kings XI Punjab versus Kolkata Knight Riders (Preity Zinta versus SRK) was an interesting contest. As the players walked out, the public announcement system played '*Pretty Woman*' from *Kal Ho Na Ho*, the movie in which the KKR and Kings owners engaged in a different game. When play started, Chris Gayle was in a savage mood, hitting huge sixes that cleared the stadium. But Sourav bowled an inspired spell to pick up two crucial wickets with clever swing bowling. Later, he explained his strategy: *When there are clouds, I bowl. When the sun is out, I pick up my bat!*

KKR won and celebrated late into the evening with SRK.

Dinner with Anil Kumble

As soon as we had ordered Italian food at Broadwalk, a popular eatery, the other guests recognised Kumble. *You Anil bloody Kumble*, screamed an excited fan. *Welcome to Port Elizabeth. Where is Dravid?* Good question, I thought. Dravid was back home in India for two weeks as his wife Vijeyta was expecting their child.

Anil appreciated the importance of the IPL but detected dark clouds on the otherwise bright horizon. He was concerned that players would prefer the IPL to Ranji and excessive focus on 20-over cricket would put extra pressure on the spinners, specially off-break bowlers. He thought the challenge before every team was to attract quality Indian players. He was unhappy that Kaif (with RR) had been sent back and Wasim Jaffer (with RCB) was stuck in a camp far away from the actual action.

Gautam Gambhir on Anil Kumble

At practice, Gautam Gambhir was in great touch, confidently middling everything. He was riding a great wave, having scored five hundreds in the last eight Tests to become the fastest to get 2,000 runs. Quicker than Gavaskar. A Kumble fan, Gautam thought he was a fantastic captain because he gave confidence to players. *He told me I'd play even if I made 5 zeroes. Before that I was always scared of being dropped. A good captain must identify and pick the right players—as Sourav did with Yuvi, Bhajji and Zaheer.*

Team Meeting

McGrath walked into the team room, read the names of the playing eleven on the noticeboard and found his name missing. It's sad the IPL's 'four foreigners only' rule keeps out so many greats who get benched not on merit but on team combination compulsions. The rule keeps them out of the game and robs fans of the opportunity to celebrate their superb skills.

McGrath took the blow on the chin. Overcoming his disappointment, he put his hand up and asked to be named among the 16 players allowed in the dugout. He wanted to give inputs, talk to the bowlers at fine leg and third man and distribute water bottles. What a champion! When dropped, most superstars would have lapsed into a long sulk and switched off.

With Mandira Bedi, Delhi

Watching the IPL with Shashi Tharoor and Jyotiraditya Scindia

The Need for Incentives

To encourage players to put in extra effort, the Delhi Daredevils announced a performance-based team incentive scheme. It was the first team to do so. The broad features of this scheme were that the management would contribute a certain amount to create a 'prize pool'. After that, a fixed amount would get added with each win and the pool would decrease by a similar amount if the team lost.

As with all incentive schemes, conditions did apply. The pool was subject to making the semi-finals, and all team fines (for instance, on slow over rates) had to be paid from the prize pool. The players supported the scheme but McGrath pointed out that players play for pride, not money, and don't need extra incentives as they are already doing their best. Vettori raised his hand to ask a pertinent question: What happens if there is a negative pool, with more defeats than losses? Would players then owe money to the Delhi Daredevils?

No, was the answer. The team owners would take the hit to avoid any financial exposure to the players. And, it was added, with a touch of arrogant self-confidence: *Why worry, Delhi is well on its way this season, clearly ahead in the league. A semi-final place is assured, it's a given!*

As the players trooped out, one remarked with a raised eyebrow: *Semi-final is a given? This is cricket, mate; nothing is ever a given!*

Delhi Daredevils vs RCB

Chasing a modest total of 150-odd runs, the Delhi Daredevils lost its openers early on and the game got tight in the 13th over with spinners K.P. Apanna and Kumble putting the brakes on. The asking rate climbed to 11 but DD crossed the line thanks to a blazing 60 from Dilshan, who was in hot form this season, and a decent hand from Mithun Manhas. Captain Sehwag was relieved: *Ek* stage *par gale mein aa gayi thi.*

DD's great escape wouldn't have been possible without liberal assistance from key RCB players. Robin Uthappa dropped a sitter at long-off. Jacques Kallis had a forgettable game: he went for 18 at a crucial time and was dismissed first ball. Captain Kevin Pietersen, otherwise such a champion, would want to erase this match from memory: he was bowled by Vettori trying a suicidal switch hit. Back at the hotel, Brijesh Patel was livid and boss Vijay Mallya raised questions about team performance but found no answers. RCB had come to South Africa with a squad almost as large as Tipu Sultan's army. While frontline fighters travelled to games, the reserve troops prepped for live action in Johannesburg in a high-performance camp.

Lalit Modi: Mails and Messages

Throughout the IPL, Lalit kept teams posted about developments, sending out emails (often at midnight) giving information and instructions and occasionally holding out threats to those not complying with his imperious *firmaans.* He would share news about the IPL—its growing stature, brand value, and positive media mentions. One mail forwarded by Lalit in the 'Dear All' category caught everyone's attention: a newspaper had reported that prisoners in a Kolkata jail had gone on strike because they couldn't watch the IPL on television. This invited a sarcastic comment: *Lalit should be thankful he is outside and not supporting the IPL from inside the jail.*

Asides:

- IPL memorabilia that each team was required to sign: 125 bats, 50 shirts.
- Sachin on T20 cricket: *The game changes quicker than the Cape Town weather.*

Delhi Daredevils vs Rajasthan Royals

When the Delhi Daredevils bosses arrived late for the customary pre-match meeting, pissed-off players pointed out that they would have been fined for being late, so why should they be made to wait? Already, the team think-tank thought these meetings served no purpose except that everyone shook hands and wished each other luck. This was true, but the counter-argument was that they were held because the owners wanted to remain in the loop. Which too was understandable.

In the meeting, McGrath offered an interesting insight about the Rajasthan Royals. He said Warnie was so worried about his team's batting that he had asked him to play for them as a batsman! McGrath also said Kamran Khan's action was not suspect—the bloke definitely

chucked. Coach Shipperd warned the team to expect 'verbal pressure' from Warne and said that DD were still not playing their best. But he wasn't worried because *we are winning even when not playing well.*

At the ground, IPL's Sundar Raman informed everyone about a rule clarification: only four foreigners could be on the field at any time, which meant that no foreign player could act as a substitute if four were already in the playing eleven. This mid-tournament rule change drew an angry response from Warner: *I am not playing and now I can't even bloody field!*

DD lost the match because:

- Kamran Khan continued to chuck and was not called by on-field umpires.
- Sehwag and Gambhir didn't fire at the top.
- A.B. de Villiers was given lbw on a ball pitching outside leg. Bad luck, sympathised Warne, it was only two feet outside.
- Yusuf Pathan played an innings described by Ravi Shastri as *out of the world,* hitting six sixes and smashing Vettori and Amit Mishra.

The loss triggered an angry response from the team's owners, who demanded more intensity and suggested changes, including bringing Warner back. This brought up the larger question of interference in cricket matters by team owners. One view was that owners should leave cricket to the professionals and trust their decisions. Others said the owner was *maalik*—his word was set, if not in stone, then at least on the pitch. The boss would have his way and if he asked questions, the professionals must explain.

Delhi Daredevils vs Deccan Chargers

At Centurion, one of the prettiest grounds in the world, India's conquest of South Africa was complete. The stands were full of noisy fans, Hindi film music blared full volume, spectators with colourful *pagris* and fake *mooch* were everywhere. The food menu in the presidential suite reflected the takeover: reshmi kebab, paneer tikka, even chaat paapri and gol gappe.

There were plenty of off-field needles in the game as both the teams were owned by corporate giants from Hyderabad. On this day, Delhi prevailed with stellar contributions from Nannes, Dilshan and Karthik. But there was cause for worry because Sehwag was injured and his right hand needed five stitches.

After the game, Collingwood went back home without getting to play — another instance of top foreign players missing out. What a waste!

A Day Off in Durban

Rajasthan Royals were training on the beach and the DD boys went surfing with Nannes, who was an acknowledged expert. Nehra kept a safe distance from his teammates and the water; he recalled an incident in the West Indies when Sachin had to be rescued because he almost got swept away by strong waves. Since then, he and Ganguly — who couldn't swim — stayed away from the sea.

The Indian Consul General in Durban hosted a reception and though the foreign players had a day off, de Villiers stayed on, since he had been nominated official speaker on behalf of the team. When informed about his off-field 'duty', the normally composed player panicked. *Spare me, mate*, he pleaded, *I have never done this. Easier to play in front of thousands than speak in front of a few.*

I ran into Dada, who was disappointed that things were not going well with KKR. Dada wasn't central to their plans and it seemed he had mentally switched off and moved on. He spoke about spending time in London, his favourite city, and getting back before his daughter's school reopened after the holiday break. *Are you a hands-on father, fully involved in her studies*, I asked. *Very much*, he said. *I even go to PTA meetings at 7.30 in the morning.*

Wonderful, for someone famous (notorious?) for landing up late for the toss!

Delhi Daredevils vs KKR

Cassim Docrat, the long-time boss of Natal cricket, was happy that the IPL in Durban was a complete sell-out and no tickets, absolutely zero, were available for the KKR game. I thought Cassim was exaggerating but found out that he was right — even Dada was struggling to get tickets.

The Delhi Daredevils had their own set of concerns with Sehwag not yet fully recovered and Gambhir troubled by a strained groin. But they won easily as KKR's top batsmen had a disappointing day and they were so ordinary in the field that someone remarked that they would struggle to catch a cold. Lalit offered advice to fix things for KKR. *Sack Buchanan*, he told SRK. *Do it right now.*

Bizarre Facts

- Amit Mishra bowled a maiden, 14th of the innings, to a clueless Moises Henriques.
- Dada did not bat or bowl in the game.

Like KKR, Deccan too was in a mess after three successive losses and the owners were hopping mad. They sent an angry email expressing their feelings freely, severely berating the team, belittling the players and questioning team strategy. One deadly line in the mail which, for some reason, was also marked to the IPL email address (hence the leak), said the *raging bull of DC is absent, it is only visible on the logo*!

Team owners support their team in tough times but, despite the polite posturing and kind words, demand results. Perhaps it's only natural that sometimes, when the going gets rough, pent-up anger and disappointment burst into the open.

East London Golf Course (Estd 1893)

I played a round of golf with Warner, de Villiers and McGrath. De Villiers is IPL's Tiger Woods with a smooth swing and precise, clean, powerful strokes, whether from the tee or the fairway. A naturally gifted athlete, he is an all-round champion with great balance and amazing hand-eye coordination. With a cricket bat he is a creative genius, not an accumulator. But give him a bat, racket, stick, club—anything—and he will get it right. He told me later that he used to be scratch but is rusty now because he doesn't get to play enough.

Micky Speak

South Africa coach Micky Arthur, five years into the job, revealed his mantra for success. The key is to focus on the team aspect and get players to buy into a shared vision. After that it's about giving responsibility to individuals, creating clear leadership positions and for the players to step up.

Stars in the Aid of Stars

In the IPL less is never more and sometimes it's the more the merrier. In the relentless quest for success teams look for external assistance and key decisions are influenced by favourable star positions and auspicious timings.

Cricket experts decide team composition, the batting order and field placing but another set of experts takes the call on flights, bus departure time from the hotel (11.30 or 11.37 a.m.?), the hotel to stay in and the lucky floor. Sometimes it gets even more detailed: who gets off last from the bus, should the captain carry a lucky photo or object in his trouser pocket and recite a short prayer before the toss? Of course, all this is in addition to special pujas, hawans, aartis, chanting of mantras and temple visits. Most teams do this, some going through the motions, others showing more faith and intensity.

To attract divine blessings the Delhi Daredevils invited a swamiji to talk to the team. He was extremely interesting and surprisingly entertaining (citing examples of O.J. Simpson, Boris Becker and Javed Miandad). His message was that players must control the mind to erase negativity by logging into positive thoughts. *Do not accept or justify failure*, he said. To which Sehwag had a logical question: *How do I erase negative thoughts when the bowler is running in to dismiss me?* Swamiji's equally logical answer: *Controlling the mind requires as much practice as the cover drive. You have to train yourself.*

Another time, a lengthy team-bonding exercise was conducted with a motivational guru who stressed the importance of a 'shared vision' and individual buy-in. Importantly, the shared vision was to be created by those who also had the responsibility to execute it. It couldn't be imported or imposed. He gave a lengthy lecture about players committing to collective goals—a sermon that the players had heard many times over. Some, clearly bored by the proceedings, yawned disrespectfully while others, slightly more discreet, nodded off with eyes open. Yet, the session was not a write-off. The players, when asked what they thought of the Delhi Daredevils and about the future, gave interesting answers:

- A team that's better than the Delhi Daredevils: Chennai Super Kings.
- A team equal to the Delhi Daredevils: Mumbai Indians.
- Qualities that best describe the Delhi Daredevils (according to Sehwag, Gambhir, de Villiers): Confidence and a fighting spirit.
- Team vision: Dare to succeed.

9

DELHI DAREDEVILS: AN UNEVEN RIDE

In 2008, the IPL decided to keep the winning team of the Under-19 World Cup outside the auction, arguing that youngsters should be protected from the corrupting influence of money. This seemed a bit rich given that the IPL swore by market forces and its structure was built with bricks of cash.

The Indian U-19 players were offered to teams through a draft at a predetermined price. The draft was held in Bangalore's Gardenia Hotel. The names of all the players were put up on a board, with captain Virat Kohli at the top. To decide the sequence of the draft—which team would choose first—lots were picked.

I got the first pick for the Delhi Daredevils and promptly chose Pradeep Sangwan, who was the first on our wish list. I must emphasise that, in 2008, this was a perfectly legitimate cricket decision on three counts:

1) DD already had an extra supply of Delhi batsmen with Sehwag, Gambhir, Shikhar Dhawan and Mithun Manhas. One more would have been one too many.
2) Kohli in 2008 was very much a work-in-progress.
3) DD was looking for a young left-arm quick and Pradeep Sangwan, a local lad, fit the bill.

Did the choice of Sangwan over Kohli set the pattern for the Delhi Daredevils, of misjudging talent, not spotting match-winners and making a series of wrong choices while retaining and releasing players? Was it the first of many instances where they spurned top talent? And is this one reason why Delhi Daredevils (now Delhi Capitals) remains, together with Kings XI Punjab and Royal Challengers Bangalore, one of the teams from the original eight to not win the IPL?

The Hiring of David Warner

With IPL regulations allowing for uncapped players to be contracted outside the auction teams scrambled to sign young stars. Hiring talented but untested youngsters was a risk worth taking: if the player came good, there was a huge upside. If he failed, the cost of investment would have been minor.

The buzz at the time was around Moises Henrique, a promising all-rounder from Australia. DD contacted Moises and made an offer but he went to KKR for a few thousand dollars more. Almost on the rebound we turned to David Warner, a dasher making a splash in New South Wales club cricket. He was yet to play for the state team but was a pocket-sized dynamo—a power hitter. T.A. Sekar discovered a video of Warner and, impressed by the visual evidence, the Delhi Daredevils dialled him.

The negotiation was brief because Warner was only too keen to grab the opportunity. The price wasn't an issue and terms were satisfactorily concluded. But soon after the conversation ended, his manager Peter Lovitt called back. Just one more thing, he said. In case Warner makes the Aussie side, the contract should provide for a bonus of US$ 50,000.

I wondered about this brazen ask. Here was someone who hadn't made it to the state team, who was not even in the state's second team, and yet he was talking about playing for his country. Was this amazing self-belief, or a crazy request from a delusional young kid?

From the time he first had a go, it was obvious Warner was custom-built for T20 cricket. Fearless by nature and positive in intent, he was a 'see ball, not bowler' sort of striker who lit up the IPL. From the time he joined the Delhi Daredevils, with its team of international superstars, his body language suggested that he belonged in the elite group. Clearly, in his personality and in cricket, all doubts had been permanently deleted from the system.

A Practice Session

The Delhi Daredevils had a day off, but Warner wanted a hit. *Have to get used to white ball cricket*, he said, walking out to the middle to play net bowlers arranged by the state association in Hyderabad's impressive new Rajiv Gandhi stadium, which was plastered with photos of Shivlal Yadav and Arshad Ayub. To make sure nobody missed the point of their importance, the pavilion of the stadium was named after Shivlal.

Warner, a left-handed batsman, knocked the ball around for a while before changing gears to hit shots in match-simulated conditions. He played the square cut with the intent to go over point. He pulled short balls with the intent to go over deep mid-wicket. Satisfied with his shape and timing, he then took fresh guard to switch sides and batted right-handed, hitting crashing drives and solid pulls to square leg that sailed over the ropes.

This batting *doosra* surprised many but not Trent Woodhill, Warner's long-time coach. *Warner can bat like a regular right-hander if he wants to*, he said. *No switch-hit business, he can actually hit proper cricket shots. His right-hand cover drive is as good as the left-handed one.*

The session over, Warner, who by now was drenched in sweat and drained by Hyderabad's sapping humidity, explained his batting strategy: *Batsmen must be positive and look for scoring opportunities but they must not overthink.* Having an uncluttered mindset was something teammate Sehwag also believed in; they seemed to share the same playbook.

David Warner at a practice session, Delhi

Warner was convinced that he was better than the bowler, but reminded himself to respect the ball. *At times you must play out bowlers*, he says. *But if the ball is there to be hit, I hit it.* His mantra: *play to your strength and back yourself. Field placements reveal what the bowler will do. Fielders on the fence don't worry me. I know how far I can hit.*

Warner's Masterclass for Unmukt Chand

The IPL is a crash course in cricket for young Indian players. They learn by observing the greats and some lucky ones get one-on-one lessons. In Hyderabad, before a game against the Deccan Chargers, Warner gave young Unmukt Chand a private tuition he is unlikely to forget.

It happened at one of those IPL pre-match dinners where important guests met cricketers and everyone enjoyed the kind of hospitality you thought belonged in Bollywood. With a glass of white wine in hand and barbeque prawns and lamb chops on his plate, Warner sat Unmukt down for a chat.

When I started, I knew nothing and had no idea about what to do, he told Unmukt. *But you must learn, absorb the atmosphere, go to seniors at nets and ask for feedback. Ask bowlers from your side or the opposition. They will help. To get accepted, show intent and let others know you are involved with the team. Make suggestions to the captain, no matter how senior or junior you are; he will respect that. On the field, be competitive regardless of who is in the opposition. Off the field, all are mates. Play to your strength, force the bowler to adjust and make him bowl where you want him to. Respect the ball, trust your routine and stick to what works for you.*

Unmukt heard him in silence, an attentive student making mental notes before the next exam.

The Mystery Spinner, Sunil Narine

IPL teams spent more time decoding KKR's Sunil Narine than discussing other aspects of preparation. The Delhi Daredevils held a special meeting at which batsmen agreed they struggled against him because:

- He was a finger spinner who turned it big.
- He was an off-spinner who bowled a deadly doosra.
- He was a slow bowler who surprised batsmen by firing a 95 kmph quicker one.

- He was tight and did not offer easy scoring opportunities.

Unable to pick Narine, the batsmen switched to survival mode and decided to see him through and not get adventurous—happy to get 25 from his four overs, which was wise considering you didn't know which way the ball was going.

The team watched slow motion videos of Sunil Narine to pick up clues. Did he follow a routine in the beginning or at the death? Was there a pattern of bowling slower ones, doosras and those which rushed through straight? The consensus after repeated viewing of slo-mo and freeze frames: changes are visible in delivery stride, arm and wrist position but no conclusive evidence.

Sehwag offered a solution: the only way to play is to dominate, attack upfront and unsettle him; else, he will get on top. Warner, on the other hand, was more cautious: pick singles, play the sweep and see him off.

After the meeting, one young Delhi batsman was convinced that he had cracked the mystery. I know what to do, he said confidently. But at the game the next day, the story was different: he played and missed five balls in a row, beaten each time. On the last ball, still clueless, he crudely heaved across the line, only to be caught at short mid-wicket.

This shows that all the planning, preparation and video analysis is useful only up to a point. After that, it's best to have faith in God.

A Sorry Tale of Drugs and Disaster

Pakistan's Mohammad Asif was the hot new bowler at the time, celebrated for his mastery over swing and a probing line. He was a prime asset for the Delhi Daredevils, his hammer price a massive US$ 650,000. However, Asif got his lines mixed up and when awkward questions were raised about his conduct, he had no answers. He was the first player to flunk a dope test in the IPL when nandrolone, a banned substance, was detected in his urine sample. He defended himself, pleading that this was because he was using Keratyl, an eyedrop.

At one level, Asif was fighting a personal battle, but the Delhi Daredevils became an involved party since he was contracted for three seasons. Back then, the IPL contracts had a binding lock-in period of three years and teams couldn't release players even if they turned out to be non-performing assets.

A dope-tainted star was harmful for the brand and the Delhi Daredevils examined legal options to terminate his contract. When Asif was caught with recreational drugs in Dubai, detained in jail and then deported, the franchise decided they wanted to end this toxic relationship.

An elaborate legal process had to be followed, which started with Asif's desperate pleas to the Delhi Daredevils to release the last instalment of his contract. He was in a financial mess as legal battles in Dubai and Pakistan had wiped out his savings and his only lifeline was the money that DD owed him.

DD's lawyers felt that Asif had a fair claim for payment for services already rendered as per his contract. However, there was a catch. Because Asif had hurt the Delhi Daredevils by attracting negative publicity, the latter could withhold his remaining salary and, taking a hard line, claim damages to make good that loss.

Asif came to Delhi for the settlement meeting accompanied by Shahid Karim, his London-based lawyer. He paid for his travel but requested DD for hotel accommodation. The meeting in Delhi's Lalit hotel played out as expected. Asif's position was that he would voluntarily exit the contract if DD agreed to release his salary and also pay him for year two. DD's position was that they would release the remaining salary for year one, provided Asif exited the contract and released the team from any future liability.

Initially, both Asif and his lawyer were aggressive, almost belligerent, despite being on a bad wicket legally. It was only when discussions stretched over two days and DD's lawyers stuck to their stand that Asif's counsel read the writing on the wall. He told Asif to accept the offer or risk losing everything.

Asif got a financial lifeline and the Delhi Daredevils released a player who, once an asset, was now a liability. This closure, though legally satisfactory, wasn't without a tinge of sadness. Asif was a wonderful bowler known for his controlled aggression and strict discipline. Unfortunately, these professional qualities did not reflect in the choices he made in his personal, non-cricketing life.

PS: After his forgettable IPL stint, Asif lurched from one controversy to another. He was convicted in a match-fixing case and despite a brief return to first-class cricket, his career nosedived.

When Kevin Pietersen Moved to DD

Kevin Pietersen was a match-winner and an absolute superstar, but there was also chatter about him creating dressing-room friction wherever he went. That he was first chosen by RCB seemed appropriate: the franchise was known for the flamboyant lifestyle of its owner and the cricketer loved attention and believed in playing the game king-size.

Imagine my surprise when someone very senior at RCB sought me out during an IPL auction. *I want to give you a friendly tip,* he confided, as though letting out a state secret. *Stay away from Kevin Pietersen. He is not good news.*

PS: Delhi Daredevils bought Kevin Pietersen. He wasn't a successful leader but he was a crowd-puller and an outstanding pro.

DD Releases Aaron Finch

On a lovely, sunny day in July 2014, in an MCC versus Rest of the World match to commemorate 200 years of cricket at Lord's, the sold-out crowd was treated to a brilliant hundred by Yuvraj Singh. Dravid, on the other hand, fell first ball, bowled by Collingwood.

The standout knock was an unbeaten 181 by Aaron Finch, who once played for the Delhi Daredevils. After the game, at a reception in the Long

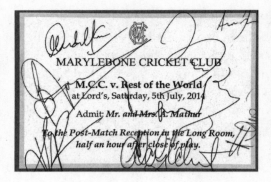

Room, when I congratulated him, Finch responded with a naughty glint in his eyes: *Thanks, mate but you sacked me at Delhi Daredevils.*

Finch wasn't the tiger he became later, but DD missed a trick in not judging his potential correctly.

Discovering Talent

Andre Russell: On a West Indies A team tour to England, Andre Russell made waves as a strong sixer-hitting batsman and useful medium-pace bowler. DD's scouts had a quick word with Pravin Amre, the coach of the India A team, who confirmed the promise of the big-built West Indian. Armed with this input, the Delhi Daredevils went hard for him in the 2012 auction, paying US$ 4,50,000 for the relatively unknown youngster.

Little was known about Russell in cricketing circles but Sangeeta Jaitley, of all people, thought it was an inspired selection. Like many others, she took keen interest in the fortunes of the Delhi Daredevils and closely followed the team's matches. Unfortunately, Russell got limited opportunities with DD and was released after 2013.

Russell the muscle became one of IPL's biggest stars—an impactful, game-changing finisher. But not for the Delhi Daredevils.

Glenn Maxwell: In 2012, Delhi discovered an uncapped foreign player and signed him as a replacement for Travis Birt at US$ 50,000, the base price. Maxwell, at the time, was finding his way in Aussie cricket. He took the opportunity offered by Delhi but got limited game time, played a few matches and was released after one season.

No one could have guessed what was to follow. Maxwell's stock rose on the strength of strong performances in Australia and in the 2013 auction, the bidding for him was intense. When the paddle finally fell in favour of Mumbai Indians, it was at a jaw-dropping price of 1 million US dollars. Yet another instance of the Delhi Daredevils identifying a gem but not realising its value.

Maxwell's IPL journey has been astonishing—and baffling—because his auction price went up despite ordinary performances which, in most cases, would have killed a player's career. Starting with ₹5.3 crore in 2013, his IPL price kept climbing in a bizarre upward curve—to ₹6 crore in 2014, ₹9 crore in 2018, ₹10.25 crore in 2020, and a whopping ₹14.25 crore in the following year. Ahead of the 2022 auction, RCB retained him at ₹11 crore.

PS: Interestingly, after 2020, when Kings XI Punjab released Maxwell due to his dismal form, Sehwag ripped into him savagely. He said Maxwell treated the IPL as a picnic and was only interested in drinking beer and partying.

Umesh Yadav: When Umesh Yadav attracted attention with a fiery spell in a Duleep Trophy game, the Delhi Daredevils called Dinesh Karthik for a quick reaction. The DD player confirmed that the young Nagpur player was sharp and hit the bat hard. A second opinion was obtained from Vidarbha veterans Pritam Gandhe and Prashant Vaidya.

Umesh Yadav was picked in 2009 at the base price of ₹30 lakh and accompanied the team to South Africa, where an injury forced him to return midway. He was later released and entered the auction where the Delhi Daredevils bought him for ₹3.45 crore. After long stints at KKR and RCB, Umesh went back to DD in 2021, purchased at a discounted price of ₹1 crore. In 2022, in an interesting U-turn, he returned to KKR at ₹2 crore.

Retaining Talent—Or Not

Is Delhi Daredevils the Rajiv Chowk metro station that every IPL player must pass through for a quick change to another line? It's a standing joke that the Delhi Daredevils are good at spotting talent and great at managing it sloppily. The team has been a consistent underperformer with a great flair for assembling talent and an equally marked talent for losing it. Over the years, it has recruited and lost superstars Virender Sehwag, Gautam Gambhir, Shikhar Dhawan, A.B. de Villiers, Glenn Maxwell, Andre Russell, Aaron Finch, David Warner, Ravichandran Ashwin and Shreyas Iyer.

DD is known to have created turbulence within its leadership group, tossing the captaincy from Sehwag to Gambhir to Karthik to KP and Mahela Jayawardene. Coaches too came and left in a revolving door policy. Greg Shipperd was succeeded by Eric Simons, then came Gary Kirsten, who was followed by Rahul Dravid, Paddy Upton and Ricky Ponting.

This unsettling churn reflected the confusion over the franchise's business and cricket objectives. While CSK opted for experience over youth, DD swung from one side to the other, unable to decide which way to go. While RR chose the 'low-cost airline' model of financial austerity, DD alternated between carefree splurging and severe belt tightening. While MI spared no expense in hiring top pros, DD hesitated to take bold decisions.

The pattern of inconsistent decision-making was noticeable in 2010, ahead of the first big auction. When the IPL started, players were given the security of a three-year contract and franchises could not offload non-performing players. The only way to get rid of someone was separation by mutual agreement, invoking the 'buyout' clause which stipulated that players had to be paid to exit. As a consequence, most teams remained stable except for the occasional trade. With contractual provisions for release heavily loaded in favour of the players, there was continuity of personnel too.

This changed in 2010 when new player retention and release rules kicked in. Teams now had the option of retaining four players, three of whom could be Indian, on mutually agreed terms. Biggies like Sourav, Yuvraj, Dravid were sent back to the auction and only 12 players were retained. Mumbai Indians and CSK showed faith in their top four (Sachin, Kieron Pollard, Harbhajan, Lasith Malinga; MSD, Murali Vijay, Suresh Raina, Albie Morkel). The Rajasthan Royals stuck to Watson and Warne and RCB kept Kohli for his connect with the youth, a quality consistent with the United Breweries' brand image.

The Brain Fade Moment

DD's defining moment came in the 2010 auction when it released everyone except Sehwag and decided to reset its player combination. The wholesale purge was surprising because the team had had two semi-final finishes in the previous three years.

The players were released after negotiations on retention amounts broke down. During a game in Chandigarh, the franchise owners met the players to start a conversation about the upcoming season. DD wanted to end its partnership with Gambhir but were keen to retain Sehwag, de Villiers and Nehra. Nehra remembers an unpleasant meeting in Bangalore where he was made an offer he had to refuse. Unable to retain its core, the Delhi Daredevils then changed track and decided to rebuild the squad around 'value for money' players. Hindsight tells us this was a huge error.

With only Sehwag in its dugout, the Delhi Daredevils went shopping with a budget of US$ 7.2 million. Its prime target was David Hussey, who could be counted on to lead a young squad. Also high on the list of must-haves was an Indian all-rounder.

Aashish Kapoor recalls that the quest for Hussey backfired because his name came up late in the offer list and DD passed over all the other options in anticipation of getting him. *I kept urging Shipperd to consider other options*, says Aashish, *but he was adamant*.

When Hussey was finally offered, a bidding war erupted with the Deccan Chargers and the price kept climbing. Once it breached the 1 million dollar mark DD pulled out, but by that time their planning stood thoroughly exposed.

If the Hussey bid was botched, hiring Irfan Pathan was another monumental cock-up. Going into the auction, Irfan seemed a great option (swing bowler in powerplay, powerful lower-order striker), the only worry being that he had missed one season due to injury and was undergoing rehab at the NCA.

When the coach insisted on an Indian all-rounder for team balance, we made enquiries with the physio and Aashish and I met Irfan to get a first-hand fitness update. Assured by him that he would be match-fit by the time the IPL started, it was all systems go at the auction. The end result: Irfan Pathan 'sold' to Delhi Daredevils for a record-breaking US$ 1.9 million.

Auction Fiascos

Yuvraj Singh: Delhi Daredevils set a new IPL record by paying a whopping ₹16 crore for Yuvraj. It turned out to be another case of hope trumping reality. Anyone slamming Stuart Broad for 36 from 6 should be able to put away lesser bowlers with ease. Yuvraj threatened to take down the opposition each time he stepped into the middle—but the magic didn't work. That is why, in the IPL circus, Yuvraj became a cricketing nomad, moving camp and pitching his tent with different teams.

The lesson: There is no point splurging 20 per cent of the total player purse on one individual—the ROI never works.

Venugopal Rao: DD's aggressive bid for Venugopal in 2010 was out of desperation as the team was one Indian batsman short, and nobody else of quality was available. In the bidding war with the Deccan Chargers, the price went through the roof, settling finally at ₹3.2 crore. In three previous IPLs Venugopal had fetched the minimum price for a non-capped player.

A senior Indian pro consulting with another franchise summed up the Venugopal auction: *Delhi Daredevils saw something in him that nobody else noticed. They paid for a motorcycle thinking it was a Mercedes.*

DD Lose HERO

In year one, the Delhi Daredevils pulled off a major coup by signing HERO as its principal team sponsor. The deal was worth a staggering ₹54 crore over three years.

HERO paid a premium to get on board when the going rate across teams was far lower. For Delhi it was a lottery: top price, top partner. HERO was a respected corporate entity and its support enhanced the value of brand DD. The partnership worked fine, but at renewal time disagreements cropped up on the new asking price. A US-based media agency released a report that put a much higher value on DD's uniform properties. Armed with this dodgy data, DD pushed HERO for a disproportionate increase.

A presentation was made with complex diagrams and even more complicated financial calculations quantifying the media return basis the IPL sponsorship. HERO's senior management sat through it, clearly unimpressed by the research and shocked by the higher price demanded. They quickly decided this was a no-ball, a waste of time, and pulled out. But not before giving the Delhi Daredevils some frank advice. *We are open to a fair proposal*, they said, *but this research is disconnected from the ground reality in India.* Then came the final blow, the wicket-taking delivery: *In our business, relationships and trust matter more than rupees.*

HERO moved to the Mumbai Indians. In 2020, its main uniform property fetched the Delhi Daredevils all of ₹12 crore.

The Hiring of Eric Simons

When Coach Shipperd left for personal reasons, the Delhi Daredevils invited applications and held interviews to pick the next coach. Among the shortlisted candidates was Darren Penny, who had worked earlier with Shane Warne at the Rajasthan Royals. He made an impressive presentation that drew parallels between cricket and the corporate world.

Cricket teams, he said, *consist of 11 MDs running a business and winning isn't everything—it is the only thing! The team must play to a plan and think of winning from any situation. The role of the coach is to create the right environment, assign specific roles and act as a facilitator to help players execute plans.*

Former South African cricketer Eric Simons was clear about the role of the coach: *Identifying a problem is commentating, which is easy. Solving the problem is coaching, which is difficult.*

Trevor Bayliss, another applicant, was uninspiring. He spoke vaguely about the four styles of batting (technically orthodox, stroke players, power hitters and nudgers) and forcing batsmen to make decisions, which is when they also make mistakes. This might be perfectly valid, but his disjointed speech and flat presentation left the interview panel cold.

Coaching in the IPL is more challenging than working with a state or national team because there is no time to work on skills or technique. Teams assemble at the last minute and the squad is a mix of domestic players and international superstars. With 14 matches in six weeks, it is a mad race to plan strategy, get the team balance right and put the best eleven in the middle.

In this rush, do coaches really make a difference? Why have top coaches failed to lift their teams? Is it a reflection on their calibre or is the unforgiving T 20 format to blame?

PS: Trevor Bayliss, turned down by the Delhi Daredevils, had a wonderful career with KKR. England won the 2019 World Cup with him as coach, after which he went to Sunrisers Hyderabad. Then, in another lateral shift, he replaced Anil Kumble as head coach of Kings XI Punjab.

Dismiss!

One of the ironies of the IPL is that team owners are not included in the decision-making process. Teams collectively pay millions to run their franchises and, in addition, contribute 20 per cent of their annual revenue to the IPL. They have commercial muscle and loads of managerial experience, yet the IPL refuses to give them a role in managing the league. While owners are usually included in a post-season debrief, there is no structured coordination mechanism between the teams and the league. Team owners are excluded from the IPL Governing Council which comprises only BCCI insiders. Owners are not consulted before the council meetings nor are they informed about any decisions that have been taken; for the latter, they have to work the backroom channels or check media reports. A smug BCCI is unwilling to concede space. *What is the need? We know how to run cricket. It is our business, not theirs.*

In the initial years of the IPL, attempts were made to change this way of working. During an IPL workshop in Goa, the team owners created a small group to engage with the IPL. Following extensive discussions, a note was prepared which listed the merits of regular engagement. Afterwards, a delegation set off for Lalit Modi's Taj Village cottage, much like political parties marching to Raj Bhavan to petition the governor on some important matter.

The meeting was cordial but brief and completely unproductive. As soon as Lalit realised that the agenda was to involve owners in running the IPL, he declared stumps and announced his decision. *Forget it*, he said, ending the meeting. *This is not how the BCCI works.*

The team owners got a cup of tea from Lalit Modi but not one inch of space. Not even an insincere 'I will see what is possible' assurance.

Celebrity Shenanigans

In the IPL, each franchise adds its distinct flavour to the festivities. If RCB is colourful and splashy, the Daredevils are sober and understated, the owners supportive but non-interfering, concerned but not control freaks.

Srinivas Bommidala led the GMR franchise. An astute businessman, he was an extremely generous and large-hearted person. He gifted expensive watches to players but his great love was vintage cars, of which he had a vast collection at his Hyderabad home.

The IPL saw exciting action away from the field, at least in its early years. It was a whirl of matches, travel, parties and events at a dizzying speed. Not surprisingly, the gaze sometimes shifted away from cricket, the core business.

One such instance was Tillakaratne Dilshan's wedding at Delhi's Lalit hotel, organised by the Delhi Daredevils. Dilshan and his wife were already married and were expecting their first child. However, as she was keen on an Indian wedding, an elaborate ceremony was set up—the couple wore Indian clothes and went through a traditional wedding ceremony with mandap, pooja, pandit and, of course, *saat pheras*. Dilshan's teammates were his *baraatis* and McGrath raised a celebratory toast. Kingfisher, DD's commercial partner, covered the cost of *khaana peena* and the event was aired on NDTV Good Times.

The notorious after-match parties were annoying distractions and also a source of potential corruption. Sponsor events and promotions consumed time and energy and it was like one big circus with one act leading to the next. Players had to meet the families of sponsors, interact with kids, do staged media interactions and even walk the ramp.

In Delhi, a city with the highest density of well-connected VIPs, the biggest challenge wasn't winning home games but managing the endless demand for free passes. The bigshots demanded high-end invites and government agencies squeezed you for that extra ticket before granting the permits required for staging matches. If you refused to play ball, you could be accused of violating the terms of the liquor licence or the fire department would discover or invent hundred irregularities in the temporarily constructed dining area where booze was served.

Sometimes, celebrities added to the mayhem. Lalit Modi wanted his car to be parked inside the stadium, next to the pavilion, a privilege not accorded even to Arun Jaitley, the president of DDCA. The police refused outright and the impasse became one more pain point.

Many of Lalit's dictats were conveyed by Sunder Raman, the COO. A flashpoint was reached at DDCA when he barged into the Delhi Daredevils office, aggrieved that he had been stopped by security personnel carrying out their usual pre-game check. He threw a fit, speaking insultingly about the franchise and its owners, which incensed Sunil Valson, DD's mild-mannered, gentlemanly technical expert, and the other staff present in the room. There was an argument and a brief altercation during which the IPL COO was pushed around but saved from harm by Valson and escorted out.

Sundar speed-dialled Lalit to allege 'assault' and physical abuse. Armed with this one-sided account, Lalit blew a fuse and threatened to call off DD's evening home game. To resolve the matter, a meeting was held in his suite in ITC Maurya, where Sundar repeated his dramatised version of the incident. Further 'evidence' of misconduct by Valson and DD staff was produced by an IMG employee.

After much discussion, with no resolution in sight, Valson offered to resign, and so did I. At which point DD's owners prevailed upon us to 'cool it'. Finally a truce was agreed on, keeping the long-term interest of the franchise in mind. Valson, completely innocent of any wrongdoing, was suspended from the IPL for the season and had his accreditation revoked.

Shah Rukh Khan, Kolkata Knight Riders

This was sad and unfair because everyone in the IPL knew where the truth lay in this particular case. The incident was best summed up by a Delhi Daredevils employee: *I regret we did not do what Sundar alleged we did.*

But not all visitors were unwelcome at IPL games and the steady supply of celebrities was one of the charms of the home games. Nita Ambani arrived for Mumbai Indians matches, her visits preceded by an elaborate recce done by an advance party which satisfied itself about all arrangements. SRK came for KKR matches and, seeing the full house at Kotla, jokingly asked for a commission for pushing ticket sales. Preity Zinta descended with queenly swag, accompanied by a videographer who captured her presence for posterity. This was a special privilege granted to her because IPL guidelines prohibited teams from having their photographers at games.

CSK, Rajasthan Royals, Sunrisers Hyderabad were undemanding and unfussy, while RCB added a dash of colour to the proceedings, especially when Deepika Padukone came to cheer Virat's team. Local Delhi VIPs too were regular visitors. CM Sheila Dixit watched some games, as did the Vadras and various other bigshots and ministers. Each time there was a high-profile visit, the security managers were summoned to temporarily disable the turnstiles to allow their hangers-on to enter.

The ED Raid

Lalit's departure amidst a series of controversies led to events that shook the league and the tremors were felt at the Delhi Daredevils too.

Manoj Badale, Rajasthan Royals

We got caught in the mess when, one morning, government personnel landed up at the Barakhamba office to carry out a raid, as part of a nationwide investigation into the murky world of the IPL.

With Sunil Valson and Colonel Vinod Bisht, colleagues at Delhi Daredevils

What unfolded over ten hours was, in some ways, a surreal experience—rude officials spitting orders and demanding prompt compliance as if dealing with criminals; inspectors emptying drawers as they searched for papers. Everyone in the office was told to gather in the conference hall with instructions not to move. Mobile phones were confiscated.

I was the only one allowed some freedom. I was permitted to move around and, in order to assist with the search operations, allowed to keep my mobile phone. I was asked pointed questions about the business of the IPL, its revenue sources and the likely income. It became clear that the raiding party suspected the franchise teams were involved in betting because, to them, that seemed the only possible reason for participating in this loss-making business.

Nita Ambani, Mumbai Indians

The person leading the raid was initially bossy, trying to fit facts into a predetermined narrative, but he backed off when he realised that I had worked in *sarkar* much longer than him. When he asked what was in the files in my office, I told him to read them. When he asked for specific papers, I told him to take away whatever he wanted.

The stressful drama lasted all day and it was early evening by the time the female staff and junior personnel were allowed to leave. By that time, the mobile vans of several television channels were outside the office building and anchors were reporting breathlessly in true 'breaking news' style on the IPL's shameful scandal.

The raid ended around dinner time. The investigating team marched out, taking with them lots of documents. When I reached home and switched on the television, a news channel was describing Operation IPL and a ticker at the bottom of the screen screamed: 'Raid going on at Delhi Daredevils' office … Amrit Mathur detained!'

10

IPL: THE ROAD AHEAD

In 2008, Lalit Modi's announcement of launching the IPL triggered disbelieving smirks, widespread scepticism as well as sharp criticism. Traditionalists disapproved of the showy tournament that reduced cricket to a crude Bollywood item number with dancing cheerleaders and leering spectators. They were appalled that cricket was changing from sport to spectacle and disliked the vulgar cocktail of cricket, commerce and entertainment. Other non-believers wondered if 20-over cricket would work.

That was then. Today, the doubts have disappeared. The IPL invited private enterprise into cricket and successfully created a commercial property that aligned with changing social trends and lifestyles. In a fast-paced world with low attention spans, the IPL is the perfect, result-oriented sporting event – short, snazzy and spicy. It has succeeded in converting cricket into a three-format sport, with T20 driving its economy. The shorter format has taught batsmen to be aggressive and bowlers to discover new tricks. And as cricket evolves and run rates go up, Test cricket stands energised, as happened at Edgbaston in the Ashes in the summer of 2023.

The IPL is India's sole creative contribution to world cricket since Ranji invented the leg glance one hundred years ago. It taps into India's recession-proof cricket economy and connects with its huge fan base. It is also Indian cricket's greatest export, which has changed the power dynamics of the global sport. Because of the IPL, India is an entrepreneur, not a customer, and a world leader.

Launching the Cash Revolution

The IPL did to cricket what the Green Revolution did to Indian agriculture and liberalisation to the Indian economy. It changed the system. It did so by 'auctioning' players and determining wages through the interplay of market forces. Players got paid according to merit, not on a fixed scale decided by the BCCI, and this injection of cash made the IPL the ideal fast track to fame and riches.

Players seized this opportunity to earn money and secure their future. Market-driven salaries reduced the dependence of domestic players on government jobs and temporary PSU contracts. Fortunately, the BCCI designed the IPL as a 'domestic tournament' and granted reservation (seven Indians in the playing eleven) and gifted financial benefits—contracted players would get their full salary even if they were not picked for a single game.

The IPL's cash revolution has created cricket crorepatis. In the 2022 auction, Ishan Kishan went for a staggering ₹15.25 crore, fast bowlers Prasidh Krishna, Harshal Patel, Avesh Khan and Deepak Chahar breached the ₹10 crore mark and teams bet big on uncapped Shahrukh Khan, Rahul Tripathi and Abhishek Sharma. Top Indian players commanded top rupee – K.L. Rahul: ₹17 crore; Rohit and Jadeja: ₹16 crore; Kohli and Hardik Pandya: ₹15 crore; Sanju Samson: ₹14 crore.

The 2022 mini auction set new records with teams bidding big for overseas all-rounders. Sam Curran (₹18.50 crore) became the most expensive player in IPL history, while Ben Stokes (₹16.25 crore) and Cameron Green (₹17.5 crore) fetched serious money. Harry Brook (₹13.25 crore) lucked out and Nicolas Pooran's case was even more interesting. Released by the Sunrisers after a poor season, he found himself in great demand in the auction and ended up with Lucknow for ₹16 crore, substantially higher than his previous salary of ₹12 crore.

Kane Williamson, the Sunrisers captain, wasn't so fortunate – his salary dropped sharply from ₹14 to ₹2 crore, as he moved to the Gujarat Titans. Prominent among those who suffered huge pay cuts were Kylie Jamieson (₹1 crore from ₹15 crore), Jhye Richardson (₹1.5 crore from ₹14 crore) and Romario Shepherd (₹50 lakh from ₹7.5 crore).

Auction prices don't accurately reflect a player's worth, they only indicate the franchise's desperation to acquire a particular player given the demand–supply situation. Also, mini auctions have their own dynamics because teams are targeting specific players to fill gaps in their squad. In a regular auction, with 25 slots to be filled within the player purse of ₹95 crore, it is unlikely that Curran/ Stokes/ Green/ Pooran/ Brook would attract the price they did.

Given its reach, the IPL is the perfect platform for product launches ranging from movies to new automobile models and mobile handsets. Each team has roughly 25 commercial partners. Duff and Phelps, the brand experts, have valued the IPL at US$ 8 billion and KPMG, in a recent report, acknowledged the IPL's role in raising economic activity, creating cricket and non-cricket jobs and contributing to tax revenue.

The 2020 season added a new twist with Dream 11, a fantasy sports platform, becoming the IPL's lead sponsor. This is the first instance of a cricket corporate, an insider, stepping up instead of an outside entity such as a real-estate player, a cola brand or a mobile handset manufacturer. The IPL's association with Dream 11 demonstrates the rising influence of the fan and the economic possibilities that open up. Earlier, fans were useful for buying tickets and merchandise; now, the boundaries have been extended for deeper engagement. Evolved fans (with knowledge, smartphones, cheap data and good connectivity) are active participants in virtual contests, not merely passive consumers of the sport. That fans are directly funding cricket is a game-changing development—Indian cricket's *atmanirbhar* moment.

The IPL first smashed box-office records in 2017 by netting ₹4,000 crore annually from sponsorship deals. The 'achhe din' promised by Lalit Modi arrived when the STAR media deal amounting to more than ₹16,000 crore over five years kicked in and each team's share of central revenue went up. This changed the colour of balance sheets from red to green and the teams turned a financial corner, moving from certain losses to guaranteed profits.

What followed in 2022 was even more astonishing. Media rights for the next five-year cycle fetched nearly Rs 50,000 crore, a staggering jump, with the digital space outstripping traditional television in value. The upward trajectory is captured by the following numbers:

2013: ₹8,000 crore; ₹13 crore per game
2018: ₹16,000 crore; ₹53 crore per game
2023: ₹48,000 crore; ₹117 crore per game

It is not surprising then that IPL team valuations have soared. In 2018, JSW bought 50 per cent of the Delhi Daredevils for ₹550 crore. The Rajasthan Royals in 2023 were worth approximately ₹18,000 crore. When the new teams of Lucknow and Ahmedabad sold for ₹7,090 crore and

₹5,625 crore respectively, the high price shocked industry experts. But going by recent trends, those numbers look very workable.

The Fitness Impact

Aware of the IPL's life-changing opportunities, players have been working on their fitness and developing the skills needed for the 20-over format. There has been a huge aspirational shift with the IPL being perceived as the end goal and the traditional career pathway of Ranji–Duleep–India is no longer as attractive. The Ranji is, in the eyes of the modern-day player, too much effort for too little gain—essentially, a waste of time. On 'days cricket', as players describe Ranji, the sun has set. A total eclipse.

Those lucky enough to reach the IPL dugouts upgrade their skills by learning from the best and soaking in the atmosphere of top-quality cricket. Think of Yashasvi Jaiswal opening the innings with Jos Buttler, Mukesh Choudhary and Simarjeet Singh sitting next to MSD in the CSK dugout, Hrithik Shokeen getting tips from Rohit Sharma. Akash Madhwal gets fast bowling lessons from Jofra Archer at MI and when young Yash Dhull is Warner's colleague at DC, the positive rub-off travels downstream to mates in the Delhi Ranji dressing room—like the adventurer merchants on the old Silk Route sharing their learnings with others once back home.

The IPL has thrown up new and confident players who are ready to take on the best. Rahul Tewatia demonstrated this when he hit five sixes in one over to take down Sheldon Cottrell and three sixes off Andre Nortje. Rinku Singh smashed 31 in the last over to seal an incredible victory for KKR. Abdul Samad hit a last ball six to take SRH across the line against RR. Jaiswal deposited the first ball of the innings from Nitish Rana into the stands. Left-arm quick Mohsin Khan conceded just 5 when defending 11 in the final over despite having big hitters Cameron Green and Tim David at the crease.

The league has created 'white ball' specialists Yusuf Pathan, Pawan Negi, Krunal Pandya, V. Chakravarthy, M. Ashwin, Nitish Rana, Shahrukh Khan, Shivam Dube and Venkatesh Iyer. Because of the IPL, Ranji bowling attacks have begun to revolve around quicks and a leggie or a left-arm spinner, and fielding standards have gone up, as has the run rate. Ranji games produce more results because teams are chasing wins.

It may not have been intentional, but the birth of the IPL became cricket's moment of *azaadi*, the tipping point that gave it freedom from control and restrictions. Just as India's liberalisation policies in the 1990s unshackled an economy chained by regulation and control, the IPL freed up cricket and unlocked its potential.

Players no longer have to slave for years in domestic cricket to get rewarded. Instead, they can paradrop to the top by taking the IPL shortcut. Talented players without Ranji experience could get noticed in local state leagues by IPL 'spotters' and find themselves sharing a dressing room with MSD and Kohli. This is possible because the IPL has made BCCI selectors redundant and removed them from the equation. Ajay Jadeja, a sharp cricket mind, explains: Earlier, players were desperate to please five selectors who controlled the careers of 1,000 first-class players. But the IPL has appointed hundreds of selectors and spotters who search for talent and this has broken the BCCI's monopoly on selection.

Jadeja astutely points out that the IPL has moved cricket from consistency (needed in Ranji and Tests) to intent and impact, from solid defence to tactical aggression. Instead of teaching strict discipline and self-denial, coaches now encourage players to express themselves in a style that suits them. With old methods (getting in line, foot close to the ball and elbow up) losing importance, batting is about making runs using any technique – with a straight bat, a scooped hit, a paddle shot, a reverse sweep or a switch hit.

Players, liberated in spirit, don't have to attend formal coaching in cricket academies anymore because they receive online education by watching live television coverage. When Brain Lara breaks down the finer points and performs live demos from a television studio dugout, it is invaluable *gyaan* available for free.

Battle of Brands

While IPL teams battle in the middle, a different contest is fought away from the public eye. This is the battle of brands where franchise teams compete to create distinct identities to connect with fans.

There are those who dismiss branding as mere perception, a hazy concept for generating goodwill and a positive image. But in the commercial context of IPL, the brand is at the core of the franchise-based business, more important than the players or the team. It is an asset to encash, and as the league matures the focus will increasingly shift from players to brands. That is why the ILP has been positioned as a long-term valuation game.

Initially, iconic players helped by attracting attention to the brands they represented. Later, their role diminished and players became passengers on a long-distance train, arriving and departing only to be replaced by others. They have a limited shelf life and the list is long, of top performers moving on, being retained or released, or remaining unsold.

The brand, on the other hand, is more permanent and, released from the grip of celebrity players, it develops its own distinct identity. Occasionally, the star value of players continues to work for the brand, as with MSD and Virat Kohli. Attached like glue to their teams all these years, their influence is such that the distinction between team and brand stands blurred. In public perception, MSD and CSK are inseparable. As N. Srinivasan put it, *There is no CSK without Dhoni.*

Earning the loyalty of fans is critical to the brand, and unlike politicians, who reach out to voters at election time, brands engage with their fan base regularly. It is the emotionally invested fans (with their faces painted in team colours) who make the brand. That is why the battle of brands is fought fiercely on social media platforms, with likes, tweets and number of followers becoming the measure of victory.

The Future

There are questions about the IPL that demand a deep dive. The first: has the IPL delivered on its promise of making domestic cricket robust?

It is true that exposure to top players and the experience of competitive cricket in the IPL has been immensely beneficial. The modern Indian player is self-confident and better prepared for a higher grade of cricket, his education fast-tracked by sharing a dressing room full of legends. India could field two international sides simultaneously (in Ireland and Sri Lanka) because the IPL created the bench strength. Impressed by the depth of talent, Faf du Plessis made a telling observation that, thanks to the IPL, India could field three competitive T20 teams. 2022, in particular, was a breakthrough year for young Indian talent, the IPL lit up by the brilliance of Tilak Varma, Rajat Patidar, Mohsin Khan, Yash Dayal and Mukesh Choudhary. The 2023 season saw the emergence of new stars Yashasvi Jaiswal, Rinku Singh, Dhruv Jurel, Jitesh Sharma and Nehal Wadhera.

But is there a downside to this success story? Possibly, yes. One concern, articulated by Rahul Dravid when the league started, was that it would devalue traditional cricket in the eyes of young players. If it is possible to make serious money and become a star on the strength of the limited skills required in the 20-over format, he argued, why would anyone work hard to play Test cricket? Facts confirm Nostradamus Dravid's prediction: players don't want to play *any* red ball cricket. Not even Ranji.

Non-believers are certain that once the dazzling lights dim and the loud music subsides, the harmful side-effects of the league will rise to the surface. Like long COVID, IPL's long-term impact on cricket's ecosystem is still not fully known. But there is no denying that the cricket climate has changed forever.

One criticism of IPL is that unequal player salaries create conflict in the dressing room. This imbalance is a reality that everyone (diplomatically) chooses to ignore, but large differences in player contracts inject negativity into domestic cricket. In Delhi, veteran Ishant Sharma was priced at ₹1 crore, much lower than Nitish Rana and Rishabh Pant. In Punjab, Yuvraj was at ₹1 crore while Prabhsimran Singh, the U-16 keeper who had not yet played Ranji, went for ₹4.8 crore. In Chennai, Murali Vijay earned a fraction of V. Chakaravarty's salary. And Cheteshwar Pujara must have wondered what made his Ranji colleague Jaydev Unadkat hot property at the box office.

The skewed salary structure places uncapped players like Rahul Tripathi and Shahrukh Khan above Virat Kohli, Rohit Sharma and Jasprit Bumrah, who are in the BCCI's ₹7 crore A-plus annual contract category. Gavaskar has strong views about disproportionately high salaries for uncapped and U-19 players. He feels this disturbs the balance among domestic players, creates disharmony and devalues the Ranji Trophy. According to him, salaries of uncapped players should be capped (maybe at ₹50 lakh) but once they play for India, market forces in the auction should determine their value.

The bizarre nature of the IPL contracts was noticed when K. Gowtham was bought by CSK for ₹9.25 crore but did not play a single game in 2021. Tim David of MI had a pay cheque of ₹8.25 crore in the IPL but his salary in England's Hundred was a mere £50,000. K.L. Rahul (₹17 crore) was more expensive than an entire team in the Big Bash League or the Caribbean Premier League.

Besides affecting dressing-room morale, the IPL is criticised for messing up the batting techniques of youngsters, Unmukt Chand being one example. Players are encouraged to play too many shots too soon, and patience, previously seen as a virtue, has become a grave sin. Fed a steady diet of the

T20 format, young players don't learn the art of building an innings. And even more damaging than technical confusion is the disrespect that has developed for other formats. Ravi Shastri famously said that the IPL is the best physio (because everybody reports fit) and the best energy supplement (because nobody wants rest). These positives aside, it is toxic in the sense that it creates an environment where players play Ranji only for the purpose of playing the IPL and seniors skip Ranji to 'save' themselves for the IPL.

The stark reality is that top Indian players are getting richer (with demand exceeding supply) but the vast majority (1,000-odd Ranji/first-class players across 38 teams) exists outside the reach of the IPL's commercial lottery. Ruturaj Gaikwad, Devdutt Padikkal, Venkatesh Iyer, Harshal Patel and Rahul Tripathy made spectacular gains, leaping from ₹20 lakh to astonishing multi-crore contracts. Shahrukh Khan, Rahul Tewatia, Avesh Khan and Prasidh Krishna were handsomely rewarded, but substantial benefits (contracts upwards of ₹20 lakh) have reached only a small group of domestic players.

What the IPL has done is create job opportunities for a larger number of Indian support staff. After an initial phase when foreign professionals were hired as a package deal with foreign coaches, retired Indian crickets, including Sanjay Bangar, Chandrakant Pandit, L Balaji, Pravin Amre, Arun Kumar, Mohammad Kaif, Hrishikesh Kanitkar, Ajit Agarkar, Abhishek Nayar, Mithun Manhas, Ajay Ratra, Sairaj Bahutule, Vijay Dahiya, Wasim Jaffer, Sunil Joshi, Ashish Nehra and Aashish Kapoor were appointed as teams realised that Indians are best suited to provide intelligence about Indian players who make up two-thirds of each squad.

However, in terms of future growth, a big stumbling block could be IPL's policy that players can only be contracted through auctions. In previous years, 'uncapped' foreign and Indian players could be signed through mutual negotiations and this allowed teams to hunt out and secure talent. Now, with everyone going into the auction, teams don't see value in developing players. It doesn't add up, remarked an official, because all that effort and money goes down the drain if a competing franchise raises the paddle one extra time to outbid you in the auction.

For the IPL to grow the BCCI needs to look at creating an enabling environment where team owners are encouraged to invest in the properties they own. Currently, teams have no say in the governance of the league as they don't sit on the IPL governing council. There is also the possibility of extending the season beyond eight weeks. For the multi-million-dollar business to be sustained, the league needs more teams, more matches, a bigger season, perhaps even two seasons. Obviously, such expansion would throw up challenges in scheduling and player availability, including conflicts with national bilateral commitments. It could also jeopardise the future of Test cricket and reignite the club versus country debate.

Yet, for the IPL to live up to its potential, teams must view it as a 365-day business and not lapse into sleep mode post June. They need to create activities to remain busy and engage fans instead of having them fall off the radar. This won't be easy because the players are contracted for only ten weeks and, unlike the big international football clubs, IPL teams don't have 'touch points' such as stadiums or other facilities that fans can relate to.

A women's IPL is already a reality and a junior IPL is an option that could strengthen the brand and allow teams to connect effectively with fans. Until this happens, teams could take steps within their control to partner with their state associations and embed themselves in the existing structure. Also, they could explore new sources of revenue to reduce their dependence on the share of central sponsorship they receive from the IPL. Ticket sales and uniform sponsorship numbers are likely to soon hit saturation point and any future increase would only be incremental. To achieve financial independence, running subsidiary businesses (customised video content, cricket academies, merchandising and licensing) could become an important priority.

There is a catch though, because alternate revenue streams can only materialise if the brand is strong. The teams recognise this reality now and are paying attention to building their brands—a change from the past, when it was thought that a strong brand would emerge organically. MI have been running an extensive education programme, the Rajasthan Royals are helping to preserve Rajasthan's rich cultural heritage and DC has formed cycling and running groups in Delhi.

But it is KKR which has had the clearest vision about its brand and its critical importance. Initially, like the others, they relied on players (like SRT in MI and MSD in CSK), brand ambassadors (like Shilpa Shetty for Rajasthan Royals and Akshay Kumar for DD) and high-profile owners (such as Vijay Mallya at RCB, Preity Zinta at Kings and of course, SRK).

In the beginning, SRK was all over KKR and the two were difficult to separate. He appeared in television promos, led ad campaigns and pulled in his personal sponsors to support the franchise. It was Venky Mysore, KKR

CEO, who recognised the long-term implication of this connection. He felt that the KKR brand was being smothered by SRK's overpowering presence and realised that while this was good to get the franchise off the ground, it would stunt its future growth. For brand KKR to evolve, SRK had to recede to the background. The challenge was, how to put this across to SRK and get him to step aside. Venky pulled off this feat by explaining that distance between the two entities (KKR and SRK) would benefit both, especially the latter. While pushing KKR, SRK was actually diluting his personal brand because he could be accessed through cricket at a cheaper price. From a business perspective it made sense to ring-fence the SRK brand and maintain its exclusivity. It is to SRK's credit that he grasped this logic and separated himself from KKR. He also distanced himself from day-to-day decision-making and left the cricket to carefully chosen professionals. His is still a powerful presence, but KKR is a thoroughly professional unit.

This was not the only smart move that Venky, the seniormost CEO in the IPL, made. The next step was to shift the focus to the brand, away from the players, and put it on a high-growth trajectory. KKR stopped using players and players' images in their communication and travelled abroad to carry the brand into new areas. Its first stop, in 2015, was the West Indies, where it bought the Trinidad team in the Caribbean Cricket League (CPL). The Trinidad Knight Riders have since become the most successful team in the competition, winning the title three times. KKR was also part of the aborted T20 league in South Africa and acquired a stake in the US Major League Cricket tournament. In addition, they operate the Abu Dhabi team in Dubai's ILT20.

This global expansion is good business because of the cricket synergies between different teams. Brendon McCullum has been head coach in the CPL and IPL, and Sunil Narine and Andre Russell played for KKR across different leagues. KKR's global footprint helps them acquire new fans and keeps the brand alive throughout the year.

The business strategy of CSK and RCB, meanwhile, has remained unchanged. Both brands remain chained to the powerful personalities of their star players, MSD and Virat Kohli. While this will continue to be effective for as long as these players are active, once they move on, as they must, both teams will have to rethink their strategy.

Ultimately, brands are about fans, loyalty and engagement. So far, the IPL's franchise teams have taken their fans for granted and used them for financial gains. However, as the league matures, they are becoming aware that they have to go beyond a transactional relationship and forge an emotional bond with fans based on a sense of participation and ownership.

Allies or Enemies?

Fans complain about the nonstop churn resulting from player auctions that change the team composition every year. Jaydev Unadkat has represented 7 teams in his career and with players regularly shifting loyalties, it's difficult to remember whether the previous year's Super King is now a King or a Royal, a reborn Titan or a Giant.

From a governance perspective, IPL teams presently exist in private bubbles, removed from the Indian cricket ecosystem despite being part of the BCCI. Their role in domestic cricket is limited to contracting a maximum of 18 players to build their squad. Avishek Dalmiya, president of the Cricket Association of Bengal (CAB), voiced this sentiment when he said the last Bengali player to make the KKR squad was Sayan Ghosh in 2017.

Some feel that the IPL teams are merely feasting on the best players and should become constructive shareholders who contribute to Indian cricket. For this, franchises must invest in talent in their regions and partner with state associations to promote the sport. This was originally on the IPL's agenda under the 'catchment area' scheme but was sadly abandoned.

That said, the BCCI also needs to set a development agenda that involves franchise teams by giving them a meaningful role. It can persuade franchise teams to take a cue from MI, which has an elaborate cricket promotion and talent development programme that is independent of the IPL team. Their Talent Search Group headed by John Wright includes T.A. Sekar, Rahul Sanghvi, Kiran More, Abey Kuruvilla, Robin Singh, Vinay Kumar and Parthiv Patel. These experts scour India looking for youngsters with the spark that separates the good from the ordinary.

MI has invested heavily in a plush cricket facility in Navi Mumbai which has a state-of-the-art ground (with international standard LED lights) a High Performance Academy (with fulltime coaches, physios and trainers), a modern gym and indoor nets. When COVID-19 struck, MI had a month-long camp for their players in a secure bio bubble. MI's domestic players practised there through the monsoon on the centre wicket which was covered with transparent fibreglass. In 2022, the franchise took young players drawn from all over India to England as a part of their talent scouting strategy.

But there is a depressing side to those domestic players who exist on the fringes of IPL dugouts. Many don't get to play a single game, for them the IPL is limited to pre-season training camps and random team meetings. Yash Dhull got a few starts with DC and Prabhsimran Singh, Punjab Kings' batting star who scored a hundred against DC in 2023, played just 6 games in the previous four years. Even big-ticket players are starved of opportunities. Parthiv Patel didn't get a single game one season and India players Umesh Yadav, Ishant Sharma, Amit Mishra, Navdeep Saini and Karn Sharma have warmed the bench for extended periods.

Compared to Indian talent, overseas players have it much worse, with top stars missing out because of the 'only 4 foreign players rule'. Joe Root was benched by RR for ten games before he got one. De' Cock sat out for a month with LSG and Punjab Kings' Kagiso Rabada struggled to make the team.

Still, from the perspective of Indian domestic players, especially those striving to break through, the IPL is an invitation to the Oscars, a passport to the dream world. Getting picked at the auction is an achievement, getting a game is a massive break and in case one makes a mark, the sky is the limit. Even an accidental brush with cricket's A-list celebrities is a huge positive. Young players benefit from sharing net sessions with top stars, if only to see how Virat Kohli straps on his pads or Jasprit Bumrah marks his run-up at practice.

Many of the problems of domestic players would be resolved if the BCCI were to insist that the IPL teams provide opportunities for Indian coaches and support staff, and foreign experts share their knowledge, perhaps through the NCA. Learning from franchise teams, the BCCI could adopt the best practices of cricket management and governance used in the IPL. For instance, Ranji teams desperately need professional data analytics support for enhancing performance and, going by the experience of the IPL, there is a case for empowering coaches and reducing the interference of officials. There is also a growing perception that IPL performances receive excessive weightage in the national team selection and on some occasions, a soft approach has been taken when players have prioritised the IPL above India.

Observers gazing far into the future worry about a possible confrontation sparked by the growing ambition of IPL teams. Will a stage be reached

A Delhi Daredevils brand promotion event

when assertive team owners flex their economic muscle to create their own destiny, defying the BCCI? Given the IPL's growing clout, it is possible that the league could snarl at, if not bite, its parent.

There are some visible signs of the changing equation between the board and the franchise teams. Quietly, almost unnoticed, the BCCI has been ceding ground. Its regular pathway of junior cricket stands disrupted. Players prefer taking the IPL elevator to the top instead of climbing the many stairs of domestic cricket. The BCCI's normal selection policy has also been short-circuited by the IPL's elaborate network of spotters. The franchise teams are powerful stakeholders who collectively invest in excess of ₹1,000 crore (salaries and other expenses) every year but take away almost ₹2500 crore collectively as profit, a large amount that escapes from cricket's ecosystem. Presently, the team owners are without a role in governance, but their influence is growing. MI has created an elaborate structure to support its cricket business. RR has set up academies in Nagpur, UAE and England and ventured into women's cricket. KKR, RR, CSK, DC, Sunrisers and Kings have taken their brand overseas. RCB is pushing for matches to be played abroad, to tap into the Indian diaspora market. DC is running a network of academies and tournaments in the National Capital Region (NCR).

As the teams scale up their activities, they might end up stepping on the toes of state associations and trespass into space that the BCCI presently owns. The gradual encroachment on territory has the potential of triggering friction and conflict. Thinking ahead, could it be that in the event of an ugly dispute with franchise teams, they might declare *azaadi* and establish their own league? The teams have the financial muscle and the cricketing expertise to manage their own affairs in their own stadiums with their own players. Franchise cricket could just as easily go the Liv Golf or football way with 8 or 16 teams and one or more IPLs in a season.

The big unknown in this, of course, is whether top Indian players would switch ships mid-stream to support a private, non-BCCI venture. Perhaps this too would be decided by market forces and if firm financial guarantees were available, the offer on the table might become too good to refuse. Top golfers recently switched sides, persuaded by huge sums of Saudi money; cricketers could do likewise, if promised staggering riches.

For the moment, a rebel league is not on anyone's agenda, nobody has spoken about it, nor is it likely to happen tomorrow morning. But it is a possibility in the future. Will the teams take the big Bob Beamon leap to break away? Do they want to? Do they have bold leaders to guide them through unknown territory? Is there a 'finisher' willing to put his hand up to take control and get them across the line? Is a cricket tsunami round the corner? There are no signs of it as of now. But *kal kisne dekha*?

It is true that the BCCI is all-powerful, rich and influential; other cricket-playing nations view it as a big brother or a dominant uncle who controls the ICC. Lately, its financial might has multiplied many times over, with the revenue sharing formula of ICC giving it a massive 40 per cent share, which translates into ₹2000 crore annually. England gets the second-best share, a meagre 6.89 per cent. While the BCCI is protected from any future upheaval, the ICC senses serious trouble coming. When IPL owners snapped up franchise teams in South Africa/ Dubai/ US, alarm bells rang about an imminent takeover of world cricket. This was exactly what critics of cricket's commercial takeover had feared—multiple leagues destroying bilateral cricket and Tests, IPL teams seizing control and replacing national boards to hire players by offering them year-round contracts. The trend started with Test star Trent Boult severing ties with NZ to focus on the lucrative T20 league circus. Others could follow his example. Brendon McCullum said it would be naive to think players would refuse such offers. Alive to this prospect, CA and ECB are scampering to restructure their annual contracts system to retain talent. But they are on the backfoot because they lack the resources to match what the market offers to attract the best players. A few years down the line, international cricket could morph into a series of T20 leagues playing in a loop, with the IPL being the richest and the best, its marquee event, the equivalent of Masters golf and Wimbledon. The IPL owners would then call the shots, writing large cheques with a carefree flourish and setting ground rules.

In the short run, CA's Big Bash League (BBL) and ECB's The Hundred are most at risk. The BBL, whose schedule clashes directly with the SA20 and Dubai's ILT 20, has reduced its matches and is struggling to find ways to keep its players from flying off to foreign leagues. The Hundred fortunately has a clear window in England's summer but it could also do with extra cash. Its top salary of £125,000 (compared to almost £500,000 in South Africa and Dubai) isn't good enough to attract top talent.

The BBL and The Hundred are both non-private leagues, fully owned by the CA and the ECB respectively, and the easiest way for them to raise funds would be to replicate the IPL copybook and invite private investors. But this is a difficult choice because the solution is itself a problem. As soon as the doors are opened for private investors, rich IPL owners are bound to rush in and outbid others. And this is a scenario neither the CA nor the ECB would be comfortable with.

11

BCCI AND I

Question: Who does Indian cricket belong to?

Does it belong to the BCCI or the 305 Indian players who have played Test cricket since 1932, or the 1,000 Ranji players who represent 38 first-class teams?

Short answer: Cricket belongs to everybody, yet, it belongs to nobody; it's a national treasure.

My first memory of the BCCI from the late 1980s is its dingy two-room office on the north side of the CCI in Mumbai. There was no air-conditioning, hardly any furniture, and papers were piled untidily on iron racks that needed a coat of paint. There wasn't even a washroom; the BCCI shared a common facility with others in the building.

When I first attended a BCCI meeting at the Taj Mahal Palace hotel in Mumbai, I was awed by the presence of luminaries I had only heard about. The list of stalwarts included M.A. Chidambaram, Fatesinghrao Gaekwad, Raj Singh Dungarpur, P.M. Rungta and Madhavrao Scindia. With them were Jagmohan Dalmiya, I.S. Bindra, Judge Kanmadikar, P.R. Mansingh, Niranjan Shah, C. Nagraj, J.Y. Lele and Ranbir Singh Mahendra. Such was their aura that newcomers like me stood up when senior members of the BCCI entered the room. When they debated points listed on the agenda, we listened in respectful silence.

Debates were common, and they were always animated and occasionally angry. Yet, they were never uncivil or acrimonious. It wasn't unusual for members to have a go at each other at a meeting and share a friendly glass of expensive wine a little later. Judge Kanmadikar and P.R. Mansingh ensured that the minutes of the meetings were precisely recorded, a young Jagmohan Dalmiya looked at the accounts with a fine-toothed comb. Raj Singh-ji talked at length, mostly about English cricket. Srinivasan was meticulous, his papers neatly arranged, all the important points highlighted and flagged. He argued his case with clarity and force. As did Bindra sa'ab.

The BCCI was always splintered into 'camps' but the prospect of sharing power kept the members together. If the Indian bureaucracy is known for perpetuating itself, the BCCI can claim credit for looking after its family. If India believes in unity in diversity, the BCCI is a shining example of diversity leading to unity. Different political parties were represented in the BCCI but they played as one united team to protect its turf. The BCCI was always politically loaded—N.K.P. Salve, Madhavrao Scindia, Sharad Pawar, S.K. Wankhede and Anurag Thakur served as presidents and other heavyweights, including Farooq Abdulla, Amit Shah, Rajeev Shukla, Arun Jaitley, C.P. Joshi, Narhari Amin and Manohar Joshi were prominent players.

The BCCI's annual general meetings (AGMs) buzzed with activity, for this was when important business was transacted which directly impacted members. Primarily, they were about electing office-bearers and sharing the spoils of office. All the members had a stake in this game and once the main business was concluded, minor items on the agenda (annual budgets and accounts) were signed off in as much time as a CEAT mid-innings strategic timeout at the IPL.

Elections were bitterly contested and every method was used to influence votes. Threats, incentives, promises, contact tracing—all of these were legit weapons in the battle to secure support. To gauge the direction of the electoral *hawa*, rival candidates hosted dinners on the eve of the election where the headcount demonstrated who was ahead in the race. As with any election, this could change after a late-night drink, an ominous phone call or a friendly knock on the hotel door. Long before political parties discovered the formula, the BCCI had perfected 'resort politics', with presidential candidates ensuring that their team members did not cross over to the opposing side's dressing room.

Once the votes were counted, the day ended with a *jaadu ki jhappi* and all was well. In the BCCI, I was in Mr Scindia's team which meant directly opposing P.M. Rungta (Bhaiji), former president of the BCCI, a much-respected senior who was a close family friend from Jaipur. I consistently voted against his group but he never held that against me. Bhaiji was large-hearted, generous and affectionate, and remained so without showing any hint of annoyance or displeasure. Except when he complained, in jest, to my father that I was disrespectful and didn't listen to him.

The AGM also constituted various operational committees and representatives of each zone would huddle in a corner to decide who should get which committee. After a bit of give and take, a friendly compromise would be reached and all the nominees 'adjusted'. This inclusive system ensured that status quo was maintained. The voting members were happy with their gifts and the BCCI was happy that the voting members would not rock the boat.

This might seem like a creative way of running a sports body but can one fault a democratic system where officials are legitimately elected through a transparent process? It's just that this democracy was tightly controlled, dissent was discouraged and decisions taken in backroom deals instead of the boardroom. The norm was to 'unanimously authorise' the president and the secretary to take 'appropriate steps' on all policy issues.

The BCCI works on a presidential system where the president has almost unlimited powers of patronage, which he uses for building and maintaining loyalty. In a small house of 38 the electoral balance can change rapidly, so the ruling dispensation governs in a manner that ensures voters are not displeased. Over the years, the board has had many powerful presidents but none could match the stature of Jagmohan Dalmiya and N. Srinivasan, both men of extraordinary ability. Even as secretary, BCCI, they held the remote instead of the president.

The BCCI places officials above cricketers in administrative positions. The new constitution grants 'reservation' to players on various apex councils but cricketers were always represented, from Vizzy, Ghulam Ahmad and Raj Singh-ji to Kishan Rungta, Mahendra Pandove, Sanjay Jagdale, Bishan Bedi, S. Venkataraghavan, Brijesh Patel, 'Doc' Sridhar and Niranjan Shah. This tradition has continued with Shivlal Yadav, Aunshuman Gaekwad, Kiran More, Arshad Ayub, Anil Kumble, Srinath, Azharuddin, M.S.K. Prasad, Vikram Rathour, Ranjib Biswal and Jaydev Shah. Lately, Ganguly and Roger Binny have been at the crease in the BCCI headquarters at Cricket Centre, Mumbai.

Polly Umrigar and Sharad Diwadkar were professionally employed by the BCCI, as were Suru Nayak, Doc Sridhar (highest Ranji score of 366 and an efficient administrator), Saba Karim (first-class batting average of 56.66) and K.V.P. Rao (212 Ranji wickets). Professor Ratnakar Shetty, a pillar of the BCCI, took on diverse responsibilities during his 20-year innings. He had all the rules, regulations and previous BCCI decisions on his fingertips.

I remember the time when Polly Kaka, the executive secretary, used to sit behind the office-bearers at meetings because he was only required to discharge the clerical function of keeping notes. President Scindia noticed this slight and insisted that he sit with the members and participate in the deliberations.

For some time a debate has raged about the ability of past players as cricket administrators. Sanjay Jagdale, M.S.K. Prasad and Brijesh Patel are held up as examples of forward-looking administrators but many retired players, when placed in positions of responsibility, realised that cricket administration is a difficult ball game.

Raj Singh Dungarpur and Sanjay Jagdale (both without Test experience) were respected selectors. Saba Karim, Vikram Rathour and M.S.K. Prasad were no less competent than players with more matches to their name. But India's obsession with superstars won't allow a situation where a former captain (Paul Collingwood) becomes an assistant coach under someone who never played international cricket (Trevor Bayliss in this case).

Such appointments would be unthinkable in India. Chandu Pandit, Amol Majumdar, Mithun Manhas, Sujith Somasundar, Bhaskar Pillai, Vijay Dahiya, Hrishikesh Kanitkar, Rajat Bhatia and Sitanshu Kotak are excellent pros on the domestic circuit but unlikely to get national coaching jobs or leadership roles in cricket administration. The Indian cricket culture that attaches a disproportionate value to star power won't allow a senior Ravi Shastri to play second fiddle to juniors like Sanjay Bangar.

The BCCI places officials above players in other ways too. Cricket stadiums in Chennai, Bangalore, Mumbai, Delhi, Mohali — all international venues — are named after officials (Chidambaram, Chinnaswamy, Wankhede, Jaitley, Bindra) and the pecking order is best illustrated by Mumbai where the Wankhede stadium has a Polly Umrigar gate and stands named after legends Gavaskar and Sachin. Shivlal Yadav took a bold step to correct this wrong — as president of Hyderabad cricket, he put his name on the pavilion complex of the newly constructed Rajiv Gandhi stadium.

Photographs of Tiger Pataudi, Jaisimha and Abbas Ali Baig were placed in the reception area.

The Melbourne Cricket Ground, on the other hand, has statues of past greats in the concourse, Hobart has a museum section dedicated to Ponting and David Boon, the Oval and Lord's celebrate the feats of legendary cricketers. We have a Dravid 'wall' at Bangalore but the Karnataka State Cricket Association (KSCA) stadium is yet to remember the contributions of Karnataka superstars Vishwanath, Chandrasekar and Prasanna, and Mumbai is yet to acknowledge Vijay Manjrekar, Ajit Wadekar and Ravi Shastri.

— —

The Perks of the Job

The BCCI is generous in granting perks to itself and members receive handsome benefits which are built into the system to ensure general wellness and discourage dissent. Free tickets and passes to big events are handed out; I too lucked out many times with these gifts. When Abdul Rehman Bukhatir's CBFS announced 'benefit matches' for retired players, the BCCI cleverly negotiated an agreement that allowed it to nominate four guests for the annual desert cricket circus in Sharjah. BCCI's 'holiday package' for its members at Bukhatir's expense included business-class travel, luxury hotel stays, top-end hospitality and an allowance for shopping. Everything was free, free, free.

The Sharjah stadium was rather basic then, the ground located in the middle of nowhere, surrounded by sand and manned by rude Yemeni soldiers. Invited guests watched cricket from first-floor corporate boxes and popular support was overwhelmingly for Pakistan. The smaller (and less vocal) pro-India contingent was led by businessman Kanak Khimji from Muscat, who hosted Raj Singh-ji and Lata Mangeshkar. Khimji's box was a popular pit stop for anyone looking for delicious homemade Gujarati vegetarian

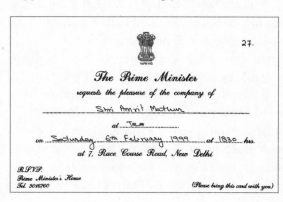

food. Indians were in a minority in Sharjah but there was one gentleman, a mysterious guest with a large entourage, who turned up to make a strong statement from the front-row box every day. He was among the few brave persons who dared to fly the tricolour.

Before the 1992 World Cup final the BCCI asked Cricket Australia for tickets and I was told that they could be picked up on match day. Knowing the last minute gadar in India at cricket matches I decided to collect them a day earlier. I watched Pakistan trump favourite England and have vivid memories of Wasim Akram's twin strikes to *chalta karo* Allan Lamb and Chris Lewis, Imran batting at number three ahead of Miandad and Inzamam. When temperatures rose before the tense finish, captain Khan sa'ab stood at mid-on, an indulgent schoolmaster letting his boys have some fun.

At the 1996 World Cup final, as one of the four members of PILCOM from India, I had the best tickets in Lahore. I watched Sri Lanka stun Mark Taylor's fancied Aussies from an exclusive four-seater box where attendants served coffee and kebabs. At Lord's, invited to the MCC enclosure by Derek Brewer, the secretary, I watched cricket on a sunlit afternoon with cricket royalty (Mike Gatting, Tony Lewis, Ted Dexter, Mark Waugh, Graeme Pollock), politicians (John Major, former prime minister and president of Surrey) and non-cricket celebs. Seated next to me at lunch was Sam Mendes who, unfortunately, I knew nothing about about till the startled host whispered in my ear that he was married to Kate Winslet and had directed the James Bond blockbusters *Skyfall* and *Spectre*. Mendes watched cricket with the intensity Bond reserves for his evil adversaries.

Cricket in England is marked by tradition and polite civility but Australia is informal and the protocol is less strict. At Sydney, when Sachin made that famous 200 without playing the cover drive or any other shot, Cricket Australia (CA) officials got up to make the mandatory speech at lunch in the president's box. He welcomed — in order of priority — guests from India, Aussie Test players, members of CA and, in the end, casually mentioned that the prime minister of Australia was also present. Did I hear right? The PM himself? Yes, it was John Howard, the cricket enthusiast who said he'd come to watch 'Laaaxman', his favourite batsman. Nobody fussed over the prime minister, there was no *shosha*, or aggressive security. He fetched his own drinks from the bar.

--

Among the officials at the BCCI that I worked with closely were Ranbir Singh, C. Nagraj, J.Y. Lele and Niranjan Shah, all of whom served as secretary of the board at different times. Each had his distinct way of handling things but all were devoted to Indian cricket.

Nagraj was very hands-on, meticulous and autocratic in a benign and benevolent manner. He would be at his desk at the Chinnaswamy every day and pay attention to every minor detail. Lele worked not only from a regular office but even while sitting on a *jhoola* in his Baroda residence. Niranjan, another long-serving official, was extremely prompt with paperwork. Kishore Rungta was a very efficient treasurer, no surprise considering the background he had in business, as the owner of a company that manufactured steel communication towers.

Interacting with Ajay Shirke, the BCCI secretary based in London, was a challenge. Shirke came to the office when in India, but this too was not without problems. He would fly in from Pune in his private plane and be at his desk around lunch. We had a four-hour window to get business done before he flew back to beat the deadline for landing at Pune airport.

Shirke was very professional and clear thinking. A man of strong views, he controlled Maharashtra cricket with an iron hand and a dog squad which was let loose on spectators to control disorderly behaviour. The Pune stadium has a detention room next to the VIP enclosure — an informal prison for those found misbehaving during a game. It's not uncommon for venues to have dress codes and guidelines for spectators and miscreants are evicted from the premises under certain conditions. But detaining people and locking them in a cell was taking things to a different level.

Another stalwart was Delhi's C.K. Khanna, a unique package of hustle and instinct who understood elections better than the Election Commission does. Ideologically agile, CK is always in campaign mode, not the *neta* whom you meet only at election time. He is more like the Delhi Police — with you, at you, all the time. He lives in the present but has one eye on the future. If Munnabhai's motto was *lage raho*, CK's is *aage badho*.

Facing the Media

Team India has a prickly *saas-bahu* relationship with the media; they are in the game together but look at one another with suspicion and distrust. The Indian team is a bunch of popular icons, role models and, lately, social influencers. Players have a sense of entitlement; for them, luxury is a right, not a perk. They are not different from yesteryears' princes looking for a privy purse in a democratic and egalitarian system.

Strangely, for a group that exists in an artificial bubble of celebrity, cricketers often suffer from a siege mentality. They feel targeted by the media and Team India is super-sensitive to criticism. As media director of the BCCI, I realised that most players are convinced that journalists are ignorant and biased, driven by their personal agendas. In this us-versus-them scenario, the players and the media sit in opposite corners. Well-known media persons have taken a hit for criticising the team, removed from commentary positions because of a passing negative whisper from a cricket legend.

Those inviting player displeasure pay a price that ranges from Gandhian non-cooperation to aggressive boycotts, angry verbal duels and churlish behaviour. Valid questions at press conferences attract a sharp putdown. MSD's responses would drip with sarcasm; Virat, even more fluent and articulate, often got riled. Most Indian cricketers dismiss any comment or observation from outside the dressing room with contempt, describing it as 'noise'.

Interestingly, knowledge is equated with the number of matches played, and you often hear that toxic question: *kitna khela hai?* Players believe that only those who play cricket know cricket, and those who have played more know more. Many support this view, arguing that war is understood only by soldiers who have seen actual combat, not by armchair strategists.

The *kitna khela hai* question resonates through Indian cricket; it is legal currency that is accepted across playing fields and dressing rooms. Cricketers swear by a pecking order that seats international stars at the high table and first-class players in a faraway corner. Looked at dispassionately, numbers do matter and players have 'domain' knowledge. But the number of games and runs scored can give you an advantage, it cannot hand you an automatic, permanent, lifelong perk. However, all key cricket appointments (India coach, membership in the Cricket Advisory Committee, the IPL Governing Council and the NCA) are 'reserved' for legends, others need not apply. Some feel that numbers lie — or, at least, conceal the full truth — and it is not essential to have played a lot of cricket to understand its nuances better. And about those who become experts without having played serious cricket, there is this classic comment: *You don't have to lay an egg to criticise an omelette.*

The media feels that players think they are above criticism and consider a negative report an unacceptable affront that demands brutal retaliation. Interestingly, retired players who work with the media are not exempt from 'friendly fire' in their new roles. With them, the '*kya khela hai*' jibe doesn't work, but their career stats don't give them diplomatic immunity either.

When a past legend (rightly) questioned Team India's decisions on an overseas tour, the response was a rocket, that people sitting far away should not 'fire blanks'. When Sanjay Manjrekar described Jadeja as a 'bits and pieces' player, the latter savagely put him to the sword by pointing out that he has played more cricket. Instances of, say, Gautam Gambhir talking tough about Virat Kohli's IPL captaincy record are rare. Most past players carefully filter their public content, not wanting to ruffle feathers and jeopardise dressing-room *dosti*.

'Captain Is King'

Ashok Malhotra (Test player, former selector and president of the Indians Cricketers' Association) observed that cricket's bhakti tradition converts players into gods and after one Test, every player thinks he knows as much as Bradman. Which, as the talented actor I.S. Johar said famously in a film, is *half right, half wrong*. Partly right because the virus of arrogance infects young players on getting an India call. Partly wrong because not all players suffer from this disease.

Many cricketers seem to believe in the myth that they are 'out there for the country', working for a noble cause. However, this talk of 'national duty' is a colossal hoax because scoring runs or taking wickets is a sporting achievement, it does not have a higher subtext. It is the soldiers in Kargil and Tawang who are putting their lives on the line fighting for the country, not someone asking for a leg stump guard on a green wicket. To equate the contributions of frontline troops with

King Kohli

cricketers is inappropriate and disrespectful.

An equally seductive myth is the one about former players wanting 'to give back' to the game. In reality, with rare exceptions, they are putting in a post-retirement job application, a request for re-employment. Many past legends chase jobs, their hunger for money and relevance couched in fake words which nobody believes. Retired players are, of course, perfectly justified in offering their experience and expertise, and in their expectation to be compensated for their time, skill and knowledge. Just spare the world the hypocrisy of the urge to 'give back'.

Another new trend is the OTT glorification of current performances and the GOAT (greatest of all time) fixation that is overtaking cricket. In this world view, Virat is King Kohli, deserving of a 21-gun salute for bossing all formats. MSD is a national treasure, the greatest leader since Gandhi and Nehru, and Rohit the 'hit man' who takes down opposition bowlers. In the frenzied adulation of current players, most people seem to overlook the fact that Indian cricket has always had brilliant performers. Gavaskar was an absolute superstar who brought respect to Indian cricket. Kapil Dev was bankable at the box office, equally popular with the masses and the critics. Sachin ticked all the boxes of greatness, the *Sachin Sachin* chant evidence of his mass appeal and sustained excellence. Dravid was everyone's inspiration and Ganguly led from the front. Sehwag and Kumble were great match-winners.

Strangely, the present-day players share an uneasy relationship with seniors from the previous generation. Living in a bubble of entitlement and self-importance, they think the past is romanticised and are convinced that cricket before their time was easy. Many past players feel their achievements are not appreciated and resent the commercial success of the present lot. In this past-versus-present comparison, one universal favourite is G. Viswanath, admired for his square cut and respected for scoring runs when others failed. People logged into the cricket circuit confirm that Vishy is personally endearing and a thorough gentleman.

Just as the Khans rule Bollywood, Indian cricket is dominated by a 'superstar syndrome' where top players call the shots. The era of powerful players started with Tiger Pataudi who, ironically, was rudely removed from captaincy by a selection panel headed by Vijay Merchant, another legend. After Tiger, Gavaskar and Ganguly had a (relatively) free hand but Indian cricket's unique 'Captain is King' culture peaked with MSD and Kohli. Such was their power that they controlled everything, from minor details (the suitcases to be used by players) to policy matters (whether the yo-yo test score should be 16.5 or not applied at all).

The 'superstar syndrome' surfaces at different levels. Established players ignore the Ranji circuit and umpires hesitate to give star players out in close lbw and bat-pad decisions. It manifests itself in interviews, such as the one where Hardik Pandya and K.L. Rahul made crass boasts about their off-field accomplishments.

Is the superstar syndrome evidence of the cricket administration's negligence, an example of dereliction of duty? Or is it clever delegation that allows urgent matters to be decided by the captain, the domain expert? It's difficult to tell, but the perception is that Indian cricket's superstars are, if not bigger, at least as big as the game. And as it turned out, excessive power in the hands of the captain was not entirely a bad thing because both MSD and Virat used it for the good of Indian cricket.

MSD was supremely self-assured and led in a friendly, non-abrasive manner, often stumping others by remaining silent. He didn't talk to anyone—not the media, not colleagues (remember Laxman?). The whisper in the cricket world was that you couldn't get MSD on the line or get him to fall in line. He is a limited-edition celebrity who lives behind carefully drawn curtains and only communicates through chance remarks, letting his achievements speak for him. He avoids publicity, yet the media chases him. MSD is a cricketer minus the spin.

He carries this aura of mystery to the middle. When batting, it is impossible to decipher his game plan. With balls running out and the asking rate rising, he is annoyingly cool—pushing singles, knocking the ball around, taking the game 'deep'. Then, just as desperation sets in, he turns red-hot to 'finish' the game. He is a batsman with a bowler's mindset who believes in keeping others guessing. When he abruptly abdicated the Indian captaincy (midway through a series in Australia, ending a 90-Test career) players in the dressing room gasped in shock.

For all his reticence and laidback attitude, MSD is not shy of making a loud statement. He wears his love for the armed forces on his sleeve and, occasionally, on his keeping gloves. During the 2019 Champions Trophy, when the *Balidaan* logo became a cause of controversy, the BCCI, TV channels, political leaders and assorted celebrities supported him. At the Rashtrapati Bhavan to receive the Padma Shri, Hon. Lt Col Dhoni delivered a crisp salute that would have gladdened instructors at the Indian Military Academy.

MSD didn't give angry send-offs to opposition batsmen and sledging was not a part of his gameplan. Yet, he ran the Indian team single-handedly with an iron fist inside his soft keeping glove. At CSK, *Thala* MSD is the final, and only, word. Whenever he decides to call time on his career, he will most likely send a brief mail to the BCCI and then jump on to his Harley Davidson Fatboy to kick off on another journey.

After MSD, Virat raised the superstar syndrome to a new high. Consider the facts: the ICC discussed future strategy, Australia commissioned an independent review to reboot its cricket and England released a vision document listing 26 priority activities. But in India, Virat Kohli set the Indian team's agenda:

- Test cricket is of paramount importance.
- Team India's goal is to win overseas.
- Fitness is non-negotiable.
- The bowling attack should revolve around pace.
- Players must embrace a culture that puts the team ahead of individuals.

Virat was best described by an observer who said he was not a music director who set a tune for others to sing. Instead, he was the tough sergeant whipping new recruits into shape.

People worry about the superstar cult and the uncontrolled power that is vested in individuals. This is a genuine concern because, without checks and balances, neutral umpires and DRS, things can go wrong and while cars need accelerators, a handbrake is also necessary. Still, on balance, the

'Captain is King' syndrome has done more good than bad for Indian cricket. History tells us that from the time of Pataudi, Indian cricket's path—the destination and the route—has been set by the captains and each era has been defined by what Gavaskar, Ganguly, MSD or Virat stood for. The ultimate team game allows space for individual expression too.

India is currently the 'surya' of cricket's universe around which everyone spins and to which every cricket body must do namaskar. The BCCI controls cricket's commercial lifeline and can destroy opponents by switching off their oxygen supply. As former PCB Chairman Ramiz Raja said, India funds the ICC, which in turn funds Pakistan. India can shut down Pakistan cricket the day it wants.

The BCCI is celebrated for its commercial conquests but it also has an elaborate domestic structure with age-specific tournaments starting from U-16 and reaching up to Ranji. Once criticised for its mediocrity, the tough grind of Ranji is now getting appreciation. If the system was actually dysfunctional, India couldn't have simultaneously fielded two international sides in England and Sri Lanka in 2021. The Indian bench is so strong that Karun Nair (a triple centurion in Tests) is not in contention and Sarfaraz Khan (a Ranji run machine) struggles to get his foot in the door of the Indian dressing room.

The BCCI has done well to take cricket to remote areas by building quality infrastructure. More importantly, cricket is now an attractive career

BCCI AGM. Key attendees, front row: Ranbir Mahendra, Kishore Rungta, P. C. Mahanta, Jagmohan Dalmiya, P.M. Rungta, C.K. Khanna; back row: Sanjay Jagdale, Brijesh Patel, S.P. Bansal, Rajeev Shukla, N. Srinivasan, Professor Shetty, M.P. Pandove, Samarjitsinh Gaekwad, Anurag Thakur

option, a passport to fame and riches. Opinion is divided on whether this happy situation came to be by accident or as a result of careful planning. Clearly, led by Dravid, the focus on U-19 cricket and A-tours has created a smooth talent pathway.

However, with 38 teams, the Ranji Trophy is bloated. The BCCI needs to cut fat by adopting the England model and run it at two levels, allowing for relegation and promotion. When Bihar's Sakibul Gani created a world record by scoring 341 runs on debut, he not only made a statement announcing his talent but also highlighted a weakness of Ranji — his history-making effort came against a weak Mizoram team.

The welfare of first-class cricketers also deserves greater attention. Given the BCCI's wealth, top Indian stars are generously compensated, but Ranji players are without the financial safety net they so desperately need. They are paid handsomely for playing Ranji but without annual contracts they are dependent on match fees where 'conditions apply' — payments are subject to selection. If not picked, because of injury or loss of form, they get nothing. Zero. And so, especially with public jobs shrinking (since the government and PSUs have stopped recruiting), vulnerable Ranji players are financially dependent on the BCCI, which is their *mai-baap* and de facto employer.

As an aside, I was pleased to find that Ramachandra Guha, a former member of the Committee of Administrators appointed by the Supreme Court, while flagging the problems faced by domestic players in his resignation letter, had referred to a proposal I once shared with him. 'The experienced cricket administrator Amrit Mathur,' he wrote, 'prepared an excellent note on the need for fairer and better treatment of domestic players but this wasn't taken forward.'

A related argument that keeps surfacing is that Test specialists like Pujara, who miss out on IPL's financial lottery, should be compensated for this 'loss' and possibly even incentivised for protecting cricket's traditional format. But this does not fly because Tests would be better served by being made more competitive and meaningful. When market forces decide IPL contracts, why would the BCCI step in to right a perceived wrong?

Cricket has changed a great deal, shrinking from five-day games to 50 and 20 overs, and now 100 balls. The run time too has reduced to 2 hours and 30 minutes. In 1964, Bapu Nadkarni bowled 21.5 overs without conceding a run; in 2013, RCB made 263 in a 20-over IPL game. Other things have changed too. Once, fans stood outside hotels to catch a glimpse of stars and get their autographs. Now they hang out in hotel lobbies and thrust their mobiles forward saying, *Please talk to my son Babloo.*

For a long time now, there has been talk of cricket being practically a religion in India. Cricket is indeed a mass entertainer that unites people in the same way as Bollywood films and music, cutting across divisive boundaries. But there is little to suggest it has a higher, uplifting purpose. Certainly, if religion is a way of life and intent on building up noble values, cricket fails the test. What we see instead is a slavish bhakti that makes idols of cricketers, not cricket. For committed followers, Sachin is the God of Cricket and fans have built temples where MSD is worshipped. Top players are national heroes and role models and it seems that players have grabbed all the respect and affection, leaving nothing for the game of cricket itself.

Such adulation comes at a price. Often, fans see qualities in a star performer that don't exist and judge him by standards he never claimed to meet. Rahul Dravid, everyone's bhai, made a telling observation that Indian cricket's only objective should be producing quality cricketers who make the Indian team win. Everything the BCCI does should be aligned to that goal.

The players too must play their part by becoming professional in the true sense of the word. Bishan Bedi bowled a straight one when he noted that *many players have a limited understanding of being professional; they mistake it for money whereas it is an attitude and a guiding principle that shapes your conduct.*

Indian cricket has to emerge from its self-manufactured bubble and reach out to society. Presently, apart from transactional contacts, it exists in its private universe — isolated from all that surrounds it. It must put its power behind causes that matter. If sport has the power to change, the BCCI should be playing a long Test match innings to make a difference.

12

GAMECHANGERS

TIGER PATAUDI

While Tiger Pataudi's career record compared to other legends may be modest, he is Indian cricket's most enduring and endearing star, an all-time great. Impact, not numbers, defines Tiger, one of the finest to wear the India colours.

I met Tiger through his nephew, my friend and collegemate Aamer Bin Jung. When Aamer joined the St. Stephen's College cricket team, he looked like a younger version of Tiger and even batted like him. On weekends, Aamer would visit his grandmother (Begum of Bhopal) on Dupleix Road and some of us tagged along. Tiger Mamu would be around and, occasionally, he would spare a few minutes to enquire about our cricket and casually throw in a few encouraging words. We looked at him with respect and awe; he, after all, was *the* Pataudi we had all grown up admiring.

Through these brief meetings, I got to know him a little. And sensing my interest in cricket, he agreed that I could write a fortnightly column about non-serious, gossipy cricket *khabar* for *Sportsworld*, the magazine he edited. He also commissioned me to do a story on Rao Raja Hanut Singh of Jodhpur, polo's Bradman, and a cover story on the mess in the DDCA, with whom he had a frosty relationship. Given that the DDCA is one place where controversy has permanent residency rights, the subject remains relevant even today.

I remember the annual trips to Sharjah in the 1990s, when Nawab sa'ab had to write a daily column for a local paper. Not a great 'watcher', Tiger found the cricket tedious. He didn't like the heat either and would leave mid-afternoon after instructing me to meet him at his hotel after the day's play to help with the article. Every evening, I dutifully filled him in on what had happened, which he then converted into a sharp piece that appeared the next morning under his byline. He was a pioneer of remote work, much ahead of WFH.

In my youthful exuberance, I addressed him as Tiger, only to find out later that not many enjoyed this liberty. Sunil Gavaskar recalls that, as a youngster playing under Tiger, he was at a loss as to how to address him. *Tiger was captain of our team in the Moin-ud-Dowlah tournament and my team mates asked me to check with him about how he should be addressed. During play, when a wicket fell and before the next batsman walked in, I went to him at cover where he was fielding. He was bent down, tying his shoe laces, when I posed the question. He looked up, finished tying his laces, got up, smiled—and walked away!*

Gavaskar wasn't alone in being confused about this. Other friends, colleagues and teammates faced a similar challenge, unsure how to deal with Tiger's intimidating personality and casual aloofness. Most played it safe: Tiger remained 'Skip' or simply 'Captain' even to players who played alongside him for over a decade.

There is so much about Tiger in the public domain that is unconnected to reality, more perception than fact. Having known him on and off for almost 30 years, I can confirm that some of the things that have been said about him are not entirely correct. If he appeared distant, it was less due to his royal aura and more because he was an intensely private and self-sufficient person. He enjoyed a quiet drink and was happy playing bridge with a few chosen friends. But attending social functions was a drag, an avoidable punishment because he disliked crowds and meeting people he didn't know. Forced to attend cricket events, he would ask me to come along. *I won't know many around*, he would say, so *stick around. We will have one quick drink and leave*. His strategy for such evenings was simple: quick entry, quicker exit.

He spoke little, but whatever he said was measured and he didn't say one word more than was needed. Strangely, for someone so articulate, he hated public speaking. He accepted invitations to attend functions only after setting non-negotiable rules: *will stay only for a short while, and no speech*. When asked to attend social cricket matches (for example, Parliamentarians versus Media), Tiger showed up in churidar kurta, sunglasses and a Panama hat to umpire a few overs. But not once did I see him hold a bat or knock a few balls. After his retirement, as far as playing cricket was concerned, he practised total renunciation.

At home, Tiger spent time in his study that opened onto a veranda with a small lawn in front where he casually hit a shuttlecock for exercise on some evenings. Surrounded by books (mostly biographies and histories), newspapers and his pet parrots, this is where he met people over tea or a glass of whisky. I once took Shashi Tharoor to meet him and, naturally, cricket dominated the discussion. Shashi did most of the talking, with Tiger making strategic contributions.

Tiger's public image is of a rockstar cricketer and inspirational captain. Much has been said about his dry sense of humour, easy elegance, and the force of his personality. In private, he was disarmingly charming and also very punctual (even a five-minute delay hassled him). His dislike for air travel has been well documented and he was known to refuse outstation engagements if they involved a plane journey. I once accompanied him on a flight during which he was genuinely terrified despite being suitably fortified with 'confidence-boosting liquids'. I was also his railway travel agent: he booked his Bhopal and Mumbai tickets in advance but would call to ask for an AC first-class lower-berth reservation.

My meetings with him were mostly without a specific agenda, and sometimes to bring him up to speed on the latest developments in cricket. Tiger watched games on television but wasn't really connected, and, when asked to do interviews or appear on shows, wanted to know about current players and their performance. Despite the obvious rustiness from being not fully tuned in, he was a difficult-to-please pro, not easily impressed by statistics. When informed that someone had scored a double hundred, he would quickly introduce quality control filters: Bowler *kaun tha*, pitch *kaisi thi?*

When asked to name the best Indian captain, Tiger voted for M.L. Jaisimha, with whom he shared a special bond. At Hyderabad, Tiger, captain of India, happily played Ranji under Jaisimha, a non-regular India player. He was less impressed with Hanumant Singh, another astute cricket mind. He thought Hanumant Singh was too 'theoretical'.

Asked to name the cricketers he admired, Tiger mentioned quite a few. He thought highly of Vijay Manjrekar (best player of spin) and Gavaskar (best all-round technique). Vishy, Subhash Gupte, Bishan Bedi, Prasanna and Kapil Dev were his other favourites. But his highest praise was reserved for Salim Durani. Approached by a newspaper to name his best-ever Indian eleven, Tiger initially refused, but relented when I pleaded with him, saying it wouldn't take more than ten minutes. He first picked the players who selected themselves: Merchant, Gavaskar, Kapil, Sachin, Kumble, Hazare. After this, he thought hard, searching for other names to complete the list. He weighed options, picked someone and then changed his mind. Mankad or Bedi? Dravid or Vishy? What about Subhash Gupte? Confused and bored, he decided to opt out. *You put in anyone you want*, he told me, *as long as you have Salim in the list.*

About himself, he said almost nothing and on the many occasions I probed, he gave little away. Questions about his cricketing career and major innings drew a blank; with a *shararti* glint in his eyes, he would deflect the conversation neatly to some other topic. In his self-effacing style, he played down his contribution to Indian cricket. He thought captaincy was simple and that people saw too much in it and complicated it. In his opinion, captaining a side was about common sense.

Tiger was only 16 when he first played first-class cricket for Sussex. When he scored a hundred in each innings for Oxford against Yorkshire, the county champions (with Fred Trueman leading the bowling attack) observers acknowledged his sensational talent. He was modest and utterly understated, with the self-confident attitude of someone supremely comfortable in his skin. Tiger had swag and style; fame and adulation sat lightly on him.

When Raj Singh Dungarpur named him India's greatest fielder ever, ahead of Azhar, Eknath Solkar and others, I asked him for a reaction. The response—brief and direct—was typically Tiger. *You know Raj, he is mad.*

On another occasion, I asked about his popular image as a god-gifted natural who didn't have to work hard and arrived at Ranji games rubbing his eyes minutes before the toss. This time, he spoke a few words to put the record straight. *That's what people like to think. In England, in university and county cricket, I slogged hard.*

Much has been said about Tiger's role as captain and his contribution in shaping the Indian team. His '*hum ek hain*' formula for Indian cricket united a fractured dressing room, he invented the spin-to-win formula and set high fielding standards in an era when dropped catches and misfields were accepted without a sign of disappointment. Tiger injected confidence and self-respect into Indian cricket and made runs abroad in Australia and England against pace. But his lasting legacy is the affection, admiration and adulation he continues to receive from his fans and colleagues.

Nobody is more profuse in praising Tiger than Bishan Bedi. *He was the best thing ever to happen to Indian cricket*, he says. *Tiger was simply outstanding as a captain, player and person.* When Bishan organised an event in the memory of Tiger, the large turnout of past and current cricketers confirmed this. Among those present that evening were Virat Kohli, Sehwag, Jimmy Amarnath, Vishy, Aunshuman Gaekwad, Gautam Gambhir and many other stalwarts.

When the IPL started, Tiger was on the governing council, lending the league credibility and stature by associating with it. But his role was only peripheral and he was uneasy being part of the set-up. Yet, when removed from the IPL council (without reason), he was deeply hurt and, quite against his character, went to court to claim his contractual dues. The ugly episode was settled only after he passed away.

IPL and T20 cricket weren't Tiger's cup of tea. I once invited him to a game in Delhi and he agreed after much persuasion. He spent one hour getting to the Kotla from his Vasant Vihar home. He watched for a while before his patience ran out; he was put off by the bright lights, loud music and noise in the stadium. Four overs into the game, he asked to be dropped back and made the return journey, another hour in Delhi's crazy evening rush hour. Cricket's hottest, money-spinning product left Tiger stone cold.

When he suddenly fell ill, I went to see him at Sir Ganga Ram Hospital and was depressed to find him struggling to breathe due to a severe lung infection. The doctor said he was on the mend, but sadly, it wasn't destined and a few days later he was gone. Too soon, only 70.

I was away in England when Rinku called to give me the sad news. *Tiger has passed away and an announcement will be made a little later,* she said, sounding extraordinarily stoic, her voice firm despite the crippling loss. His nephew Saad bin Jung (Aamer's younger brother) wrote a piece in the *Asian Age* about Tiger and I was moved by his mention of the fact that one of the persons his mamu last mentioned was me.

It is almost 50 years since Tiger retired and over a decade since he passed away. But he will always be remembered fondly by all those who love cricket.

JAGMOHAN DALMIYA

Early in 2004, a meeting was held in Jagmohan Dalmiya's office at the CAB to discuss the BCCI security team's visit to Pakistan to assess the on-ground situation. It was a day before our departure for Lahore and I was sitting with Jaggu-da when the phone rang. A senior (very senior) minister in the Union government was on the line and the conversation was brief.

The minister wanted Dalmiya to cancel the tour citing security concerns, thus taking the onus away from the Government of India for a politically loaded decision. Jaggu-da heard him out respectfully before responding in a clear, firm tone: *I am the president and the BCCI wants the cricket to go ahead. You are the government; if you don't want the tour, please go ahead and order its cancellation.*

Indian cricket has seen legendary players and formidable administrators, but Jaggu-da was in a league of his own. He was blessed with a 360-degree understanding of the business and administration of cricket, and was absolutely the right man in the right job at the right time.

Jaggu-da stood up for friends and allies and carefully nurtured personal relationships. Beneath his tough exterior was a caring individual who joked and laughed easily. However, to those who didn't know him well, he remained a stern figure with a steely gaze, generously oiled hair (as if hit by a slick, wrote Rohit Brijnath) and trademark grey or beige safari suits. His command of the English language wasn't the best, but those who underestimated him for this quickly regretted it because he spoke with clarity and made his points forcefully and with sound logic. You could disagree with the grammar but the message was always clear.

Like all good players, his success lay in doing the small things right. Jaggu-da was disciplined, he believed in the 'process' (the current buzzword for cricketers) and had a strict daily routine. He arrived at his Shakespeare Sarani office around noon. The next few hours were devoted to his real estate and construction business, followed by a working lunch consisting of simple, homemade dal, roti, rice and vegetables; fried bhindi was his favourite.

Around 3 p.m., he reached his sparse, windowless CAB office on the first floor at Eden Gardens. Switching roles from private businessman to cricket administrator, he worked into the night, only heading back to his Alipore Road residence once all the business of the day was concluded. Then he settled down to watch the daily soap operas.

Cricket embraced Jaggu-da's personal, professional and social life in a lifelong *jhappi* – he had no time for anything else and little outside of cricket interested him. Fiercely focused, he worked very hard and I never saw him looking tired and don't remember him ever wanting a break. BCCI members soon got used to being woken up by his calls at odd hours. To use a cricket analogy, he was a hungry batsman who combined the work ethic of Dravid and Kohli. First to arrive at practice and last to leave the nets.

Despite being at the centre of many things, he was never caught off guard. Whether attending or chairing meetings at the BCCI, Jaggu-da was one step ahead of the others. He was always ready, his papers neatly arranged, key portions carefully flagged and marked for quick recall. His strengths were attention to detail, solid preparation and flawless paperwork. While others walked into meetings unaware of the agenda, he came with his homework done and lessons revised. His mastery over documents and records was such that he could pull up minutes of past meetings and previous correspondence quicker than a computer.

These qualities stood Jaggu-da in good stead when facing investigations by the Enforcement Directorate, Income Tax Department and CBI. No administrator has been put under the scanner as much as Jaggu-da, but despite all manner of allegations and thorough probes by multiple government agencies, he came out unscathed. Not one charge was proved.

Initially, Jaggu-da treated me like any other member of the BCCI who had a vote—I represented the Railway Sports Control Board—in a small house of 27. Later, our relationship changed. When he became secretary of the BCCI, he saw me as someone who had the ear of the board president. As our interaction increased, he began to find me worthy of sharing responsibility with, a decision that I suspect was driven not by my competence but by our common Rajasthan connection—all conversations between us, except in official situations, were in our native Marwari.

Jaggu-da appointed me to key positions and gave me important assignments even when I wasn't a member of the BCCI. I was invited to attend BCCI meetings and he created the position of Director, Media Coordination in Delhi so that I could have an office and a role within the BCCI. Our equation created heartburn and I recall a BCCI meeting at which a member rose to confront him about my holding the position. Angered that he was being questioned, Jaggu-da responded firmly as only he could: *Let us not go into who can do what*, he said. *I know who is capable and who is not. Don't ask me to elaborate.*

Though a control freak, Jaggu-da consulted people he trusted and sought their opinion. He would then digest the information and process it in his mind before taking a calculated decision. But once he decided which way to go, whether to hit through the line or play across, he entertained no self-doubt and saw no need to course correct. Not the type to be shaken or stirred, the only physical sign of things not going to plan would be his eyes darting around in different directions.

Jaggu-da was never on the backfoot and his reputation for getting into scraps was well-earned. He was the proverbial street fighter who took on the

ICC's white establishment that ruled cricket until the Indians came along, shattering convention and rewriting, not rules but the game's financial statements. He stood up to match referee Mike Denness (over the ball-tampering controversy around Sachin) and protected Muralitharan and Shoaib Akhtar (because Pakistan and Sri Lanka were allies) when they were charged with suspect bowling actions.

Irked by the insulting attitude of the ECB and Cricket Australia (CA), who sent 'inspecting teams' to check facilities in India before a tour, Jaggu-da decided to hit back and teach them a lesson. Ahead of a tour to England in 2002, he dispatched a two-member BCCI team—Jyoti Bajpai and I—to travel to England to review arrangements for the Indian team. To me it felt like a fully paid two-week holiday to England with a large daily allowance. There was, however, one snag: it was a bit embarrassing to go to Lord's to assess whether it was good enough to host the Indian team. Lord's is the Mecca of cricket, the dream venue for everyone wearing whites. Could one possibly fault the famous slope or the wooden benches outside the Long Room or the cramped home team dressing-room balcony?

Still, you do what you have to do. To appear professional and business-like, we landed in England with a detailed wish list to do with dressing rooms, hotels, food preferences and security. The ECB, fully aware of the background of the visit, cordially showed us around various venues, fixed meetings with county officials and explained the arrangements they had put in place. We dutifully went around England 'inspecting' Old Trafford, the Oval, and meeting officials who appeared bemused by our visit but were too polite to comment on it.

We submitted a report to the BCCI giving England the thumbs up, declaring it worthy and ready to receive the Indian team. But nobody was interested in the feedback, least of all Jaggu-da. To him the messaging was important and what mattered was optics and perception. And on this occasion, the point was to tell the ECB not to mess with the BCCI.

Another time, Jaggu-da interviewed John Wright regarding the coach's contract. Ahead of the interview at the Taj Palace, Delhi, I put up a briefing note flagging some points for him. We both knew that the interview was a formality. John's job was secure but Jaggu-da wanted to send out the message that he meant business and that everyone was accountable.

In the interview, Jaggu-da came straight to the point. He said that the team's performance must improve and, mincing no words, issued a direct warning to Wright: *I am under pressure and want you to be under pressure.* Wright handled this with impressive calm and accepted the challenge, saying he was happy with the arrangement. Jaggu-da was satisfied that Wright had got his message and announced that he was extending the contract till the 2003 World Cup. Wright thanked him graciously and slipped in a quicker one. *It's fine*, he said, *but three months down the line, if results are not to your satisfaction, I will be happy to step down.* Jaggu-da must have wondered whether Wright was brave, super-confident or just reckless.

Like a batsman in tricky conditions, Jaggu-da was quick to assess length and his footwork was precise. In the words of someone who was at a meeting with him to discuss a business proposal: *Mr Dalmiya is not only single-minded but single-handed; he knew exactly what he wanted and didn't budge. No on-one-hand and on-the-other-hand stuff. He seems to have only one hand. It was his way or … nothing.*

Jaggu-da was a clever strategist with an uncanny talent for keeping people together and managing elections. He knew how to handle power and used patronage to create a loyal group of supporters. At CAB, the club members swore by him; in the BCCI, his word was law for voting members from the East zone. In the ICC, he consolidated the subcontinent votes to ensure India, Pakistan, Bangladesh and Sri Lanka remained united. It was due to his deep understanding of election *rajniti* that Zimbabwe's Peter Chingoka became a lifelong friend of the BCCI.

Jaggu-da understood money and grasped numbers on a balance sheet as quickly as Mohandas Menon processes cricket stats. His negotiating skills were legendary and he could squeeze more rupees out of a commercial deal than anyone else. I recall an occasion when a potential sponsor approached him with a final figure already worked out in his mind. Half an hour later, he emerged from the meeting with a smile, having happily agreed to a much higher amount. Jaggu-da had convinced him that paying more was in his best interest.

Jaggu-da was a natural leader who led the BCCI with distinction, but the same board conspired to file charges against him in a court, leading to an inquiry and extensive interrogation. But the wheel turned and, in a spectacular somersault, the BCCI turned to him when hit for a six by the Supreme Court. By then, Jaggu-da's health was failing.

During that stint, he asked me to work with him and, for a short while, I spent a few days every week in Kolkata. He was far from the confident, energetic man we had known; his magical touch was gone. Like a past superstar struggling to time the ball, Jaggu-da had difficulty finding the middle of the bat. But this was only a minor glitch in an otherwise magnificent career. Jaggu-da was Indian cricket's original Don, feared and admired. He was also the first Indian whose voice was heard with respect in world cricket.

SACHIN TENDULKAR

Despite the claims of Sachin's countless fans, including Virender Sehwag, Sachin is no god. Nobody is. But legend, icon, master, GOAT—all of this he certainly is. The hard evidence is 664 matches for India, 35,000 international runs, 200 Tests and 100 hundreds. In his 24 years of bossing cricket, Sachin Tendulkar has set the bar so high that others can only pass under it. Sachin has created his own mountain, a cricket Everest, that others crane their necks to admire and reflect on.

My first interaction with Sachin was on the 1992 tour to South Africa, when he was only eighteen years old. There was something awe-inspiring about him even then. Seasoned cricket administrator Ali Bacher thought Sachin was in the same league as Graeme Pollock and only one step away from Don Bradman. In 1999, in Chennai, Pakistani players respectfully stepped aside to make way as Sachin came out of the Indian dressing room. During the 2003 World Cup in South Africa, the Netherlands team and their families lined up after the game at Paarl to get photographed with him.

Many years later, at Lord's in 2019, I saw the respect he commanded among fellow players. Aakaash Chopra and I were in the media centre with Sachin, who looked dapper in a sharp Italian suit and Hermes tie, when he was approached for a photo. It wasn't the usual fan request. It

With Sachin in Sharjah, 1998

was James Anderson, the fast bowler with the highest wickets in Test history, asking Sachin if he could have a photograph with him.

You understood where that awe came from. During overseas tours with the Indian team, I observed Sachin in action and it was obvious he was special. At team meetings, he would make sharp points, expressing his views logically and clearly. At the 2003 World Cup in Harare, when the team was getting slammed for underperforming, he fronted an emotional appeal to fans through the media to reassure them that the players were trying their best.

I saw him at work in the dressing room—choosing his spot and spreading his kit before a match, bats neatly lined up against the wall, pads, gloves, helmet and elbow guard kept ready. I saw him play in acute discomfort and pain after taking cortisone injections for his injured shoulder. I watched the fussy pro going through his pre-match routine. Gentle stretches, a quick look at the wicket, some high catches and, finally, knocking a few balls to get the right 'feel'. He was self-sufficient and listened to others but carefully filtered the advice he received. Cricket never caught him in two minds—the one he had was excellent.

Sachin the player was a Ferrari on cruise control. Coach John Wright said he never had to remind him about anything. Trainer Andrew Leipus said Sachin knew his body and did what was needed to 'maintain' fitness. For Sachin, preparation was key. He was a master who remained the student, never rushed, always ahead of the class, having revised his lessons twice before every exam. He had the time and the steely resolve to succeed. He was aggressive but in a non-demonstrative, non-Virat way. Sachin's cricket DNA didn't allow him to play a false shot and he wasn't one to lose his shirt or take it off. On off days, he would play pool or a game of table tennis with his teammates. Relaxed yet competitive, he battled hard for every point because he hated losing. He said the only people he could bear losing to were his children.

Sachin prepared by staying in his self-created bubble while chasing excellence. Most observers look at his numbers but Imran Khan made a perceptive comment about his real genius: no player maximised his natural ability like Sachin did. Respecting the process was an important part of his preparation. Once, in England, on the night before a three-day practice match, teammates invited him to join them for dinner. He declined politely, saying he had to get ready for the game. Not a Test, just another first-class match, a 'side' game.

During the 1992 South Africa tour, as the team manager, I often helped the team at practice, hitting high catches and helping batsmen (with knocking) because there was no support staff to assist coach Ajit Wadekar. With Sachin, even if he was patting the balls gently, the ball came back quicker than I expected.

During the 2003 World Cup, he didn't bat in the nets for a long time, relying instead on knocking and throwdowns. His explanation: *I am*

batting well and feeling good. When Sachin ordered an extra pair of pads midway through the tournament, the consignment was delivered to me. The carton containing the Morrant pads was so light I thought it was empty.

While most batsmen obsess about the pitch, Sachin was equally worried about sight screens at the ground. Shane Warne admitted Sachin gave him nightmares, but there was another group of people who had sleepless nights thinking about the great man—the ground staff. They dreaded Sachin landing up at the last minute to demand the height of the sight screen be raised.

Ahead of the World Cup clash with Pakistan at Centurion, Sachin looked at the track and the outfield. He observed that batsmen could run two to third man because the blades of grass were facing the other way and would slow down the ball. It's normal for batsmen to factor in opposition bowlers, pitch and weather conditions, but examining the direction in which blades of grass near the boundary grew? Extraordinary!

Such attention to detail is not surprising, if you consider that Sachin is cricket's Google. Once, when he casually mentioned that he remembered every dismissal in his career, I challenged him by asking about a first-class game on a previous tour of England. He reeled off his score and the bowler's name and provided additional info: *After lunch I cut a short ball from the left-arm spinner and was caught at point.*

In all these years and multiple tours, Sachin's respect for cricket always stood out. Cricket for him was not about amassing runs and scoring hundreds but a commitment, a duty to perform and a sacred debt to repay. God blessed him with gifts that he accepted gratefully, and he surrendered himself completely to cricket. He touched the ground each time he entered the field and looked up at the sky for inspiration and thanksgiving. Even his autograph is a personal statement: always signed with full attention, neatly written and never a hurried scrawl.

I often think that the dialogue writer Kader Khan's classic line—*bachpan mein pachpan* (a child wiser than his years)—aptly describes Sachin, for he seems to have been born mature, with a monk-like humility and composure.

In the late 1980s, when Bombay's Ranji team was practising at Baroda's Moti Baug ground, captain Dilip Vengsarkar pointed to Sachin, who was standing quietly behind the net and said: *That kid is the best batsman in Bombay after me and Sanjay Manjrekar but I am not playing him—he is too young.*

The person behind the player has remained charmingly modest and self-effacing even though he has so much to be immodest about. In the team set-up, he was the first among equals and was always treated with respect, but in his demeanour I saw a superstar with his feet firmly grounded, who loved playing childish pranks on Yuvraj (whom he nicknamed 'Young') and Harbhajan.

On the 2002 tour to England, I remember, Sachin had committed to another engagement around the same time that the team was to attend a performance of the musical, *Bombay Dreams*. I said to him that the organisers were looking forward to his presence and a last-minute change would be awkward. He agreed instantly, turned up and also went on stage to meet the actors before the show. When the lights dimmed and the formalities were done, I told him to quietly slip away.

I always saw him treat my role as tour manager with respect and courtesy. A Wisden Awards function at Wembley on the same tour ended late one night, the venue a longish drive away from the team hotel. As we boarded the bus, Sachin asked me if his wife Anjali could ride with us. She had come with some friends for the event and they had left early. It took a moment for me to understand what was happening—this was India's most senior cricketer, not a schoolboy, asking for permission which he didn't really need. According to team tradition, wives are allowed to travel on the team bus for official functions and social events. Sachin knew this, but chose to follow protocol. His sense of courtesy and propriety are innate—it didn't matter who he was, what mattered was that he did what was right. If he took a break to be with his family, away from the tour for a week in London, there would be a thank you afterwards—formal but sincere.

I saw a superstar who chewed his nails nervously in tense situations. A friendly senior who never raised his voice or threw his weight around but helped create and maintain a tension-free dressing room. He expected no favours and made no demands. Didn't pull rank or use his stature to extract privilege. We got used to his modest manner, an exception in a world where dressing rooms have been damaged by the egos of superstars less skilled and with lower performance standards.

In terms of setting an example, he ensured he did everything right, down to the smallest detail. If the luggage had to be collected by 11 p.m., Sachin was the first to keep his bags outside his hotel room. He was never late for the bus or a team meeting or a gym session. If a contest was held for the most neatly organised room, he would be a runaway winner. Everything about him was organised and thoughtful, whether it was making a list of questions to ask his motor racing hero Michael Schumacher ahead of their dinner meeting at Silverstone or giving Sehwag technical lessons on how to open a bottle of wine.

Not that Sachin was always even-tempered and unruffled, but his was a controlled anger. When match referee Mike Denness penalised him for ball tampering in the Port Elizabeth Test in 2001, he felt he was being deliberately targeted by a vindictive person bent on publicity. He said Denness's mind was made up—*he questioned my integrity and I could see anger in his eyes.* During the 2004 Multan declaration crisis on the historic tour of Pakistan, Sachin was upset at being called in at 194 but he and captain Dravid settled their misunderstanding like two mature adults.

Sachin is India's most loved celebrity but the fame and adulation extract a heavy price. He misses leading a normal life, misses taking his kids for *nariyal paani* at the Bandra bandstand. A private person, he guards his personal space by erecting walls around himself; to the outside world he is the batsman always wearing protective equipment. When the guard drops, we see the 'normal' Sachin. At dinner, he dominates the conversation while eating his favourite seafood with his teammates. Like others, he stresses about gaining weight and once went on a severe 'soup only' diet to get back to 72 kg.

In personal interactions he is correct to a fault and if he gives you his word, the chances of him forgetting it are zero. Even if you do. Once, on a flight back from Dhaka (after Hrishikesh Kanitkar hit a last ball four to win the final), I asked him for an interview to discuss the craft of batting. He agreed and promised to do it on his next visit to Delhi. A few days later, I was astonished to get a phone call from Sachin, ringing to fix a time for our chat.

During our longish conversation (carried in four parts in the *Hindustan Times* and, later, as a cover story in *Outlook*) he spoke freely about his game. To two of my questions he gave answers that would have seemed immodest coming from someone else. When asked about his childhood heroes, he replied he was too busy playing his own cricket. On the burden of the expectations of fans, he said he was more concerned about meeting his own expectations. He was not being boastful, just stating facts.

During the Pakistan tour of 2004, my twin boys were participating in a school sports quiz which was being aired on STAR. One evening, in Lahore, the hotel phone rang; it was Sachin on the line, calling to say that he had seen them on TV and was happy they had won that round.

At the start of that tour, I asked Sachin for an autographed bat but forgot about my own request. After the last Test in Rawalpindi, everyone was busy packing and rushing about as an Islamabad–Delhi flight had been arranged outside of the normal protocol. The day before we were to leave Rawalpindi, there was a knock on my hotel door; it was Sachin holding a bat, neatly autographed. He said, *Aapko dena tha.* I had forgotten, he had not.

Sachin is cricket's royalty, a Bharat Ratna and a role model for youngsters. He wears his eminence lightly but is acutely aware of the responsibility that comes with his stature. Which is why he supports a wide range of social causes in a spirit of 'giving back' and is that rare public-spirited celebrity who refuses to endorse any cigarette or alcohol brand. Despite tempting offers, it is a strict 'well left' from the master.

SRT's cricket heroes: Don Bradman, Sunil Gavaskar, Viv Richards.

An early cricket lesson: *My coach would punish me for not grounding the bat or getting dismissed playing a loose shot.* Mujhe bahut daant padi hai. *As a kid I was scared of fielding.*

LALIT MODI

Once the undisputed king of Indian cricket, Lalit Modi has been in exile since 2010, a fugitive according to the Indian government. Friendless and forgotten by India's powerful who once courted him, disowned and discredited by the board he ruled, Lalit's contribution seems to have been erased from Indian cricket.

Time, an unbiased third umpire, will assess Lalit's brief cricket innings and pronounce a verdict. It is likely to describe him as a man of extraordinary contradictions who played the double role of creator and disruptor—a remarkable builder and bulldozer. A maverick who built a unique property, but in doing so, triggered a series of events that singed him and almost brought down the BCCI.

Lalit was a cricket outsider who crashed the BCCI party and ended up wrecking it from the inside. Many myths surround him; one popular version attributes the launch of the IPL to a personal vendetta against Subhash Chandra, who owned Zee's Indian Cricket League. The truth is that it happened as a consequence of Lalit returning to India from America, excited by the idea of a cricket clone of the NBA or NFL. He dreamt of a privately owned made-for-television league, masala cricket laced with money and *mauj masti.*

Rewind to Bombay in the early 1990s. Lalit met the legendary ad guru and worldwide CEO and creative head of O&M, Piyush Pandey, who put him in touch with Arun Lal and me, to explore the idea of a privately owned cricket league. The three of us worked on the project and developed a blueprint, down to identifying teams, selectors, coaches, players, and even office spaces in different cities.

This was the original IPL, but with two key differences from the final product that was launched 15 years later. Our league had 50-over games (since T20 didn't exist then) and the tournament was to be owned and operated by a private entity which would receive a licence from the BCCI for a commercial consideration.

BCCI President Scindia supported the idea and a formal proposal was presented to the board through his home state association, the Madhya Pradesh Cricket Association (MPCA). The BCCI junked it in no time. To salvage the deal, a meeting was arranged between Lalit and Jagmohan Dalmiya, and I travelled with him to the Shakespeare Sarani office. The meeting lasted barely ten minutes and was a total disaster.

Jaggu-da thought the league was a non-starter because its commercial numbers (projected revenue from media rights and sponsorship) were way over the top. His blunt, almost rude, conclusion was a sledgehammer blow: *This is a fool's paradise.* Years later, he explained the real reasons for the BCCI rejecting the Modi league. *Cricket,* he said, *is BCCI's property and we have a monopoly to run our dukaan. Why allow someone else to start a similar business and create competition?*

Lalit realised that the league would only work with support from within the board and so he began to make his moves on various fronts. He joined hands with J.Y. Lele in Baroda to became vice president of the Baroda Cricket Association, with Lalit's firm (Godfrey Philips India, owners of Four Square cigarettes) sponsoring its Ranji team. He also shared a working relationship with Punjab through I.S. Bindra, but the ball started rolling for him only when he was elected secretary of the Rajasthan Cricket Association with government support. It gave him a seat in the BCCI and a direct say in decision-making. Allowed a free hand by the then president Sharad Pawar, it didn't take long for Lalit to convert his dream project into reality.

At an IPL franchise workshop in Bangkok in 2009, Lalit informed stakeholders about the years of hard work that had gone into the IPL launch and mentioned my association with him in the long journey. But when the league finally got underway in 2008, I almost missed the opportunity. Lalit offered me a job, taking into account my experience as a cricket administrator and my previous association with him. But accepting a full-time responsibility meant I had to resign from my government job, which was not an easy decision. To protect myself from future upheaval, I made outrageous financial demands, all of which he readily agreed to. With the deal done, I took the flight back to Delhi.

Almost immediately, doubts began to crop up in my mind about this new assignment. The IPL was exciting, the deal with Lalit was terrific, but I felt uneasy that a friend would effectively become my employer and write

How the Board slept over its own ICL

Chandresh Narayanan | TNN

Mumbai: So, is the Indian Cricket League (ICL) really a novel concept? On the face of it, yes. But a closer look at it reveals that the ICL was really an old idea put forth in the BCCI circles, much before the TV wars began.

What's more, the idea got shot down not once, but thrice in Board meetings. So, the fact that the Board has finally woken up to the idea of a league of its own is a tacit admission of dragging its feet.

The ICL was an idea initially floated by current Board vice-president Lalit Modi way back in 1996. He had registered a company called Indian Cricket League with the late Board president Madhavrao Scindia as chairman.

That ICL was also supposed to be a six-team city-centric league to be played under lights with four foreigners per team. Teams like Mumbai was to be called Mumbai Lions and the stage was set for the league to be

rolled. The only difference being the BCCI's ICL was to be in 50-over format and not the current ICL's Twenty20.

The basic research for this league was done by former Board media manager Amrit Mathur — adman Piyush Pandey and former Test opener Arun Lal.

Modi had presented his case to then Board bigwigs like president I.S. Bindra and secretary Jagmohan Dalmiya. The idea found favour and few world greats of that era had even been contacted to participate. But eventually it was shot down as one top official did not agree with the idea of having foreigners playing in India.

A few years later in 2003-04, the ICL changed its shape again and this time was to be a 40-over affair to be run like an inter-corporate tournament. Again the Board officials got together and decided that the league "would not make any sense."

Regimes changed hands, a few more heads rolled and

the idea got buried.

As the TV wars began to rule the vision of Indian cricket, the ICL returned once again this time as part of a three-point plan presented by a production house in June 2006.

The plan was: (a) re-brand domestic tournaments, (b) scrap the zonal structure, (c) introduce a club structure for Twenty20 to be run as a franchisee with public-private ownership. The idea was revolutionary and for some within the Board 'threatened' to strike at the very root of its existence. It was, for some in the Board, 'blasphemous' to suggest the scrapping of the zonal structure, because of the vote-driven culture.

The idea was quickly put in cold storage only to be dusted and re-drawn just as the new ICL began to rear its head. Ironically, the old ICL is still registered in the name of Modi. Now, his idea may finally fructify. And, in all probability, BCCI will not be the first to capitalise on it.

my salary cheque. This changed equation bothered me and on landing in Palam, I called Lalit to tell him it wouldn't work. He, expectedly, blew a fuse at my sudden U-turn and screamed in his familiar hyper voice that we had agreed on everything just hours back. We had, and I had changed my mind. Simple enough.

My mind was made up: working with Lalit would be playing with fire, more dangerous than handling Malcolm Marshal on a green wicket. I appealed to my friends Arun Lal and Piyush Pandey to douse the fire, which they did quite well.

My misgivings weren't unfounded. Lalit behaved more like a czar than a commissioner. He was whimsical and unpredictable, the sole decision-maker, and anyone who crossed his path had to take a hike. Given a free hand in the IPL, he had no hesitation in showing anyone the finger.

The BCCI was not unfamiliar with autocrats but Lalit pushed the bar higher. He ran the IPL single-handedly from a laptop and a Blackberry, sitting in his office, hotel suite or private aircraft. He was a one-man army who brushed aside the BCCI and the IPL Governing Council as effortlessly as Viv Richards could put away a leg stump full toss.

Unconcerned about being polite or civil, Lalit never held back. During an IPL workshop in Goa, he raged at a senior BCCI office-bearer in the hotel lobby in full view of guests, volume turned up full, using language a Daryaganj *ka dada* would have been proud of. He had no time for a second opinion or an alternate view. When the IPL moved to South Africa, he summoned the franchise operating teams for a workshop. A long agenda was on the table but Lalit ticked off each item with a quick yes or no. What would have normally taken a full day was sorted out in less than one hour.

Lalit kept total control over the IPL by remaining switched on at all times; one wondered whether he slept at all. Given his limitless energy and relentless drive, he always answered calls and responded to messages; teams got used to receiving mails (mostly instructions not to be disobeyed or delayed) late in the night and early in the morning. Nothing remained pending with him; you always got an answer.

To keep the IPL moving in real time, Lalit got his hands dirty by getting involved in relatively minor issues, even personally checking tickets at games and evicting guests without proper invites. At the slightest opportunity, he'd be on the phone shouting instructions and demanding compliance, whether it was for tickets for a sold-out game or wanting changes in the seating arrangement in a hospitality box. Always in a hurry, for him tomorrow was yesterday.

The IPL was Lalit's Mission Mangal, a magnificent achievement to be accomplished by him alone. He was a climber who wanted a selfie on Mt Everest without anyone else in the frame—a paradoxical situation where one individual bossed over a team sport.

Never short of self-confidence, he was sure of his role in the IPL universe and was not shy about projecting himself. He used the media to create a personality cult, doing interviews and photo shoots as film stars do before a major release. It was difficult to decide what he loved more—himself or the power and reach that the IPL provided him. He was a performer and always on stage. At IPL games, the joke was that a Modi-cam followed him.

On a personal level, Lalit was warm and charming, a gracious and generous host. He lived life king-size, everything about him was magnified. He stayed in the most expensive suites in luxury hotels, drove the biggest cars and wore designer suits with his trademark blue linen full-sleeve shirts. I once travelled with him in a chartered plane from Jaipur to Chandigarh to watch an ODI. We were there for barely a few hours—we reached post lunch and flew back before play ended. Life in the Lalit stream was bizarre but heady.

In Jaipur he is remembered for the daily darbar outside his Rambagh Palace hotel suite. At the RCA he is remembered for the funds he raised using his considerable clout with the government. Apparently, he set financial targets for senior officials; some of the funds raised were used wisely (to build infrastructure, the famous academy), others for questionable purposes (RCA voters were informally assigned monthly allowances to ensure loyalty).

Today, Lalit is caught in all kinds of legal complications but it would be unfair not to give him his due. If India takes pride in having gifted the IPL to world cricket and inventing a magic formula which every country has put into copy mode, Lalit deserves at least a grateful nod of acknowledgement, if not praise.

His vision for the IPL was clear. The 'domestic' BCCI tournament had to be the best in the world, bigger and better than anything cricket had seen. He was uncompromising, going for the best players playing for salaries they would only have dreamt about. Lalit insisted on small things that made a big difference: the design of the accreditation card, the lanyards, the look and feel at the stadium, the decor of the marquee and the design of match tickets and invites. He chose the food menu, customised crockery, decided branding and personally approved the t-shirt design, IPL memorabilia and giveaways. If the IPL installed turnstiles at venues and created a better stadium experience for spectators and had dancing cheerleaders and rocking after-match parties, all these came with a Lalit Modi stamp.

He created the IPL's business model where everything—player auctions, strategic timeouts, cheerleaders and even umpires' uniforms—was monetised. He understood money and the cricket market better than others. His mind converted everything into money (dollars, not rupees!) and came up with top numbers that others thought were unrealistic and outlandish.

Lalit sold the IPL, a concept still on paper, to eight investors to raise almost US$ 700 million. Broadcasters and sponsors paid serious amounts and money poured into the IPL. Every financial deal, every contract, every player payment was noted in dollars and figures were always mentioned in millions, never crores. This was a deliberate business strategy to dazzle the cricket world into believing that a spectacular, never-before global product was being launched.

Lalit did more than just market a concept through a clever pitch. His lasting contribution is getting the league off the ground. Thinking of an idea is easy, putting words into action is a rare and very un-Indian quality. In a country full of wise men with great ideas, Lalit was a rare doer who talked (a lot) but also walked the talk.

Equally remarkable was his unique gift of making enemies and rubbing people the wrong way. Lalit did not feel the need for friends and had a talent for converting friends into enemies. Teamwork was an alien concept given his impatient, undiplomatic, cocky nature and it was only a matter of time before things unravelled and the wheels came off. A colleague in the IPL described him best: *Lalit was an out-of-control boxer who threw wild punches even when asleep*. He was a cocktail of swagger and substance and if the credit for launching the IPL must go largely to him, so must the blame for his stunning fall. He streaked briefly across the cricket sky only to disappear into the darkness beyond.

In a casino, regardless of the game you play, it is the house that eventually wins. In a twisted way, the same holds for Lalit Modi, who played his cards well for a while, but in the end, was dismissed by the BCCI. In cricket the law of averages comes into play and over time the good and bad decisions balance out.

Any kind of DRS would find it tough to decide Lalit's case. But it is certain that the spike mark he scratched on Indian cricket won't disappear so easily.

SOURAV GANGULY

Sourav Ganguly is best remembered for:

- His debut hundred at Lord's in 1996.
- His aggressive captaincy.
- His bare-chested act on the Lord's balcony after India's NatWest win in 2002.

I remember Sourav the elegant left-hander who drove fluently through the offside. And captain Sourav who changed the mindset of the Indian team and made them believe they could win overseas. But these are not the 'qualities' that define Sourav the person, the cricketer or the captain.

The popular view is that Dada was aloof and arrogant and believed he was an entitled cricketing prince. I saw a different person who was grounded, self-confident and insecure at the same time. Someone who struggled with the burden of responsibility, the expectations of others and his own ambitions, but kept a lid on all the pressure simmering inside. Someone deeply superstitious, who changed his jersey number, apparently advised by Sanjay Bangar, and wore many threads and chains around his wrists and neck to attract luck. Someone who prayed in the dressing room when India batted and silently consulted the third umpire above to arrive at the right cricketing decisions. Depending on the *tashan* of the day, Sourav was the first to get off the bus or  the last. I saw a charming and generous person who deliberately 'leaked' information to the Bengali media surrounding him because, in his words, their editors would otherwise give them *bamboo*.

I saw in Sourav the contradictory figure who loved England despite having been attacked by racist hooligans on the tube. *It was a scary experience,* he recalls. *Sidhu tried arguing with them but I kept quiet and luckily, we escaped unscathed.*

Sourav had a set routine and hated waiting for his turn once padded up. Batsmen are fussy about their bats but nobody was more fastidious than Sourav. His kitbag contained seven to nine bats, each with three extra grips sticking out above the handle. He used different bats depending on the situation—heavier ones when getting into top gear—and changed bats even mid-over. With Sourav in the middle, the twelfth man was a harassed person, always on high alert.

Sourav's understanding of Indian cricket history could be sketchy but he was up to speed on runs, averages and strike rates of players. While he admired England's cricket structure, he had difficulty adjusting to county cricket's discipline and professionalism. He was a modern pro with charmingly old-fashioned ideas about fitness, fielding and training. He would turn up late for meetings, miss a gym session, fix a net for practice and not land up.

Sourav changed Indian cricket, his captaincy marked by some fundamental principles, such as:

- Win toss and bat first.
- Play with a three-men pace attack because *what will I do if one has an off day, can't have spin from both ends before the first drinks.*
- Ensure boundaries at grounds are extended, so opposing batsmen think twice before attacking Indian spinners.

Away from the dazzling glare of fame and adulation, I saw an emotionally frail Sourav scarred by doubt and uncertainty. The protocol on overseas tours is that the team management decides the playing eleven with inputs from senior players. Sourav often defied this and would overturn decisions taken the night before while walking out for the toss. *It's my neck on the line,* he would say. *Everyone has suggestions but nobody is certain. That's why in the end I listen to my inner voice.*

There were occasions when Dada the captain felt the heat. In Harare, before a must-win game to stay alive in the 2003 World Cup, team morale was down as players were being slammed for underperforming and faced mounting criticism. Dada surfed the net in the hotel's business centre, his face visibly darkening as he read unpleasant reports from back home. The corrosive tension that goes with captaining India is best described by him: *My hair turned grey and I lost weight.*

He was aggressive in a quietly confident manner. He would be strong in a tight match situation, but in private spaces, the pressure occasionally rose to the surface. On an off day in South Africa, the players went to a shooting range to hit targets in an enclosed space. This was done with real weapons—automatic carbines, pistols and Kalashnikovs which went off with a loud noise. Some of the players enjoyed the experience, but not Sourav, who came out of the cabin looking deeply disturbed.

Did Dada deliberately make other captains wait at the toss to rile them? That's more myth than reality. In the 2003 World Cup league game against Australia at Centurion, by the time he walked down the steps, the others were already waiting in the middle. Reason: the team couldn't decide what to do on winning the toss. In the general panic I was asked to contact Ravi Shastri to get his opinion. I called frantically (while Sourav waited, team sheet in hand) but couldn't get him on the line. Turned out the panic was pointless. He lost the toss.

Dada was as much manager as captain, a leader of men whose main accomplishment was creating a happy dressing room and maintaining peace.

This wasn't easy given that he had towering seniors on one side and a group of seriously talented young players on the other. Driven more by instinct and intuition than inspiration, he discovered the best working arrangement. His relationship with seniors was built on unconditional respect and he left them alone to go about their business. He praised the genius of Sachin, admired the discipline of Dravid and the consistent brilliance of Kumble. The toughest decision for him was having to choose between Kumble and Bhajji.

He related an incident when the selectors decided to drop Kumble for the Australia tour. They had made up their minds but an adamant Dada wouldn't agree. He refused to sign the team sheet. The discussion went back and forth for hours with neither side willing to take a step back. Dada wanted experience and proven ability. The selectors wanted to give a break to a promising youngster. Ultimately, Dada prevailed.

Dada's relationship with his juniors was based on genuine trust. Players believed they would get a fair deal with him. He was, quite literally, the caring older brother. On selection matters, especially when it came to younger players, Dada was guided by a simple principle: pick players who can win matches. Based on this yardstick, he always voted for Yuvraj, Harbhajan or Sehwag. Once convinced of a player's potential, he supported him wholeheartedly. A day before the 2003 World Cup final, when Yuvraj was belting bowlers in the nets at the Wanderers, Sourav watched with admiration. *Isme bahut dum hai. He doesn't know the talent he has but has to get rid of distractions and focus on his game.* Watching Sehwag score a triple hundred in Multan in 2004, Sourav predicted he would play more than 100 matches for India. Sure enough, Sehwag retired in 2013 after 104 Test matches. The tea lover had read the tea leaves right!

Two memories stand out for me. The first is of Dada the vanquished leader. In 2003, in Johannesburg, India had lost the World Cup final to Australia. The Wanderers dressing room resembled a disaster zone with players holding their heads in disappointment, some shedding tears. After the post-match ceremony, where Sachin was presented the award for Player of the Tournament, the team returned to the Sandton Sun hotel for a final meeting. Little was said. Players shared their grief and rued the missed opportunity. Sourav made a stirring speech, a general vanquished in battle applauding his troops for the fight. He spoke from the heart and praised individuals for their efforts. He had a special word for Srinath, who had announced his retirement after the game. His unscripted speech was emotionally charged and sincere, the words pouring out spontaneously.

My second memory is of Dada the triumphant leader. India had just won a historic series in Rawalpindi in 2004. In the dressing room, celebrations were in full swing. The team was rejoicing, and as is customary, expensive champagne was being wasted. Some poured on players, the rest spilt on the floor.

Sourav congratulated his mates on the victory and profusely thanked everyone for making the fantastic achievement possible. All standard stuff, the usual nice things that are said on happy occasions such as this one. What followed, however, was extraordinary and has stayed with me since. Dada turned to Akash Chopra (who is now Aakaash) and Ajit Agarkar and apologised to them because they had not got a chance to play. Captains don't normally say these things and neither did the situation demand it. He could easily have had a private word with them, but he chose to publicly seek pardon. That is the kind of empathy and humility he was capable of.

In Indian cricket, Dada stands apart as a leader of men.

MADHAVRAO SCINDIA

One afternoon, when I was away at some remote railway station, people in the office were frantically trying to find me. Urgent messages were repeated on the Railway control telephone network with instructions that I must rush to Rail Bhavan. The messages were heard by everyone and, understandably, created great *hulchal*. Why, wondered station masters and senior officials who were logged into the system, was the Railway minister looking for a junior Railway officer?

It was about cricket, I found out on reaching his office. *The selection of the Railway Ranji team in Bombay is badly messed up*, he said, from behind a desk cluttered with a mountain of files, coming straight to the point. *Go, sort it out*. When I pointed out that selectors and coaches should take these calls, his response was quick. *You have my authority, just go fix it.*

This was my first contact with the Railway Ranji team, and the incident marked the start of a long association with Mr Scindia. As secretary, Railway Sports, he gave me a free hand in making policy and, more importantly, in its execution. He ordered that all sports files and papers should be directly routed by me to him, bypassing the many layers of the slow-moving Railway bureaucracy. This created heartburn and considerable jealousy in the bureaucratic hierarchy, but some saw the positive side of it. One officer, directly my senior, said: *It's great the minister has faith in you. Just keep us informed about what is happening.*

Mr Scindia was more of a professional CEO than the usual *neta mantri*. With him, the ground rules of official interaction were clear: every paper and file marked by him had to be discussed the same day. Which meant a late evening meeting in his Rail Bhavan office before he called it a day. He also had a (dangerous) habit of keeping track of papers marked by him to officers and would ring, sometimes late at night, to enquire about something that had been sent a few days earlier. With him you had to be alert at all times.

He was extremely fussy about the letters he signed; the language had to be right and he preferred to see a typed-out draft first. Only when fully satisfied would he sign, with a flourish, using a fountain pen with black ink. Never a ballpoint. Never blue ink.

As Railway minister, he is remembered for two important sports initiatives. One was about the Railway teams wearing a corporate logo on their playing kit, an idea much ahead of its time. I had persuaded Lifebuoy's Ravi Dhariwal to 'sponsor' all (about 40) Railway national teams and provide clothing and equipment to the players. When this landmark proposal (in my opinion) went to the minister for approval, it came back immediately with a line in red drawn across the noting sheet with a bold 'NO'!

That same weekend we were playing a social cricket match. A wicket had fallen and as we waited for the next man to come in, he casually asked why I wanted Railway athletes to wear private corporate logos. *Can't be for money*, he said, *because we can pay for the stuff*. I explained that it was for creating a consistent look and a sense of pride that every national-level Railway athlete was smartly dressed. To support my argument, I pointed out that our own team members, fielding at the time, were wearing different shirts with different logos, which didn't look good.

Send the file back, he said, walking back to his position at mid-off. The next day, he approved the Lifebuoy deal.

Mr Scindia wanted Railways to form a women's cricket team, an idea that left me cold. The standard of the women's game was very ordinary, not many players were seriously committed to it, and fielding and fitness were major issues. The quality of play wasn't anything to write home about, though there were exceptions, notably Diana Eduljee, a skilful left-arm spinner,

Shanta Rangaswamy and a few others.

My objections were dismissed with a wave of his imperious hand. *Let's hire the whole Indian team*, he instructed. That's how the great cricket defection happened: the entire Indian team employed with Air India resigned their jobs to switch overnight to the Railways. Diana led the defection, making the personal shift herself to become the captain of Indian Railways and the captain of the Indian cricket team.

Mr Scindia's election, when he stood for president, was amongst the most bitterly contested in the BCCI's history. There he was, the candidate from Haryana, North Zone in one corner and opposite him, Jagmohan Dalmiya backing B.N. Dutt from Bengal. I had a ringside view of the drama that unfolded.

Mr Scindia's supporters camped at the Oberoi Grand, Calcutta, the hotel gripped by a war-like atmosphere. The group of supporters had to be protected and kept in a secure, unreachable bubble, away from rivals desperate to poach them. This was the resort politics of those days — voters protected from temptation and terror.

I found myself in the middle of this intense battle, a minor pawn in a high-stakes game. With each vote so crucial, every effort was made to influence voters to change loyalties, cross the pitch and go to the other end. In this unusual (to me) power game, my wicket was the first to fall. The night before the election, the anti-Scindia lobby persuaded the Railway ministry to change its representative for the election meeting. A communication was sent to the BCCI that instead of me, the duly authorised secretary, some other officer was nominated to attend the meeting.

The sudden switch drastically disturbed the delicate vote count. Aware of its implication, Mr Scindia picked up the phone and spoke to someone (really) high up in the V.P. Singh government. The call worked and soon — past midnight — Minister of Railways George Fernandes came on the line to assure Mr Scindia of his support with a promise to restore my vote. The phone was passed to me and the minister directed me to vote for Mr Scindia.

While the conversation was going on, Mr Scindia signalled frantically that I ask the minister to send a fax reinstating me as the Railway representative and also convey written instructions to me. I dutifully mumbled the request and within minutes a fax landed in Mr Scindia's suite confirming the arrangement.

The election was held the next morning. The result: Mr Scindia was elected president of the BCCI by one vote. I was amazed that the election of a cricket body could go right up to the biggest and most powerful in the country.

PS: This election also saw the first appearance of Rajeev Shukla in the BCCI. The evening before voting, he arrived to meet Mr Scindia, bringing with him Pashupathi Singhania, the UP vote.

Mr Scindia was by nature a pro-player and a progressive president willing to look ahead while maintaining the traditions of the game. He knew most of the Indian players at a personal level and, as president, kept a line open with them on a one-to-one basis. Before the 1992 World Cup, he met the team in Mumbai and when players brought up the issue of single rooms and business-class travel, he readily agreed to the request.

As Railway minister, he granted Sunil Gavaskar and his wife free unlimited AC first-class travel which the master used when traveling to Mussoorie. Years later, following a change of policy, the Railways withdrew this special pass.

During his years as the BCCI president, I ran his office, attending to routine matters, putting up back-up information and giving advice, though only when asked. He was the rare BCCI president who understood the difference between inswing, outswing and reverse swing. One of his first tough calls was to sell media rights to a foreign bidder, and by doing so, he took on both Doordarshan and the Government of India.

This was against my advice, for I thought it would put him in an awkward position, considering he was a senior member of the cabinet. But he chose what was in the best interests of cricket. The BCCI approached the market to get the best price for its asset and that bold decision transformed Indian cricket economics forever—it made the BCCI the cash-rich Kuber it is today.

In the debate on whether or not the BCCI should sell to the highest non-government bidder, the Prime Minister's Office (PMO) got involved, as did other heavyweights. On one occasion, a meeting was held with Arjun Singh, a senior cabinet minister. We briefed Mr Scindia, giving him points he needed to argue the case. He appeared distracted as the phone kept ringing and various visitors kept dropping in. We thought he hadn't grasped the key points and possibly missed some important details.

To our surprise, Mr Scindia gave a lucid presentation at the meeting, as if he had rehearsed it for days. Arjun Singh heard him in complete silence, at times with eyes closed. I feared he would lose the thread but he too captured all the arguments, the pros and cons of the deal, picking up relevant details from the complex narrative. This experience taught me a lesson: our politicians are a rare breed – incredibly sharp, champion multitaskers who can process many things simultaneously. Like good batsmen, they have excellent judgement and quickly assess the conditions.

Mr Scindia was keen on restructuring Ranji by splitting it into two groups, a change that did take place many years down the line. He supported the move for better fees for players and called for professional administration. At MPCA, he was a hands-on administrator and engaged Ashok Mankad, Sandip Patil and other professionals to raise the standard of the Ranji team.

He was open to advice but retained a veto on decisions. When Raman Lamba chased Rashid Khan around the ground, waving a threatening bat following an argument in a Duleep Trophy game, Mr Scindia was appalled. An inquiry was held which split the blame—Raman for assault, Rashid for provoking him. I pleaded for a milder sentence for Raman because Rashid had started it, but he did not relent. Raman was suspended from all cricket for one year.

Mr Scindia's aura occasionally made him inaccessible to BCCI members, so it suited them to reach him through me. Mr Dalmiya had a direct line to the president, despite being on the opposite side during that bitter election. Mr Scindia respected his competence and election management skills and joked that Dalmiya-ji should shift to Delhi to manage his political affairs.

He also shared a warm personal rapport with Arun Jaitley. The two were close friends despite different political leanings. Both had a deep interest in cricket and collaborated closely on BCCI affairs. Many times, I was told to check things with Mr Jaitley and seek his advice on complicated cricket matters. I distinctly remember one meeting at Mr Scindia's residence, just ahead of the BCCI elections, where they reviewed the likely voting position, discussing the status of individual members. Each voter was slotted into one of three buckets: pro, anti and iffy. The paper on which these remarks were scribbled by Mr Scindia and Jaitley-ji is still with me.

One of my fondest memories is from the Founders Day of Scindia School, when a School versus Madhavrao Scindia eleven cricket match was played at the school's magnificent ground on top of the Gwalior fort. All of Gwalior, bureaucrats and businessmen, parents and public, were present on this grand occasion.

The cricket wasn't exactly Test level and the school team made a little over 100 runs, batting first. Mr Scindia and I chased that down easily with him blazing to 60 not out, the best I saw him bat. Normally, his batting was disciplined and determined. He valued his wicket and grafted for runs, nudging singles to square leg and point while waiting for the big cover drive. But that day he was in fifth gear from the start, swinging his bat with unusual freedom.

Pleased to have played the way he had on an occasion that mattered, he invited a few people to dinner at the Jai Vilas Palace. It was a fun evening with much laughter, wine and great food. And then the best part: close to midnight, Mr Scindia took us on a tour of the palace, getting rooms opened and telling us the history associated with the place. I knew I had got lucky: a private tour of the royal palace conducted by HRH Shrimant Madhavrao Scindia, the Maharaja of Gwalior!

I worked with Mr Scindia for almost 15 years and in that period a strict partition existed between the official and the personal. For official work, his office set up time and delivered the relevant papers in advance. Like all busy men who lack time, he demanded competence and didn't tolerate inefficiency. At work, he weighed all options carefully, keeping an eye on the bigger picture, and acted decisively. He listened to contrary views but made up his own mind.

With anything non-official, the protocol was completely different. Golf games were always fixed over a direct personal call from him, never a message from his staff or office. We often went together to the course, and he would drive (no driver, no attendant), park the car in the designated slot and wait for his turn at the tee. At the golf course, the maharaja was an ordinary member who did not seek special treatment, except at the refreshment hut where, not able to remember his membership number, he simply signed Scindia.

I feel privileged to have earned his trust and worked with him for so many years. He played a great part in shaping my career and went out of his way to put me in positions others thought I did not deserve. It is to him that I owe all the lucky breaks in the BCCI, the Railways and the Ministry of Sports. Interestingly, the mere fact of working with him turned out to be a great recommendation. I remember a Delhi party where the host introduced me to an influential guest as someone who worked closely with Mr Scindia. The guest sized me up and asked, *How long have you worked with him?* About five years, I answered. *Oh*, he replied, impressed. *Then you must be good.*

I remember Mr Scindia for his grace, generosity and extraordinary kindness. When my twin boys were born, he (the minister of Railways) sent a cake, flowers and a handwritten note to the hospital. Whenever he called on the mobile during office time, he enquired whether it was okay to talk. After meetings at his home, he would always walk his visitor to the door.

I can't forget the time I spent with him in London in the cricket season, when we would walk through Mayfair and Green Park and Piccadilly, taking shortcuts through lanes to reach our destination. He would point out shops on Jermyn Street which stocked good shirts and also the best tailoring establishments on Saville Row. *How come you know these*, I once asked, rather stupidly. His answer: *I have been here every summer of my life.*

St. James' Court, just off Buckingham Palace, was his summer home. He stayed in the same suite every year. One year, he had tickets to the Wimbledon final and I (travelling through Europe) was instructed to reach on match day to make it in time for the big game. Landing that morning in London, I arrived at St James' a little early and found Mr Scindia already dressed for the occasion, nursing a glass of wine. One glass led to another, then another, then one more.

After a while, he announced, *Why go all the way, let's enjoy the wine and watch on television.* So, that was that. I looked at the match invites lying on the table and thought of the many who would give an arm and more to have them.

For Mr Scindia, golf was a stressbuster, an escape from endless appointments, hundreds of visitors, millions of hangers-on and non-stop calls on his mobile. Golf was a release from tension, but such was his competitive nature that it was always fun, yet never a joke. He played to win and nothing thrilled him more than a big strike down the middle with his Callaway ECRC ll. He rejected coaching and refused to hit balls at the range because practice was a waste of time. He treated golf as exercise, a pleasant activity to stay fit and test his physical limits. He had no nakhra about heat or cold and it was normal to tee off at noon in peak summer and be the only four-ball on the course. He had no use for a cart or sunblock cream.

A slow group in front annoyed him, anyone taking extra swings on the tee or taking too long to line up a putt invited his displeasure. He played for enjoyment, which increased when he played well. He anguished over missed putts and sliced drives that missed the fairway. For someone who excelled at everything he touched, the inconsistency of golf exasperated him and he would have liked few things more than lowering his handicap.

Over the years, we played endless rounds of golf, hopping from one course to the other. Starting with the Air Force course next-door to his house on Safdarjung Road, then moving to NOIDA, and later to the Army course, Dhaula Kuan. After that to Delhi Golf Club, to ITC Classic Manesar and finally DLF, Gurgaon.

My last meeting with him was golf related. Driving back from a round at DLF, he mentioned he wouldn't be in town the next day, but a game was fixed for the first day of October. I excused myself from this because Uma Bharti, the sports minister, was to inspect the Nehru Stadium that day. *Okay*, he said, *then we will play on 2nd October*, a national holiday.

That wasn't to be.

RAHUL DRAVID

Rahul ('*naam to suna hoga*') is Indian cricket's bhai, but not the filmi Khan who rips off his shirt and raises a muscular arm to demolish enemies. He is the caring elder who is a guide and a helpful friend.

He is also a diligent student, a curious sponge who observes and absorbs. For him, cricket, and life itself, is an opportunity and a challenge (two words he loves) to improve and expand his knowledge. He is a teacher and a *chalta firta* coaching clinic. The buzz in the Indian dressing room : *Want to become a successful Test player? Follow Rahul bhai, copy whatever he does.*

Dravid is everyone's go-to person, a selfless giver who is cricket's 'champion sure shot guide', the kunji to crack cricket exams. In the past five years he has hand-held every young Indian cricketer and even when Kevin Pietersen struggled against spin, India's helpful bhai mailed him friendly tips. A colleague described Rahul Dravid in one sentence: *He is the 'good man the laltain' who thinks of others. Always ready to help.*

Unlike Bollywood bhais, Rahul raises his hand only to volunteer for difficult missions in the team's interest. He (India's best slip fielder with 210 catches) kept wickets in 73 one-day matches to achieve better team balance. He struggled to make out whether Kumble was coming in or going out but never complained.

I have hard evidence of Rahul bhai sacrificing his personal interest. Soon after the 2003 World Cup, he and I were contracted by a publisher to write a book, an insider account of the Indian team. As the deadline neared, we were hopelessly behind schedule, a lot of work remained and Rahul had an important matter—his wedding—to attend to. But he didn't let this inconvenient distraction come in the way of fulfilling his responsibility. In true bhai style, having made a commitment, there was no going back. He sent emails even while on his honeymoon. Eventually, the book wasn't published because BCCI's contract prohibited players from 'engaging in media activity' and Rahul, not one to cross a line, decided to let the opportunity pass.

When the high court appointed me administrator of Rajasthan cricket (after suspending the association led by Lalit Modi), Rahul called to say there was a promising young fast bowler, Nathu Singh, who was good. And to look after him.

In South Africa, during the IPL, while others saw the glittering lights and the dazzling spectacle, he detected dark clouds in the distance. Over a seafood dinner, he introduced me to fried calamari and warned about the disturbing trend in domestic cricket: *It is worrying that young kids will give this priority over Ranji and Test cricket.*

Dravid himself revelled in the challenge of five-day cricket. He is a champion worrier who, in his own words, strives to become the best version of himself. Before every Test, nervousness makes him study videos to check his backlift for non-existent flaws and he fusses over foot movement. Processes takes precedence over performance but ultimately his bat talks and his record speaks.

Dravid the batsman was not a Mercedes speeding on the motorway. His runs were extracted by digging deep, with determination and discipline. He set high standards for himself and often talked about tough match situations and the need to make 'tough runs'.

To describe him as a wall of cement or stone is incorrect. I have seen steel first-hand. Ahead of India's famous match against Pakistan at Centurion in the 2003 World Cup, a pre-game handshake and exchange of mementos was proposed to lower temperatures. Dravid, the professional, disliked the idea. *Why do this?* he objected. *We are not politicians.*

During the Multan declaration, when a storm was blowing because Sachin had been denied a double hundred, captain Dravid stood his ground. In making his point, he displayed a tough streak many believed was alien to his system.

Attention to detail and making informed choices is second nature to him, especially in matters of diet and fitness. He is the obsessed type who reads food labels carefully and makes a mental note of calories while eating his favourite Italian food. Dravid devotes himself entirely to what he commits to and it is rumoured that he breathes only after doing a quick cost-benefit analysis.

Such a work ethic makes Dravid a universal favourite. Sponsors adore him because he is non-fussy, prompt, polite and professional. He happily signs autographs, smiles when posing for photographs, enthusiastically chats with the MD's wife and shows genuine concern about the low math scores of the marketing manager's son.

Rahul once visited me in my government office and caused a stampede because everyone landed up for the usual autograph and photograph routine. He did it all with a smile and even suffered a cup of tea with my senior without a trace of impatience or annoyance.

Much more revealing was the time when we went to meet Tiger Pataudi at his Delhi residence. Tiger and Dravid were from the same cricket school, somewhat alike as persons. Low-key, cultured and understated, they represented the best of cricket's values and traditions. The talk was about cricket, the usual this and that. Tiger was typically economical with words but Dravid asked questions to keep the conversation rolling. More important than the discussion was the occasion, a current great meeting a past legend.

While most other players are predominantly about cricket and a tiny bit of something else, Dravid is a man of many facets, with a lot of this and much more of that. On tours I saw him reading Mandela, Mohammad Ali and Lance Armstrong, and he kept an open mind on all things.

In Pakistan, interacting with the bright minds at LUMS, he was the statesman speaking about the positive energy of youth and cricket's power to unite people. This was genuine sentiment, straight talk without spin. A few days later, he was engaged in a serious conversation on Kashmir with Shiv Shankar Menon. Evidently, Dravid is a 360-degree person who can bat on different wickets.

His colleagues might behave as though their tails are on fire but Dravid is *shaant*; there is an air of serenity and reassuring calm about him. Crowds and fans embarrass him and praise makes his face go red. When a group of young fans in Karachi screamed his name as he checked in at the hotel reception, you could see he wanted to hide.

Modern yet traditional, Dravid is unlikely to march in a dharna to protest the ill-treatment of street dogs in distant Nairobi, but he has an impressive list of social campaigns in his off-field portfolio. He is unflashy, stylish, but never over the top. He will sport trendy clothes and smart shades. But a tattoo on his forearm, ear stud or distressed jeans? No way!

Once, when offered a huge amount of 'appearance money' to attend an event, he declined politely citing a prior family commitment. While other stars find it hard to miss out on a commercial half-volley, Dravid controls want and desire.

When I requested him to speak to young kids in Jaipur on the 'Spirit of Cricket', he promptly made time. I was witness when Jaggu-da gave him various choices in the BCCI system but he let them pass. Anyone else in his position would have latched on to the gift without a second thought.

Looking back, I remember jogging with him in a golf course, one late evening in Zimbabwe. Also, a putting session in Arundel during the NatWest tour of 2002. Dravid approached it with focus; having read up on putting technique, he understood the importance of dropping short putts.

Rahul and I collaborated in the TOP scheme initiated by the Ministry of Sports to support potential medal-winners at the Olympics. He brought a reasoned perspective to the meetings, supporting the athletes and explaining the pitfalls and bumps they would face in their journey.

Contrary to his somewhat dour image, Dravid is pleasantly relaxed and has a delightful, self-deprecating sense of humour. In Multan, after Sehwag smashed 300, dressing-room chatter turned to others replicating the feat. Dravid commented: *The rate at which I score, you'd need an eight-day Test match.*

When asked about his greatest challenge at a press conference in Pakistan, he deflected the question neatly. *No, not Inzamam, not Shoaib Akhtar—just trying to keep my son quiet at night.*

On a Zimbabwe tour, over dinner in an Indian restaurant in Harare, players were discussing post-retirement life. Various options were mentioned and Dravid, with a huge grin on his face, announced his plans. *I will become a commentator and give gyaan to you guys.* Only, everyone knew how unlikely that was. Dravid the TV guru? Possible. But bhashan and unwanted gyaan? Unlikely.

Rahul bhai kept his promise. He shuns social media and prefers to remain on mute. The nation might want to know but Dravid is not telling.

Dravid rapid-fire

- Bowling style: *Flighted off-spin, did everything right but no turn.*
- Memorable bowling moment: *My only wicket in 163 Tests. Ridley Jacobs batting on 100 (WI 700), big slog—caught in the deep.*
- Best ball received: *I saw the Brennan delivery that came in but it moved out. Bowled off. Also, Shoaib Akhtar yorker in Calcutta when I was quite set.*
- Worst shot played: *Batting at 93 at Perth. Slog sweep off Symonds. Not a shot I play, and the ball was too far out. Caught and bowled after doing the hard work.*

ARUN JAITLEY

During the initial years of the IPL, the phone would ring early in the morning. *Arun bol raha hoon*, a slow, deliberate voice would say before asking whether everything was fine at the Feroz Shah Kotla.

These phone calls said something about the gentleman at the other end of the line. Protocol and courtesy demanded that I (as chief operating officer, Delhi Daredevils) make the calls to keep him, the president of the DDCA, updated about what was happening on his turf. But he was that

rare person who is high on stature, low on ego. To those close to him, he always remained Arun. Each time he called, I visualised him in his study on the first floor of his house in Kailash Colony, a room lined with cricket memorabilia and a photo of Madhavrao Scindia on a side table, relaxing after the customary morning walk, a cup of tea by his side and newspapers waiting to be read.

Cricket was dear to him, and his ability to recall dates, players and performances was astonishing, especially since he had so much else on his plate. He followed the progress of Delhi cricketers closely and was known to surprise selectors, coaches and team managers by reeling off scores of Under-16 and Under-19 players they had not been paying attention to. It wasn't unusual for him to watch cricket at Kotla or Palam, spending hours tracking some young kid rated to be the next Virender Sehwag or Gautam Gambhir.

In the years that I knew him, Mr Jaitley's love for the game always shone through. My initial interaction with him was at Mr Scindia's behest when he wanted his inputs on BCCI matters. We watched some 1999 World Cup matches together in England and, each time we spoke, it became clear to me that he wasn't just a passionate fan but also an astute analyst. He could access facts and extract little known details about players from his formidable memory. His recall was extraordinary and scary because he remembered chance remarks—by me and others—made years ago, as if spoken the day before.

When the IPL started, franchise owners approached me for a professional role with their teams, some of them serious options, others only exploratory in nature. I knew I had to seek voluntary retirement from the Railways before accepting a full-time responsibility in the private sector and waited for the right offer to come my way.

It came from an unexpected quarter, totally luck by chance. The GMR group, which had paid US$ 84 million for operating the Delhi franchise, called on the president of the DDCA to discuss plans for the upcoming league. During the meeting, when Mr Jaitley enquired about who would manage the franchise, my name was mentioned in passing. At which point, Mr Jaitley intervened to give me a solid recommendation, then picked up the phone. *Arun bol raha hoon*, he said as usual. *The GMR people are with me and they are looking for someone for their team. I have said yes on your behalf. Tum mana mat karna.* That is how I was hired.

As president of the DDCA, he was a huge support when the IPL came to Kotla. Delhi is not the easiest place to work in and the DDCA not an easy pitch to bat on. In this minefield, Mr Jaitley was friend and ally, protector and insurance cover. He helped the Daredevils sort out government procedures and gave helpful (insider) tips on how to work with the DDCA, including who to steer clear of.

Whenever there was a hiccup, a minor disagreement or dispute, all I had to do was ask for help. To me he was the single-bench court that resolved issues speedily, on merit and with complete fairness. Surprisingly, Mr Jaitley took a keen interest in the commercial results as well as on-field performance of the Delhi team. He spent time discussing matters ranging from auction strategies and sponsorship deals to ticket rates and new hires. When Delhi recruited a young Andre Russell (unknown then, even to some franchise support staff), he surprised us by commending the selection of the impactful all-rounder. He had tracked his progress and respected the choice.

Despite being pressured from all sides for tickets—because everyone in Delhi wants a free ride—he never made any demands, choosing to handle the pressure himself. On the few occasions when there was only a dead end in sight, his request was that someone be *accommodated*. He would say hesitatingly, his tone almost apologetic: *Usko dekh lena.*

He watched IPL games from his allotted box number 1 in Kotla's New Club House located above the home team dressing room. Half of Delhi would land up there to enjoy food and drinks and rub shoulders with celebrity guests, making it tough to push back the flood of gatecrashers and uninvited guests. The chaos bothered Mr Jaitley, so he found a solution: no liquor in his box. The crowd thinned.

For someone so busy, Mr Jaitley, like a good batsman, was never in a hurry and always had time and patience at hand. Whenever I took a problem to him, the meeting would end in a few minutes but he would insist on a cup of tea and talk shop—even as 20 others waited in the adjoining room to meet him.

Everyone in Delhi knew about Mr Jaitley's morning walk in Lodhi gardens—for the sake of his health and an adda with friends. Sitting on a bench, chai and *nimbu paani* at hand, everything was out for airing— national politics, films, cricket and plain gossip. Within this close group he was friendly and open with no hint of hierarchy or rank. If you ignored the security persons close by, it could have been just another group of seniors meeting as they did every day. Every year, his birthday (28 December) was celebrated in Lodhi Gardens, and an elaborate feast laid out for all the Lodhi regulars, known and unknown. Local rasgulla king Gopala from Meherchand Market would serve chaat, chhole, chai and cake.

During the BCCI's power tangles—of which there were many— Mr Jaitley was the go-to person on the strength of his personal charm, universal acceptance and proximity to power. On matters of policy and complicated issues he was the DRS: regardless of the persons involved, he would be objective and fair. In the fragmented, unruly world of the BCCI, Mr Jaitley was adviser, problem-solver and consensus-builder, a selfless individual who played for the team.

Much has been said about Mr Jaitley's taste in food and his fondness for stuff he should not have touched for the sake of his health. He loved street food and was partial to the dal gosht served at Embassy, the restaurant at Connaught Place. At the DDCA, there were standing instructions not to serve pakoras during meetings because he couldn't stop himself from snacking.

Mr Jaitley's other major interest was films. He was a hardcore Dev Anand fan, an admirer of Mohammad Rafi, and his all-time favourite was Sahir Ludhianvi, whose lyrics from *Naya Daur* and *Gumraah* he could recite. He recommended Sahir's biography by Akshay Manwani to everyone who chatted with him about music and movies.

You couldn't help but notice that Mr Jaitley was a man of refined tastes, from his upmarket Church's shoes to the limited edition fountain pens and exquisite Jaamawar shawls. To me he was gracious and kind, and whenever I met him—at home in Kailash Colony or Krishna Menon Marg, at the High Court or in his Parliament office, or Lodhi gardens—he enquired about my wife (an economics professor at his alma mater, Shri Ram College of Commerce) and my twin boys who graduated from the same college.

The last time I met him, in his tastefully decorated wood-panelled North Block office, he looked tired and preoccupied. He was India's finance minister, but as always, we had a cup of tea and chatted about cricket without any particular agenda. I left the meeting wondering, yet again, how he managed to find time when so many things were spinning around him.

Mr Jaitley was a man of many aspects, but in all his roles, one quality stood out—he always played straight. Hitting across the line was never an option, his was a bat that had a big middle and no edges. Cricket is about scoring runs, but equally important is the manner in which you make those runs. By this yardstick, the verdict is unanimous: Jaitley-ji was pure class.

SUNIL GAVASKAR

Among the many mysteries of Indian cricket, Sunny Gavaskar features prominently in two.

One: Was he actually out caught bat-pad in his last Test innings, batting at 96 in the 1986 Test against Pakistan in Bangalore?

Two: Why did he announce his retirement in London—at Lord's—in 1987?

Gavaskar has gagged himself; he is not telling. He wants the suspense to continue, but I have background masala to share. That time in Bangalore, we knew he wouldn't play anymore and this was sort of confirmed when he sent handwritten invitations on the last day, asking friends to dinner at the Taj West End hotel. This, we thought, was a significant moment in cricket history, a giant walking away after an extraordinary career.

Sunny said nothing that evening in Bangalore and instead of hitting the exit button, he merely pushed pause. Till the next summer when, after 188 at Lord's in the MCC bicentennial game, having scored a century that had eluded him on four previous visits to England, he decided to put away his bat.

When Gavaskar came to the Feroz Shah Kotla stadium for a benefit game after his triumphant West Indies tour of 1971, I stood in a long queue to get his autograph.

Years later, I met him in Chennai in 1982 during the Sri Lanka Test when my friend Arun Lal made his Test debut. He was sitting in the players' area outside the Indian dressing room reading a book while play was on. Arun introduced me to him and, on an impulse, I asked him whether he would answer some questions for an article I was writing. To my surprise, he said yes and put the book down. I got an *exclusive*.

When I sent him an invitation for my wedding, he wrote me a letter in which he pointed out that 'from now on you will look at other girls and feel bad'. A few years later, when he was editing *Indian Cricketer*, Aajkal's English monthly magazine, I became his Delhi correspondent.

Gavaskar is as prolific with the pen as he was with the bat, and much more aggressive in this field. He wrote his columns himself, occasionally from a noisy dressing room, and had the remarkable ability to block all distractions and focus on the job at hand. Exactly the way he batted in the middle, shutting out the chatter of chirping fielders and the deafening stadium noise. But, mindful of maintaining his 6/6 eyesight, he never wrote or read anything in a moving car.

Gavaskar made the forward defensive look cool and, like Bishan Bedi's silky-smooth action, it was sheer perfection. His technique, a cocktail of art, science, geometry and physics, enabled him to make what Dravid calls 'tough runs' against bowling that was scarily fast. He earned respect from opposing batsmen and bowlers, including Viv Richards and Imran Khan, as well as his teammates. At a social function, Kapil Dev introduced his teenaged daughter Amiya to him. *Meet my captain*, he said, in a manner that conveyed respect and admiration.

Gavaskar was the first cricket superstar after Tiger Pataudi, the Rajesh Khanna of his time. He became a pioneer who unlocked business opportunities, opened commercial doors and monetised celebrity cricket. He understood numbers and read the direction and swing of commercial trends better than the rest.

Sunny's business venture, the Professional Management Group (PMG) was cricket's one-stop platform that supplied everything—television content, newspaper columns, celebrity management, events and sponsorships. When the Railways organised the national hockey championship at the newly installed Astro Turf in Gwalior at Mr Scindia's insistence, he found a commercial partner and despatched a young executive, Harsha Bhogle, to make sure it went well.

His astonishing gifts of concentration and relentless desire to excel are well documented. But what isn't well known is that his memory is sharper than that of an elephant. When he was introduced to Shashi Tharoor at a function, he waited till the introductory handshakes and pleasantries were done before casually slipping in an arm ball with a reminder to Shashi about a cover story he had written many years ago in the *Illustrated Weekly,* in which he called Gavaskar the worst captain to have led India. Soon after that article was published, Sunny led the Indian team to a memorable win at the World Championship of cricket in Australia. Tharoor, caught and bowled Gavaskar!

Unlike other past greats, Sunny remains connected with cricket because he is always on the road, with eyes open and ears to the ground. Nothing escapes his attention; he knows all there is to know and what he doesn't know is not worth knowing. He has a deep understanding of cricket's need to evolve and its commercial dynamics. He celebrates the past, yet lives in the moment and is cued into the contemporary. It's not just about connecting the dots. Sunny knows where the dots are — he probably put them there in the first place!

If there is a cricket debate and he is a participant, it's safe to punt on Sunny. He can defend batting left-handed in a first-class game and give a convincing explanation for using a Duncan Fearnley bat with four holes drilled into the blade. Given his standing, he has a ready platform and a powerful voice. There is an old jungle saying that trees trembled when the Phantom got angry. Well, Sunny isn't Phantom and he is not in a jungle, but when he speaks there are tremors. Maybe not trees, but administrators shake and wickets fall.

He is unafraid to call a no-ball when he sees one and can punish the loose delivery that presents itself. He questioned MSD's long absence after the 2019 World Cup and drew attention to the raw deal given to Ashwin over the years. After India's loss in the ICC World Test Championship in 2023, Sunny did not hold back on what he thought was wrong and demanded greater accountability from players.

He has a dim view of players missing India games, wanting breaks on account of excessive workload, fatigue or stress. *As retained players of the BCCI they are contractually obliged to be available*, he says and asks, *how come none of these issues arise at the time of the IPL?*

Sunny is a proud Indian who deplores the tendency to distribute the India cap to undeserving players, likening it to handing out freebies to passers-by at Flora Fountain in Mumbai. He regularly stands up for India and leads the pushback on what he believes is the excessive importance of English cricket. He is immensely passionate about Mumbai cricket and hosts an annual dinner for his club and Ranji colleagues.

Yet, Sunny isn't just about bat and ball. Away from cricket, he is an excellent mimic who can do Miandad better than Miandad and has a delightfully mischievous sense of humour. When asked why he hadn't taken to golf like so many others had (including brother-in-law Vishy, Kapil Dev, MSD and Sachin) he said he wasn't good enough. *The coach taught me never to hit the ball in the air.*

Sunny is a man of refined tastes, with a love for Chinese food (crispy Peking duck, a favourite), is a good judge of red wine and knows the difference between wine from Stellenbosch, Chile and Colombia. I once attended a wine-tasting session with him in Delhi where Champagne's India representative explained the intricacies of red, white and pink, all of which pretty much sailed over my head but Sunny, not surprisingly, was on the ball.

In his personal life, Sunny is a great accumulator with a vast collection of watches and hats and unconfirmed mischievous rumours indicate he probably owns 10,122 pairs of shoes, as many as his Test runs.

It has been more than half a century since Sunny Gavaskar announced his arrival in international cricket in 1971. All through this wonderful journey, he has been on the cricket treadmill, logging miles at a furious pace. Unlike younger players who look to take a break, the thought of missing action in some kind of 'rotation policy' or break to recharge batteries is the last thing on his mind. He does rest, but only briefly. Every summer, he spends time at his home in Swiss Cottage, London.

Sunny Bhai is Indian cricket's soft power, its popular export. When Prime Minister Modi visited Australia, Sunny was part of the delegation.

PS: I grew up watching Gavaskar play. He was the best in the business and his batting, viewed on a neighbour's grainy black and white television, was a coaching lesson to anyone wanting to play. So supremely good, you could watch him defend all day, marvelling at his brilliance, elegance and grace.

Perhaps I am biased because I have known him for about 40 years and received a merit certificate from him. On live commentary during a Test match, he mentioned that I was one of the best managers Team India had. A great compliment from the great man himself.

Sunny or Sachin

Milind Rege is the typical hard-nosed Mumbai cricketer who played Ranji for ten seasons and was a state selector for another ten. He is intensely *khadoos*, remarkably astute and a difficult man to please. Few read the game as well as he does.

I once asked him, who was the greater player: Sunil Gavaskar or Sachin Tendulkar?

He voted for Gavaskar. *Without question*, he asserted confidently. *Just think of Indian cricket at that time and what he did. Alone. Single-handedly. Not just that, he kept getting better and better. Gavaskar changed the way the world looked at Indian cricket.*

RAJ SINGH DUNGARPUR

If a poll were held to pick India's Mr Cricket for the all-time hall of fame, it would be a landslide in favour of Raj Singh Dungarpur. He played many roles, wore several hats and was a popular figure in cricketing circles across the world. His was a stylish head that fit every stylish hat.

Raj Singh-ji and cricket were inseparable. He talked and walked, lived and breathed cricket. He thought only the prime minister had a job tougher than that of the captain of the Indian team, and the selection of the Indian team was as important as a cabinet reshuffle.

His early years were spent bowling gentle medium-pace for Rajasthan, outswing delivered from a run-up longer than that of Dennis Lillee. In a first-class career stretching 15 years, he bagged 206 wickets.

He remembered those years not for his personal exploits but the privilege of rubbing shoulders with Indian cricket's legends: Vijay Merchant, Vijay Hazare, Vijay Manjrekar, Vinoo Mankad, Subhash Gupte and Polly Kaka.

Topping his list of all-time greats was Col. C.K. Nayudu. Over several cups of mint tea at the Cricket Club of India (CCI) lawns, Raj Bhai narrated stories of days past, of incidents involving yesterday's giants, laced with analysis and admiration. *CK*, he said, was special, *he stood out in any group. Such was his aura, you couldn't leave a dinner party unless you walked up to him and wished him goodnight. Didn't matter who the host was.*

No less special was Vijay Hazare, for whom cricket was sadhna, a religious duty. According to Raj Singh-ji, Hazare took special care of his bat and had a habit of cleaning and oiling it soon as he was out—the ritual unchanged even

if he had been dismissed for zero. Raj Bhai adored Tiger Pataudi for shaping Indian cricket and Salim Durani, colleague and teammate from Rajasthan, for his sheer brilliance. Duleepsinhji was another favourite.

Raj Bhai was cricket's living Wikipedia. He had a sharp memory and a fund of stories which he happily shared with anyone willing to listen. I often pushed him to put things down on paper and write a book. *Come to England in summer,* was his standard reply, *I have time there and we will get it done.* The book never happened, though I spent many summer days with him in London and have happy memories of morning walks in Regent Park, a short distance from his flat opposite Lord's.

When I ran into him once at Wimbledon, he gave me his Centre Court tickets as he was leaving early. His kind-hearted nature made him reach out to anyone in need, especially if they were from Jaipur—young Parthasarathy Sharma looking for a break in Mumbai, a retired Salim Durani requiring help to tide over tough times. Anyone in distress could always knock on Raj Bhai's door.

Cricket wasn't just in his blood, it was Raj Bhai's life. In Mumbai, he lived at the CCI, which was home and office. He took great pride in making it an institution that celebrated Indian cricket and even now, one can't walk in there without feeling his imposing presence. I owe him a personal debt of gratitude. After the 2003 World Cup, he made me a member of the CCI, couriering the membership card, out of the blue, to my Delhi residence.

In his long innings, Raj Bhai batted at different positions and occupied many posts to handle a wide variety of responsibilities. He was manager of the Indian team, chairman of the selection committee and head of the NCA. He headed the CCI, was chairman of the Rajasthan Sports Council and later became president of the BCCI, although this last innings was scratchy at best. He spoke with authority on all things cricket, often citing the example of England, but non-cricket matters concerning finance and accounts defeated him. Raj Bhai had no head for numbers; he only understood cricket scores.

The underlying political cross-currents of the BCCI frustrated him but, despite this, he remained a popular figure. Untrained in the skills required of a career administrator, he made questionable choices in annual elections, sometimes switching sides to make friends with people he had opposed the previous evening. But nobody held that against him; members knew Raj Bhai lacked malice and his cricket DNA was pure.

Kishore Rungta, former BCCI treasurer and Raj Singh-ji's colleague in Rajasthan, summed up the paradox neatly: *He was a cricket person and a good man, but simple to the point of being naive in many matters. Administration wasn't his strength.*

He was immensely popular in England's cricket circuit and enjoyed a strong personal rapport with many past greats. When Colin Cowdrey visited India on his invitation to inaugurate the NCA in Bangalore, Raj Bhai asked me to be the officer-in-waiting. I spent two memorable days with the legend, showing him around the city and escorting him to the church close to the Chinnaswamy Stadium where he had been baptised. The priest there pulled out old records to show him the original entry in the church register.

Raj Bhai once took me on a free holiday to Muscat, Oman, where his friend Kanakbhai Khimji had organised some cricket. Harsha Bhogle was also on the trip, which was an eye-opener in terms of cricket in the Middle East and also the deep influence of the Khimjis in Oman. It was said that they funded the kingdom in the pre-oil days when the Indian rupee was still official currency in the country.

In 2003, Raj Bhai visited South Africa during the World Cup and in the middle of an important meeting appeared to have nodded off. At that time I attributed it to jetlag after a long flight from Mumbai to Johannesburg. Another time, he invited me to lunch with Ali Bacher at the CCI. We met in the dining room and spent time chatting about cricket. He was in top form, regaling us with stories and incidents nobody could describe better. Imagine my shock when, later that same evening, he called to ask why I didn't turn up for lunch.

Raj Bhai was an old-world, unadulterated cricket romantic. A gentleman like none other, completely devoted to the gentlemen's game.

IMRAN KHAN

Every country has its cricket heroes. India has placed Sunil Gavaskar, Kapil Dev, Sachin and MSD on a pedestal beyond the celebrity tag; they are national treasures. In Pakistan, Imran Khan is a top player and a legend who is feared, revered, respected and admired.

A minor incident provides perspective. Some time ago, at a game in England, Wasim Akram, a popular figure in the press box, was chatting with colleagues over coffee when his phone rang. After a brief conversation, Wasim excused himself. *The Skip is here*, he said. *I'll go meet him.*

Skip to Wasim, Khan sa'ab to most. Imran to a few.

I first met Imran Khan in 1987 in Hyderabad, Sindh, at a World Cup game where I was working for Sunil Gavaskar's Professional Management Group (PMG), writing match reports and 'ghostwriting' Imran Khan's column. This had seemed simple to begin with, but getting access to Imran in Pakistan was like getting a private audience with SRK in Mannat on Eid. He was captain, coach, selector, the entire PCB itself—too powerful and too busy. I approached him at practice where he was surrounded by admiring subjects, introduced myself and mentioned the column. *It's ok*, he said, and added in a voice loud enough to be heard across Sindh: *How much am I getting paid?*

Ask Sunny, I replied. *I have no idea.*

We decided to chat for the first column a day after the Hyderabad game— in Lahore. After play ended, there was a crazy cross-country scramble, a taxi ride (Hyderabad–Karachi) and a late-night flight (Karachi–Lahore). To my surprise, the next morning, Imran was at the Gaddafi Stadium, running laps of the ground. I had not even played a game but was exhausted; Imran, on the other hand, was fully switched on.

Celebrated for his flamboyant image, his achievements in cricket and his non-cricket conquests, Imran's hard work as an athlete has unfortunately receded to the background. Nor is he given credit for the profound impact he has had on Pakistan and world cricket.

Like Sunil Gavaskar in India, Imran created respect for Pakistani cricket; he proved that they were good enough, if not better, than others. It was Imran who pitched for neutral umpires in Tests—two years after that Hyderabad meeting—to remove the taint of biased umpiring in Pakistan. This was in 1989, well before the ICC woke up to the idea.

He did all this by wielding his powerful personality, his aura of absolute authority. No player has enjoyed as much influence and unchecked power as Imran, and he wasn't shy of using his clout. Once, when he spotted a player taking it easy during practice, he gave him the full treatment in raw Punjabi, over which he had an impressive command. I saw national selectors wait for as long as it took to get a minute of Imran's time. Not to discuss team selection, only to know the names of the players chosen by Imran which they could announce to the press. The imperious Imran often kept them waiting or simply waved them away.

Sometimes, his choices defied logic, but everyone in Pakistan knew it was unwise to take *panga* with him. For Imran played cricket on his terms. He transformed from a lower-order batsman to a fast bowler to a top-order batsman who bowled only when in the mood. He played Tests depending on the quality of the opposition, the weather and the nature of the wicket. He retired and returned, bowing gracefully to public pressure, and re-retired after winning the 1992 World Cup.

Imran was every journalist's dream because he never ducked a question and expressed himself freely and fearlessly. But sitting him down for 'ghosted' columns in 1987 during a World Cup was another matter altogether. We did a few with great difficulty and then worked out a practical solution. *You write what you want*, he said. *Just be careful—the usual non-controversial cricket stuff.*

This, from my point of view, was perfect. I wrote what I wanted, didn't have to chase Imran and was paid by PMG for easy work. I don't think Imran read or cared what went in his name.

Some years later, when I met Imran in Sharjah and asked for an interview, he readily agreed. *Get on the team bus with me, we'll do this on the way to practice.* During the bus ride, as we went about our business, the other players were respectfully silent. In the background, a tape of Nusrat Fateh Ali Khan, Imran's favourite Sufi singer, played softly. I asked my questions and in his usual candid manner Imran had a direct answer for everything thrown at him. I got a great interview but my joy evaporated later when I realised the tape recorder had malfunctioned. I had to depend on my memory to reconstruct all that Imran had said.

During the Indian team's tour of Pakistan in 2004, Imran was part of the commentary team but his most interesting comments came during informal chats when he was off the air. When Dravid declared with Sachin short of a double hundred in Multan, Imran supported the move. *It's always team first*, he said.

When Pakistan succumbed meekly, Imran blamed the PCB (for a domestic structure that promoted mediocrity) and the players (for lacking intelligence and cricket education), his voice at top volume as he said, *Zillat hai. It's a disgrace.*

Imran the captain was like Ian Chappell, who spoke his mind and had no time for coaches. The captain is boss and the coach should only run practice. Like Tiger Pataudi, he thought captaincy was simple but complicated by so-called experts. He rated Sourav as a good captain because 'he manages bowlers well'. Incidentally, both Imran and Sourav shared the 'match-winner' eagle eye, identifying and supporting players who could perform in pressure situations and win games. Imran chose batsmen who knew which shot to play at what time instead of those *jo befizul chalate hain.*

On the 2004 tour, Zakir Khan (director, cricket operations, PCB and former Pakistan medium-pacer), Professor Shetty and I were invited for a post-dinner coffee with Imran. It was pretty late when we rang the bell at Imran's apartment. All the lights were off and for a longish while there was no response.

As we contemplated retreat, the door opened to reveal a frazzled Khan sa'ab. Motioning us to remain silent, he ushered us into the flat, which resembled a war zone. Toys strewn all over the place, used dishes on the table, clothes on the sofa. Enough evidence of unruly young children in the house.

We had caught Khan sa'ab at an inconvenient time. His wife Jemima was away in Afghanistan, setting up an orphanage for kids, and Imran was fulfilling his role of parent diligently in her absence. After struggling with the children's dinner, he had just succeeded in getting them to sleep. We settled down in the living room and Khan sa'ab left the bedroom door open a crack to keep a careful watch, jumping up each time a sound emanated from within.

After retiring from cricket, Imran entered politics, a new field, spurred by a desire to take Pakistan forward and give hope to his people. Initially he was the favoured new batsman on the block and the establishment offered him positions in high office. But he refused the half-volley, realising he was being tempted by a team of people whom he called 'icons of corruption'. His mind made up, Khan sa'ab took on the opposition—Sadr Musharraf, the powerful faujis and the civilian Sharifs of Punjab.

Since that meeting, much has changed. But he remains at the centre of every durbar and whatever the issue, he is an active participant, never a silent observer. His mind entertains no doubts, no confusion. In cricket parlance, he has always had decisive footwork and a big forward stride.

Imran on Indian cricket

- 1996 Bangalore Test: *Both teams misread the wicket. Salim Jaffer didn't bowl a single over in the game and I bowled three. Gavaskar was out before he got to 96, perhaps wasn't out that time.*
- Sunil Gavaskar: *He was best at building an innings. Both he and Miandad knew* kab maarna hai aur kab rokna hai, *who to pick runs from and when not to do anything.*
- Irfan Pathan: *He will be a match-winner if he increases pace.*
- Balaji: *Love his passion, he is a fighter. I became his fan when he fell down while bowling but still appealed.*
- Dravid: *The batsman most likely to succeed in a tough situation.*

Imran on Pakistan cricket

- *Pakistan cricketers are shohde (show-offs) who lack 'intellectual capacity' and education.*
- On Inzamam: *I picked Inzy in five minutes because he had time. He was playing quality fast bowlers off the front foot, could cut and pull them without being hurried. Once, against Allan Donald, I couldn't see the ball but he was not in any trouble. His greatest quality is that he doesn't give in to pressure. I would always back him in a crisis but he is lazy—at times you can see he is sleeping at the wicket.*
- On Mudassar Nazar: *The best brain in the team. Great analyst.*

Imran on captaincy and cricket

- *Captains must play to win. You can't be scared of defeat and play safe.*
- *Captaincy is what you do with the bowlers; all successful captains must understand when to bowl whom, when to take them off and what fields to set.*
- *Key to good batting: Performing in tough situations and being diler.*
- *Key to good bowling: Look for pressure on the batsman's face. Aankh dekho.*

13

LOOKING BACK

Not wanting my association with cricket to be limited to that of an official or an administrator, I once decided to become a first-class umpire. The qualification process was frightfully difficult because candidates had to clear a tough written test (pass mark 90 per cent) and an even tougher interview. I prepared hard: mugged up cricket's 42 laws, consulted past papers, did mock interviews and took tuitions from senior umpires Rajan Mehra and Bansal sa'ab. To me, this was Delhi University and UPSC combined, an exam I had to pass.

Which I did, to become the second sitting BCCI official (after J.Y. Lele) on the umpiring panel. I stood in Ranji games, including one in Bilaspur when Delhi was led by Kirti Azad, my friend and colleague from St Stephen's. At Delhi's NIS ground I umpired an MPs versus Indian Veterans game where Prasanna bowled to Chetan Chauhan. When the ball left Prasanna's hand, I could hear it spin, a humming sound.

The over went like this. Ball one: Flighted off-break, Chetan stepped out and hit it for six over the straight 50-yard boundary. Ball two: Repeat, action replay—similar ball, similar shot. Another six. Ball three: Flighted ball but no off-break, this one floated out with the arm. Chetan Chauhan, sold a dummy—stranded miles down the pitch, stumped by a yard—could only scowl in disappointment. Prasanna, wizard of subtle treachery and deception, was delighted to have nailed one more.

Umpires are pretty low in cricket's power hierarchy. They are treated shabbily by senior players and often face aggressive sledging. But nobody dared step out of line with Venkat (former India captain, later international umpire), who was greatly respected and much feared. Apparently, when one brave batsman on being judged lbw gestured that he had played the ball, Venkat was furious. *Good bat*, he said through clenched teeth. *Next time, use it.*

My umpiring career ended quickly because I couldn't make time for it, but my other interest—writing on cricket—lasted longer. I started when still in college, thanks to Ranjit Bhatia (Olympic athlete, head of sports at St. Stephen's), who put in a good word for me with Jigs Kalra, then editor of the Weekend Review at *Hindustan Times*. Bhatia sa'ab's colleague Avinash Singh, a respected sports journalist, took me to meet Jigs and praised my work though he hadn't read a word of it. The HT gave me a platform, closer contact with cricket and cricketers, a byline, and ₹80 per article.

I also started writing for *Sportsworld* and other magazines. In 1987, I went to Pakistan for the World Cup in the pre-fax days when you wrote on the typewriter and sent your copy through telex. Once, after a game in Lahore, I took an overnight bus to Peshawar for a match that was scheduled for the next morning, sleeping in the aisle between the seats. I reached in time for the toss but rain and bad light restricted play to a few overs. With great difficulty, I put together a non-cricket story, but the telex lines were down and the report didn't go through. Net outcome: wasted trip; too much effort and zero result.

For the 1992 World Cup, Dr Narottam Puri and I were on a 'package deal'; he went to New Zealand while I covered the games in Australia. Interestingly, besides covering the World Cup, Narottam and I were contracted and given a handsome advance to write a book on India's campaign. But when India was knocked out early, the publishers lost interest and abandoned the project. Still, our contracts were honoured and Doc and I were paid for a book we did not write.

I remember India's first game in Perth where, at practice the day before, The Western Australian Cricket Association (WACA) stadium was practically deserted, so different from the mad frenzy at Indian grounds ahead of a big match. At first glance, the Perth wicket looked no different from the Indian pitches but Kapil Dev described it in his trademark drawl: *Shakal pe mat jaana, ball tej nikalta hai.*

After the 1992 tour to South Africa, I started writing a fortnightly column for the prestigious *Sportstar*, thanks to R. Mohan, their cricket writer. Mohan

With Kapil Dev

was the star in the press box; he knew what was happening before anybody else and was also known to influence decisions. I wrote for *Sportstar* for ten years and remember being surprised that they retained the Hindi words I used in my copy.

Early in my career as a writer, I went to meet Vijay Hazare, one of India's greatest cricketers. He wasn't very well, but thanks to a word from Aunshuman Gaekwad, agreed to see me. I was told not to take long because he tired quickly, but when I reached his Baroda residence, I found him waiting for me wearing the India blazer and a BCCI tie.

I asked him about his two Test hundreds at Adelaide in 1948 and the time when India was 0 for 4 at Headingley in 1952. *Was Trueman a terror,* I wanted to know. Hazare took a while to respond, carefully assessing line and length, then said in a calm voice: *He was okay. We made him look good.*

In those days, the weekend social cricket circuit in Delhi was very active. The MPs played regularly, and K.P. Singhdeo (useful medium pace), Digvijay Singh (technically correct batsman), Anand Sharma and Mukul Wasnik were handy players. J.P. Agarwal brought delicious samosas and mithai from Chandni Chowk. Chetan Chauhan, Kirti Azad and Azharuddin, cricketers turned MPs, were allowed to field but not bat or bowl.

As part of this circuit, I went to Chiang Mai, Thailand to play a six-a-side tournament. Abbas Ali Baig captained a team that included Ajay Jadeja, a promising schoolboy, and India players Gursharan Singh and Surinder Khanna. The cricket was surprisingly competitive and the bonus was watching South Africa legends Mike Procter and Graeme Pollock play. Pollock was way past his prime but you couldn't miss his supreme skill. Even a lazy push in defence raced past mid-off. Pure class.

My professional career pulled me away from cricket and I served five years as secretary, Sports Authority of India (SAI), the arm of the government that implements its programmes. The assignment provided fascinating insights about Indian sport and how it is harmed by the endless squabbling

Sports minister's meeting on match-fixing: Madhavrao Scindia,
J.P. Singh, SRT, Amrit Mathur, Azharuddin

between a directionless ministry, an assertive Indian Olympic Association (IOA) and rogue federations.

At SAI, many ministers came and went, some competent, others dreadfully clueless. Vijay Amritraj once invited a senior NBA official from the US to meet with the sports minister, who listened to him patiently but distractedly. Fifteen minutes into the meeting, he stirred to ask an innocent question: *How many gold medals in basketball in the Olympics?* An embarrassed Vijay realised this was game-set-match and decided to end the meeting.

S.S. Dhindsa, the Cycling Federation of India boss, presided over the sports ministry during the match-fixing controversy. On his instructions, a mega meeting was held where every prominent person in Indian cricket was invited: BCCI presidents (Madhavrao Scindia, Jagmohan Dalmiya, I.S. Bindra, Raj Singh Dungarpur, A.C. Muthiah), captains (Pataudi, Gavaskar, Bedi, Kapil Dev) and current players (Azhar, Sachin). The meeting received huge media coverage but produced little and was neatly summed up by an observer: *The only definite thing we got to know is Mr Dhindsa is India's sports minister.*

For the Delhi 2010 Commonwealth Games (CWG) I joined the Organising Committee (OC) secretariat and worked with its chairman, Suresh Kalmadi. The OC operated almost casually, in total disregard of established processes and protocols governing the use of public funds.

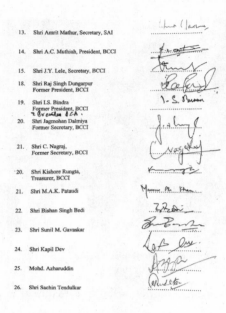

13.	Shri Amrit Mathur, Secretary, SAI
14.	Shri A.C. Muthiah, President, BCCI
15.	Shri J.Y. Lele, Secretary, BCCI
18.	Shri Raj Singh Dungarpur Former President, BCCI
19.	Shri I.S. Bindra Former President, BCCI
20.	Shri Jagmohan Dalmiya Former Secretary, BCCI
21.	Shri C. Nagraj, Former Secretary, BCCI
20.	Shri Kishore Rungta, Treasurer, BCCI
21.	Shri M.A.K. Pataudi
22.	Shri Bishan Singh Bedi
23.	Shri Sunil M. Gavaskar
24.	Shri Kapil Dev
25.	Mohd. Azharuddin
26.	Shri Sachin Tendulkar

Budgets were manufactured and amended over a cup of tea and justifications for mega projects prepared within minutes.

When I joined the OC, Randhir Singh, a senior from St. Stephen's, gave me brotherly advice. Never sign a paper where money is involved, he warned. He followed this mantra himself—despite his position as vice-chairman, he refused to touch anything that involved a financial decision. The two of us used to share a dark joke about requesting Neeraj Kumar (IPS officer, senior colleague from St. Stephen's and then the head of Tihar jail) to block a good room for us in case we landed up there.

Fortunately, we didn't have to pull that favour but many senior members of the OC became guests of Tihar, including Suresh Kalmadi. I avoided the visit because I followed Randhir's advice and, sensing the arrival of the tsunami, left in time. I was the first officer to join in 2006 and the first to leave in 2008—two years ahead of the Games.

After this close call, I had a second innings with the sports ministry, this time as an advisor. In this stint, I put together the Target Olympic Podium (TOP) scheme with the help of Nandan Kamath, the brilliant lawyer who is passionate about Indian sport. The scheme was designed to identify talent capable of winning Olympic medals and providing them with everything they needed to succeed. When I approached Rahul Dravid, Abhinav Bindra, Pullela Gopichand and others to join the programme, their response was brutally frank: *Working with the government is a waste of time.*

After much persuasion, they reluctantly agreed and the TOP scheme started with Anurag Thakur as chair of the committee. Dravid came for meetings with his homework done and made intelligent suggestions. Abhinav presented his points in a reasoned manner and was always disarmingly modest. *I won an Olympic gold,* he said, *not on talent but because I could work harder than others.*

The TOP scheme is the sports ministry's flagship initiative for nurturing excellence, but its efficiency was eroded by a delivery mechanism that was painfully sluggish, strangled by red tape. After a while, Anurag

At the Abhinav Bindra Targeting Performance centre, Bangalore

Thakur, who was the chairman, distanced himself, citing his election as BCCI secretary, and I resigned to take the GM (coordination) position at the BCCI.

Looking in the rear-view mirror now, I am struck by the sheer chance of my association with cricket and the element of 'luck' that is fundamental to cricket itself. I wasn't a cricket person, nor a professional player; for me the BCCI and official cricket existed on some other planet in a distant universe. It still feels like a *chamatkar* that the stars moved in mysterious ways to grant me access to this fascinating world.

I think of myself as a concussion sub, someone not supposed to play but unexpectedly pushed into the middle. Through many lucky breaks I became a cricket administrator and official—on the sidelines of action—stationed in what observers describe as a close catching position. For this opportunity I am happy, and grateful.